**REVIEW COPY
NOT FOR SALE**

HISTORY
An Interpretive Overview

Thomas R. Gildersleeve

PUB DATE 6/1/97

HEP Publications

For my wife,
Jeanne

HEP Publications

All rights reserved. No part of this book may be reproduced or transmitted in any form or by any means, electronic or mechanical, including photocopying, recording or by any storage and retrieval system without written permission from the publisher, except for the inclusion of brief quotations in a review.

Copyright © 1997 by HEP Publications
Printed in the United States of America

Library of Congress Cataloging-in-Publication Data
Gildersleeve, Thomas R.
History, An Interpretive Overview
Includes a bibliography and an index.
1. Civilization — History   I. Title.
    909   96-94723
ISBN 0-9653630-3-1

Contents

Introduction 9

ONE • Prehistory 15

TWO • The Middle East 23

THREE • Greece 45

FOUR • Rome 65

FIVE • Islam 91

SIX • The Dark Ages 99

SEVEN • Feudalism 107

EIGHT • The Rise of Nations 121

NINE • The Reformation 143

TEN • The New World 157

ELEVEN • The English Revolutions 167

TWELVE • The American Revolution 183

THIRTEEN • The French Revolution 209

FOURTEEN • The US Expands 237

FIFTEEN • The Civil War 267

SIXTEEN • Reconstruction 283

SEVENTEEN • The Industrial Revolution 293

EIGHTEEN • The First World War 305

NINETEEN • The Great Depression 319

TWENTY • The Second World War 331

TWENTY-ONE • Russia 367

TWENTY-TWO • India 409

TWENTY-THREE • China 419

TWENTY-FOUR • Latin America 431

CHARTS AND LISTS 439

Time Line 441

English Royalty 453

Russian Rulers 463

Order of Entry of States into the US 469

Presidents of the US 473

BIBLIOGRAPHY 477

INDEX 483

Introduction

In Greek, the word *historia* originally meant learning by inquiry. By the time it had been adopted into Latin by the Romans, it had come to be used to refer to a narrative of past events. In general, a history can relate to the past events of almost anything. We can have a history of economic thought, beer brewing, cats as pets, or anything you like. But to aspire to the title of History with a capital H, unmodified, and without an introductory a, the past events must relate to civilization.

The word civilization is rooted in the Latin *civilis*, which means "pertaining to citizens, particularly with respect to their rights under their government". From this beginning, the word civil came to mean several things. One of these is political organization. Thus, if you can remember as far back as I, when you were in junior high school, you studied the organization of your government in a course, the name of which was Civics.

The suffix *ize* is used to convert a word into a verb. Thus, in the sense of the word civic as it refers to political organization, to civilize is to organize politically. The suffix *ation* means "the state or condition of". As a consequence, in one of its meanings, the word civilization refers to the state of being organized politically.

Every group intent on a common goal has a leadership structure, no matter how temporary. Thus, even the most rudimentary tribe or clan has some political organization. However, for historians, such a structure isn't sufficient to qualify a people as a civilization. To meet the historian's criteria, a people must have evolved enough of a division of labor so that a group, whose function is to govern, can be identified. As a practical matter, from the historian's point of view, to qualify as a civilization, a people must also have developed a written language, because it's the written record that a civilization leaves behind that constitutes the historian's source for reconstructing the life of the civilization. Typically, a people that meets these two criteria has also established itself permanently in a geographic location.

For much of history, civilizations existed in enclaves surrounded by lands over which tribes roamed. Historians make a distinction between these civilizations and those people who didn't live within the confines of civilization. These other, "non-civilized" people are referred to as barbarians.

The Greeks coined the word barbarian. To be *barbar* was to not speak Greek. To Greeks, those foreign languages sounded like barbar, the Greek version of our blah-blah. The suffix *ian* means "of or belonging to", so a barbarian was one who belonged to those not speaking Greek. As was their wont, the Romans took over the word barbarian from the Greeks. The Romans used it to refer to those people not part of the Roman empire. And since, to the Romans, the Roman empire was civilization, barbarians weren't civilized, which is how we use the word.

Historians have a hard time ignoring the barbarians, for they were forever invading and conquering civilized areas. But with the exception of this, if you will, barbaric activity, historians are happy to relegate barbarians to the same dustbin into which they've dumped pre-civilized human activity. Pre-civilized and barbaric societies are acceptable for study by archeologists and anthropologists, and historians are only too glad to take advantage of the knowledge unearthed by these specialists. But when it comes to research and the publication of original work, historians confine themselves to the study of civilizations.

Civilizations first arose on the flood plains of great rivers where rain was scarce. The lack of rain kept down wild vegetation, so that the soil could be worked with the wooden tools that were the only farming implements available at the time. The annual flooding left a new top dressing each year, which solved the problem of soil exhaustion that had previously plagued farming. The difficulty was that, to farm the flood plains, an irrigation system was necessary to compensate for the lack of rain. Irrigation systems required specialized work gangs whose activities were coordinated by a specialized managerial group. Division of labor and a specialized governmental function were necessary to the survival of flood-plain society.

Four flood-plain civilizations developed thousands of years before the birth of Christ: Mesopotamia, surrounding and between the Tigris and Euphrates rivers; Egypt, on the Nile river; India, on the Indus and its tributaries; and China, on the Yellow. Western civilization is an offshoot of Mesopotamian civilization and first made an independent appearance in Greece. The Middle East ultimately became Moslem. In the 12th century, another civilization, the Russian, began to evolve in the forests north of the Black and Caspian seas.

By 525 BC, Egypt had ceased to be a factor in the evolution of world civilizations. The Moslem, Indian, Chinese and Russian civilizations still exist, but each exhibited a flaw that caused it to become rigid. Only Western civilization kept itself open to change. Around 1500, it began to pull ahead of the other civilizations with which it shared the world. Since then, it has just increased its dominance and shows every indication of continuing to do so. As a result, History is preeminently the study of Western civilization, with a side look at other civilizations to see why they haven't fared as well.

In writing this book, I've tried to maintain enough of a long-range view to allow the broad outlines of historical development to come into clear view. As a consequence, the detail making up these long-term trends disappears from sight. One of the effects of this approach is that this book fails to document the fact that, far from being irresistible movements, these broad patterns were composed of a multitude of both long and short term forces, many of which ran counter to the overall trend. The result is that the progress of civilization has been more characteristically fitful with frequent backslidings than monotonic. In fact, tendencies surviving long enough to constitute a trend were, not infrequently, near things that could have almost as easily gone the other way at any one of a multitude of points and, therefore, come to naught. So if you find this book entertaining and informative, you ought to look further into the subject by reading my sources and the many other fine history books that are available in your local public library and bookstore.

And now, a note on the organization of this book. First of all, each chapter is a freestanding essay, the topic of which is identified by the chapter's title.

Second, the first 21 chapters constitute the history of the Western world and are arranged chronologically. The final three chapters cover, respectively, the history of India, China, and Latin

America for purposes of comparison with the development of the Western world.

Third, this book constitutes a framework within which to organize the many details of history that you'll collect in your further pursuit of the subject.

Despite the fact that the large majority of the material in this book comes from my sources, this material has been subjected to a significant amount of selection, rearrangement, summarization and rewording, all done from my point of view. As a result, I'm happy to issue the caveat found in all acknowledgments: Any errors in this book are mine and mine alone.

The other part of the standard acknowledgment also applies, in spades. In a sense, this book is just an extended series of citations. I've unblushingly taken advantage of the research and scholarship of my sources. The selection of those events that represent turning points in history and the insights that pinpoint their significance are the priceless results of their work. No matter to what extent I've woven my account beyond that provided in these sources, without them, I couldn't have gotten started. These sources are identified in the bibliography at the end of this book.

In addition to my obligation to my sources, I have three other debts to acknowledge. At one point in this book's development, I sent each chapter to a number of historians for review. For those professionals who graciously gave their time to look over and comment on my work, I'm forever indebted. Their suggestions were invaluable.

I also owe a debt to my wife, Jeanne, who not only put up with me during the preparation of this material but also gave generously of her time to review this book in its various drafts, provide me with encouragement, and draw my attention to ways in which this book could be improved.

My third debt is to the research librarians in the Darien, Connecticut public library. Without their help in guiding me through their library, my task would have been much harder. Particular thanks is due to Blanche Parker, the inter-library loan librarian, who found all sorts of material for me in other libraries.

All the drawings in this book are mine. For each, a work, such as a photograph, painting, or other drawing, has been used as a model. For each such work, every effort has been made to get the appropriate permission to use the work as a model. However, some of these efforts weren't successful. The trail ran out before the appropriate party was reached. In such cases, I've given credit to the extent that I was able to unearth the information. If I've stepped on anybody's toes, I apologize and hope that the credit and apology given will suffice.

The eagle on the cover of the dust jacket comes from a photograph taken by Jim Reardon of Alaska Photo that appears on page 23 of *Eagles*, written by John Bonnett Wexo and published by Creative Education of Mankato, Minnesota.

A Stone Age Hunter. *From an illustration in the Mary Evans Picture Library.*

CHAPTER ONE

Prehistory

The term, prehistory, refers to the time before the appearance of writing. that is, before the emergence of civilization.

We're not sure where man arose. The latest in paleoanthropological thinking is that man began life on the African savanna, and in addition to the requisite appropriate bones found in the area, there's a logic to the thesis. As a large bodied predator, man needed a broad area over which to range, and this the savanna provided. As a peltless animal without the ability, at least initially, to fashion clothes, man could survive only where the temperature didn't get too cold. Once more, the savanna fitted the bill. As a defenseless mammal bearing offspring with a maturation cycle of well over ten years, man needed a place of sanctuary. The high, broad branches of the widely separated trees growing on the savanna offered at least an approximation of this essential refuge.

Man had an evolutionary ancestor, and apparently, he shared this ancestor with other hominids (manlike animals) such as the Neandertal man and the Beijing man. We know these hominids existed, because we've found their bones, and these bones tell us that these hominids were physiologically different from man. All these other hominids are also not around any more. One group of theorists maintains that there was little interbreeding between man and these other hominids and that these other hominids died out, for reasons that only novelists are brave enough to propose. Another group holds that these other hominids interbred with and melded into man. In any case, man is now one. He breaks down into racial types on the basis of superficial characteristics such as skin color, hair texture, and eye shape, but to an overwhelming degree, man is the same the world over. All specimens breed successfully and without difficulty with all other specimens, and the offspring are healthy, sound and whole.

Man migrated to Europe after the last ice age, around 40,000 years ago. At that time, Neandertal man was in residence, but by the time another 10,000 years had passed, he had become extinct,

A Less Idealistic Depiction of a Stone Age Hunter. *From an illustration by Victor Ambrus for the book* The Story of Britain *written by R. J. Unstead and published by Thomas Nelson & Sons Ltd.*

as we've said, for reasons unknown.

Fangless and clawless as he was, man would have made a remarkably unsuccessful predator without the use of weapons and other tools. Some animals other than man exhibit tool use. That cute, little otter floating on its back and using a rock to crush shells on its chest invariably comes to mind. But man is the only animal who resorts to tools as a matter of course. And he *is* the only tool maker. Man couldn't have existed without tools, and fashioned tools are a uniquely human artifact. One couldn't have developed without the other. They had to have evolved contemporaneously.

Man's first tools were made of wood, stone, bone, antlers, hide, sinews, and other such readily available materials. Relatively soft materials, such as bone and antlers, man shaped to his purposes by rubbing and polishing. For sharp tools, like arrow and spear heads, knives, and scrapers, man used brittle stone like flint, which he chipped to create the desired sharp points and edges. He also used hard stones to create such things as battle axes, but these stones he used as is, with no shaping involved. It's because of this fact that the period, when man first occupied Europe, is known as the Paleolithic (Old Stone) age. The characteristic Paleolithic artifact is the tool made of unpolished stone. Obviously, we're eventually going to get to the age where the characteristic artifact is the tool made of polished stone. Please be patient.

Another defining characteristic of man is his use of language. As we've already seen with respect to tool use, Mother Nature doesn't like to draw clear lines between her creatures, and we find gradations of intelligence among her species and some signs of primitive language use. But when it comes to conceptualization (so that experience can be expressed, stored away, and generalized upon), sophisticated language is a prerequisite, and only man exhibits this attribute. Again, this characteristic is so unique that, as we've said, it's in the nature of a definition. Animal without language wouldn't be man, and language wouldn't exist apart from man. Once more, they must have evolved together.

Fire is different. It could be considered as just another tool. But it's so unlike man's other early tools that it's given a unique status. Fire is also different in that it's possible to conceive of man existing without having adapted fire to his uses, so the concurrent development of man and utilization of fire wasn't a necessity. Nevertheless, man is the only animal that has come to terms with fire and shaped it to his purposes, and he did it early in his development. Use of fire by man predates the Neandertal.

So Paleolithic man was a predator, a hunter, aided in his quest by tools, language and fire. He was also a gatherer. Thus, he lived, not only on the game he slew and the fish he caught, but also on the berries, grubs, roots, and other edibles he gathered. The results of these efforts were unpredictable. If the hunting was good, there was more than enough for all. But if the hunting was poor and the gathering lean, man could experience some extremely hard times.

To rise above the feast or famine level provided by the hunter-gatherer way of life, tools, language and fire weren't enough. Man needed a fourth asset — domestication of his food supply.

How the transition from hunter-gatherer to farmer-drover occurred is another of those historical mysteries. We simply don't know how it happened. But it marks the beginning of the Neolithic (New Stone) age. So here we are. The hallmark of the Neolithic age is the fact that the stone in the tools used by Neolithic man was polished. Why this should be the case we'll explain shortly.

The agriculture practiced by Neolithic man was, in every sense of the word, primitive, which was a result of the fact that his ground preparation tools were primitive. Most unfortunately, the only material he had with which to fashion them was wood. So his tools would stand up and do the job only in especially forgiving soil. The ground couldn't be covered with underbrush or full of roots, because Neolithic man's wooden tools weren't capable of clearing such land. Moreover, the ground had to be soft, because hard soil broke his tools. So the Neolithic farmer looked for heavily forested land (because the leaf canopy inhibited the spread of brush) where the soil was soft (chalk or light loam). Such land was usually found on hillsides, and it was here that Neolithic man did his farming.

The first grains to be domesticated were barley and wheat. This practice began around 9000 BC in the hills around Mesopotamia, and for some time, grain growing was restricted to this locality. But by 7000 BC, it had spread to cover the area from Turkey to the region south of the Caspian sea.

Neolithic man's farming technique was what we call slash and burn. When he found a suitable plot, the first thing be did was "slash" the trees. That is, he would girdle them — cut away all the bark in a circle around the trunks. This would kill the trees; the foliage would, as a consequence, disappear; and the sun could then reach the ground to nourish the farmer's crops. The ground around the trees was prepared (that is, the surface was scratched) with digging sticks, hoes, and spades, all made of wood. The seeds were then planted in the scratched up soil.

After a few years of growing the same crops on the same plot, the soil would begin to wear out. By then, the dead trees, still standing in the field, would have been well seasoned. These trees were cut down and burned, and the resulting ashes were spread on the field to renew fertility. When the land became depleted for the second time, the only thing left to do was to find a new plot on another hillside and start over again.

As opposed to wooded hillsides with no undergrowth, grassland was hard to work with wooden farming equipment. Moreover, even if the land was cleared and planted, the wild grass tended to grow back and suffocate the farmer's grain. Consequently, the Neolithic farmer avoided the grasslands (the steppes), and they became the nomad's (drover's) domain.

Transition from hunter to nomad was less wrenching than from hunter to farmer. Possessions were still limited to what could be carried, and the prime virtues remained vigilance, endurance, and courage in the face of danger.

As we've already noted, flint made fine arrowheads, knives and scrapers for the hunter, but it was too brittle for slashing bark and cutting down trees. What was needed was a sharpened ax head made of the hardest material at Neolithic man's disposal — stone, specifically, granite or basalt. In this way, it came about that the roughhewing and polishing that was heretofore confined to forming bone and horn tools were transferred to the creation of polished stone tools, particularly axes, that came to symbolize the Neolithic age.

Man's domestication of his food supply had a lasting effect on the animals and plants involved. Sheep that looked to a shepherd to find grazing land and water holes for them, that depended for defense on the shepherd and his dog, that no longer even grew horns, such sheep could never have survived a return to the wild.

The impact on plants was perhaps less obvious but just as telling. Before their domestication, wheat and barley grew wild in the Middle East. The seeds of wild grain were loosely attached to the grain stalk, since the propagation of the grain depended on having the wind or other natural disturbances dislodge the seeds so that they would be broadcast on the ground. This may have been fine for wild grain, but it was a drawback to domestic grain, where the object was to first harvest the stalks and then thresh the seed from the chaff. If in this harvesting process, most of the grain dropped from the stalks, the procedure would have been very inefficient.

The first farmers tended to plant seed that had remained on the stalk throughout the harvest. This probably wasn't even conscious selection. The seed available for planting was the seed the farmer succeeded in harvesting, which was the seed that had remained on the stalk. As a result, domestic grain became characterized by seed that natural disturbances wouldn't dislodge. Consequently, the grain became a better domestic crop but lost its ability to survive in the wild. This process of selectively breeding hybrids for particular purposes continues to this day.

The Neolithic farmer didn't confine himself to crop growing. He also kept cattle. Of course, he didn't have the herds the drovers maintained. But he did raise cattle to, among other things, vary his diet with meat and dairy products. And being confined to one spot by crop growing, he couldn't lead his cattle to new pasture when local grazing became inadequate. Consequently, he had to supplement the diet of his cattle with grain. As a result, the farmer's way of life was dedicated to growing, to feed both himself and his cattle.

With the coming of the semi-settled way of life called for by his reliance on grain, the Neolithic farmer was more prone to establish a home and collect big, hefty, and easily broken household articles, such as pottery. Tillable land tended to appear in batches. Consequently, more often than not, a number of Neolithic families would construct their homes in close proximity. The Neolithic farmer characteristically lived in a village.

The oldest examples of cloth have been found in the remains of Neolithic villages. This doesn't mean that cloth-making necessarily began in the Neolithic age, for it was an offshoot of basket weaving, a Paleolithic skill. But cloth-making on any kind of scale had to wait until flax became a crop and hair and wool from tame animals were at hand.

A new technology, the baking of clay vessels, was also practiced in Neolithic villages. Once the process had been developed, clay vessels became easier to make than stone ones.

The foot-plow had been created more or less contemporaneously with the hoe and spade, and was a variation on the spade. It had a twisted handle, which let the farmer turn the soil by pushing down on the handle, and a footrest near the bottom of the handle permitted him to force the blade into the ground at a slant. The Neolithic farmer eased his effort and enhanced his productivity by hitching his plow to his cattle. The critical ingredient of this innovation was to see that animal labor could be substituted for manual by hitching the plow to a beast. Even this change took time to develop. The original, inefficient hitch was probably from the plow to the ox's horns.

The first plows were wooden. They did little more than scratch the earth. Plowing a plot twice to form a crosshatch was usually necessary to break the soil sufficiently for planting. As a result, to accommodate this type of plowing practice, the typical farm plot was square.

River plains on which rain fell throughout the year developed into jungles, which kept away the Neolithic farmer. But in dry regions, the alluvial soil of the river plains both attracted and repulsed the Neolithic farmers. The sediment left behind by the spring floods was fertile and easily worked, so seed could be planted with little effort. But unless some artificial way could be devised to supply the growing grain with water, the plants shriveled in the summer heat. The solution to this problem was irrigation.

The way of life on the flood plain was different from its counterpart in the Neolithic village. For one thing, flooding left a new top dressing each year, so exhaustion of the soil wasn't a problem. Consequently, there was no need to ever move to a new location. Agricultural settlement on the flood plain was permanent.

Second, constructing and maintaining the canals, dikes and aqueducts making up an irrigation system required the coordinated effort of work gangs. With respect to maintenance, not only was constant repair necessary. There also had to be continuous effort to see that the works didn't silt up.

The coordination of this work was provided by a managerial group, and to support them and their work crews, farmers had to produce a surplus over what the farmers needed to sustain themselves. Fortunately, the level, stone-free bottom land made plowing easy, and production of a surplus was feasible.

Once managers made good their claim to surplus crops, larger and larger groups could be supported, not only to work on the irrigation system, but also to serve in the army and construct public buildings and granaries to store the surplus of good years against future poor harvests.

To carry out such activities, record keeping was necessary, and pictographs and numeric notation performed this function. Measurement and calculation also became important. Controlling grain consumption, reserving surplus against a bad year, calculating what part of the crop should be set aside for next year's seed and how much land to cultivate — all these functions required at least crude measurement and calculation. And the construction of complex irrigation systems and public buildings called for even more accurate techniques.

When people with a common cultural identity establish themselves in a permanent location, exhibit a significant degree of division of labor, make political decisions on how to maintain themselves in the future, and use record keeping and measurement to carry out their activities, they're justifiably called a civilization.

CHAPTER TWO

The Middle East

The first flood plain settlements were established along the lower Tigris and Euphrates rivers in Mesopotamia around 4000 BC by the Sumerians. At that time, the Tigris and Euphrates had separate entrances into the Persian gulf. It wasn't until later that the accumulating silt formed the land through which the confluence of the two rivers now flows. Mesopotamia is a Greek word meaning "(land) between the rivers".

The beginnings of these Sumerian settlements are shrouded in mystery. We know nothing about the Sumerians before they appeared in Mesopotamia, we don't know where they came from, and we don't know how their civilization evolved. All we know is that it existed and what its structure was. So we'll begin with what we know. We simply have to accept the existence of this civilization and be satisfied with an after-the-fact description of it.

Sumerian civilization began in a number of independent cities grouped in the lower part of the Tigris-Euphrates flood plain. Each city had a patron god and contained one or more temples dedicated to the god. Each temple was surrounded by a body of land, the god owned this land, and the temple priests managed the god's land. Thus, the priests made up the managerial group that coordinated the population's activities. As we've said, we don't know how these temple communities evolved. But we can speculate on how they were maintained.

The farmer was at the mercy of the weather, and the weather was unpredictable. If a community of farmers came to believe that the weather was determined by the gods and that the gods' priests knew how to influence the gods, then it became important to do what the priests said. Under such circumstances, if the priests asked for a portion of the farmers' production for the purposes of the gods, the only thing to do was to see that the priests' requests were satisfied.

However, a Sumerian city wasn't just a farming community. Fishing, snaring of water fowl, and stock raising also flourished. In addition, there was commerce, which came about as follows.

Stone, timber and metals were necessary for construction and maintenance in the city and were also used in fabricating various tools and other products. The absence of these raw materials in lower Mesopotamia meant that the Sumerians had to either go and find and bring back these materials or convince indigenous tribes to trade these materials for the products of the city — surplus grain and manufactured products. The transportation facilities necessary to carry on this trade were available. Boats had no trouble navigating the valley waterways, and there was no difficult terrain to obstruct the movement of overland pack trains. This trade gave rise to a class of merchants, who conducted it. For each merchant, there were dozens of artisans turning out exportable products and using imported raw materials in their work. Merchants also carried on local trade, where produce was exchanged for the artisan's products.

In contrast with Egypt, where flooding of the Nile was a reliable annual occurrence, in the Middle East, the seasons didn't signal their arrival in any clear way. This lack of regularity presented Middle Eastern farmers with the problem of how to determine when to schedule their agricultural activities, particularly plowing and planting, so that these actions would be coordinated with the seasonal growing pattern. A calendar was what was needed, and the Sumerians were able to overcome the formidable difficulties involved in developing one. The critical insight was to recognize that the rising sun moved through the signs of the Zodiac almost exactly once every 365 and a quarter days.

The Sumerians also get the credit for inventing the wheel.

By 3500 BC, the cities of Sumer had reached a high state of development. Each city was an independent entity, but the homogeneity of their culture made clear that there was frequent contact and interchange of expertise among them.

These amicable relations began to deteriorate when, as a result of a growing population and the consequent spread of cultivated land, the fields of one city began to run up against those of another.

Political organization by temple community wasn't able to deal with the conflicting water claims that then arose. The argument that we should do it this way, because that's the way my god says we should do it, wasn't able to carry the day. It was too easily countered by the contention that, no, we should do it *this* way, because that's the way *my* god says we should do it. The resulting stalemate created discord between neighboring cities.

Such disagreement led to escalating conflicts between work gangs as their labor on their respective irrigation systems became increasingly intrusive. In such a face-off, the gang that came out on top was commonly the one whose straw boss had better prepared, deployed and led his men in the conflict. As a consequence, military prowess became, more and more, a desirable trait.

Sumerian city government had already established its right to a portion of the people's produce in return for interceding with the gods on their behalf and for looking after the well-being of the community by maintaining an irrigation system. As the importance of military capability for the defense of the city grew, it was only reasonable that the people should support a fighting force as well.

Work gangs had long been a feature of city life. So the idea of following a leader's orders wasn't new. But if obeying orders was necessary to, for example, supply water to a field, such obedience became even more critical in battle, where performance could be a matter of life or death as well as the difference between victory and defeat. Since following a commander's orders could mean putting one's life in danger, it became essential that the commander be able to count on his orders being carried out. To this end, within his unit, a field commander became endowed with judicial as well as executive authority. Not only did he give the orders, he also decided whether they had been effectively and expeditiously carried out. If they weren't, the results could be catastrophic, and the commander exercised the right to mete out punishment accordingly. A field commander's authority was extraordinary, amounting to the ability to make decisions regarding the life or death of those he commanded, not only on the battlefield, but also by calling for their punishment, including execution, when in his opinion, orders hadn't been obeyed.

Ultimately, conflict between cities escalated into open warfare. By 3000 BC, such intercity engagements were common. The result of such a face-off could be the defeat and occupation of one city by another. The question of how to govern the occupied city then arose. The most immediate answer was for the victorious commander to extend his extraordinary war powers to include the subjugated city so that cooperation would be assured. Over time, this expedient rigidified into practice. And because tyrants were frequently driven to the conclusion that their home cities were as difficult to deal with as conquered ones, they weren't immune to the idea of applying what worked on the conquered cities to their home ones. In this way, the governmental institution of kingship arose. Once a king had established his unquestioned authority over more than one city, resolving problems arising between the cities became nothing more than having the king decree what was to be done.

We've already determined that the authority of the field commander over his troops was extraordinary, consisting of both the executive and judicial functions, and extending to matters involving the life and death of his troops. As this authority moved without diminution from the baton of the field commander to the scepter of the king, one can get an idea of the unlimited power over his subjects that became vested in the king. In Sumer, this all-encompassing power ate into the prerogatives of the priests, and management of the peoples' activities passed from the priests to the kings. This process began around 3000 BC.

Out of intercity conflict grew imperial aspirations, as cities successful in military conquest sought to extend their sway over larger and larger territories. Lugalzaggisi of the city of Umma was the first ruler known to have extended his empire beyond his own locality. "Lugal" is king, literally, "big man". Thus, Lugalzaggisi is King Zaggisi.

Lugalzaggisi set out on his course of conquest about 2375 BC, and by 2350 BC, all of Sumer had been incorporated into his empire. All early Mesopotamian dating depends on how sequences of events unfolded, and since multiple interpretations of how these sequences occurred are possible, all dates should be considered approximate.

The Empire of Lugalzaggisi

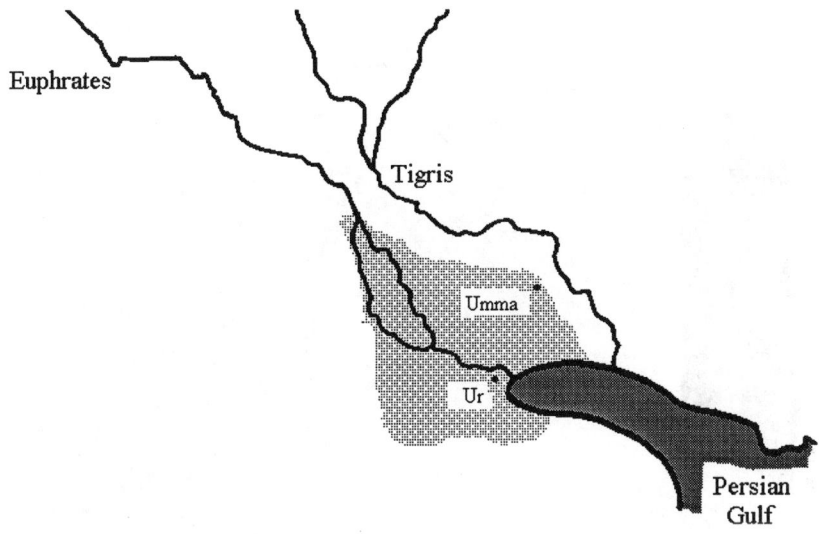

Lugalzaggizi's dominion was short-lived. Around 2334 BC, Sargon of Akkad defeated Lugalzaggisi and brought Sumer into his empire. Sargon's real name is unknown. In Akkadian, Sargon is Sharrum-kin, which means "true king" and has to be an adopted name.

Akkad was upriver from Sumer, and its population was Semitic, which the Sumerians were not. The distinction is linguistic. Akkadian, like other Semitic languages, was flectional, while Sumerian was agglutinative. The Akkadians were the ancestors of both the Babylonians and Assyrians.

In Sargon's time, Akkad was a transition area between civilized Sumer and the surrounding land controlled by barbarians. As a consequence, the Akkadians were able to merge barbarian skill in warfare with civilized technology to forge a strong military force, thus constituting the first known historical example of a recurring pattern of marcher lords establishing empires by exploiting the marchlands, the border between civilization and barbarism. Sargon came originally from the city of Kish but established his capital upriver at Agade, the exact location of which has yet to be determined.

The only thing validating the Akkadian king's right to rule was

The Akkadian Empire

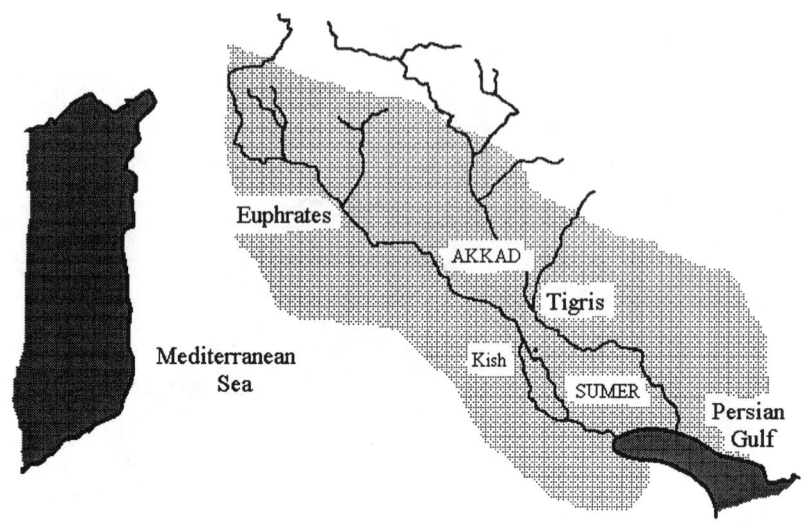

his might. His army enforced his rule, and consequently, be had to keep it in readiness. There were three choices.
1. He could disperse his troops and station them at strategic locations. But Sargon and his successors lacked the administrative structure needed to hold such separated forces together, and fearful of losing control, none of them opted for this choice.
2. An alternative was to keep a united army immediately under the ruler's direction. But just as lack of an administrative structure made a dispersed force impractical, it also made the logistics of maintaining a standing army in one location impossible.
3. The remaining choice was to stay on campaign, for then the army could live off the land. This may account for the endless military activity characteristic of the Akkadian empire.

Just as lack of an administrative structure prevented the Akkadian kings from maintaining a peacetime military force, it also kept them from giving their empire consistent governance. The Akkadian empire reached its high point during the reign of Naram Sin, Sargon's grandson. Naram Sin means Beloved of Sin, a Mesopotamian moon god. As a first attempt at forming an administration, Naram Sin supplanted local rulers with his relatives, a step that turned out to be questionable from a control point of view, let alone from the perspective of trying to move toward administrative consistency.

The Akkadian empire lasted about a century. Shortly after Naram Sin's death, regional interests tore at the fabric of the Akkadian empire, and invasion by barbarous Guitians from the upper Tigris and Amorite tribes from the west contributed the extra weight needed to swing the balance and smash the empire into bits.

The history of the Akkadian empire forms a pattern that was repeated several times in Mesopotamian history as well as in the subsequent history of other peoples. A war leader from the marchlands would forge an empire by force of arms. After a few generations, generally very few, these conquerors would give up their warlike ways for the more comfortable life of the city. The time was then ripe for domestic revolt, external conquest, or a combination of the two.

The Guitians occupied the Mesopotamian plains for nearly a century. There was no central government, just a number of military estates.

The Third Dynasty of the city of Ur then restored governmental unity to what had been the Akkadian empire. We'll explain about "dynasties" after we discuss the Sumerian king list, which we'll do shortly.

This governmental consolidation was accomplished during the rule of the first king of the Third Dynasty of Ur, Ur-Nammu (2112 - 2095 BC), and was achieved by diplomacy rather than by warfare. The empire of Ur lasted about 100 years.

It was during the Third Dynasty of Ur that a system for administering an empire was first developed. The administrative unit was the city, and in each city, the administrator was the "king", with the king of Ur being, by far, the first among equals. These subsidiary kings were administrators in every sense of the word. They could be appointed, dismissed, and transferred from city to city.

Communicating with and coordinating these city administrators would have been impossible without writing. Writing originated in

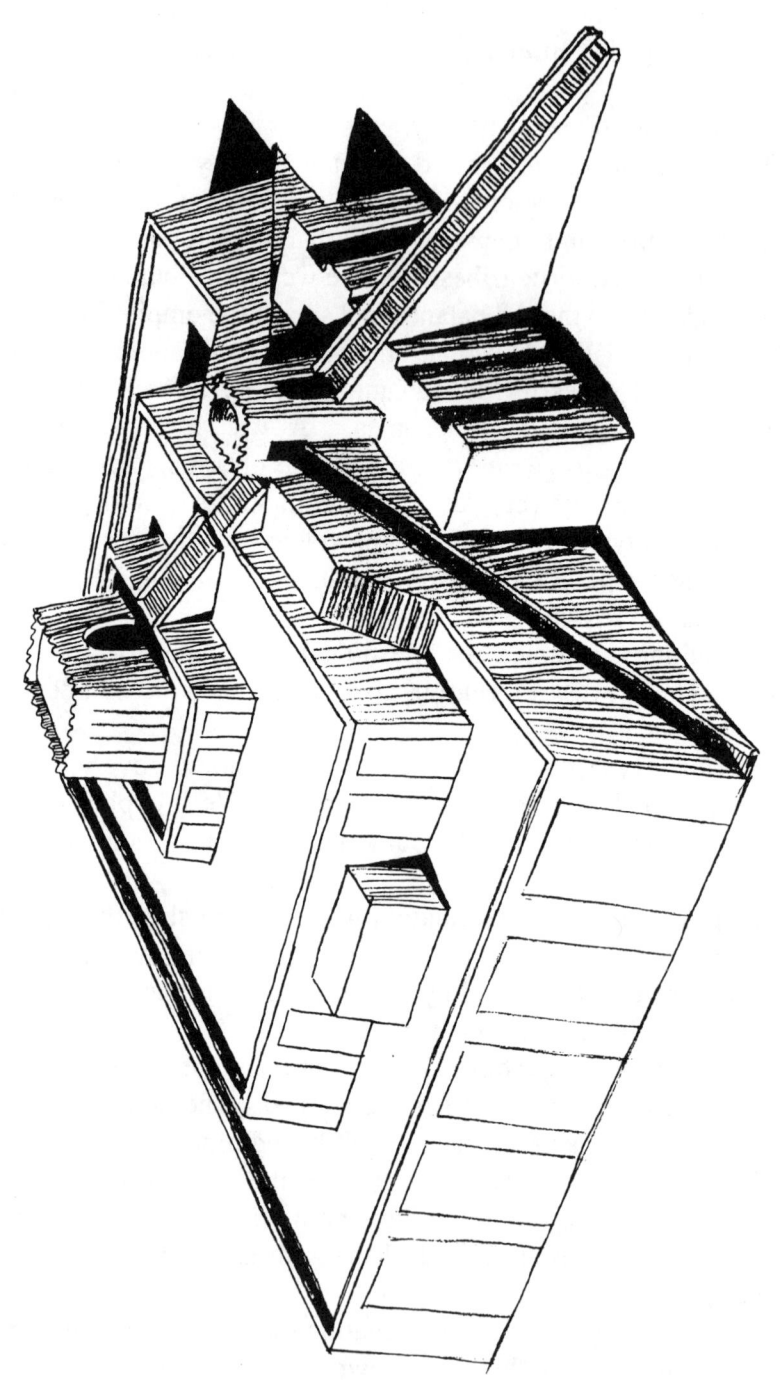

Sumer to keep records of goods brought into and disbursed from storehouses. Pictographs and numeric notation performed this function, except when it came to recording names for the personal accounts of those who had or hadn't paid their debt to their god. It may have been this requirement that caused Sumerian scribes to associate phonetic meaning with specific symbols. A broadening of this practice allowed the conversion of all speech into writing. But for some time, the possible uses of this skill weren't pursued.

It was probably the increasing complexity of civilized life (property ownership, individual commitments, judicial rulings, etc.), which could no longer be kept in men's minds, that caused writing to be more generally used. It then became available for communication across a distance.

Shulgi (2094 - 2047 BC), Ur-Nammu's son and successor, established a new system of taxation and set up an organization to collect these taxes, which were paid primarily in the form of cattle, sheep, and other agricultural products. He reorganized the system of weights and measures and introduced a new calendar. He was also the author of the oldest known law code.

At about this time, civilization began to spread beyond the confines of the flood plain. One factor permitting this encroachment was the development of fallowing. Plowing made possible the cultivation of more land than that required to sustain the resident population. By leaving part of this cultivated land unsown for a year and plowing it a number of times to help the soil hold onto moisture, the fertility of the soil could be rejuvenated. As a result, it became possible to develop the agricultural base for a civilization on land watered only by rain as well as on the flood plain.

Another factor encouraging the spread of civilization beyond the flood plain was trade for timber, stone and ore, which allowed settled communities to support themselves in areas where local

---

The Ziggurat of the Moon God Sin at Ur. *From a reconstruction after Woolley. A ziggurat was a stepped tower surmounted by a small shrine. It was set in the middle of a large open space. Ziggurats were first constructed during the reign of Ur-Nammu of the Third Dynasty of Ur.*

The Babylonian Empire of Hammurabi

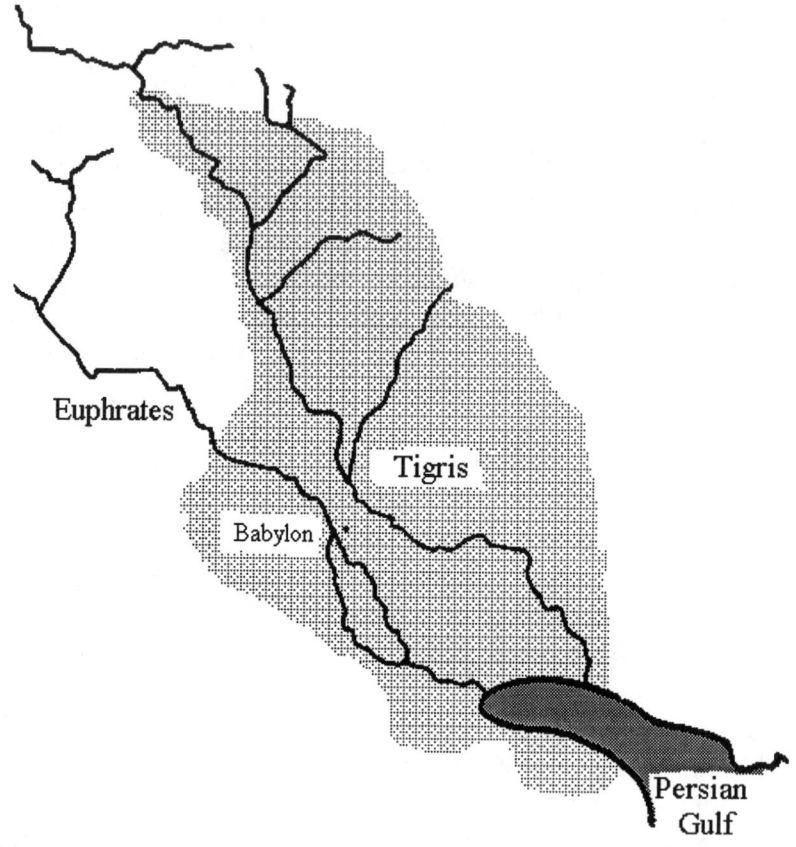

food supplies were otherwise insufficient.

Wasted by battle with the Elamites to the east and Amorites to the west, Ur was overcome around 2004 BC. For the next two centuries, Mesopotamia was in disarray. It was reunited by the Amorite leader, Hammurabi, around 1792 BC. He moved the capital north to Babylon.

By the time of Hammurabi's conquest, Mesopotamian administrative procedures had evolved to the point where he could post soldiers at strategic points. To do so, records had to be kept of these soldiers' names and locations, and communication with them had to be feasible. Both of these functions were carried out by writing. Writing also allowed Hammurabi to publish a uniform code of justice for his empire. The code was modeled on that of the Third Dynasty of Ur.

Of course, consistent administration of an empire required more than a written code. A panoply of officials (judges, tax collectors, and administrative officials) was needed, and by Hammurabi's time, thanks to the innovations introduced by the Third Dynasty of Ur, it was possible to put such a bureaucracy into place.

The Babylonian realm was the last Mesopotamian empire. Future Middle Eastern kingdoms extended beyond the borders of Mesopotamia. So at this point, let us note that the Mesopotamians struggled with a recurring problem of government: On what basis do those in power rule? What legitimates their position of authority?

Of course, the fact that central administration is necessary justifies a central authority. The example we've already met was the resolution of the problems created by abutting municipal irrigation systems. But such justification doesn't make any particular government legitimate. The ultimate answer to this question is, of course, the power that the government has to coerce its subjects. But even as far back as the early Mesopotamian empires, the king recognized that he was most secure when his subjects were convinced that his government was legitimate and not based solely on the raw ability to coerce. Out of this fact rose the ceaseless quest of those in power to justify their reign and, thus, gain the voluntary cooperation of their subjects.

Mesopotamian rulers recognized the benefit of being sanctioned by religious authority. As a result, some of the Mesopotamian kings laid claim to being gods. Naram Sin tried this technique, and it was the general practice during the Third Dynasty of Ur. This approach didn't endure in Mesopotamia, but the king continued to identify himself with the gods through participation in religious rites. Since then, such religious legitimation of secular authority has been fairly consistently pursued. It was long after the Reformation before the king was able to feel secure without the endorsement of a state religion that knew no rivals. Even today, in the most secular of societies, political leaders don't embark on significant undertakings without first petitioning God for His blessing.

The Sumerian king list was another attempt to legitimate the king's authority. The contention was that the land had always constituted a single realm, and to buttress this position, traditions and records were modified to create the king list. This fabricated record of an unbroken succession of kings became the basis for the argument that, since the land had always been the domain of a single king, it was only proper that the realm remain united under a single ruler.

In its mixture of fact and fantasy, the Sumerian King List is an interesting document. Like the Hebrew genealogies, it includes kings that reigned and, therefore, lived over a thousand years. Like the Greek myths, it incorporates heroes, such as Gilgamesh, who in legend was two thirds god and one third human. But buried in this accumulation of myth is probably an actual historical king of Umma.

The basic thesis of the king list was that there had always been a single king of Sumer. These kings came from various Sumerian cities. Thus, a series of Sumerian kings came from Kish, followed by a series of kings from Umma, and so on. Each of these series was referred to as a dynasty. Thus, according to the king list, Sumer had been ruled by two series of kings from Ur before the advent of the Third Dynasty of Ur, even though, in fact, the "Third" Dynasty was the first to actually enjoy the undisputed rule of all Sumer.

Babylonia was in uncontested control of Mesopotamia for about a century. Then Kassites from the Iranian plateau began to challenge the Babylonian empire. More than a century later (about 1595 BC), they brought the empire down. The agent instrumental to this conquest was a superior, new weapon, the light, two wheeled war chariot.

Agricultural communities had developed in the more watered parts of the Iranian and Azerbaijanian plateaus. Barbarian nomads lived on the grasslands around these agricultural settlements. By means of these agricultural communities, the nomads became exposed to Mesopotamian civilization. Here, somewhat before 1700 BC, the war chariot was either created or perfected.

Nomads domesticated horses around 3000 BC. In the beginning, they constituted just one more source of food. It was the Sumerians who first conceived of hitching horses to wagons. Originally, horses were yoked and controlled with nose rings, like oxen. It was the development of the bit around 1700 BC that made the war chariot possible.

The only way to turn Sumarian four wheeled wagons was to slide their heavy, solid wheels sideways. As a consequence, they weren't maneuverable enough to be effective in battle. Light, spoked wheels and harness designed so that the horses carried part of the weight of the vehicle were prerequisites for a maneuverable, two wheeled chariot. The carpentry and leatherwork needed for these purposes were developed in Mesopotamia.

Also essential to the success of the war chariot was the compound bow. A wooden bow, reinforced with bone and sinew, could be made more compact without giving up power. With such a weapon, it was possible to be an effective archer even in the confines of a chariot. There's evidence that the compound bow was around before 1700 BC. But it first came into large scale use with the introduction of the war chariot.

With these weapons, charioteers could move over a battlefield at will and shoot as they went. Infantry was no match for these mobile archers safe behind the parapets of their chariots.

For forces still relying on now out-of-date fighting techniques, success against this new form of battle array was possible only by striking at the charioteers when they had unharnessed their horses. To defend against such an eventuality, earthwork fortifications were thrown up in open country. It was here that the chariots, horses and charioteers were stationed when not harnessed for battle.

The war chariot made the barbarians awesome opponents. Their nomadic life, which joined veneration for reckless bravery with unquestioned obedience to authority, added to their prowess on the battlefield.

By 1500 BC, civilization was no longer confined to the Mesopotamian plain and its borderlands. It had spread over the Fertile Crescent from the Mediterranean to Mesopotamia.

The Chariot incursion into the Middle East was carried out by

The Fertile Crescent

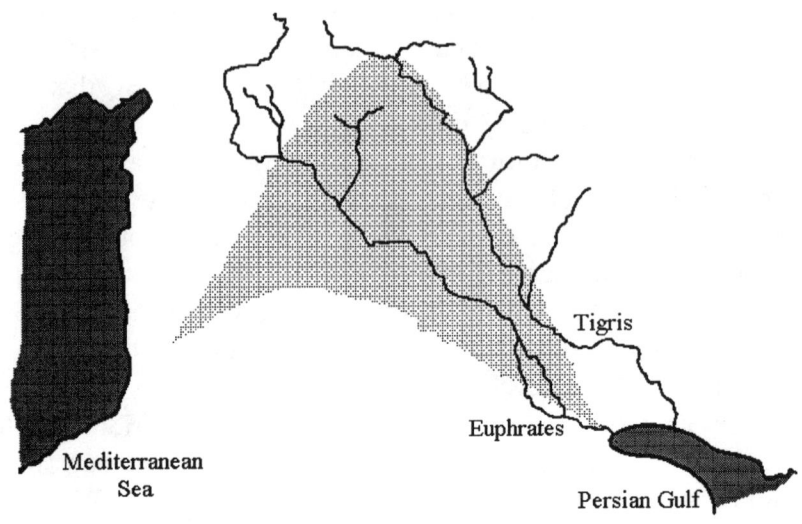

the Kassites and the Mitanni, a Hurrian people, and ended about 1500 BC. Each Kassite and Mitanni military chieftain divided the land he occupied between his lieutenants, thus establishing military estates answerable to the chieftain.

The war chariot not only allowed barbarians to take over the Middle East. Another tribe, the Hyksos, conquered Egypt. Kindred peoples rode their war chariots into regions from the Indus river valley in India to the Balkan peninsula in Europe. And wherever these chariot warriors went, they carried their language with them. This language has been lost, but it has been given a name, Indo-European. It's the root for languages as varied as Sanskrit, Greek, Latin, German, Slavic and the languages that sprang from these older tongues. The ancestors of the Medes and Persians were Indo-European.

The kings of Assyria led a reaction against the Indo-European invaders, gained their independence around 1380 BC, overturned the Mitanni empire around 1330 BC, and then took over the Kassite kingdom. The Hittites, who occupied Turkey, assisted in throwing off the barbarians. As a consequence, the Assyrians and Hittites came to share domination of the Middle East with the

The Mitanni and Kassite Occupation of the Middle East

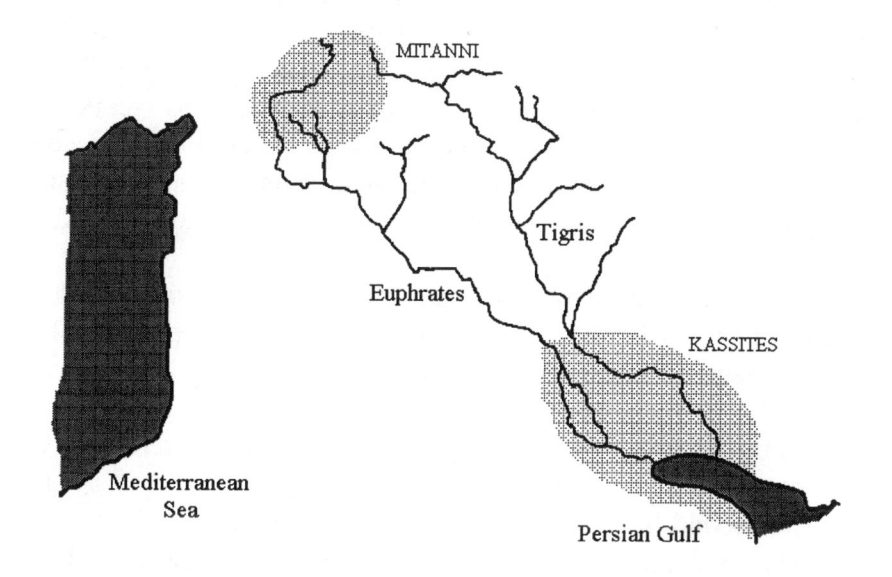

Egyptians, who had dislodged the Hyksos.

Not long after 1200 BC, barbarians once more swept over the Middle East. It was during this second wave of barbarian invasion that the Hebrews, Philistines, Aramaeans and Phrygians settled into their historic homes. This second wave was less destructive than the first, in that neither Assyria nor Egypt was completely subjugated.

Sometime during this period, the smelting of iron ore was perfected. Some historians say that this event occurred before the second wave of barbarian invasion into the Middle East and that it was the resulting steel weapons that enabled the barbarians to make the inroads that they did. More recent academic theory holds that steel tools weren't generally available until three centuries later, in which case the barbarians effected their invasion without the benefit of steel weapons.

In any case, the general availability of steel tools had a profound effect on agriculture, the crafts, and warfare. The steel produced at the time was seldom functionally better than bronze, which it replaced. The significance of steel was that, compared to copper and tin (the ingredients of bronze), iron ore was plentiful.

Steel, thus, was, in relation to bronze, inexpensive. As a consequence, farmers could afford metal plowshares, sickles and scythes. Heavy and stony soils which remained impervious to wood and stone tools could be tilled with a steel plowshare. Thus, because of steel tools, both the productivity and scope of agriculture, which was the underpinning of civilization, were increased. Steel held an edge better than bronze, with the result that steel tools revolutionized crafts such as carpentry and masonry.

Just as the farmer and craftsman could afford inexpensive steel tools, infantry could now be equipped with steel corselets, shields and helmets. Protected in this way, infantrymen could stand up under the arrows of the nobility mounted in chariots. The determining factor in warfare tipped from the maneuverability of chariots to massed infantry.

The second barbarian invasion ended not long after 1100 BC, and a second uprising began, once more led by Assyria. In a continuing series of campaigns marked by their cruelty, the Assyrians expanded their empire until, at its height (750 - 626 BC), it virtually blanketed the Middle East.

It was in Assyria that Middle Eastern administrative techniques were, for the first time, strengthened. Starting with the reign of Tiglath-Pilestar III (744 - 727 BC), the land making up the core of Assyria was arbitrarily partitioned into provinces run by governors who saw to tax collection, conscripted men for imperial labor and military service, and adjudicated legal matters, all under the direction of the crown. Further afield, where it was harder to control matters directly, local rulers were made servants of the state. But as time passed, the trend was to transform these tributary territories into provinces.

Tiglath-Pilestar took several steps to curb local uprisings. He appointed eunuchs as provincial governors, since eunuchs had no children and would, therefore, be more likely to be loyal to the king. He also pursued large-scale resettlements of peoples.

To further control its large empire, Assyria built road systems to speed messengers on their way. At regular intervals of about a day's trip there were, on the major roads, stations where messengers could rest and get fresh mules to pull their chariots.

The Assyrian Empire

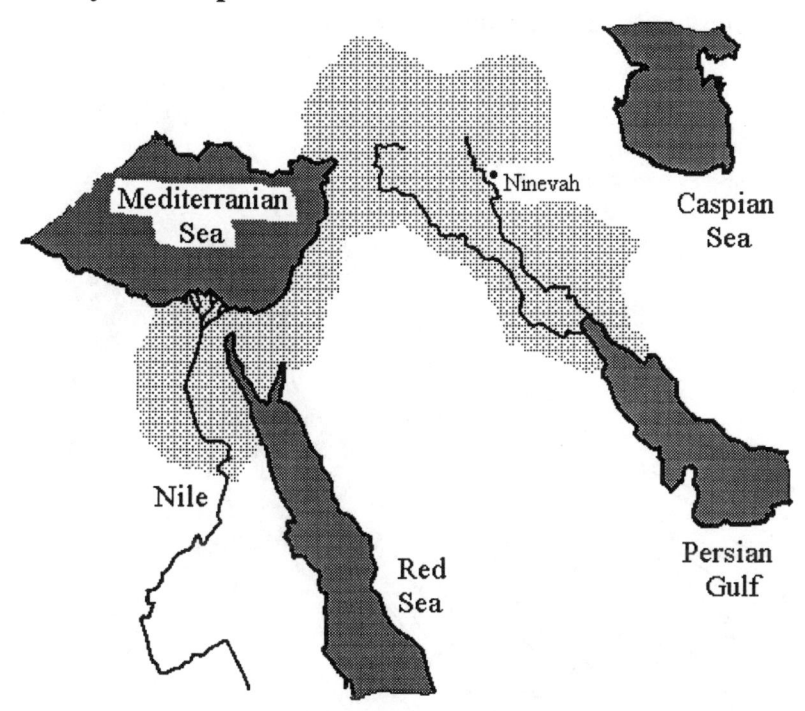

[Map showing the Assyrian Empire with labels: Mediterranian Sea, Ninevah, Caspian Sea, Nile, Red Sea, Persian Gulf]

In keeping with prior example, the Assyrians instituted written law, some parts of which were adapted from Hammurabi's code.

In the beginning, Assyrian soldiers were natives. But as the empire grew, the demand for soldiers outran the native supply. As was to be repeated time after time in the history of subsequent peoples with the same disastrous results, Assyrian soldiers were supplemented with personnel from conquered lands, until when Assyria finally fell, the army was made up primarily of subject peoples.

The immediate cause of Assyria's ruin was the usual combination of barbarian incursion (by the Medes from Iran) with internal uprising (originating in Babylonia). In 612 BC, Nineveh, the capital of Assyria, was destroyed, and the Assyrian empire was no more.

For a short while, the Medes, Babylonians and Egyptians shared the rule of the Middle East. Then around 550 BC, the Persians, led by Cyrus, emerged from the southwestern part of the

.An Assyrian Guardian of the Palace Gates *The guardian now resides in the British Museum in London.*

The Persian Empire

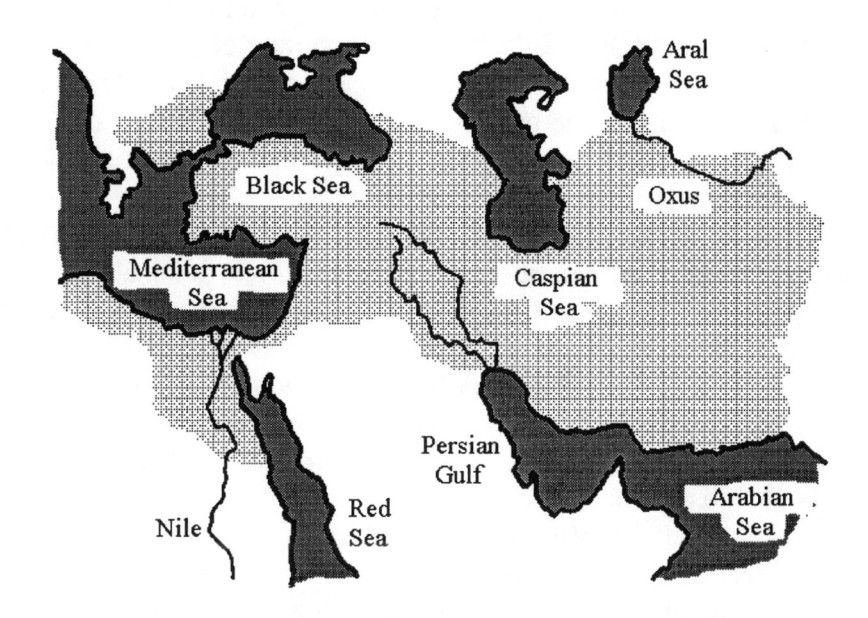

Iranian plateau and conquered most of the Middle East. In 525 BC, Cambyses, the son and successor of Cyrus, subdued Egypt. The Persian empire then reached from the Nile to the Oxus river (now the Amu Darya), which empties into the Aral sea.

The Persians adopted Assyrian techniques of administration. Under Darius the Great (521 - 486 BC), the Persian government assumed its final form, which was that of provinces, or satrapies. The Persians enlarged the Assyrian road system to help integrate their empire. It was Herodotus, the Greek historian, who said of the Persian messengers who used these roads, "Neither snow, nor rain, nor heat, nor darkness, are permitted to obstruct their speed."

Darius introduced one improvement on Assyrian administration. Periodically, he dispatched officials from his court, "the king's eyes", to advise on the condition of the satrapies and the loyalty and capability of their administrators, or satraps.

With the Persian conquest, Egypt disappears from the historical scene as an imperial power. It's instructive to inquire into why Egypt came to this insignificant end, while the nations centered around Mesopotamia continued to flourish.

Egypt and Mesopotamia had much in common. Although Egyptian civilization began somewhat later than the Mesopotamian (3000 BC versus 4000 BC), both arose on the flood plains of great rivers, in the case of Egypt the Nile, in Mesopotamia the Tigris and Euphrates, and in some respects, particularly architecture, to which its great pyramids and temples bear testimony, Egyptian skills surpassed those of the Mesopotamians.

It was in the political realm that the significant difference between Egypt and Mesopotamia lay. In contrast to the 2000 years over which Mesopotamian empire developed, Egypt was brought under a single ruler around 2850 BC. Archaeologists now think that the name of this ruler was Narmer. Traditionally, he has been known as Menes. The pertinent question here is how a king, bereft of the administrative structure that slowly grew in Mesopotamia, was able to control an empire.

First of all, in Mesopotamia, habitable land radiated beyond whatever the current borders of civilization were, with the consequence that Mesopotamia was continuously surrounded by other peoples, who were frequently hostile. As a result, both the threat and actuality of invasion demanded that Mesopotamia pay a good bit of attention to its borders. Egypt, on the other hand, was surrounded by deserts. This didn't mean that Egypt couldn't be invaded. It could and was. But invasion was infrequent. To a great extent, Egypt was free to concentrate on its own concerns.

Secondly, any given Mesopotamian empire was made up, in large part, of conquered peoples with memories of their former power and independence. The consequence was that Mesopotamia had to devote a good bit of its time to keeping these subject peoples in line, either through supervision or efforts to convert their allegiance from their former affiliation to the current empire. Egypt, on the other hand, was ethnically homogeneous. Dealing with enclaves of culturally diverse peoples wasn't an Egyptian problem.

Finally, Mesopotamia was dispersed geographically. To function as a political and economic entity, it had to develop both an extensive political bureaucracy, made up of a variety of skills to handle tax, administrative and judicial matters, and a market economy made up of merchants and artisans. Egypt, on the other hand, was geographically concentrated, a green ribbon of land of which the Nile was the backbone. The Nile flows from south to north, while the prevailing winds in Egypt blow from north to south. As a consequence, boats could move down the Nile by drifting with the current and up the Nile by catching the wind in their sails. As a means of transportation, the Nile was both available and reliable, and there was no alternative. Consequently, the king, or pharaoh, found it easy to control the movement of goods and people and, thereby, possessed the means for dominion.

From the first, the pharaoh was considered an immortal god. Thus, all of Egypt resembled one giant Sumerian temple community. Egypt was made up of a peasant mass and the household of a god. Egyptian civilization was the product of the royal household. All significant economic activity was administered by the pharaoh's household. As a consequence, Egypt never achieved the population variety that was forced on Mesopotamia by the multiple challenges with which it was faced. Egypt's political and economic structure was underdeveloped and lacked the adaptability and capacity for evolution present in Mesopotamian civilization.

When the states set up by the war chariot barbarians broke up, Egypt spread into the resulting vacuum. Yet even at this peak, the Egyptian empire was no more than an exercise of influence over a cluster of principalities. Egypt never developed the administrative organization, written law, and merchant class that characterized Mesopotamian civilization.

Egypt looms large in most history books, because the preponderance of archaeological work has been done there. Yet it never amounted to more than a byway on the path of civilization. It's to Mesopotamia that we must look for our roots.

While the Middle East was the cradle of Western civilization, it never became part of the West. Perhaps it's for this reason that, after describing the history of the Middle East as we've just done, historians slip into the practice of referring to the area with the more inclusive term of "the Orient", which indicates the ultimate direction in which the Middle East moved. In keeping with this practice, we now also adopt this terminology.

Athena. *Based on a photograph by Roloff Beny of a statue of her discovered in Piraeus in 1959. The photograph resides in the National Archives of Canada in Ottawa.*

CHAPTER THREE

Greece

We call the Greeks Greeks because that's what the Romans called them. The Greeks called themselves Hellenes, after their mythic progenitor, Hellen. And historians call the spread of Greek civilization Hellenization rather than Greekification.

We know more than usual about Greek history. The reason for this is that the Greeks were concerned with history and made efforts to write it down. Nevertheless, Greek history concentrated on Athens and Sparta. And in reading Greek history, we must keep in mind that it was written by Greeks, primarily Athenians.

We don't know when Greek speaking people began to migrate to the Balkan peninsula. The best guess is that the first Greeks appeared not long after 2000 BC.

The Greeks remained barbarians for centuries. Then around 1600 BC, civilization began in a few towns, such as Mycenae. The people who lived in these towns were Achaeans. Their towns were heavily fortified, and weapons were a feature of their archeological artifacts. Achaean society was martial.

The foundation of the Achaean state was a chariot aristocracy. However, unlike other similar states (such as the Kassite and Mitanni), the Achaeans weren't only chariot warriors. They also went to sea as traders and pirates. Agamemnon, the legendary leader of the Greeks in the Trojan War, was a king of Mycenae.

Other Greek tribes continued to filter down into the Balkan peninsula. They avoided the warlike Achaeans and settled in less fertile areas. Attica, for example, where Athens is located, was peopled by Ionian Greeks. In the 12th century BC, the Achaean state collapsed, probably because of internal conflict, and it may be that the Dorian Greeks, who moved from the north not long after 1200 BC, finished off the Achaeans. The Dorians settled in Laconia, where Sparta is found. Some of the Achaeans migrated to Attica, where they merged into the Ionian population.

As with other nomadic peoples, the original Greek political structure was built around a tribal king. Over time, military

Ancient Greece

organization began to effect changes in this political structure.

The way in which the early Greeks waged war is unclear, but cavalry was a major factor. Since grass was so rare in Greece that horses had to be fed grain most of the year, only men of agricultural wealth could become cavalrymen. As a consequence, noble landowners became politically influential. They found common cause and began to place restraints on the royal prerogative.

At first, the nobility effected this limitation of royal authority by assigning representatives to work with the king. But because the actions of these appointees weren't always to the benefit of all the landowners, a council of nobles started to convene and get involved in government affairs. Eventually, the nobility took over most of the king's authority. In Athens, the king became nothing more than an official named for a limited term and concerned primarily with religious matters. In Sparta, hereditary kingship was retained, but it was a duarchy — there were always two concurrent kings. Their power was restricted. They performed the sacrifices of the state religion, headed the judiciary, and commanded the army in war. In all matters, they were subordinate to the council of elders.

Because they were involved in government, noble families began to live where the government was centered. In this way, towns were established. The towns attracted artisans and merchants. Thus, Greek political organization came to be centered around the polis, a city encompassed by farms and pasture land. Polis is a Greek word that means both "city" and "state". The Greeks didn't distinguish between the two. Thus, a polis is a city-state, which is the way we translate the word.

Over time, the dominance of the nobility grew. A poor farmer might have to borrow seed or food. As collateral, he put up his land or freedom. Noble landowners, with their greater holdings, could survive lean years, made these loans, and benefited from them.

Then in the 7th century BC, the hoplite, a heavily armed and armored infantryman, supplanted the cavalryman as the major factor in warfare. Use of hoplites was first adopted around 670 BC by the tyrant Pheidon of Argos. Hoplites fought as a phalanx — a wing of men eight ranks deep. They carried shields and nine foot long spears, and moved in such close order that each man's shield gave protection to both him and his neighbor on his left. Because of their length, the spears of several ranks of the phalanx extended beyond the first rank. The phalanx was able to maneuver rapidly on the battlefield without losing its close order because it kept pace

The Discus Thrower. *From a photograph of a Roman copy of the original sculpture by Myron, a Greek. The copy is in the National Museum of Rome. The original has been lost.*

by means of a shouted cadence. These formidable infantry units could best cavalry.

In the phalanx, every man was an equal. Each hoplite's life depended on his neighbor's performance. Wealth and status were unimportant. Strength, courage and discipline were the essential characteristics of a man. In addition to the leveling effect of the phalanx, the close order, discipline, and action in unison gave the hoplites a strong group identification.

As a consequence, aristocratic ostentation came to be looked on with disfavor. The model man became the independent farmer, owning enough land to live decently, able to equip himself with spear, shield and helmet, and ready and able to take his place in the phalanx. Thus arose the Greek principle of moderation in all things.

The stronger the phalanx, the more secure the city-state. A system in which wealthy landowners took over small farms and turned farmers into slaves became counterproductive. In Athens, in 594 BC, Solon was given extraordinary powers to revise the laws. Solon outlawed debt-slavery and, by voiding current debts and freeing those who had previously been enslaved, returned small farmers to the land.

The phalanx also widened participation in civic affairs, since the hoplites, who were the defense of the city-state, could hardly be denied a voice in the government, and the "hoplite franchise" saw to it that they weren't.

Around 825 BC, the Greeks adopted the Phoenician invention of an alphabet as the basis for a written language. All pictorial and syllabic characters were abandoned, and words were formed from combinations of characters whose only meaning was phonetic — they represented various sounds in the spoken language. To the Phoenician contribution, the Greeks added most of the vowels. Together, these characters made up the alphabet (from "alpha beta", the first two characters of the Greek alphabet — the familiar ABC's).

Over time, the nature of agriculture changed from grain crops to an emphasis on wine and olive oil. Wine was always in demand, and olive oil was an important supplement to what was generally a fat-poor Mediterranean diet, a substitute for soap, and fuel for lamps. Moreover, wine and olive oil could be stored in jars and relatively easily shipped. By exporting wine and olive oil, the city-state got in return more grain and other goods than it could have produced locally. Grape-olive agriculture also added to the amount of productive land, for grape vines and olive trees could grow on the uneven and rocky slopes of Greece not conducive to grain cultivation.

Grape-olive agriculture also contributed to the democratization of the city-state. Food for the Oriental city came from the surrounding countryside, much of it in the form of rent and taxes. As a consequence, the Oriental farmer was only peripherally involved in city life and accepted political change as little more than a turnover of masters. The Greek farmer, on the other hand, made a vital contribution to his city-state in the production of exports, bought the products of the city as readily as any urban resident, and thought of himself and was thought of by his contemporaries as a model citizen. Market relationships reached further down into society in Greece than in the Orient and bound more of the populace into a united, aware, proud political unit.

In 491 BC, a Persian fleet of 600 troop ships moved across the Aegean and reached Euboea. After putting up minor resistance, Euboea surrendered, and the Persians crossed the bay to Attica, where they camped at Marathon.

It was at Marathon that about 16,000 Greeks from just two city-states, Plataea and Athens, battled around 20,000 Persians. The smaller Greek force routed the Persians, and if Greek testimony can be believed, 6400 Persians but only 192 Greeks were killed. Marathon was the end of the first Persian invasion of Greece.

Darius was succeeded by his son, Xerxes. At that point, Xerxes' most critical concern was an uprising in Egypt, which was finally crushed after prolonged resistance. A rebellion in Babylonia then had to be put down. After dealing with these distractions, Xerxes turned his attention to Greece.

In the meantime, in 485 BC, the Athenians discovered rich veins of silver at Laurium. These mines were worked with slave labor, and each year, the output of the mines was distributed among the labor, and each year, the output of the mines was distributed among the citizens of Athens. In 483 BC, Themistocles built, for Athens, a new harbor at Piraeus. In 482 BC, he persuaded the Athenians to forgo their annual distribution of silver from Laurium so that the Athenian fleet could be expanded from 70 to 200 triremes. A trireme was a galley with three banks of oars.

In 481 BC, Xerxes moved out with an army of about a million men, the largest ever heretofore mustered. It was a mortally heterogeneous host. There were Persians, Medes, Babylonians, Afghans, Indians, Bactrians, Sogdians, Sacae, Assyrians, Armenians, Coichians, Scyths, Paeonians, Mysians, Paphlagonians, Phrygians, Thracians, Thessalians, Locvians, Aeolians, Lydians, Carians, Cilicians, Cypriotes, Phoenicians, Syrians, Arabians, Egyptians, Ethiopians, Libyians, and many more. In the spring of 480 BC, the army arrived at the Hellespont, where engineers constructed a bridge consisting of a road resting on the decks of 674 (Herodotus's number) ships. It took the army seven days to cross the bridge. It marched through Thrace into Macedonia and Thessaly accompanied by the Persian fleet, made up of possibly 3000 ships of various sizes, which moved down the coast.

Against this horde stood a shaky league of not many more than 20 city-states. The Athenians sailed north to meet the Persian fleet, and a troop of 6000 under King Leonidas of Sparta went to delay Xerxes at Thermopylae.

The two fleets came together off the northern coast of Euboea. When the Greek leaders saw the size of the Persian fleet, they were inclined to retreat. The Euboeans, afraid of incursion by the Persians, offered Themistocles 30 talents (a talent was 57 pounds of gold) if he would see that the Greek fleet fought, which he did by dividing the money among the ship captains. The battle lasted three days and was indecisive. The Persians withdrew to Aphetae, the Greeks to Artemisium.

Leonidas held the Persians back for two days at Thermopylae. His flank was then turned, and he realized that the battle was lost. He dismissed all of his troops but the 300 Spartans whom he had brought with him. These Spartans consisted of "elders", for Leonidas had allowed only fathers of sons to go with him, so no Spartan family would be wiped out. Of these Spartans, only two survived Thermopylae. One died a year later in the battle of

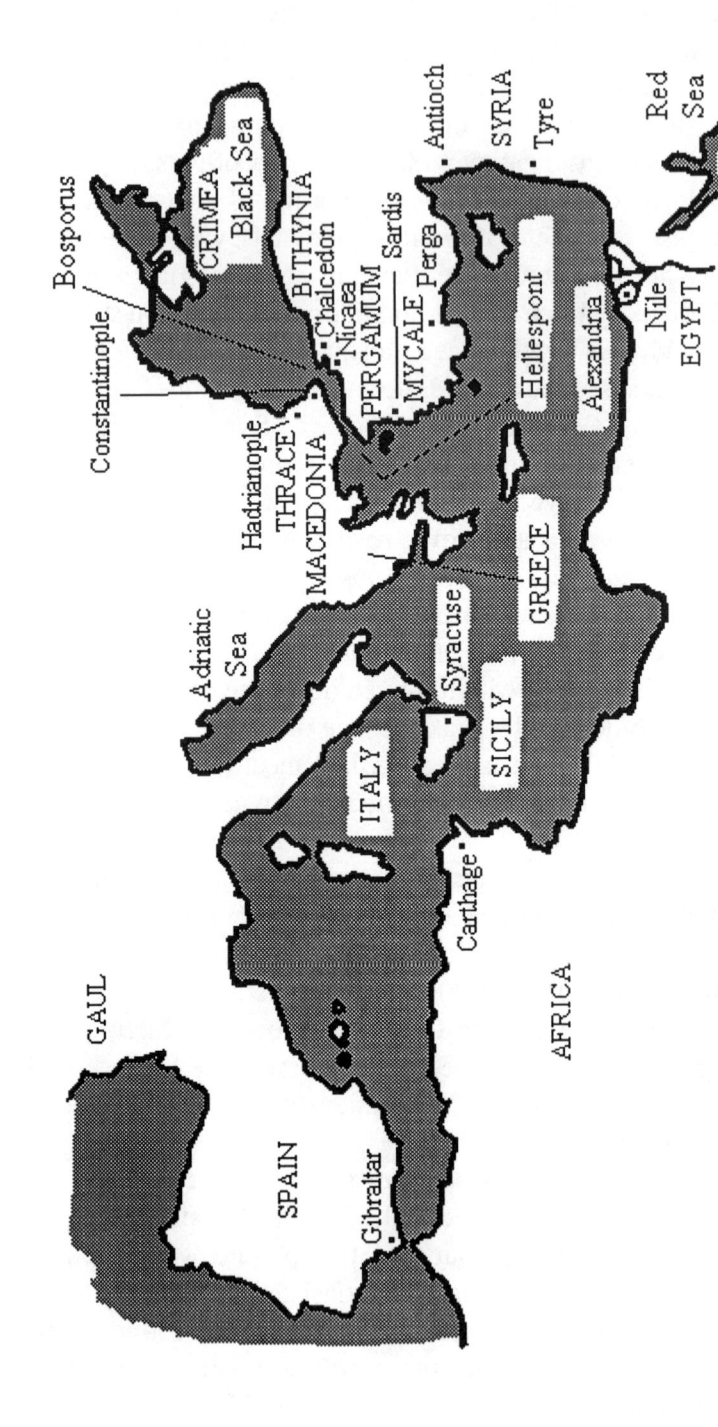

The Mediterranean Area in Greco-Roman Times

Plataea, the other hanged himself in shame. Herodotus said that the Persians lost 20,000. The epitaph on the tomb of the Spartans at Thermopylae reads, "Go, stranger, and tell the Spartans that we lie here in obedience to their laws."

When news of Thermopylae reached the Athenian fleet, it sailed south through the Euripus strait to Salamis, an island west of the peninsula on which Athens is located. Athens was abandoned. By the time Xerxes reached the city, it was almost deserted, and he sacked and burned it.

Soon after, the Persian fleet, made up of 1200 fighting ships, moved into the bay of Salamis. The Greeks, in contrast, had just over 200 triremes. Most of the Greek leaders were once more against engaging. Themistocles dispatched a slave to Xerxes to tell him that the Greeks were planning to escape and that he could forestall this by surrounding the Greek fleet. Xerxes acted according to the counsel, and the Greeks had no choice but to fight. Persian captains were hampered by lack of a common language, and the Greeks carried the day. According to Diodorus, the Persians lost 200 ships, the Greeks 40. The Greeks lost few men, for if a Greek ship sank, the crew just swam to shore.

What was left of the Persian fleet retreated to the Hellespont. Xerxes left 300,000 men in Greece under Mardonius, his nephew and son in law, and withdrew the rest of his forces to Sardis, since without his fleet, he was unable to keep his troops supplied. A large part of the retreating army died of plague and dysentery along the way.

Mardonius set up his camp near Plataea on the Boeotian plain. A year after the naval battle at Salamis, 110,000 Greeks, led by the Spartan king Pausanias, engaged Mardonius in the largest land battle of the Persian wars. The non-Persians under Mardonius abandoned the field as soon as the Persian soldiers, who made up the salient, fell back under the Greek blows. According to Herodotus, the Persians lost 260,000 men, the Greeks 159. Diodorus lowered the Persian losses to 100,000, and Plutarch raised the Greek losses to 1360.

On the same day (once more, according to the Greeks), a Greek fleet met a Persian one off the coast of Mycale. The Persian fleet was wiped out, and the Greek city-states on the Aegean coast of Asia Minor were emancipated from Persian dominion.

Thus were the Persian wars concluded. They marked the end of the westward advance of the Persian empire. Herodotus may have exaggerated the difference between Persian soldiers whipped into battle and Greeks fighting of their own free will, but he, nevertheless, put his finger on a critical point.

The significance of the outcome of the Persian wars was that, for another three centuries, it allowed the Greek mind to develop free from the enervating mysticism of the Orient.

Athen's fleet, powered by citizen rowers, gave the landless Athenian, who was too poor to equip himself for service in the phalanx and whose only asset was a strong back, an essential part to play in the defense of the city-state. As a consequence, he earned the right to participate in the government, and Greek democracy spread further.

Nevertheless, in several respects, Greek democracy was foreign to what we're familiar with. First, for the Greeks, the essence of democracy was a collection of citizens who could gather periodically (typically, once a week) at a single meeting place to consider the problems they faced.

Second, Greek democracy was limited. No democracy has an unrestricted franchise, but the Greeks went further than most. No women could vote. In fact, women had no say over their lives. They lived under the guardianship of a male, a father, or if he were dead, the male next of kin, or a husband. They could own no property and spent their lives in the women's quarters of their homes.

No alien could vote, and to be a citizen, both of your parents had to be citizens. To be able to vote, a citizen had to be in a position to make himself available whenever and for whatever length of time was required to carry out whatever public role he might be assigned. Many citizens couldn't meet this requirement. Finally, the Greeks had slaves, and in some city-states they were numerous. Slaves, of course, couldn't vote. Consequently, those who voted were a rather aristocratic lot. They had the leisure to engage in political activity because they had slaves to do their work for them.

So the Greeks get the credit for originating democracy. In fact, even the derivation of the word democracy is from the Greek. But it was democracy reserved to a small in-group, and as we'll see shortly when we look at the Delian Confederacy, it could be combined with an indifferent, despotic attitude toward less fortunate groups. At best, it was a model for the type of town-meeting government found in small New England villages. The representative form of government, which we practice today, developed from sources unconnected with Greek tradition.

Finally, Greek democracy didn't work that well. Not uncommonly, strong minded men would tire of the debate over governmental decisions and assume power on the basis of military might. These men were called tyrants. But in those days, the word, tyranny, didn't carry the unequivocal connotation of exploitation that it does today. Typically, the rule of a tyrant was benign if not actually beneficial to the city-state involved.

While on the subject of political organization, it's pertinent to ask why the Greek city-states never merged, either voluntarily or forcibly, into larger political units. The answer seems to be that, with their orientation toward city government, they were never able to create a political system suitable to the purpose. The best that they could achieve were intercity leagues or confederations, and this usually occurred for only short periods under pressure of external threat.

The Greek answer to population press was colonization. This movement resulted in Greek cities scattered from Africa to Thrace and from Gibraltar to the eastern end of the Black sea.

Greece also served as a source of mercenary troops. For instance, after the Persian wars, Persian satraps paid Greeks the ultimate compliment of hiring them for military service.

While giving Greece its due, we should also note that trial by jury is of Greek origin, even though the jury was typically larger than ours. For example, the jury that condemned Socrates to death was made up of 1200 men, although because of the importance of the man on trial, this was unusually large. More characteristic was a jury of several hundred. Such numbers were practical because a Greek trial seldom lasted more than a day, and minor cases were settled by a panel of judges without resort to a jury.

In 477 BC, the Greek city-states of Asia Minor and the Aegean organized, under Athenian leadership, the Delian Confederacy, ostensibly to defend against future Persian invasion. Athens provided the administration for the Confederacy, while the other city-states made annual monetary contributions to a common fund kept in the temple of Apollo on Delos. Because of its dominance, Athens exercised de facto control over the other members of the association, and the Confederacy was transformed into an Athenian empire. It was the Confederacy's funds that, in 454 BC, Pericles had transferred from Delos to Athens to pay for the vast construction that represents what art historians refer to as the "Golden Age". The contribution of the other city-states to the common fund became an annual assessment used to beautify Athens. By 432 BC, the yearly amount had grown to around 460 talents per city-state.

The distaste of the subject city-states for such despotism, and the fear of other city-states that they might become subject to Athens, resulted in an alliance with Sparta to end Athens' domination. The consequence was the Peloponnesian War, which was fought intermittently from 431 through 404 BC. When the devastation of the war was over and Sparta emerged the victor, it turned out to be more despotic than Athens. It exacted an annual tribute of 1000 talents from each of the city-states in the former Athenian empire and set up a Spartan governor, backed by Spartan troops, in each of them.

There then followed a period of shifting political balance in Greece. The spread of Greek economic practices to its colonies worked to the detriment of the home country. In Thrace and along the Black Sea, Greek colonies developed the manufacturing skills previously found only in city-states such as Athens and Corinth. In the West, Greek and Etruscan cities followed suit. Wine and olive oil production multiplied in Sicily, southern Italy, and Carthage, and grape growing expanded in central Italy, Thrace, Bithynia, and the Crimea. The trade patterns (which had brought fortune to the Aegean city-states) then shifted, and the colonies became the ones to get the benefit of the favorable terms of trade for wine and olive oil vis a vis grain. As a result, economic decline set in at the center of Greek civilization. Depressed living conditions propelled the lower classes into the mercenary armies that were becoming common. Civil discord, which crippled city-states, grew to be the rule. These disorders, and endless and savage intercity wars, prepared the way for the coming of Philip of Macedonia.

Macedonia was a barbarous state of tough but illiterate mountain men when Philip became its king in 359 BC. But in contrast to the Greek city-states, it was territorially large. Philip had lived for three years in Thebes as a hostage, and his overriding ambition was to unite Greece under his rule and then rid Asia Minor of the Persians. He maintained a Greek court at his capital, Pella, and his nobles were semi-Hellenized. He borrowed the Greek concept of the phalanx but armed his infantrymen with pikes longer than the spears carried by the Greeks. To the phalanx, he added cavalry, which he also trained in close-order tactics. He drilled this army of 10,000 men into the most powerful fighting force the world had yet known. Philip began his incursion into Greece in 357 BC and completed the conquest in 338 BC at the battle of Chaeronea.

Philip was generous in victory. He freed his prisoners and guaranteed the independence of each city-state, which spoke to their pride and also prevented the growth of any one city-state, at the expense of the others, into a potential Macedonian enemy. He called an assembly of the city-states at Corinth and organized them into a federation. At a subsequent assembly, be proposed that liberation of Asia Minor from the Persian yoke be undertaken. His proposal was adopted, he was put in charge, and each city-state committed itself to supplying him with men and arms.

Philip's plans were cut short when he was assassinated. There are various proposals for the explanation of the assassination. But whatever the particulars, the motive for the assassination was personal. It wasn't a commentary on Philip's political activities. As a result of the assassination, Alexander, Philip's son, then 20 years old, took his father's place at the head of the Greek federation.

Thus, when Alexander invaded Persia in 334 BC, he did so as a champion of Hellenism at the head of a combined Macedonian and Greek army about 40,000 strong. He reestablished the independence of the Greek city-states of Asia Minor. In Persia, he

Alexander's Empire

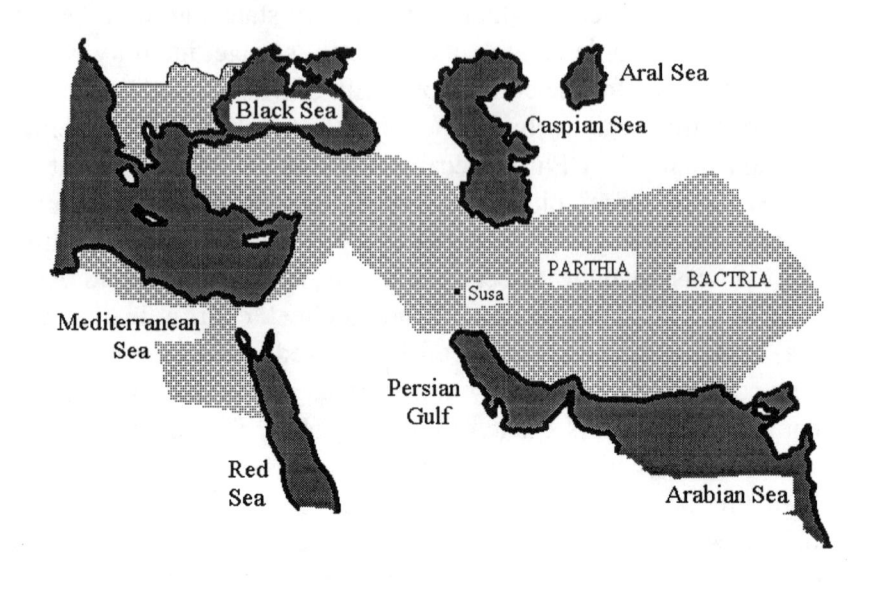

promoted the practices of Greek civilization. He set up Greek cities on the borders of his empire. Most of these cities were in eastern Iran, but Alexandria, in Egypt, was the most successful.

In just three years, Alexander subdued the Persian empire. He owed his success to the superbly trained fighting force he inherited from his father and application of a fundamental principle of siege warfare. If on the appearance of his army outside a city, the city opened its gates to him, he treated the citizens with benevolence, spared the city, and asked only for its allegiance. But if a city resisted, then when it was vanquished, the inhabitants were massacred or sold into slavery and the city was pillaged.

The effect of Alexander's conquests on Greece was profound. In the wake of Alexander's army, thousands, maybe hundreds of thousands, of Greeks moved to seek their fortunes in the Orient. Alexander never returned from Asia. In 323 BC, at the age of 33, he died.

After conflict that lasted almost half a century, Alexander's generals ultimately divided his empire between them. Three states emerged: Macedonia, consisting of Macedon and Greece, and ruled over by Antipater; Egypt under Ptolemy; and the Seleucid empire, in western Asia, under Seleucus. In each case, local methods of government were retained. Macedonia remained a collection of city-states with a free peasantry. Ptolemy and his offspring assumed the role of pharaoh. And government by satrapy prevailed in the Seleucid empire.

Ptolemy and Seleucus had no authority for their claim to power and were strangers in their own land. The justification for their rule was their Macedonian troopers. They needed Greek administrative talent to take advantage of the resources of their empires so that the revenue to pay their troopers could be collected and, at every opportunity, appointed Greeks to official roles in their states. Even so, not all Greek immigrants ended up in governmental posts. Many were merchants, doctors, teachers, athletes, actors and architects — the upper classes of society.

To reduce the expense associated with standing armies while, at the same time, appealing to the desire for land of Macedonian peasant-soldiers who had joined the army to improve their lot, the Ptolemies and Seleucids established military enclaves for their soldiers, where in exchange for plots of land, the soldiers agreed to return to active service on call. In the Seleucid empire, such military enclaves, on occasion, grew into Greek-style city-states.

Those who lived in these and other Hellenistic cities came from a variety of origins. Even in the cities that completely adopted Hellenism for their own, the chances were that the Greeks were in the minority. But the people in these cities who flourished were those who at least passed as Greek or Macedonian. Consequently, the indigenous upper classes of cities such as Antioch and Susa were encouraged to adopt Greek ways. Being Greek was no longer so much a matter of birth as it was of a person's culture. As a result, these cities and dozens of others became Greek islands in an Oriental sea.

Thus it was that Greek civilization, after having incubated on the Balkan peninsula, spread, in a variety of ways, throughout the Orient. And it wasn't over yet. For another 100 years, Greek culture continued to grow.

Over time, the Seleucid empire was subject to erosion. In the east, Bactria (255 BC), and then Parthia (247 BC), broke away. At about the same time, in Asia Minor, Pergamum gained its independence. What was left of the Seleucid empire was basically Syria.

The Greeks had a gift for creating beauty, to which their statuary testifies. However, it would be hard to describe the Greeks, themselves, as beautiful. What more readily come to mind when describing Greeks are words like treacherous, duplicitous, selfish, grasping, exploitive, envious and ungrateful. Besides the examples we've already seen, here are a few more illustrations of less than attractive Greek behavior.

Miltiades, the leader of the Greek forces at Marathon, subsequently failed to take an Aegean island, the capture of which be had been commissioned to effect. He was impeached and fined. But he got off lucky. During the Peloponnesian War, Athens won a sea battle at Arginusae. Nevertheless, the city subsequently executed six generals involved in the battle because, in stormy weather, they had failed to rescue Athenian seamen. Athens carried out these executions even though the executions reduced its experienced commanders to a perilously low level. During this war, at least 27 cities switched sides.

Pausanias, the victor over the Persian forces at Plataea, subsequently captured Byzantium, which opened the waterway to the grain grown around the Black sea. Nevertheless, Sparta accused him of treasonable negotiations with Persia. On his recall to Sparta, he avoided arrest by claiming sanctuary in a Spartan temple. He was walled in and left to starve.

Themistocles, whose efforts made defeat of the Persian fleet at Salamis possible, was anti-Spartan, and because Athens was pro-Spartan, it ostracized him (exiled him for ten years). The Spartans accused him of complicity in the alleged treason of Pausanias. Athens then condemned Themistocles to death. As a result, he approached the Persians, who gave him a princedom, which he held for the rest of his life.

Leonidas lost the battle at Thermopylae because a Greek collaborator showed the Persians the way through the mountains, which allowed them to turn Leonidas's flank. Cimon, the son of Miltiades, who paid his father's fine, served at Salamis and subsequently led several successful expeditions against the Persians. Nevertheless, he was ostracized. Pericles, the Athenian leader at the beginning of the Peloponessian War, was elected over and over as an Athenian general. However, ultimately, he was driven from this position, accused of embezzlement, and fined.

We know more about Greek mythology than most ancient religions for two reasons. First, Homer and Hesiod recorded it, so it was a written rather than an oral tradition. Second, Greece has long been recognized as one of the direct ancestors of the West, and as a consequence, its mythology has been both studied and popularized more than others.

We have difficulty understanding and identifying with Greek mythology. And in this, we're not alone. Greeks were also troubled by their mythology.

One difficulty with Greek myths was the gods' weaknesses. Greeks were just as human as the rest of us. As a matter of fact, they may have been more human than most. They undoubtedly could recognize themselves in the gods and goddesses who contended with one another, hoodwinked and lied to god and man alike, and engaged in all kinds of morally questionable acts. But the Greeks, in their own lives, no matter how fallible they were, aspired to a life regulated by law and administered with justice. That their gods not only didn't exhibit these traits, but didn't even strive for them, was troubling.

The other difficulty with Greek religion was the ambiguity in Greek myths. Sometimes Zeus was described as omnipotent. At other times, he was depicted as subject to fate. This ambiguity was a consequence of the fact that Greek mythology resulted from a mixture of myths developed over time. Of course, in this respect, the Greeks were no different than other peoples. What was different was that, in Greece, religious officials were elected. As a consequence, the Greeks had no authoritative, organized, self-sustaining priesthood to resolve such difficulties and interpret the world to the populace.

Because of these deficiencies in their religion, Greeks were more inclined than others to take an objective view of the world around them and try to figure out what was going on. Perhaps as a reflection of the law regulated city-states in which they lived, the Greeks developed a frame of mind that saw the natural world as physical phenomena subject to laws, and they were convinced that, if these natural laws could be uncovered, the behavior of things could be explained accordingly. It's this way of thinking that's the priceless birthright handed down by our Greek ancestors.

As in any field, those that contributed to Greek science were many, and we can't note them all. In fact, with all due respect to all those we don't mention, here we speak of only a few.

The first we consider is Aristotle, who lived from 384 to 322 BC. Aristotle codified virtually all the knowledge of his time. He placed great emphasis on logic and invented the syllogism, which is the logic of classes. In keeping with this frame of mind, it's not surprising that he was most at home with biology, in which taxonomy is prominent.

Medicine also advanced in Greece. Herophilus of Chalcedon practiced dissection in Alexandria about 285 BC and described the retina, optic nerves, cerebrum, cerebellum and meninges. He classified nerves as sensory or motor, and distinguished between the cranial and spinal nerves. He noted the difference between arteries and veins, and identified arteries as the conveyer of blood from the heart to the rest of the body. He used a water clock to take the pulse as part of his diagnosis. Erasistratus studied in Athens and practiced in Alexandria around 258 BC. He differentiated more precisely between the cerebrum and cerebellum, identified the function of the epiglottis, the lacteal vessels of the mesentery, and the aortic and pulmonary valves of the heart.

The Greeks didn't excel in arithmetic, probably because they never developed the concept of zero as a place marker in numeric notation. Geometry was their forte. Euclid started a school in Alexandria, and around 300 BC, he wrote his Elements that, until the 20th century, remained the standard textbook on geometry. He maintained that he was just collecting the geometrical knowledge of Pythagoras, Hippocrates, Eudoxus, and other Greek geometricians. It was his organization of this knowledge into a progression of proofs that was his vital contribution. Appollonius of Perga, after attending Euclid's school for years, did the definitive work on conic sections, the curves that can be generated by the intersection of a cone and a plane, and assigned three of them (parabola, ellipse and hyperbola) their names. The fourth is the circle.

Hipparchus of Nicaea (in Bithynia), who died in 126 BC, improved, probably on Babylonian models, the astrolabes and quadrants that were the main astronomical instruments of the time. He invented the technique of describing terrestrial position in terms of latitude and longitude. He invented trigonometry and developed a table of sines. He fixed the year at 365 and one quarter days less four minutes and 48 seconds. He was off by six minutes. Hipparchus was the creator of what has come to be known as the Ptolemaic system of describing the universe. Ptolemy followed Hipparchus by 250 years and put the finishing touches on his theory.

The Ptolemaic system was geocentric (that is, it assumed that the Earth was the center of the universe) and explained planetary motion in terms of "epicycles". In Greek, planet means wanderer.

Hipparchus's theory was wrong, but it was the first attempt to fit a geometric model to the mass of astronomical data that had been collected about the heavens by the Babylonians, and it was capable of a high degree of explanation and prediction.

Perhaps the quintessential Greek was Archimedes. He was born around 287 BC at Syracuse in Sicily. He went to Alexandria and worked under Euclid's followers. He then went back to Syracuse. We still have ten of Archimedes' works. In them, among other things, he set the value of pi at between 3 and 1/7 and 3 and 10/71; determined by methods approximating integral calculus. the area cut from a parabola by a chord; and investigated techniques for finding the volume and surface area of a pyramid, cone, cylinder and sphere.

According to Vitruvius, Hieron, the king of Syracuse, entrusted a jeweler with gold to make a crown. When the crown was presented, it weighed as much as the supplied gold. But Hieron suspected that the jeweler had mixed silver with the gold to achieve the desired weight and retained the leftover gold. He asked Archimedes to set the matter to rest. For weeks, Archimedes worked on the problem. Then one day, when he stepped into a tub at the public baths, the solution struck him. He ran out naked into the street and hurried to his house, while exclaiming over and over,

"Eureka (I have it) !" First he emersed the crown in water and preserved the runoff. Then he emersed gold equal in weight to the crown. The gold displaced less water than the crown, which proved that the crown had been debased with lighter weight silver.

To emphasize the power of the lever, Archimedes said, "Give me a place to stand on, and I'll move the world." Hieron, drawing Archimedes' attention to Hieron's men, who were having trouble beaching a ship, asked him to do as he said. Archimedes arranged a series of cogs and pulleys and, using this device, was able to pull the ship onto the beach by himself.

After Hieron died, Syracuse was attacked by the Roman Marcellus. Archimedes was then 75, but he supervised the defense. When Marcellus's ships approached the shore, the sailors were bombarded by arrows shot through holes that Archimedes had bored through the city's walls. He built cranes that, when Roman ships came within range, dropped heavy stones on them and sank many. Other cranes, with huge hooks, snagged ships, lifted them into the air, and smashed them against the rocks or dropped them end-foremost into the sea. Marcellus called back his fleet and advanced by land. But Archimedes attacked the troops with stones shot from catapults. Marcellus was reduced to blockading the city. After eight months of starvation, Syracuse gave up. Slaughter and sack followed, but Marcelus made clear that Archimedes wasn't to be harmed. While the city was being plundered, a Roman soldier found Archimedes engrossed in figures he had drawn in the sand. The soldier ordered Archimedes to follow him to Marcellus, but Archimedes begged off until he had solved his problem. The soldier killed him.

CHAPTER FOUR

Rome

Most of the people who came to inhabit the Italian peninsula were Indo-European tribes who had moved down from the north across the Alps in recurring waves during the period 2000 - 1000 BC. The Romans descended from the Latin people who settled the plain of Latium on the west coast south of the Tiber river between 1000 and 900 BC. They were well established when the adjoining district of Tuscany, north of the Tiber, was occupied by the Etruscans some time before 800 BC. The Etruscans weren't Indo-Europeans and were more civilized than the Latins.

In the 7th century BC, the Etruscans started to move south. For the majority of the 6th century BC, the Etruscans occupied Rome and the adjoining Latin cities. As a result, the Etruscans made major contributions to the growth of Roman civilization.

Near the end of the 6th century BC (the traditional date is 509 BC), the Romans successfully rebelled against their Etruscan king and set up a republic. In this republic, the already present class difference between the aristocratic patricians and the plebeian mass was legally sanctioned. All offices and senate membership were restricted to patricians. Intermarriage between the two classes was outlawed. Executive and judicial power resided in two concurrently serving consuls, who were elected for a one year term each. The consuls were advised by the senate, the 300 members of which were appointed for life by the consuls. Legislative power was the prerogative of the comitia centuriata, an assembly of citizens who elected the consuls and other officers. However, legislation passed by this assembly had to be approved by the senate before it became binding. As its name implies, the assembly was organized into groups, called "centuries", and it voted by century — that is, each century had one vote. Most of the centuries were made up of patricians.

With typical Roman perseverance and respect for law, the plebeians organized, maintained constant political pressure sporadically supplemented by mass withdrawal of labor, and in

Roman Italy

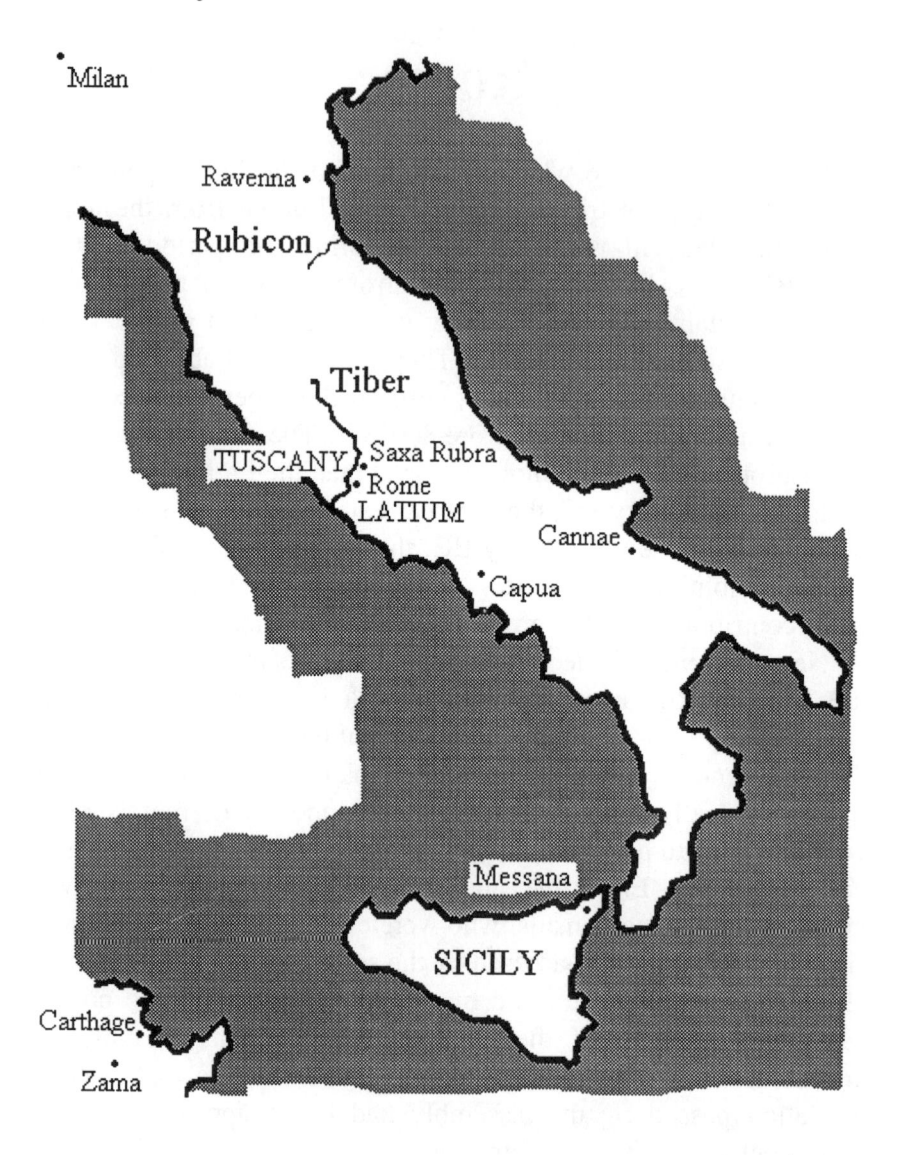

about a century and a half effected a gradual and peaceful equalization of the political situation. They were aided in this effort by the fact that they supplied the soldiers needed by Rome to fight its wars.

At the beginning of the 5th century BC, the plebeians earned the right to elect tribunes — officials to represent them. There were ten tribunes. They were elected by the plebeian assembly, or comitia tributa. The plebeians were organized by tribe, which accounts for the name of their assembly and officials.

The power of the tribunes and the plebeian assembly grew steadily until, in 339 BC, the plebeian assembly was granted the right to make laws, which were subject only to the approval of the senate, and this qualification was soon removed. At the same time, it was eliminated for laws passed by the comitia centuriata.

The plebeians also acquired the right to marry patricians and fill almost all offices. One of the consuls could be a plebeian, but the other had to be a patrician. In effect, the legal distinction between patrician and plebeian had been all but eliminated.

The Roman republic was a city-state, one of several Latin city-states on the plain of Latium. It was also a city-state that, unlike the Greek city-states, succeeded in making the transition from city-state to empire, as we shall see.

In 343 BC, Capua, another city-state, was attacked by Samnite tribes. Initially, Rome came to the support of Capua. But this first Samnite war soon evolved into a battle between Rome and the Samnites. Rome won. One of the consequences of this victory was that Capua became a dependent ally of Rome.

The other Latin city-states then became concerned about Rome's ascendancy and attacked it. The outcome of this Latin war was a Roman victory and the assimilation of the Latins into the Roman empire as partial citizens.

The second and third Samnite wars consumed the majority of the period from 326 to 290 BC. During these wars, other Italian peoples joined the Samnites to resist Rome's growing power and went down with them. When the fighting was over, Rome was in control of all Italy below the Lombard plain except for the Greek cities at the southern end of the peninsula. These she occupied 15 years later.

With respect to defeated cities and tribes, the Romans insisted on being responsible for military and foreign policy matters. In all other affairs, however, the cities and tribes were left to govern themselves. Thus, although there was no question of Rome's dominance, these cities and tribes were considered to be, and considered themselves as, allies of Rome.

Rome's expansion on the Italian peninsula brought it into contact with Carthage. Carthage had been founded in the middle of the 8th century BC by Phoenicians. The Phoenician name for the colony was Kart-hadasht, or New Town.

By the 3d century BC, Carthage had become the center of an extensive trading empire in the Mediterranean. The Carthaginians spoke the Semitic language that they had inherited from the Phoenicians. The Romans called this language Punic.

Before Rome conquered southern Italy, Carthage had been no problem to Rome, and vice versa, since Rome's orientation was to the land and Carthage's fortune was pursued at sea. But Carthage occupied over half of Sicily and came to regard the Romans at the southern tip of the peninsula as too close for comfort. The first Punic war started in 264 BC when Rome responded to a request from the Greek leaders of Messana for help against Syracuse, which caused the Carthaginians to menace Messana with the aim of blocking passage between Sicily and Italy.

The majority of the conflict took place in Sicily. It was quickly driven home to the Romans that they couldn't win an overseas war without a navy equal to the task of ferrying men and supplies without fear of destruction. During the next few years, the Romans built and lost two fleets, about 600 warships and 1000 transports, more to storm than battle. When a ship went down, most of the sailors and soldiers being transported were drowned. The losses were appalling. And building these fleets emptied the Roman treasury.

But Rome wouldn't give up. Private contributions provided the money for a new fleet, which won a telling battle at the Aegates islands in 241 BC, and the Carthaginians left Sicily.

With the taking of Sicily, Rome embarked on a new program of administration for conquered lands. A small number of cities that had supported Rome were given the same terms as those extended to the Italians. But most of the island was converted into a Roman province committed to paying one tenth of its output to Rome in tribute and under the administration of a military praetor from

Rome. The Romans also took, from Carthage, Sardinia and Corsica, which they formed into another province.

Hamilcar Barca, a Carthaginian military leader, established colonies in Spain as both valuable in their own right and a base from which to attack Rome. Hamilcar derives from Ahimelqart, which means Brother of Melqart. Melqart was the patron god of the Phoenician city of Tyre. Hamilcar's son was Hannibal, which means Favorite of Baal, a popular Carthagenian name, since Carthage had adopted the Phoenician worship of the god Baal.

After Hamilcar died, Hannibal built an army in Spain, marched through southern Gaul, crossed the Alps, bested the Romans in several battles, and all but demolished the Roman army at Cannae in 216 BC. Hannibal knew the city of Rome was too well defended to be taken, but he had planned on a general Italian uprising after he had destroyed the Roman army. This didn't happen. Most of Rome's allies remained loyal. After Cannae, the Roman army evaded Hannibal. Hannibal could make large parts of Italy desolate. But he couldn't take Rome, and he couldn't pin down the Roman army.

Time wasn't on Hannibal's side. By 206 BC, Scipio Africanus had driven the Carthaginians out of Spain, from which was created two new provinces, Nearer and Farther Spain. He then returned to Rome and began promoting the idea of invading Africa. By 204 BC, senate support and voluntary contributions had sufficed to provide Scipio with an expeditionary force with which he crossed the Mediterranean. Carthage recalled Hannibal to its defense. The war ended with his defeat at Zama in 200 BC. It was this victory in Africa that earned for Scipio the appellation Africanus. As a result of its loss, Carthage had to pay a large indemnity, give up its fleet, and accept Roman control over its foreign policy.

During Hannibal's invasion of Italy, Philip V of Macedonia formed an alliance with Hannibal and began an independent war against Rome. Consequently, when Carthage had been subjugated, Rome invaded Macedonia. It was supported in this campaign by Pergamum. Macedonia was defeated in 197 BC. Philip retained his crown in Macedonia proper, but the Greek city-states were freed from Macedonian domination, and Philip pledged to no longer wage war without Rome's permission.

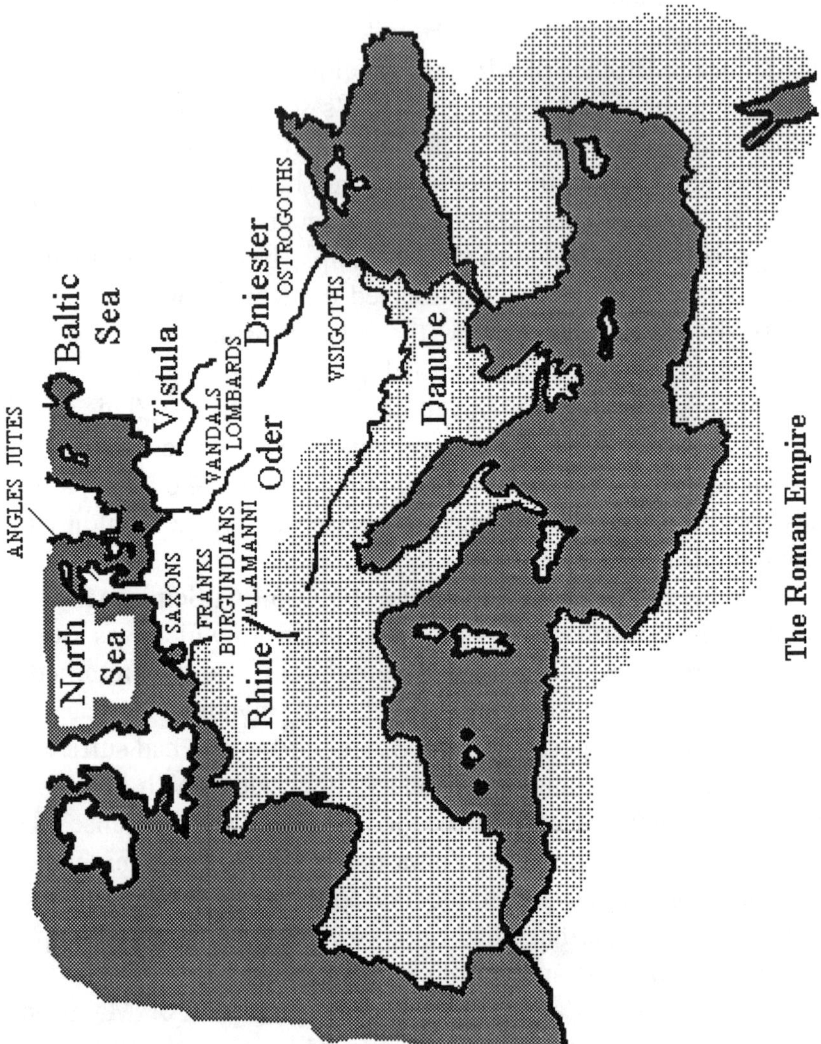

The Roman Empire

In the meantime, Antiochus III of Syria had overrun parts of Asia Minor and Thrace. In 192 BC, he crossed the Aegean and invaded Greece. Once more, Rome felt compelled to repulse an aggressor who was getting too close. In 191 BC, Antiochus was driven from Greece. Again, Pergamum had joined in. To prevent Antiochus from posing a threat to Pergamum, Rome pursued Antiochus into Asia. By 189 BC, Antiochus had been defeated. He retained power in Syria but was forbidden by Rome to move on any ally of Rome.

Philip died in 179 BC, but his son Perseus continued to intrigue against Rome. In particular, he stirred up the Greek city-states, which since once more becoming independent, had again sunk into a morass of intercity feuds and economic distress. When Rome could no longer stand idly by, it declared war on Macedonia in 171 BC. By 168 BC, Macedonia was once more defeated. This time it was divided into four republics.

In spite of these repeated defeats and the relatively lenient treatment meted out by Rome, both Macedonia and Greece continued to plot against Rome. Finally, in 148 BC, Rome converted Macedonia into a province and put Greece under direct Roman supervision.

Carthage was now beginning to show signs of renaissance, and in Rome's eyes, particularly those of Cato (who opened each day's proceedings in the senate with the words, "Carthage must be destroyed"), this return to power could mean only trouble for Rome. In 149 BC, Rome put Carthage under siege, and in 146 BC, it destroyed the city and converted Carthage into the province of Africa.

In 133 BC, the king of Pergamum willed his kingdom to Rome. It then became the province of Asia. In 121 BC, Rome annexed the province of Transalpine Gaul. In 64 BC, Syria came under Roman domination. In 30 BC, it was Egypt's turn to become a Roman province.

As a result of these conquests and alliances with other states, the city-state of Rome established hegemony throughout the Mediterranean. Over time, there was a tendency for Rome to convert its allies and protectorates into provinces. And generals continued to lead their legions into battle to keep peace in the provinces and add territory to the Roman empire.

Although the official structure of the Roman government didn't change, during this expansion, it was the senate and the leading families that provided the direction and spirit of the empire. It was the tenacity and patriotic fervor of the senate that inspired Rome and its legions. The senate appointed the generals, who came from the same family backgrounds as the senators and led the Roman legions to one success after another. More and more, the de facto government of Rome was conducted by senators and generals, who with their families, made up an aristocratic oligarchy. And even though Rome was a republic and citizens did elect their magistrates, the mass of the citizens played no part in the nomination of candidates for office. This was the exclusive domain of the aristocracy already entrenched in the republic's positions of power. In addition, officials received no pay for service, so none but the independently wealthy qualified as candidates. Finally, even though it was the assemblies that passed laws, they were under the control of the senate. In a similar way, the tribunes became agents of the senate.

As the number of Roman provinces expanded, more and more tribute flowed into Rome. The spoils from the successes of the Roman legions in the field added to this river of wealth. The military campaigns also produced great numbers of slaves, who replaced free labor. As a result, increasing numbers of these displaced and landless people moved to Rome, where they lived on a dole financed by provincial tribute.

Most Roman wealth was funneled through the senators and generals and plowed back into land. Large parts of Italy had been abandoned after Hannibal's armies had desolated them. The aristocracy acquired great stretches of this devastated territory. Scientific cultivation of money crops, such as wine, olive oil, and wool, were characteristic of these latifundia, as these large estates were called.

A significant change also occurred in the nature of the legions. Originally, Roman legions had been raised from the landed peasantry each spring for the summer campaign. The next spring, it would be the turn of a different group of peasants, the prior year's conscripts having been released at the end of the summer campaign. The peasants served without pay out of a sense of patriotism, and there was a strong bond between the army, the people, and the country. But over time, Rome's increasing military responsibility required that a trained, standing army be maintained. To satisfy this requirement, it became necessary to retain citizens in the army for more than one tour of duty. As compensation for this imposition, pay was introduced.

Ultimately, all attempts to relate military service to citizen responsibility were abandoned. The army became a mercenary force manned primarily by landless citizens. Thus, the legionnaire's loyalty was transferred from Rome in general to the military leader who had recruited him, from whom he received his pay, and to whom he swore an oath of allegiance. There was no similar oath of allegiance to Rome.

In this way, Rome entered a period of instability. Army officers, backed by mercenary troops, seized the government. The unemployed and landless crowded into the city. The state became parasitic, drawing off the wealth of the provinces to add to the riches of generals and senators, and to maintain and control the debased Roman masses on the dole. During this time, Julius Caesar led his legions from Gaul over the Rubicon river to invade Rome, as a result of which he became the military dictator of Rome. The Rubicon is a small river that constituted the border between Italy and the province of Cisalpine Gaul (the part of Gaul that lay on the same side of the Alps as Rome), one of the two provinces for which Caesar was responsible. The other was Transalpine Gaul. The Rubicon river was so named because of the rubri (red stones) found in the river bottom. Traditionally, generals returning to Rome disbanded their legions before crossing Italy's boundary (you see, Romans also knew about marcher lords and took pains to draw their teeth before they returned home), which is why Caesar said, "The die is cast," when he crossed the Rubicon.

Caesar was subsequently assassinated, and civil war followed. Ultimately, in 31 BC, Octavian, Caesar's grand-nephew (whom Caesar had adopted as his son and designated as his sole heir), emerged as the master of Rome, and Rome entered the second phase of its life.

Augustus. *From a photograph by Anderson of the statue in the Vatican Museum.*

In 27 BC, the senate bestowed the name of Augustus ("revered", a title heretofore reserved for the gods) on Octavian, and even though he assumed only the military title of Imperator (victor in battle), he was, in fact, Rome's first emperor.

Augustus exercised his authority through the institutions of the republic. The senate still convened and passed resolutions, and the assemblies still met. But Augustus was commander of the armed forces, he had proconsular power over the provinces, and he controlled the empire's finances. After death throes lasting a century, the republic of Rome was no more. Nothing remained but the former shell, and the emperor became the state. Augustus and his successors saw to it that these circumstances were perpetuated.

1. First, the problem of succession was resolved. It was to be effected by adoption. Each emperor was to select the most able man he could find and adopt him as his son and heir.
2. Second, a centralized administrative system was established. Provincial governors were replaced by imperial officers directly responsible to the emperor. However, these officers had no authority to interfere with local government. The empire was divided into civitates, or municipalities, representing a city-state, tribe, canton, or whatever was appropriate to the locality, and each municipality was allowed to govern itself.
3. Third, citizenship was expanded.
4. Fourth, Roman law grew into a universal civil code, fair and humane.

For two centuries, the world within the boundaries of Rome was at peace. Merchants could transport their goods from the Black sea to Spain, from the Nile to the Thames without crossing a border. And everywhere, the merchants met the same laws, the same coinage, the same privileges, and the protection of the same government.

Yet the ills that beset the republic remained in the empire. The bulk of commerce was in raw materials. Manufacturing remained primarily in the hands of the local artisan producing goods for a local market. Almost continual battle with barbarians took place along the empire's borders. The empire's wealth continued to flow into the land, large estates worked by slaves continued to grow, the movement of displaced commoners to an urban life on the dole kept pace, and the army remained the backbone of the empire.

The peace of Rome lasted until 180. Responsible for this feat were the administrative system set up by Augustus (which held the empire together under the reign of incompetent emperors) and the "five good emperors", Nerva, Trajan, Hadrian, Antonius Pius, and Marcus Aurelius. Difficulties began when Commodus followed his father, Marcus Aurelius, to the throne. In 192, Commodus was assassinated by mutinous soldiers.

There was then a century of disorder. Instead of providing support for emperors, the army took over command and set them up and knocked them down as it wished. Between 192 and 284, there were 30 emperors, and almost all of them met violent deaths.

In 284, Emperor Diocletian came to power and instituted a despotic regime that temporarily halted the decline of the empire. But in the long run, the cure was worse than the disease.

First, Diocletian renounced all pretense of republican government and declared himself the head of the empire with no restrictions. The senate was reduced to a municipal council for the city of Rome.

Second, Diocletian reorganized the empire's administrative system. He doubled the number of provinces from 50 to 100 and grouped them into 13 dioceses. Within this geographical structure he set up a hierarchy of administrators that reached from the emperor through prefects to vicars to governors down to the lowest level of government. At each level, these officers were supported by a large number of officials. Municipal self-government disappeared.

Third, Diocletian reorganized the army so that it would be more responsive to the emperor. The old legions, whose loyalties might lie elsewhere, were stationed along the borders as hereditary guards, and a new force, almost doubling the size of the army, was formed from German barbarians. This barbarous army served for pay only, had no connection with the Roman people, and was strictly the emperor's tool.

These changes put all the reins of control in the emperor's hands. But they were enormously costly. To pay for them, Diocletian set up a method of taxation that imposed such a heavy burden on the peasants who tilled the land and the merchants and artisans in the trades that people strove to leave their occupations to avoid the tax. To prevent this flight, the worker was bound to his land or trade, which became hereditary. Thus, not only did the people lose their right to local government, they also lost their ability to move or change occupations.

Part of Diocletian's administrative organization of the empire was to recognize the growing split of the empire into two parts, a Latin speaking west and a Greek speaking east. In 286, he selected a loyal general named Maximian to preside over the Western empire, while Diocletian retained the throne in the Eastern empire. In theory, the empire remained one, divided for governance only, and though, from time to time, administration was reunited under one emperor, in the main, the fact of two empires, with separate emperors, persisted from this time on.

Finally, Diocletian tried to boost patriotic feeling by reviving paganism. As a result, persecution of Christians reached a peak during his reign.

In 305, Diocletian abdicated. This act was followed by civil disruption. By 312, there were four competing emperors: Constantine, based in England and Gaul; Maxentius, in Italy, Spain and Africa; and Licinius and Maximus, who divided the Eastern empire between them. Constantine and Licinius became allies in their battle against their adversaries. Constantine moved quickly into Italy. The chances are that it was during this march that he decided to appeal for the support of the Christians. In any case, it was on this march that he was supposed to have seen a burning cross and the words "Hoc vince" (By this (sign), conquer) in the sky. He adopted the cross as his standard and had his men paint it on their shields. At Saxa Rubra, a few miles from Rome, he conducted a pitched battle with the vastly superior army of Maxentius, decimated it, and became the emperor of the Western empire.

The next year, Constantine joined Licinius, who had also been victorious, at Milan. There they issued a joint edict decreeing toleration of all religions including Christianity, because this was as far as Licinius was willing to go. In 323, Constantine bested Licinius. There seems to be no agreement among historians as to who attacked whom or why, but the fact that the two had been allies didn't preclude the possibility that one or both of them still had unfulfilled ambitions.

Constantine founded a new capital of the empire at Constantinople on the site of the old city of Byzantium. He became increasingly inclined toward Christianity and was baptized a few days before he died in 337.

Constantine never attacked paganism, but as a result of his patronage, Christianity essentially became the state religion. Constantine apparently believed that there was some special connection between Christ and the sun. Consequently, he decreed that the Sun's Day, rather than the Jewish Sabbath (which coincided with the Roman Saturn's Day), should be the holy day of prayer. He also called the first ecumenical council of the Christian church at Nicomedia to resolve the schisms within the church. It was at this council that the Nicene Creed, which proclaimed the common essence of Christ the son and God the father, was adopted.

This change in the circumstances of the Christian church raised some basic issues. Before Constantine, the church, except for the efforts to destroy it, was free to conduct itself as it saw fit. Would it keep this independence after it had become the state religion? And would the emperor, as a Christian, accept the advice of the church when it came to morals, a term that could be stretched to cover almost any political act? Or would the emperor determine church policy?

In the Eastern empire, the emperors dominated the church. In the Western empire, a different and surprising kind of answer to these questions was reached.

In the Western empire, the hierarchy of the church developed slowly and reproduced the structure of imperial administration. Beginning in the 2nd century, in each municipality, the bishop was the church authority. Below the bishop were the priests, who performed the sacraments, ministered to the spiritual well-being of the congregation, and took care of local financial matters. In the 3d century, councils of all the bishops in a province would meet to establish uniformity in belief and practice. By the end of the 4th century, the bishop of the provincial capital, who presided over these councils, had been acknowledged as the superior of the other bishops in the province and had assumed the title of archbishop.

And now, to make sense of the continuing development of the church in the Western empire, we have to introduce the other great upheaval going on concurrently — barbarian invasion.

All the barbarians who invaded Rome were Germanic. The German people were believed to have come from the northern part of modern Germany near the Baltic coast and the southern part of the Scandinavian peninsula. From there they emigrated west to the North sea, south to the Rhine and Danube, and east to the Vistula. By the 4th century, the dispersion of the Germans, accompanied by conquests and alliances, resulted in the creation of a number of "nations" made up of collections of tribes. Two nations had come together by the Rhine, the Franks (the free) on the lower part of the river, the Alamanni (all people) on the upper. The Angles, Saxons and Jutes settled in the northwest, along the coast of the North sea and in the Danish peninsula. The Burgundians had moved west between the Franks and the Alamanni, the Vandals to the upper Oder, and the Lombards to the east between the Oder and the Vistula. The Visigoths (West Goths) and Ostrogoths (East Goths) had taken root along the lower Danube and the Black sea. The river Dniester separated them.

The Germans were warriors, and there was no feeling of fellowship between the German nations. They were as quick to battle one another as they were to attack the Romans.

Certainly the Germans were barbarians and the Romans civilized, and certainly the two peoples embraced different cultures. But it would be a mistake to think of the barbarian invasions as some kind of incursion by a people alien to the residents. The Roman legions had been in contact with the Germans since the 2nd century BC. Roman merchants had carried on trade with the Germans for almost as long. We've already seen that the armies on which Diocletian relied were made up of German mercenaries. The officers rose in the ranks of the armies by a regular system of promotion, the highest rank being magister militum, or master of the soldiers. By the end of the 4th century, the typical master of the soldiers was a German. In 341, Bishop Ulfilas, from the Eastern empire but born a Goth, initiated 40 years of missionary labor among the Visigoths and converted many of them, including their leaders, to Christianity.

No, the barbarian invasions of the Western empire weren't unusual in the sense that they were just one more example, albeit a complicated one, of marcher lords moving in from the frontiers to overwhelm more civilized communities. The typical outcome of such an incursion was that, over time, the invaders were absorbed by the civilization they conquered, and the civilization went on, modified perhaps by the impact of the experience, but still recognizably the same civilization. The unusual thing about the Roman occurrence was that the invading Germans, while separated by different national affiliations, were, in total, so numerous that they swamped the invaded civilization. Consequently, the ability of the civilization to assimilate the barbarians was inadequate to the task, and the barbarian element of the resulting amalgam was more salient than was typical.

The cause of the first barbarian incursion was the movement of the Huns into eastern Europe. Ejected by a complicated conflict in Asia, the Huns moved west and attacked the Ostrogoths in 371. By 375, the Huns had subjugated the Ostrogoths and had turned on the Visigoths. A year later, after a failed attempt to hold the Huns at the Dniester, the Visigoths petitioned for permission to pass over the Danube and settle in the Eastern empire. After a seemingly interminable delay, Valens, the Eastern emperor, agreed to let them in if they would settle as foederati, or allies. The Visigoths accepted the terms. But the officials who oversaw the move robbed the Visigoths and turned large numbers of their young men and women into slaves. In addition, no arrangements had been made to feed the migrants. In less than a year, the Visigoths, outraged by this shabby treatment, rose to pillage Thrace.

Valens confronted the Visigoths at Hadrianople in 378 with calamitous results. Valens and two thirds of his army were slaughtered, and the rest were routed.

The Visigoths soon discovered that, like Hannibal before them, they could despoil the countryside, but they couldn't take the fortified cities and perfect their victory. Theodosius I, the new Eastern emperor, resolved differences with the Visigoths, and by 382, they were settled in Thrace as foederati.

Theodosius died in 395, the Visigoths distrusted his successor, and under the command of Alaric, they embarked on a campaign of depredation through Thrace, Macedonia and Greece. Alaric was a trained Roman soldier and had led the Visigoth forces in Theodosius's final campaign. By 397, the Visigoths had settled in the Balkans between the upper Danube and the Adriatic. In 401 and again in 403, they invaded Italy, to be forced back both times by Stilicho. Stilicho was a Vandal who had risen to commander in chief of the Roman army under Theodosius and had married his niece. He was now regent for Honorius, the son of Theodosius, who, at ten, had been made the Western emperor. In 406, to bolster Italian defenses, Stilicho withdrew his forces from the Rhine. The Vandals took advantage of this opening, moved across Gaul, and penetrated Spain.

In 408, Honorius condemned Stilicho to death on the charge that Stilicho was plotting against him. Whatever Stilicho's failings or lack of them, he was the one man who could hold Alaric back. After Stilicho's death, Alaric once more invaded Italy, and this time, he entered Rome and sacked it. He then moved south and died unexpectedly in 410.

After the pillage of Rome, Innocent I, the archbishop of Rome, managed the rebuilding of the city. Changes then began to gain momentum. The bishops in the provinces moved into the vacuum left by the breakdown of imperial administration under the blows of barbarian incursion. They performed the function of judges and governors, and negotiated with the barbarians to safeguard the lives of their congregations. With these added responsibilities, they felt the need for moral support, which general practice told them would come from Rome. This coincided with the posture of Innocent, who from the beginning, claimed primacy for the archbishop of Rome.

The Visigoths, now led by Alaric's brother in law, Ataulf, moved without direction for several years and ultimately entered Gaul in 412. In 415, Ataulf died, and led by the new king, Wallia, the Visigoths fought alongside Roman forces against the Vandals and forced them into the southern part of the Spanish peninsula. In 418 or 419, the Visigoths were recognized as foederati and settled in southwestern Gaul and Spain.

England during the Anglo-Saxon Incursion

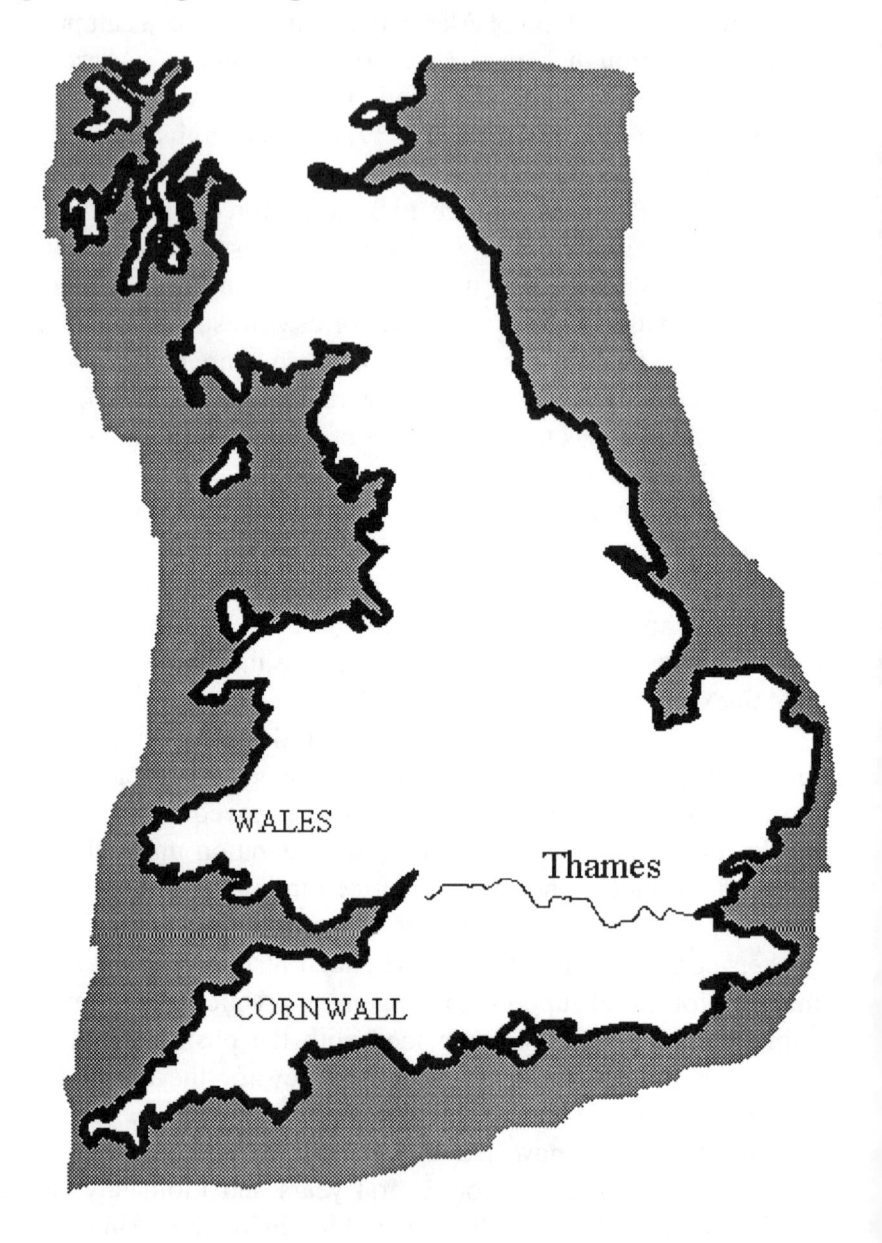

WALES

Thames

CORNWALL

When Honorius died, a usurper took control. But in 425, Galla Placidia, Honorius's half sister (and widow of both Ataulf and, then, the Roman general Constantius), came back to Rome with her infant son, Valentinian III. For ten years, she governed as regent and then was the power behind the throne under her incompetent son until her death in 450.

In 429, Gaiseric, a new king of the Vandals, led his nation across the straits of Gibraltar and subdued the North African seaboard. Rome was unable to turn back the Vandals and, in 435, recognized them as foederati.

But Gaiseric wasn't satisfied. In 439, he added Carthage to his conquests. Three years later, Valentinian abandoned all hope of resisting Gaiseric in Africa and gave up the North African provinces to him.

Valentinian named Leo I, the current archbishop of Rome, as the leader of the church, and thus, Leo became the first pope ("papa", as in "father of the church").

Shortly after 454, Valentinian was assassinated, and the government of the Western empire collapsed. This presented Gaiseric with a chance too good to be missed. The Vandals moved across the Mediterranean and entered Rome without encountering resistance. Leo entreated with Gaiseric and got his pledge that no Roman would be killed. For two weeks, the Vandals sacked the city and then returned to Africa.

After the pillage of Rome, the barbarian masters of the soldiers ruled Rome through puppet emperors whom they set up. In 476, Odoacer succeeded to the position of master of the soldiers. He did away with the practice of having a puppet emperor by deposing the current emperor, Romulus Augustulus.

In the 420's, the Roman legions in England had been called back to defend Italy and Gaul. During the next two centuries, the island was invaded by the Angles, Saxons and Jutes. The Romanized Celts (hard C; thus, "Kelts"), who constituted the indigenous population, were either slain or forced into the hills of Wales and Cornwall. They made no impact on the invaders, who continued their German and pagan ways. There were few linguistic or cultural differences between the Angles, Saxons and Jutes. In fact, historians have trouble identifying the Jutes, and some think that the Jutes were just Saxons who happened to settle in Kent, where they happened to be called Jutes. The Angles and Saxons had mingled before the migration to England. As a

The Distribution of the Germanic Nations at the Time of the Fall of the Western Roman Empire

consequence, to all intents and purposes, these invaders became one people, known as Anglo-Saxons, or even more commonly, as just Saxons.

Thus, the Western empire sank beneath a sea of barbarian invaders, never to rise again. The causes were multiple. First, the result of Diocletian's "reforms" was a subject people who considered their government tyrannical and extortionate, and to which they had no allegiance. Second, beginning in the 2nd century, Roman population decayed. Birth rates dropped, and disease depleted and weakened the populace. The barbarians defeated a worn out empire: a mercenary army, a demoralized citizenry, corrupt officials, and an unproductive aristocracy, all debilitated by disease. The only remains of the once proud empire was a shadow of its Augustinian organization reflected in the structure of the Roman church.

In 527, Justinian became the Eastern emperor. He had one overriding ambition: to return the Roman empire to its earlier grandeur. He was unsuccessful. But as part of this effort, he undertook, beginning in the first year of his rule, to codify Roman law. He set up a committee of ten jurists, the most outstanding of which was Tribonian, to accomplish this task. The result was the Corpus Juris Civilis, the body of civil law. It consisted of four parts. The Codex Justiniani, or Justinian Code, was an organized statement of all the statutes issued by the emperors from Hadrian up to the beginning of Justinian's reign, with everything out of date, conflicting, or redundant removed. The Pandects, or Digest, performed the same function for the decisions handed down by judges. A handbook to assist students was included. And the *Novels* was a compilation of Justinian's decrees.

As we've seen, other civilizations have had bodies of law. But their laws were more or less restricted to criminal and public concerns. Private matters were generally considered to be within the purview of custom alone. In contrast, Roman law was extended to provide systemization and consistent principles for all matters, public and private. Concepts such as property and contract, things so embedded in our everyday dealings that we're hardly aware of them, were, for the first time, given definition. As a consequence, disagreements could be reduced to legal cases to which particular published rules applied. The benefits were impressive, for the code made dealing with anyone, friend or stranger, predictable.

Like science, Justinian law lay forgotten during the Middle Ages, to be rediscovered and put to use when the times called for it. It was in the 11th century, when urbanism started to reappear in Europe, that Roman law provided the paradigm for establishing a legal environment to ease, standardize and broaden economic behavior. Roman law is the foundation for civil law in almost all of modern Europe, England being the exception.

The Romans were such great lawyers because of their one outstanding characteristic. They had indomitable will. They just would not give up. They persisted. If something got in their way, they worked on it until it was removed. As a result, as well as being great makers of law, they were also superior soldiers and

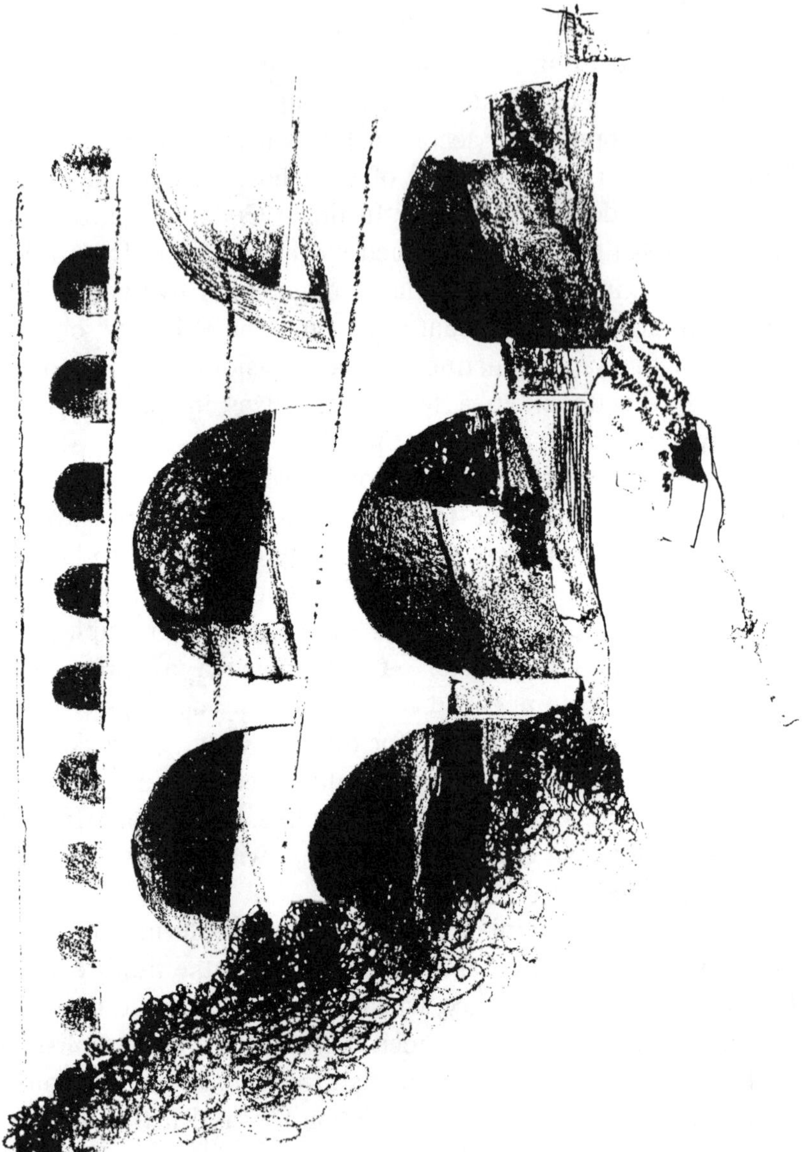

engineers, to which their dominance was attributable.

Having given the Romans their due, it's hard to say anything else positive about them. As unattractive as the Greeks were, the Romans gave them a run for their money. The Roman empire was essentially one large military camp. Like a parasite, Rome sucked tribute out of its provinces to maintain a corrupt government and a debased citizenry. On top of these undesirable traits, the Romans were just plain cruel. Their use of crucifixion as a means of punishment (it was for barbarians; no Roman citizen was ever crucified) and the bloodiness of their circuses are well known. A few other incidents add further documentation.

In 102 BC, Gaius Marius saved Rome from the Germanic Cimbri. In 88 BC, he was driven into exile under threat of his life by Sulla. Sulla then went off to conduct a campaign against Mithradites in Asia Minor. In 87 BC, Marius returned to Rome in triumph. He had the gates of the city closed, and slaughter of all notable men who had opposed him began. Thousands were killed. Burial was forbidden. Bodies were to be left to be eaten by dogs and birds. The heads of slain senators were nailed to the rostra, a stage in the forum. The houses of those marked for execution were plundered and all who were found there were murdered. All property of the slain was confiscated.

In response to this turn of events, Sulla concluded a treaty with Mithradites, returned to Rome, defeated his enemies, and in 82 BC, became dictator. He outlawed all civil and military officials who had opposed him. This meant that anyone could kill these outlaws on sight. The property of those executed was confiscated. Initially, individuals weren't outlawed. It was categories of people to which the proscription applied. Upon appeal, Sulla agreed to change his policy and subsequently identified those outlawed by name on published lists. Day after day, new lists were posted. When it was finished, about 4700 people had been executed.

When Caesar took over in 48 BC, he abstained from the usual blood bath. In 44 BC, he was assassinated. In 43 BC, a

---

A Roman Aqueduct. *From a photograph in* The Roman World *written by Michael Vickers and published in 1989 by Peter Bedrick.*

triumvirate, consisting of Octavian, Mark Antony, and Lepidus, was formed and given full power for five years. To pay their troops, replenish their coffers, and revenge Caesar, the triumvirate instituted a reign of terror. Three hundred senators and 2000 businessmen were executed. The resulting widows and orphans were shorn of their legacies. Among those slaughtered was Cicero. Antony had Cicero's head and hands nailed to the rostra in the Forum. Antony's wife, Fluvia, spat on Cicero's severed head and drove her hair pins through his tongue.

The Romans didn't even have the Greeks' saving grace of producing philosophy, mathematics and science. The little work done in these areas was derivative only.

The Eastern empire lasted until the middle of the 15th century. To the end, it referred to itself as Roman. But it was Roman in name only. It spoke Greek, and its people and orientation were Oriental. Consequently, historians adopt the name of Byzantine to refer to the Eastern empire after the disappearance of the Western empire. The name comes from Byzantium, the original name for Constantinople.

We now go back into the past to watch the development of a new method of warfare. As we've already alluded to, about 247 BC, the kingdom of Parthia arose to the east of what would ultimately be the Roman empire. It was established by Iranian tribesmen from the steppes near the Caspian sea and was a breakaway from the Seleucid empire. Like other civilized nations, Parthia was subject to incursions by nomads from the steppes. By this time, the nomads had developed the skill and most of the gear (saddle, bridle and pants) to ride on horseback, and had learned to control their mounts without using their hands. The speed of a galloping horse made the rider an elusive enough target so that armor wasn't needed. Every nomad owned horses, and a bow made him a man at arms. As a result, nomad tribes became arrow launching light cavalry.

Long before 200 BC, the Parthians developed an effective defense against such invasion. The new factor was the development of a horse big and strong enough to bear the armor needed to protect both horse and rider from arrows. A band of such armored and mounted men could stand against steppe cavalry, trading arrow for arrow, until their opponents' quivers were empty and their horses tired. An attack would then rout the nomads. The light cavalry almost always got away, because the armored cavalry couldn't catch them. Neither could the heavy cavalry retaliate, for the steppe didn't have enough pasture to support great horses. On the other hand, the same fact prevented the nomads from adopting Parthian tactics.

The problem presented by heavy cavalry was that the great horses and armor required were costly and knights had to undergo extensive training to become skilled at their trade. The Parthian solution was to link an agricultural village to a warrior. The village supported the warrior so that he and some followers could equip and train themselves as knights. In return, the knights protected the village. For more major operations, given a recognized regional authority, these scattered forces could be drawn together into a larger unit. The Sassanid empire of Persia succeeded Parthia and adopted its approach to supporting a mounted armed force.

Repeated disputes with the Persians and barbarian incursion from the Danubian steppes forced the Byzantine empire to give up the customary Roman reliance on infantry and adopt the use of heavy cavalry. The switch started at the end of Constantine's reign, and by the time of Justinian's rule, armored cavalrymen armed with bows and spears had become the element around which the Byzantine army was organized.

But the Byzantine empire never came up with an answer to the question of how to support heavy cavalry. The prominence of large land owners in Byzantium eliminated the possibility of adopting the Persian approach. The empire also rejected the idea of letting war captains organize troops of knights and use the spoils of war to compensate their followers, for it recognized the danger of creating an invincible marcher lord who saw the best source of booty in the empire itself. And the royal treasury couldn't afford to support the size of the mounted force needed to defend all of the empire's borders.

Therefore, the Byzantine emperors had no alternative but to leave at least a part of their frontiers open to continued barbarian attack. Diplomacy, subsidy, bribes, titles, and stirring up strife between barbarian tribes served the Byzantine empire as substitutes for a defended border. It was this policy that gave the meaning of complex, devious and surreptitious to the adjective "byzantine".

The explanation for Byzantine longevity was the inability of opposing forces to overpower its capital. Constantinople was situated on a narrow peninsula. The Byzantine empire was a sea power, so it could always keep its seaways open. As a result, Constantinople couldn't be blockaded. And on the one side on which it faced land, the city was protected by walls so fortified they couldn't be taken.

CHAPTER FIVE

Islam

At the time of the rise of Islam, the Arabian peninsula was primarily a desert peopled by nomadic tribes of Bedouin who lived in tents pitched in the oases where they watered their herds. Along the coastline, however, more fertile land existed. There cities provided a more civilized life supported by agriculture and commerce. But even in the cities, political organization was in the tribal stage.

The Arabs were Semitic. Idolatry was a feature of their pagan religion. They held in reverence certain temples, the most venerated of which was a small, square sanctuary named the Kaaba (cube). This temple was located in Mecca, a commercial town about 50 miles inland from the middle of the Red sea coast. Each year during the sacred months when tribal conflict was prohibited, Arabs from all parts of the country would make the pilgrimage to Mecca to worship at the Kaaba.

Mohammed was born in Mecca around 570. His life as a prophet started when he was about 40. Tradition says he spent one month a year in solitary reflection on a mountain near Mecca. It was during one of these periods of meditation that he had his first revelation. These revelations came after Mohammed had gone into a trance, which, later at least, he could induce whenever he wanted. Mohammed's first converts were the members of his family and friends, including his father-in-law, Abu Bakr, and Omar. Mohammed named his religion Islam (surrender) and his followers Moslems (those who had surrendered themselves). In the beginning, the Moslems were a secret sect. When they became public, they were persecuted by the pagan Meccans, who were afraid that Mohammed's insistence that there was but one god, Allah (Allah means "the God"), would undermine idol worship and the profitable trade with the pilgrims who arrived to venerate the Kaaba.

As Islam became more popular, the persecution intensified. In 620, six men from the city of Yathrib, 250 miles north of Mecca,

An Example of Arabic Script. *From* The Arabic Language *published by the University of Minnesota in 1969 and written by Anwar G. Chejne, who attributes the example to F. Khattat. The script is the naskhi type. I have no idea of what it says.*

النسخ

came to Mecca as pilgrims. Mohammed spoke with them. In 621, these six and a few others returned to Mecca, at which time they became Moslems. In 622, 75 men from Yathrib appeared in Mecca, assured Mohammed that they would see to his safety in Yathrib, and invited him to Yathrib to resolve their political problems. Mohammed accepted the invitation. The move of Mohammed and his congregation to Yathrib is known as the Hegira. Yathrib was subsequently renamed Medina, shortened from Medina-al-Nabi, "City of the Prophet".

Like other Arabian cities, Medina was organized in tribes. Mohammed declared Medina an Islamic community, to which tribal concerns were subordinate. He threw the Jews out of Medina, and his congregation from Mecca took over the Jewish land. But this provided only a partial solution to the economic problems of the refugees. As a consequence, Mohammed started to raid the caravans that passed near Medina en route to Mecca. This resulted in a war with Mecca that went on for years. To support themselves, Moslems continued to prey on caravans and to take over Jewish villages, which then paid tribute to the Moslems.

As a faith that guaranteed a sensual paradise after death and held out the possibility of booty in this world, Islam appealed to the Bedouin and found many converts among them. By 630,

Mohammed was strong enough to take Mecca, which he did in January of that year. He named Mecca the religious center of Islam, toward which all Moslems must turn to pray, and the Kaaba its most holy mosque, or temple. Medina continued as the political capital. By incorporating into Islam the pilgrimages, holy city, and temple of Arab paganism, Mohammed attracted new adherents. When he died in 632, most of Arabia was, at least nominally, Islamic.

Throughout his prophetic career, Mohammed published his revelations, political decrees, and commentaries on current events. This corpus was the Koran (Recitation), which constitutes a statement of the religious doctrines and civil practices on which the theocracy of Islam is based.

Moslem tradition encourages the idea that Mohammed was illiterate, since such a circumstance enhances the idea that his revelations were Allah's words. Mohammed was a merchant until after his 40th year, and as such, it's hard to believe that he couldn't read or write. However, he was illiterate in the sense that he didn't read books, not even the Bible. Nevertheless, the religious tradition, in which Mohammed grew up, conducted its business in spoken poetry, so his ability to turn out the phrases found in the Koran is hardly unbelievable.

Mohammed's death caused a crisis, for he hadn't provided for the succession to his post as religious and political leader. Finally, in June 632, with the help of Omar, Abu Bakr was chosen to succeed Mohammed. He assumed the title of caliph (successor), adopted by all the following holders of the combined religious and political leadership of Islam.

Beginning in 633, under a succession of caliphs, Syria, Persia, Egypt, North Africa, and Spain were brought into the Moslem empire, and to the east, the boundaries of Islam were pushed out beyond the Indus river. In 661, the current caliph, Mohammed's cousin and son in law, Ali, was assassinated, the caliphate was seized by the Omayyad family, and the capital moved from Medina to Damascus.

The Moslems were prevented from overrunning Europe by their inability to conquer Constantinople on the eastern edge of the Mediterranean, and in the west, their advance was brought to a halt

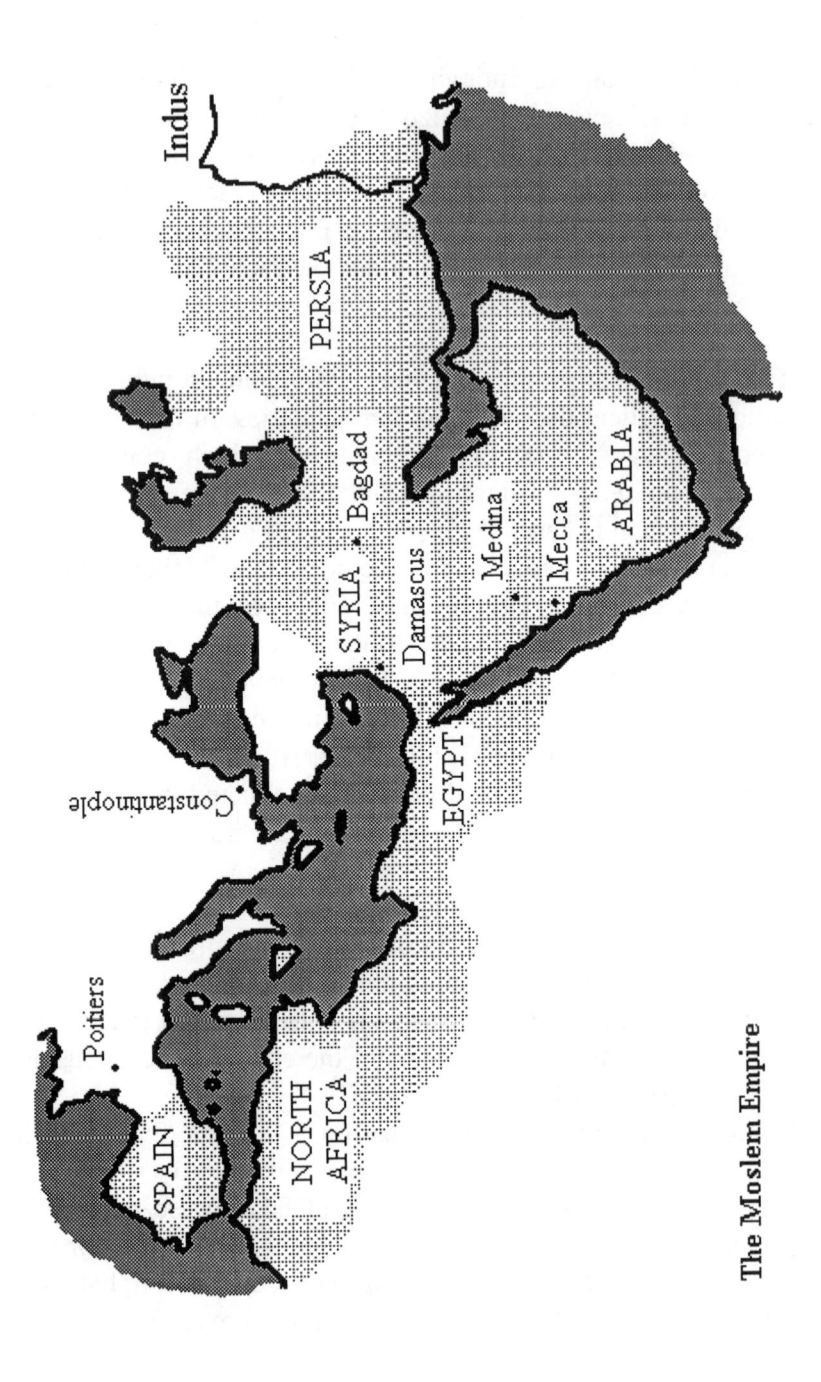

The Moslem Empire

by their defeat by the Franks under Charles Martel (The Hammer) at Poitiers in 733. The Moslems had advanced toward Tours but then fell back toward Poitiers, where the decisive battle was fought. Charles received his designation as The Hammer for his victory.

Over time, as more and more people came under the sway of and converted to Islam, the caliphs placed increasing emphasis on Moslem, rather than Arab, loyalty. The Arab nobility was replaced by a bureaucracy in which all Moslem races participated. And the capital moved from Damascus to Bagdad. This move was made in 763, after the Abbisid family had, with the help of Persian troops, overthrown the Omayyads. As a result, the caliphate in Bagdad was somewhat Arab with a flavoring of other Moslem races but was predominately Persian.

Because the Moslem empire was made up of many races, in the 9th century, it began to subdivide into multiple caliphates. Nevertheless, though politically divided, the Moslem world retained a strong religious and cultural unity. This Moslem civilization came to be known as Saracen, a name first applied by the Greeks and Romans to Arabs but then expanded to include all Moslems of this time.

The Saracens pursued learning. The works of nearly all the Greek philosophers were translated into Arabic. The same was done for Greek science: medicine, chemistry, astronomy and mathematics. To this was added the product of Saracen scholarship. In medicine, Avicenna stood out. He determined that tuberculosis was contagious, described pleurisy, and maintained that disease would be spread by contaminated water. Work in chemistry (an Arabic word) was held back by a concern for alchemy, but much information was, nevertheless, accumulated — for example, the preparation and isolation of chemical substances such as alkalis (another Arabic word), sal-ammoniac, arsenious oxide, saltpeter, and crude forms of sulphuric and nitric acids. The Saracens borrowed from India what we call the Arabic numerals (the Indians came up with this system of notation around 270), including the numeral zero (yet another Arabic word), and they did definitive work in algebra (still another Arabic word).

Thus, Islam preserved Greek science and the Greek scientific

An Example of Islamic Architecture. *From a photograph in the book* The Taj Mahal, *written by David Carroll and published by the Newsweek Book Division in 1972. The photograph was taken by the author. Yes, this is the Taj Mahal. And yes, the Taj Mahal is in India. But it was built by a Mogul emperor, the Moguls were Moslems, and the Taj Mahal is an example of Islamic (also known as Persian) architecture. Characteristic are the onion shaped dome and the minarets placed at the four corners.*

attitude so that they could be picked up by Europe as it emerged from the Middle Ages. It was from Arabic literature, translated into Latin, that European scholars in the 12th and 13th centuries first made their acquaintance with this body of work.

And how did this transmission occur? Despite the religious animosity that drove Islam and Christian Europe apart, when two civilizations come into contact, all isn't crusades and battle. The Saracens tolerated the "people of the Book" (Jews and Christians, whose "book" was the Bible) as Mohammed had commanded in the Koran, as long as they paid a special tax for the privilege. Many Christians lived under Moslem rule. In Spain, Sicily, and the realms set up by the crusaders along the eastern Mediterranean coast, Christian and Moslem came into contact in peace as well as war. And the ubiquitous merchants moved frequently between the lands of the cross and crescent.

Islam is a theocracy. It isn't only a religious belief. It's also a body of law, the sharia (sacred law), under which Moslems are supposed to live. This law comes from two sources, the Koran and sunnah, or tradition. The Moslems broke into two sects, the sunni and the shiite, over the question of the source of sunnah. The sunni maintain that it consists of the sayings and deeds of Mohammed as authenticated by the Companions of the Prophet, those Moslems who had lived and worked with Mohammed, particularly the first three caliphs — Abu Bakr (632 - 634), Omar (634 - 644), and Uthman (644 - 656).

The shiite position is that these first three caliphs were illegitimate, that Ali was the first true caliph, and that his offspring from his marriage with Fatima, Mohammed's daughter, were "imams", the spiritual leaders of Islam. This left the door open for several lines of imams, but the 12 that were ultimately fixed on by the shiite as legitimate were Ali's sons Hasan and Husayn, followed by the offspring of Husayn. The 12th in this line of imams was the mahdi, who, according to tradition, didn't die but vanished from the world to become the hidden imam who will return on judgment day. To the shiite, it's the infallible teachings of the imams, particularly Jafar, that constitute the sunnah.

In any case, the difference that separates the sunni and shiite has to do with theological dogma, not the content of the sunnah. The sunnah of the sunni and that of the shiite aren't significantly different, and thus, basically, Islam recognizes one sharia. In Islam, it's the ulema (the learned), a body of holy men who specialize in interpreting the sharia, who see that Islamic law rules Moslem life, public and private.

Ultimately, the rationalist approach of science and philosophy flourishing in the Moslem world came into conflict with the sacred teachings of Islam. The resolution of this conflict was both ingenious and disastrous for Moslem thought. The Moslem theologians used Aristotelian logic to demonstrate the inability of reason to uncover religious truth. The remaining source of theological knowledge is revelation, which had been given to Mohammed and was enshrined in the sharia. Relying exclusively on revelation provided the ulema with the sanction needed to fix the dead hand of authority on Moslem thought. As a result, legal rigidity became Islam's lot. All this occurred in the 12th and 13th centuries. Thus, at the same time that the European mind was awakening in response to Moslem scholarship, the Islamic mind was going to sleep. The result was the militant immutability that still animates Islamic thought.

CHAPTER SIX

The Dark Ages

When the Western Roman empire fell, Europe entered what has come to be called the Middle Ages. The term, Middle Ages, was invented by historians who lived and worked during the Renaissance. They thought of the ten centuries after the fall of the Western empire as a middle period of barbarism dividing a golden age of civilization from their own, in which this golden age was being reborn (re-nascent). Later historians have kept the term, but they've also demonstrated that it originated from a misunderstanding. The European civilization that emerged from the Middle Ages bore little resemblance to the one preceding this period and was, in no sense, a return to it.

The first five centuries of the Middle Ages are sometimes called the Dark Ages, because they were marked by the ebb and flow of barbarian nations as they battled for territory and domination. It has also been observed that the darkest thing about the Dark Ages is our lack of knowledge about it.

There were three significant outcomes of the conflict between the Germanic nations during the Dark Ages.

1. By the beginning of the 11th century, the peoples that would eventually make up the European nations of England, France, Spain, Portugal, Germany and Italy had settled into their ancestral homes.
2. Also by the year 1000, through conquest and missionary work, almost all of Europe had been, at a minimum, nominally converted to Christianity. Only a small region south of the Baltic (occupied by a wild and warlike people of Letto-Lithuanian stock, the Prussians) continued its pagan ways until the 13th century, when the Prussians were essentially exterminated by the Christian order of Teutonic Knights. The region, however, continued to be referred to as Prussia. Prussia was subsequently taken over by Brandenburg, ruled by the Hohenzollern's. In 1701, Frederick William I of Brandenburg was named by the Holy Roman emperor as king of Prussia. He

England in 866

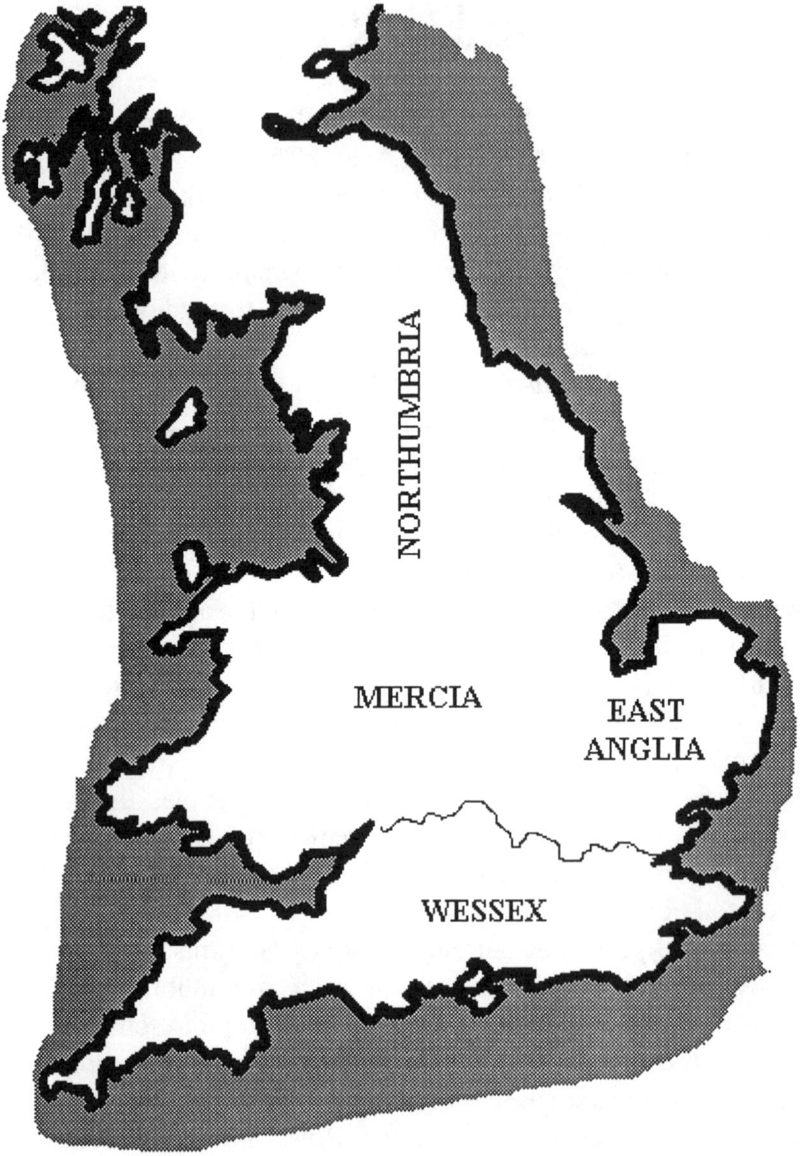
NORTHUMBRIA
MERCIA
EAST
ANGLIA
WESSEX

couldn't be named the king of Brandenburg, because Brandenburg was part of the Holy Roman empire, which Prussia was not. In this way, the sprawling domains of the

Hohenzollern's were ultimately given the name of Prussia. And Berlin, which had been the capital city of the Hohenzollern's since the end of the 15th century, became the capital of this new Prussia.

3. The first seeds of a nation had been planted in England (Angle land). We describe this event in more detail below.

In 866, England was made up of four kingdoms: East Anglia, Mercia, Northumbria, and Wessex (West Saxons (Seaxe)). In that year, the Danes (Vikings from Denmark) invaded England. In five years, they subdued East Anglia, Mercia, and Northumbria. In 871, they moved on Wessex, where King Alfred had just succeeded to the crown. He repulsed this invasion and two others, one in 876 and the other in 892. When the fighting was over, the outcome was the existence of two kingdoms in England: Wessex in the south and the Danelaw in the north.

When not combating the Danes, Alfred devoted himself to strengthening his kingdom. He added to the defense of his towns and organized a navy. He established schools and translated, from Latin into Saxon, texts such as Gregory's *Pastoral Care,* Boethius's *Consolations of Philosophy,* and the Bede's *Ecclesiastical History.* He established the *Anglo-Saxon Chronicle,* which recorded the history of his times.

During the half century after Alfred died, his son, Edward, and then his grandson, Athelstan, succeeded to the kingship, retook the Danelaw, and created a single kingdom of England. The Danes were, in any case, turning from war to farming and from paganism to Christianity. For a while after their defeat, the Danes kept their own laws. But their language and practices weren't that different from those of the Saxons. Over time, they blended into the Saxon race.

Saxon kingship prospered because of its identification with the church. The king was seen as ruling by God's grace. He was a representative of God in a Christian community. Reciprocally, the king was responsible to God for the community's protection and well-being.

Associated with the king was the Witan (the Wise Men), an assembly of the most influential men in the kingdom: lords, bishops, and the king's officials. The Witan had no clearly defined

Roland and Agrican. *From an illustration, "The Midnight Encounter", by N. C. Wyeth for* Legends of Charlemagne, *written by Thomas Bulfinch and published by Cosmopolitan Book in 1924. Roland, known to the Italians as Orlando, was the most famous of Charlemagne's mythic 12 paladins. According to legend, he battled with the Saracen Agrican at night by the light of the moon.*

responsibilities, but the king typically consulted it about matters of importance and asked it to approve his decrees and edicts. Thus, with the king and the Witan acting as a group, the king was able to back up the authority of his decisions with the endorsement of the power brokers of his realm.

For administrative purposes, the Saxon kingdom was divided into regions called shires. The king's chief administrative officer in a shire was the sheriff (shire reeve, where reeve was the king's servant), who collected the funds due the king, announced the king's laws, pursued criminals, put teeth in the pronouncements of the shire's court of justice, and called up the fyrd, the peasant militia, when it was needed. Thus, the significance of the Sheriff of Nottingham in the legends of Robin Hood.

Consequently, from the beginning, the Saxon kingdom was centrally administered.

Also identifiable on the Saxon political landscape was the borough. A borough was a town, but not all towns were boroughs. The distinguishing feature was economic. A borough had a market. Merchants, or burgesses, lived in a borough. The burgesses of a borough had the right to create guilds and establish rules for regulating trade. The king promoted the idea of having burgesses reside in boroughs, because it made collecting custom duties easier. The largest borough was London.

On the continent, the Germanic nation that became dominant during the Dark Ages was the Franks. Under Charlemagne, the kingdom of the Franks achieved its widest extent, stretching from the Atlantic to the Elbe and Danube, and from the Baltic to the Pyrenees and Rome. The Roman church was universal in this kingdom, and there were those who thought that it should also have a worldly representation, the old Roman empire. The idea that it would be an advantage for the church to be allied with a temporal power of some strength may have also been an influence here.

Consequently, on Christmas day of 800, Pope Leo III set a crown on Charlemagne's head and proclaimed him emperor. Thus was the Carolingian empire born. It isn't easy to get from Charlemagne to Carolingian, but it can be done. Charlemagne is Charles the Great. In Latin, Charles is Carolius, Carol for short, and adding "ling" means children. Thus, Caroling is Charles and his children, and the Carolingian empire is the empire of

A Viking. *Drawing based on the adventure strip* PRINCE VALIANT *by Harold R. Foster © 1938 King Features Syndicate, Inc. All rights reserved. By permission of King Features Syndicate.*

Charlemagne and his children. It was, in fact, coincident with the kingdom of the Franks.

On Charlemagne's death, the Carolingian empire began to disintegrate. Within three generations, it was no more. There were

The Carolingian Empire

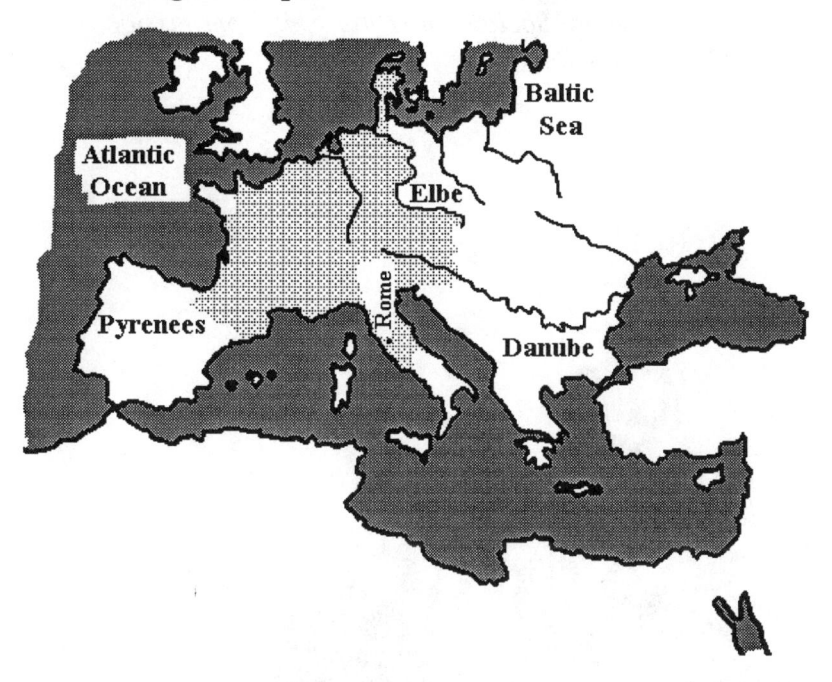

several factors contributing to this decline. For one, the Frankish custom of succession called for dividing the empire among the sons of the emperor as if it were some kind of personal estate to be bequeathed proportionately among the heirs. Even more significant in the undermining of the empire was the growing power of the lords, who began to draw away from the emperor and create enclaves of governmental power for themselves. And as if these internal difficulties weren't enough, the empire was subjected to repeated incursion by the Vikings.

Feudal Plowing. *From an illustration by Birney Lettick for the National Geographic Society in 1962. By permission of the National Geographic Society.*

CHAPTER SEVEN

Feudalism

The term, feudalism, was invented in the 17th century by lawyers. It wasn't used in its current sense until late in the 19th century.

The disintegration of the Carolingian empire coincided with the rise of feudalism, which dominated what historians sometimes call the High Middle Ages, the 11th through 13th centuries. Feudalism was the result of the fortuitous coincidence of two mutually supporting factors.

One of these factors was the rise of Islam, which, as we've seen, occurred roughly at the same time as the Dark Ages. As the Moslems expanded into the Mediterranean area, European civilization was thrown back to the north. Swamp and forest overlay almost all of the northern European plain. The moistness of the Atlantic climate and the lack of drainage on the level plains kept the land soggy for so long each year that the farming techniques that had evolved in the dry climate of the Middle East and Mediterranean could be practiced in the north in only relatively rare spots. Without any change in this situation, the paucity of such an agricultural base would have kept European civilization at such a low level that it never would have attained prominence.

There was an existing solution to this agricultural problem, which we'll now describe. Why the solution was eventually adopted we'll explain later. The solution had been developed by the Germanic tribes. It was a heavy wooden plow with a steel plowshare to cut the bottom of the furrow, a steel cotter to cut the vertical side of the furrow, and a moldboard to turn over the furrow.

The problem with this type of tillage was twofold. First, the plow was so heavy that it took a team of four or more oxen to pull it. Few European farmers could afford a team of this size. Second, such a team was hard to turn. Consequently, the efficient field layout was one of strips as long as the team could pull without tiring. After plowing a furrow in such a field, the team could be rested and then turned, and the plowing of the next furrow could begin. The problem was that most farmers' plots were small and square.

But even if these problems were surmountable, how would the heavy plow contribute to increased European agricultural output? Well, first, the heavy plow could cut and turn the clayey soil of the northern European plain. And second, if a particular plowing pattern were followed, a natural drainage system would be created. This pattern was as follows. The first furrow was cut down the middle of the field. The remaining furrows were then cut so that the current furrow being cut was next to the already cut furrows and turned toward these already cut furrows. Thus, the field was plowed from the middle out on both sides of the middle cut, and the furrows were always cut toward the middle of the field. Over time, this plowing pattern would cause the strip to become elevated in the middle and depressed along the edges, thus creating the desired drainage system.

So much for the solution to the north European agricultural problem. Let's now turn to the other factor leading to the rise of feudalism, the Viking raids of the 9th and 10th centuries, which contributed to the downfall of the Carolingian empire.

The Viking was a thorough marauder. He liked a weak victim. So what he couldn't carry away, he destroyed. He left the north European farmer on the horns of a dilemma. If the farmer was fortunate enough to avoid the Viking's sword during a raid, he was likely to starve because the Viking left him nothing on which to survive.

As we've already seen, the solution to barbarian raiding was also in existence long before the rise of the Vikings. It was the knight — the armored warrior mounted on an armored great horse. The knight of the Middle Ages enjoyed one advantage over his counterpart, who had originated in Parthia. Sometime around the 8th century, stirrups were invented. Consequently, the knight was armed with a lance, rather than a bow and arrows or a spear, because his stirrups gave him the ability to lean forward into the blow when his lance struck home. Without stirrups, such a maneuver would have just lifted the knight up over the back of his horse.

Out of these factors grew European feudal civilization. There was nothing planned or managed about its development, it evolved over centuries, and it was the outcome of innumerable bargains between individuals. The farmers in a locale would agree to give up some freedom in return for the protection of a fighting lord. This was known as "commending" yourself to the lord.

As a result, the farmers' lands were merged, and while no one farmer could afford the team required to draw a heavy plow, a community of farmers could. These merged lands could also be divided into long strips for plowing, which minimized the turning of the team. This type of cultivation, in turn, produced the agricultural surplus necessary to support the lord and his band of knights, and to finance their armor, horses and training. Thus was born the manorial system, one of the basic building blocks of feudal civilization.

The manor was ruled by the lord. At the most defensible point in the manor rose the lord's castle, which provided security for the lord and his knights and peasants, and in which the lord, his knights, and their families lived. Around the castle clustered the hovels of the peasants, which made up the major part of the village. In the village were a mill, a blacksmith's shop, a church, and the home of the parish priest. All around the village were the fields and meadows. The fields were divided into three parts. One part was sown with oats, barley and peas in the spring, the second part with wheat or rye in the fall, and the third part lay fallow. Each year the three parts were rotated. These were "open fields" — that is, they were fenced only when cattle had to be shut out from the growing crops. After the crops had been gathered, the fences were taken down and the cattle allowed to feed on the stubble.

The peasants were serfs — that is, they were bound to the land and were obligated to support the lord and his knights. This they did by paying, in work and produce, for the privilege of working the land. But even though the peasant wasn't free, he had rights. As long as he met his obligations to his lord, he couldn't be removed from the land, nor could he be kept from gathering his allotment of hay from the meadows or from pasturing his share of cattle, pigs and geese on this common land. Moreover, these rights and obligations were hereditary.

A Feudal Lord. *From an illustration that N. C. Wyeth did for the book* The Scottish Chiefs *written by Jane Porter and published by Scribners' Sons in 1921. Wyeth was depicting King Edward, but from our point of view, we're interested in showing what a lord might have looked like in the Middle Ages. Wyeth's painting now resides in the Farnsworth Museum in Rockland, Maine.*

Just as the peasant had certain rights and obligations, so did his lord. The lord had the right to predetermined amounts of his peasants' work and production. But he was also obligated to defend his peasants, set up a court for them, maintain a mill, blacksmith's shop, and church, and provide the land making up the manor. The manor was an economic and political entity. The peasant had essentially no contact outside of it.

The lord's castle keep might protect him and his knights and peasants from the Viking's sword, but it did little to prevent pillage of crops, cattle and village. To turn back the Viking, a larger military organization than that of the lord's was necessary. There's nothing to indicate that there was any direct relationship, but a precursor of such an organization was present in the Germanic comitatus, or group of companions. These men at arms pledged undying fealty to their chief and supported him in his military endeavors. In return for this commitment, the chief saw that his men were always cared for.

In any case, the other basic building block of feudal civilization was the fief. A fief consisted of one or more manors and was what a chief lord provided a companion lord in return for military support. The lord receiving the fief was, thus, the vassal of the chief lord. The vassal didn't own the fief, any more than the peasant owned the land he worked. But like the peasant, the vassal had a hereditary claim to his fief and couldn't be dispossessed as long as he carried out his obligations to his lord. These obligations were three. First was military service, both his and his knights'. Second was to participate in the lord's court of justice when required. And third was payment of produce on stated occasions.

In return, the lord had obligations to his vassals. Most importantly, he defended them from all threats. Then of course, he provided the land for his vassals. He also maintained a court for his vassals, functioned as guardian for a vassal's minor heirs, and found a husband for any unmarried heiress of a vassal. If a vassal died without heir, the fief escheated, or reverted, to the lord. Some of these obligations were, of course, also privileges. Court fines constituted revenue. While serving as guardian, the income of the fief went to the lord. And the search for a husband for a single heiress or a new vassal for an escheated manor gave the lord the opportunity to pay debts and cement relationships.

As already stated, a fief could consist of more than one manor. A fief of more than a few manors was typically subinfeudated to vassals, so a lord could be vassal to his lord and lord to his vassals at the same time. A manor, in turn, could support a lord and a group of knights or, if it were small enough, might support just one knight, who was lord of his manor but sat at the bottom of the feudal pecking order.

At the top of this hierarchy of vassals and lords was the king, to whom all the land belonged. Yet the king had limited power. He had the allegiance of only the vassals directly under him. And the benefits flowing from the land went, by right, to his vassals, not to him. Finally, the solution to Viking incursion provided by the lords and their knights was just marginally better than the problem. When the society of knights, built on the base of the agricultural community of northwestern Europe, succeeded in permanently discouraging Viking raiding, the lords turned on each other with all the exuberance and violence that they had hitherto reserved for the Vikings. In general, the king was powerless to control these local depredations. There was no state law or army, nor any state taxation to support them.

The only thing holding the feudal world together was the fealty of the vassal to his lord. In addition to all the human weaknesses that such a bond was heir to, marriage, conquest, and inheritance through the mother's family resulted in the not uncommon situation where a lord was a vassal to multiple lords, with all the conflicting demands on his loyalty that such a state of affairs generated. To take just one of the more extreme examples, until the end of the Hundred Years War, the kings of England weren't only monarchs in their own right; they were also, as the lords of several fiefs (such as Normandy) on the continent, vassals to the king of France.

The peasant's life was one of endless toil and unrelieved squalor. He worked from sunrise to sunset. His house was a crudely built hut with a thatched roof. It was filthy. It had no chimney. Conditions permitting, cooking was done outside. But in the winter, the fire was inside and the door was the only ventilation. The peasant shared his house with his geese and hens. His oxen were stabled in a lean-to adjoining the house. The peasant's diet was porridge, rye or oatmeal bread, vegetables, cheese, and whey.

The lord was only marginally better off. The goal of castle design was to make them impregnable. Comfort was secondary.

Castles were poorly lit, clammy and inconvenient. Arrow-slits served as windows. They provided little light but much cold air. There was almost no privacy. In the winter, life centered around the great hall, the floor of which was stone and spread with rushes, which became foul long before spring. Hunting dogs shared the great hall with the castle dwellers and ate the scraps and chewed on the bones tossed to them by those eating.

The lord was doomed to a life of perpetual adolescence. He lived for just one thing, fighting, for which he was born and reared. His most prized possessions were his armor, weapons and horse, for it was from these that his power, both figurative and literal, flowed. Many a lord had more regard for his heavy and finely tempered sword than he did for his wife. And he wasn't without justification. It was his sword, not his wife, on which his claim to lordship rested. Most any excuse was good enough for a local war — boundary disputes, disagreements over the terms of vassalage, family feuds, personal conflicts, avarice, or just plain boredom. Besides, fighting often paid off. It was more common for an armored lord to be captured than slain in battle, and he could then be held for ransom.

When the lord wasn't fighting, he played at it. His favorite sport was the tournament. A tournament was made up of a series of jousts followed by a melee. Not only did tournaments provide training, they could also be profitable. The loser in a joust not only lost the contest, he also lost his horse and armor to the winner. In the melee, lords could be taken prisoner. Prisoners, armor and horses then had to be ransomed.

But whether he won or lost, the lord was expected to give extravagant gifts, or largesse, to heralds, minstrels and servants. In general, the lord had a life style to keep up. He was expected to entertain guests lavishly. And he had to display himself with proper pomp and ceremony when he appeared in public.

In fact, because of the requirement to maintain such a magnificent life style, the lords, without exception, found their needs in excess of their resources. To attempt to cover this shortfall, the lord would try almost any expedient. When he could squeeze no more out of his peasants, he would levy a toll on the merchants, pilgrims and clergy who passed his castle. Or he would rob them and hold them for ransom. But his favorite recourse was a local war in search of booty. In this way, the victorious lord might temporarily improve his own position. But in general, such activity was self-defeating. It added to the impoverishment of the lords as a class, for war doesn't generate wealth, but destroys it.

On top of all their other troubles, peasant and lord alike had to contend with famine. Too much rain or too little, unseasonable heat or cold, a large number of insects, or any of the other perils of farming could result in a lost crop. In the 11th century, chronicles report 48 famine years. In addition, there were numerous local famines, for roads were so unserviceable that it was almost impossible to move food when bad weather, flood, or a raid had destroyed the crops in a locality. These famines meant a shortage of food for all. For the peasant, it could mean starvation.

Famine was frequently accompanied by an epidemic. Even when there was no famine, epidemics could strike. The chronicles often report plague and pest, names given to diseases that medical knowledge at the time couldn't more precisely identify.

When Europe entered the feudal age, there were three classes: lords, clergy and peasants. The lords looked after the defense of the realm, the clergy ministered to its spiritual needs, and the peasants provided for the physical requirements of the community. During the feudal age, a fourth class, burghers, grew up. They were called burghers because they lived in walled towns, or burghs, and they made their living by trade.

The wall that enclosed a burgh was stone and capped with towers. Around the outside of the wall ran a moat. At dusk, the town gates were locked, not to be opened until sunrise. These military precautions, similar to those taken at a lord's castle, proclaimed the town's intention to defend its rights.

First among these rights was individual freedom. The merchants who established the first towns were peasants. But having in some way escaped from their manors, they became free, because no one knew where they came from and no resident lord could claim them for his own. Freedom was acknowledged by the town as the right of all town dwellers. If a peasant could break away from his manor and live in a town for a year and a day, the town defended his right to freedom.

Second among the rights that towns defended was the right to govern themselves. The government consisted of a council and a number of executive officers, or magistrates. Only men of property could take part in the government. The government collected income and sales taxes, which were used to maintain the defense and public facilities of the town. The town also had its own code of civil and criminal law and its own courts and judges.

Possibly because the town's surroundings were hostile, and certainly because the church endorsed such an attitude, the burgher was of the opinion that the interests of the town were more important than those of its inhabitants. The medieval merchant had no concept of the workings of supply and demand in an economic market. Again with the active encouragement of the church, he believed that, for every good, there was a "just price", which should be the same in time of shortage as in time of plenty. This price was set by custom and was based on the just prices of the raw materials required plus the reasonable profit necessary to allow the merchant to live in the style recognized by public opinion as suitable. Usury was also censured. Money was loaned when one's fellow was in need. To charge interest for such a loan was both exploitive and unchristian. Of course, all this pertained only to one's fellow towns people. Town rules for trade from without the town were constructed to give the towns people the upper hand.

Regulation of trade was carried out by guilds. A guild was an association of all the merchants who made their living by selling the goods of a given craft. No one but a guild member could sell his goods at retail within the town, though foreign merchants could buy and sell at wholesale, since this was the way that local merchants obtained raw materials and got rid of excess stock. The work in which each guild could engage was closely circumscribed. Each guild had a monopoly on its given trade in the town. The guild set prices, regulated wages and working hours, and required quality in the goods produced. Guild officers inspected the merchants' shops frequently and saw to it that these standards were maintained.

The guild members were committed to helping one another. Merchants weren't allowed to try and recruit other merchants' workers. In fact, if a merchant fell behind for lack of workers, the

Medieval Italy

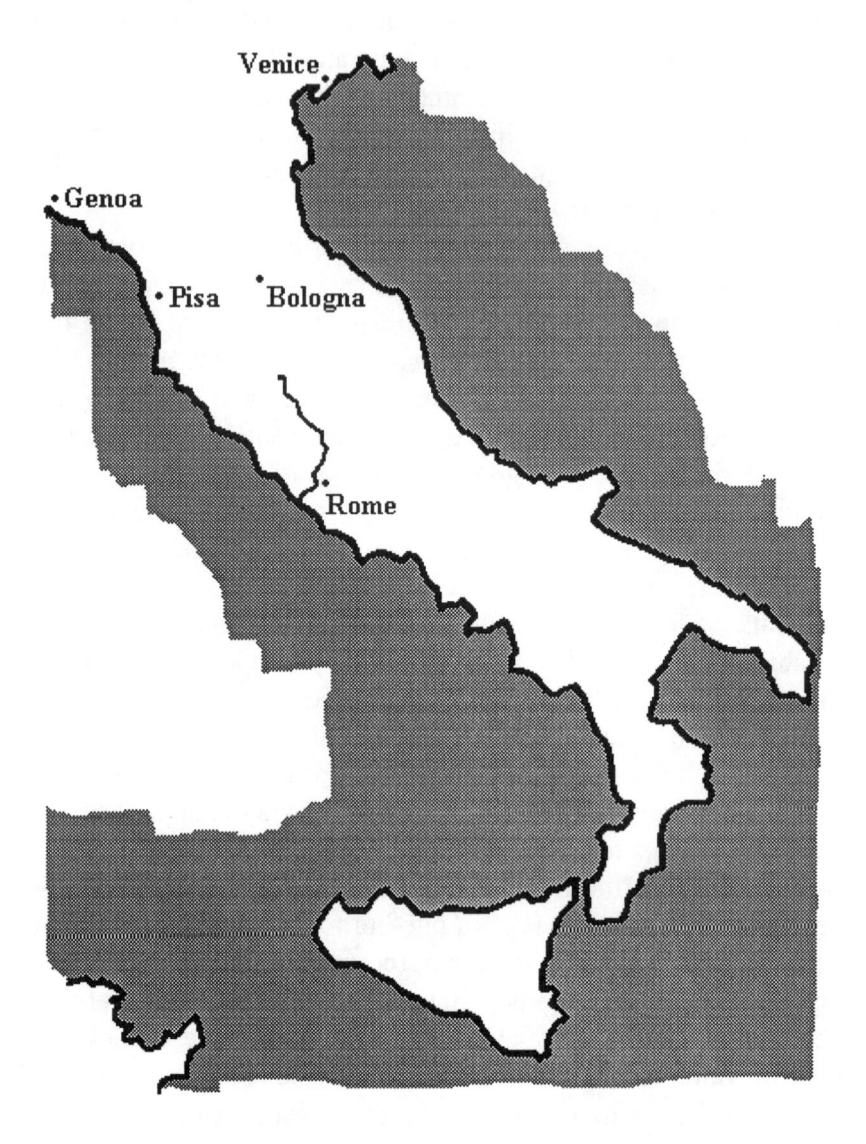

other merchants had an obligation to lend their workers to him free of charge. The guild purchased at wholesale at a lower cost than any individual guildsman could have gotten and distributed the purchase to its members at the purchase price. If a merchant got a bargain, he shared it with his guild members. When a merchant traveled, his credit was backed by his guild.

The guild was also a society. It made a ceremony of births and marriages, sponsored social affairs, and celebrated church festivals as a body. If a guildsman got sick, guild funds were used to nurse him back to health. On his death, the guild assumed the obligation for his funeral expenses, and if his wife and children were destitute, the guild cared for them.

The first step in becoming a guildsman was apprenticeship. Apprentices started their training around age ten or 12. The parents of the apprentice entered into a contract with a full-fledged guild member, a master, to take on the boy's training and generally paid a small fee. The apprentice lived with his master. He did whatever he could. In exchange, he got instruction, food, clothing and lodging. When he developed from a liability to an asset, he got a minimal wage. The guild supervised apprentice training. It established the length of the training period depending on the craft and restricted the number of apprentices a master might have at one time. This was done to optimize the quality of training, prevent any master from using too many inexpensive workers, and keep down the number of guild members.

When an apprentice finished his training, he became a journeyman (journee, French for day, man), who worked by the day for any master who was willing to hire him. He then continued to improve his skills and accumulate money toward his own shop. When he was ready, he applied for full membership in the guild; was tested by the masters; and offered an example of his skill, his "masterpiece", along with evidence of good character and religious orthodoxy. If he passed this examination, he became a master.

European trade differed from its Oriental counterpart. In the Orient, the focus of trade was the aristocracy. The wares were primarily luxury goods. These luxury goods also flowed into Europe via the Italian trading cities of Venice, Genoa and Pisa. But to the European merchant, luxury goods were just a sideline. The backbone of European trade was common goods, such as grain, smoked herring, wool, course woolen cloth, metals, timber, and the multifarious objects, tools and weapons that could be

Medieval France

- Calais
- Agincourt
- Crecy
- Harfleur
- Laon
- Rheims

NORMANY
- Paris
- Domremy
- Orleans
- Tours
- Poitiers

- Avignon
- Montpellier

NAVARRE

fashioned from these raw materials. Ultimately, European trade reached deep into the society's structure and became an integral part of its overall nature.

The feudal economy was a barter economy. The obligations between lord, vassal and peasant were primarily concerned with the delivery of produce and services. This delivery was typically direct without intervention of the use of money. On the other hand, merchants and artisans found barter uncongenial. Their work typically involved receipt of raw materials; working of these materials into products, which took time; and then, merchandising the product, which could also take considerable time. Such economic activity was next to impossible in a barter system. Consequently, a money economy grew in tandem with the expansion of towns.

A particular kind of guild was the university. Originally, guild and university meant the same thing. To assure that all those teaching were qualified, the chancellor of the cathedral issued licenses to those who had passed an examination, which required the definition of a curriculum so candidates would know on what they'd be examined. Those with licenses were referred to as masters of arts and made up the faculty of arts. Students could be thought of as apprentices and bachelors journeymen with a narrow license to give basic instruction. A master who wanted to concentrate in a profession could follow advanced studies which would ultimately result in a doctorate and acceptance into a specialized faculty such as theology, medicine or law.

By the end of the 12th century, universities had put down firm roots in Bologna, Paris, Montpellier and Oxford. When they began, we don't know. Like all feudal institutions, they just grew. These universities were open to all, because there was no language problem. All education was conducted in Latin. Thus, the section in Paris in which students lived was called the Latin Quarter.

The texts of these universities came from Saracen and Byzantine sources. We've already described them: Greek science, mathematics and philosophy as expanded on by the Saracens, and Justinian law. The method of instruction was scholastic. It emphasized reliance on authoritative texts combined with logic and gave observation and experimentation short shrift. Such an environment wasn't conducive to science (although it did maintain knowledge already developed), but under it, law thrived.

In sum, in feudal society, there were lords and peasants, living on manors. The lords were organized in a hierarchy by vassalage, at the top of this hierarchy sat the king, and theoretically, this put all ultimate authority in the hands of the king. In fact, such total royal control was far from the case. As the Viking threat declined, ascendant lords vied for dominance and often contended with the king himself.

In his struggle for control with the lords, the king found an ally in the burghs. All the burghs wanted was to be left alone to manage their own affairs. To consolidate his power over the lords, the king needed a source of revenue independent of feudalism. The burghers were willing to supply this revenue by submitting to taxation, for a strong central government would bring law and order to the countryside, a solid base on which their trade could expand free of fear of exploitation. It was in this symbiosis between the king and the burghers that the seeds of nationalism were sown.

CHAPTER EIGHT

The Rise of Nations

Saxon England wasn't feudal. The core of the king's forces were fighting lords each with his band of knights. These lords had large estates, and these estates were worked in a way similar to the way in which a feudal lord's manor was organized. But in contrast to the feudal lord, the Saxon lord hadn't received his estate from the king in exchange for his fealty. Instead, he owned his estate outright, he fought for his king out of loyalty to him and to England, and his peasants were tenants, not serfs. The Saxon lord had no castle. The distinguishing feature of his housing was a large mead-hall constructed of wood in which he fed and entertained his knights and their ladies.

In Saxon England, agriculture was carried on primarily by freemen who lived in villages. The land around a village was organized in large strips amenable to heavy plow agriculture, and farming was carried on communally by the village. However, each strip of land was divided into blocks, and the blocks were owned by individual freemen.

Like the nobles, the Saxon farmers made themselves available to king and country. They responded to the call of their sheriffs to work on roads and bridges, and to serve in the fyrd. In each village, the fyrd was organized so that, when called, half of the peasants in the village went into service. The other half remained in the village to tend to the fields. These two groups alternated in serving in the fyrd.

In 978, Ethelred II became king. Two years later, Danish raids on England began. Ethelred the Unready was unable to provide his people with the protection they required. As a consequence, freemen began to commend themselves to Saxon nobles in return for local defense. In this way, the seeds of Saxon feudalism were planted. But before this process had gone very far, England was invaded and occupied in 1016 by Canute, the king of Denmark.

As a result, Canute became the king of England. Canute's rule was a time of peace, from which England benefited, and had no influence on the political organization of the realm, since Canute ruled as an English king, according to English laws and customs. Canute's empire, which included Denmark and Norway, destructed when he died. Not many years after, in 1042, the last of the Danish kings of England died. The Witan then restored the scepter to Alfred's lineage, the House of Wessex.

In 1066, England was again successfully invaded, this time by the Normans. As a result, the English speaking Saxons came under the rule of a small minority of Normans, who spoke French. This situation, of an English speaking land ruled by a French speaking nobility, lasted until almost 1400. It was the anti-French sentiment in the Hundred Years War that caused the ultimate switch of the nobility to the use of English. The first English king, after the Norman invasion, to speak English as his mother tongue was Edward III.

However, despite the language disparity and sometime enmity between Saxon and Norman, the Normans never thought of themselves as foreigners or French. They considered themselves Englishmen, through and through.

William the Conqueror, who led the Normans to victory in 1066, was the unquestioned sovereign of all England by right of conquest. It was his to do with as he wished. Basically, what he did was superimpose the feudal organization with which he was familiar in Normandy on top of the political organization that he found in England. He confiscated the land of all those who had resisted him and replaced the Saxon nobility with a Norman one. By 1071, when the countryside had been pacified, less than one percent of English land held by Saxon nobles before the invasion remained in the hands of these owners.

However, William's English feudal system was unusual in several ways, all these differences tending to maintain and reinforce the centralized character of English government. First, William reserved a great amount of land for which he was lord, thus providing an independent income for the crown.

Second, as he had done in Normandy, he required that, no matter how far subinfeudation reached, the first commitment of all vassals was to the king rather than to their lords. Those who came after him continued this practice.

Third, William's conquest had been piecemeal, with the result that, instead of being concentrated in one large manor, the English fiefs of the Norman lords were made up of a number of sections scattered around the country, which had been parceled out to them as the conquest proceeded. As a consequence, the lords' interests tended to be at the country level rather than being focused on one locality.

Fourth, although many Saxon freemen became serfs, villages of freemen remained a feature of the English scene.

Finally, William kept the Saxon system of shires for administrative purposes, thus giving him a control over the kingdom independent of the Norman feudal system. One of the changes that did take place in the organization of the country into shires was that, instead of continuing to be called by the English name, shire, these administrative units came to be known by the French word, county. In France, a county was a taxing district, and it was run by a count.

William ruled through a court, named the curia regis (royal court), composed of a group of officials and any of his lords whom he cared to summon. And on matters of policy, William called his Great Council, consisting of the king's feudal vassals, into session for consultation. The Great Council resembled the Saxon Witan and was sometimes referred to as such. But as a Norman feudal institution, the Great Council had a different origin from that of the Witan. Nevertheless, both institutions served the same function: to get the concurrence of the influential men of the kingdom before the king took a decisive step.

For 13 years (1087 - 1100) after William the Conqueror died, his son, William Rufus (for his red face), ruled with tyranny and the goal of extorting as much personal wealth as possible from the country. While hunting, he was killed with an arrow under what could be considered questionable circumstances. But no one was sorry to see him go. His brother, Henry I, who rapidly consolidated his shaky claim to the throne, returned order and justice to the realm.

Henry had a surviving older brother, Robert, who as luck would have it, was off on a crusade at the time of William's death. Robert got back a month after Henry's coronation. But by that time, Henry had cemented his position with the church and the people. He defeated Robert in battle, and Robert spent the rest of his life as a prisoner.

With what was generally thought to be unseemly haste, Henry was crowned three days after the death of William Rufus. At the time, he published a charter in which he promised an improved government. His motivation seems to have been twofold: he recognized that William's tyranny had been resented and desired to assure his people that he didn't intend to continue it, and he wanted the rapid consolidation of power into his own hands to be as palatable as possible. Although Henry's charter was a pronouncement published by the king and not an agreement with anybody, the fact that it had been issued was general knowledge. Its existence was a factor a century later when the English lords forced Magna Carta out of King John.

One of the trends that can be seen in English history is the effort to replace local and ecclesiastic courts with a single legal system for all of the kingdom. This law was the common law, so named because it was the law established as common (universal) to all of England, and it's the only legal system in Europe not based on Justinian law. Justinian law derives from the decrees issued by the Roman emperors. In contrast, common law is case law and, thus, is dependent on precedent for its force. Ultimately, it rests on custom. The idea is that the law is the way it is because that's the way it's supposed to be. Moreover, it has always been that way. Thus, Sir William Blackstone, the most famous of the English jurists, described the law as embodying principles " ... whereof the memory of man runneth not to the contrary."

Henry widened the king's law by dividing the kingdom into circuits over which itinerant justices traveled in a regular pattern. The king's court was in Westminster. But when the king's judge presided in a county court, the law followed was that practiced in the king's court. In this way, the king's law began its journey toward the goal of being the common law of the land.

Henry was succeeded by his nephew, Stephen, who ruled from 1135 through 1154. Stephen was a weak king. During his reign, there was a tendency toward lawlessness. Stephen was the last of the Norman dynasty, the descendants of William the Conqueror through the male line.

Stephen was succeeded by Henry II, a grandson of Henry I through his daughter Matilda. The emblem of Henry's house was the broom plant, or planta genestra. For this reason, he and his successors were known as the Plantagenet dynasty.

Henry II took up the job of bringing law to England where Henry I had left off. He broadened the province of the royal court and enhanced the system of itinerant judges, with the result that the movement toward a common law for the land continued apace.

Henry's wish to have one law for all the land led to an incident that has been blown out of proportion to the contribution he made to the development of a nation of laws. In Henry's time, the Roman church claimed jurisdiction over a broad range of cases. In particular, it maintained that anyone, who in any way could be classed as clergy, must be tried in an ecclesiastic court. Henry maintained that "criminous clercs", clergy who had committed crimes, should be tried in the royal courts just like any other criminal. In 1162, the archbishopric of Canterbury (the head of the church in England) came open. In what he thought was a move to strengthen his position, Henry appointed his longtime minister and companion, Thomas Becket, to the post. Imagine Henry's surprise when Becket turned out to be an extreme defender of church rights and resisted any and all royal trespass on the prerogatives of the church.

Despite his virtues, Henry had a savage temper. After one of his many confrontations with Becket, Henry cried out in front of his court, "Will no one rid me of this troublesome priest?" Four of Henry's knights took him at his word, traveled to Canterbury, and slaughtered Becket in front of his altar.

The piety of the times converted Becket into an instant saint. Henry did public penance and withdrew his demands with respect to the trial of criminous clercs. The drive toward common law was set back only temporarily. But Henry was the victim of a bad press. His crime at most was an indiscreet remark delivered in a rage. Becket's blood wasn't on his hands and nothing could have been further from his desires than to have Becket murdered on his behalf. But like the leader he was, he acted in the way best

England, Ireland and Scotland

designed to hold his realm together even at the cost of personal abasement and a setback to his plans. Becket is, at best, an insignificant blip on the time line of history, a man with such a peculiar personality that he was apparently compelled to play to the hilt any part in which he was cast, while Henry, whatever his faults, was a strong contributor to the rule of law.

We have to be careful about how much credit we give these early English kings for the institution of a single legal system for the land, since we must remember that legal cases generate fines and fees, and every case tried in the king's court, rather than in a lord's or ecclesiastic court, was that much more revenue for the king. In addition, a king-centered legal system, rather than a church-centered one or one fragmented among lords, added to the king's power and control over his subjects. Thus, with respect to the development of the rule of law, we could say that, while doing well, the Norman and Plantagenet kings also did good.

Henry was succeeded by his son, Richard I, the "Lion-hearted". Richard was in England for only a few months of his ten year rule. Basically irresponsible, he was happier on crusade than on the throne. However, in his absence, the administrative system set up by his father performed effectively in governing the realm.

Things grew grimmer when Richard's brother, John, assumed the throne. John's rule was characterized by cruelty, extortion and failure. In June 1215, John's lords compelled him to set his seal on Magna Carta (Great Charter). If Henry II suffered from a bad press, Magna Carta has been the victim of a good one. It was called great simply because it was so long. Although it contained some ambiguous references to the rights of all freemen, in John's time, there weren't many freemen besides the lords, their knights, and the clergy. The charter was essentially just a promise by the king that he would obey the law in dealing with his people, particularly the lords. If the charter had any significance, it was in the implication (probably not thought through at the time, and as we'll see, certainly not recognized until long into the future) that the king wasn't above the law but that, instead, the law was above the king.

A second trend that can be distinguished in English history is the development of the Great Council from a consultative body of lords into a Parliament that enacted legislation and whose controlling body, the House of Commons, was converted into an institution designed to represent the people.

Henry III, John's son, ascended to the throne when he was nine. Under his regents, England returned to normal. But in 1227, when Henry took over, misgovernment once more became the rule. Protest was protracted, and finally, in 1264, Simon de Montfort, a lord with no claim to the throne, found himself in control of the

English government. A year later he was slain in battle, and Henry was restored.

De Montfort's short rule was notable for two events. First, in casting about for some way to legitimate his dominion, he hit on the idea of calling the Great Council to endorse his administration. Here was the first faint attempt to formulate the idea that the right to govern was other than the divine right of kings.

At about this time, the assemblies of the Great Council began to be called parliaments, although there was no particular significance to the name. It just meant a meeting where people talked, or parlayed.

The other notable thing about de Montfort's rule was that, when he called the parliament, he invited, not only the lords, but also representatives of the towns. For the first time, burghers took part in a government function.

A third trend that can be isolated in English history is the evolution of the king's royal court from an amorphous collection of administrators, judges and advisors into an organized cabinet and an independent judiciary.

Edward I, the son of Henry III, succeeded to the throne in his own right in 1272, although he had essentially controlled the government since de Montfort's defeat. In fact, it was Edward who led the army that bested de Montfort in 1265.

Edward's contribution was the further development of English government. Relying on middle-class ministers, who had learned their trade by long service, and on professional lawyers, he constructed a smoothly functioning engine of government and justice answering to the king. The royal court was divided into specialized courts: the exchequer was concerned with the realm's finances; the court of common pleas tried civil cases (cases brought by private individuals); the king's bench, criminal cases (cases brought by the king); and the king's council helped the king with the general concerns of government and tried all cases not handled by the special courts.

Edward planted firmly in the structure of English government the institution of Parliament. Edward called Parliament frequently and included commoners in it as a matter of practice. One group of commoners were the lesser lords who, over time, became more concerned with tending their manors than practicing war. They constituted the landed gentry, and they satisfied their obligation to provide the king with knights by substituting the payment of scutage (shield money). The other group of commoners were the burghers.

It's important, at this point in the development of Parliament, to not overemphasize the significance of commoner participation. Commoners weren't elected. The sheriffs appointed them. When Parliament was in session, the commoners stood at the foot of the hall. They were silent except when asked to consent to a proposition or express an opinion, which was done by a single member of the commoners, who had been designated as their speaker. But they did have pre-knowledge of the issues to be brought up in a parliamentary session, and they did begin to meet by themselves to discuss these matters ahead of time.

Because of their obligation to provide the king with an armed force, the lords were essentially exempt from taxation. As a consequence, taxes fell most heavily on the commoners. Therefore, proposed taxation was a subject that never failed to call for a session of Parliament, because Edward knew that the taxes would be easier to collect after the commoners had given their consent to the taxation.

In the history of England, you'll find, over and over, reference to Parliament being called to consent to taxation. To make clear what was going on here, let us point out that the taxation proposed in these instances wasn't permanent taxation. There was no piling of one tax after another on the backs of the people. Instead, the taxation referred to each time was one time taxation ("supply" it was often called) proposed for a specific purpose, generally to prepare for or to wage war.

Serfdom was an expensive agricultural technique. Between 1150 and 1280, population in England boomed. As a result, it became possible for landlords to reduce their labor expenses by pushing their peasants off the landlords' land and substituting hired laborers. By the late 13th century, serfdom in England had disappeared.

Edward II, the son of Edward I, was a weak king. Finally, in disgust, the lords replaced him with his son, Edward III, who reigned for the next 50 years. In 1337, ten years into the rule of Edward III, the Hundred Years War began.

The origins of the Hundred Years War lay in the French fiefs of which the king of England was lord. The English chaffed under the idea of their vassalage to the French king. They also had a claim to the French crown: Edward's mother was a daughter of Philip the Fair, king of France from 1285 through 1314. From the English point of view, the object of the war was to expand the number of English fiefs on the continent until all of France lay under English domination and the king of England was on the French throne. From the French point of view, the object was to drive the English from the continent, so that all of France would be ruled by French lords.

The Hundred Years War is a kind of misnomer, since in one sense, it spanned more than 100 years. But in another sense, there were periods of peace, when England and France were so exhausted or consumed with other concerns that they could no longer carry on the battle. So the years in which fighting took place total less than 100.

At first, things went the English way in the Hundred Years War. But ultimately, the tide turned. By 1453, when the war ended, England's only continental possession was the port of Calais.

The war was fought on French soil, and the French endured unspeakable suffering. However, England had to support expeditionary forces. Its resources, small in relation to France's, were also strained. Nevertheless, the war produced several significant results.

For one thing, the war was no repulse of a barbarian raid or an incursion of one feudal lord on another. This was a war in which Englishmen were trying to extend their domain and Frenchmen were endeavoring to expel a foreign invader from their soil. By the end of the war, there was no question of the existence of two nations: England and France.

From the English perspective, there were three great battles: Crecy in 1346, Poitiers in 1356, and Agincourt in 1415. Here we look in detail at just one: Agincourt.

On August 14, 1415, Henry V, the fourth of the five English kings to reign during the Hundreds Years War, and a force of 10,000 men landed on a French beach three miles west of Harfleur. This army was in the pay of the king and consisted of 2000 knights and 8000 archers. In previous encounters in Scotland, it had been demonstrated that a line of bowmen, wielding longbows that could drive an arrow through an inch of oak, could break a heavy cavalry charge. In 1337, Edward III had outlawed, on threat of death, all sports but archery and had forgiven all debts of the men who made bows and arrows.

Henry's archers are traditionally characterized as yeomen, small farmers that cultivated their own lands. To some extent, this was undoubtedly true. But it's also the case that many of the archers had enlisted to avoid punishment for various crimes including murder.

Harfleur was finally taken on September 22. Henry's plan had been to establish Harfleur as his base and then march on Paris. But by now, it was too late in the year to carry out this operation. However, it was felt that a demonstration had to be made. Henry's army had been reduced, primarily by disease, to 1000 knights and between 5000 and 6000 archers. He was convinced that he could lead this force to Calais without encountering significant French resistance. He was wrong. As a consequence, at dawn on October 22, he deployed his troops to do battle with a French force made up of some 25,000 men, primarily knights, that stood between him and Calais.

The battlefield was ploughed land about 1000 yards wide and bordered on both sides by woods. At one end of this field, the dismounted English knights formed up in three groups. Between each group of knights and on each flank were the archers, four groups in all. The whole line was four or five men deep. The archers were deployed somewhat forward of the knights. They had each driven a pointed wooden stake into the ground at an angle designed to catch a horse in the chest, and each stood to the rear of his stake.

At the opposite end of the field, about 1000 yards away, was the French formation. They were organized into three lines, each

A Longbowman. *From an illustration by Paul Williams for his book* The Warrior Knights *published by Time-Life in 1969.*

many ranks deep, the first two of which were on foot. The third was mounted, as were two separate groups, one on each wing.

Henry wanted the French to mount the attack. He waited about four hours to no avail. He then ordered his troops to advance in formation. This was a difficult and time consuming operation. But ultimately, the English found themselves redeployed within bowshot (around 250 yards) of the French. The English archers then opened fire. In return, the French attacked.

First to advance was the French cavalry in the wings, followed by the first line on foot. The cavalry was turned back, probably by the hedgehog of pointed stakes. In their return from their encounter with the English troops, the cavalry plowed into the advancing foot soldiers, which caused some disorder.

During this action, the archers had been pouring arrow fire into the attacking French, each archer being capable of releasing six arrows a minute. If an arrow hit body armor head on, it could be driven through the armor. And weaknesses at the armor joints could be found. Finally, the horses were vulnerable to arrow fire. The result was that the field became strewn with fallen horses and men, which made the footing of those Frenchmen, who had managed to retain their balance, treacherous. As a consequence, the disorder (and no doubt, the terror) in the French ranks continued to grow.

At this point, the English archers abandoned the security of their forest of stakes and, much like a pack of wolves harrying the weaker members of a herd of prey, attacked individual French knights in distress on the edges of the battle. As weapons, the archers used swords and battle axes, picked up from the field of battle, and the mallets with which they had driven in their stakes. The battlefield began to take on the characteristics of a slaughterhouse.

The second line of French knights on foot then began to move forward to aid the first line. Instead, they blocked their comrades' avenue of escape at the same time as they compressed the mass of French knights against each other, thus restricting their ability to make unhampered use of their arms against the relatively unimpeded English.

By noon, the only Frenchmen left on the field were the dead and wounded. Henry stood at the front of his line, which had now endured an hour of strenuous fighting. Before him was arrayed the third line of French, mounted and fresh for battle. Behind him were thousands of captured French knights. Because the third line of French prevented Henry from disengaging, he couldn't afford to dispatch sufficient forces to adequately guard his prisoners. They, thus, represented a continuing threat, in that they could easily rearm with the weapons strewn on the battlefield and reenter the fray. At this point, Henry's baggage train came under attack.

To lessen the odds against him, Henry ordered his prisoners slain. His knights refused to carry out this order, for what reasons we're not sure. It could be that they considered such action dishonorable. It's certain that no honor attached to such slaughter, and each prisoner represented a potential ransom. Faced with this disobedience, Henry then dispatched 200 archers to carry out his order. The archers suffered under none of the restraints acting on the knights, and the execution of the prisoners began.

Before this killing went very far, it was determined that the attack on the baggage train was being carried out by noncombatants — serfs led by three knights from the village of Agincourt, and the French third line broke formation and began to leave the field. The execution of the prisoners was then brought to a halt. It was now about 3 pm, and the battle of Agincourt was over.

In this battle, we see some of the remnants of feudalism — the taking of prisoners for ransom and the resistance of the knights to the destruction of this asset. But basically, Agincourt wasn't a feudal battle fought for honor. Instead, it began when an outnumbered but determined force, made up primarily of commoners, gained a tactical advantage over a large group of haughty, independently minded lords, and then was quickly transformed into the bloody business of slaughtering the enemy in any and every way possible.

Crecy and Poitiers had many of the characteristics of Agincourt. Crecy was quite similar. At Poitiers, mounted knights played a larger role. But in all three, the English were vastly outnumbered by the French, the English army was in the pay of the king (in contrast to the French army, which was a feudal organization), and a large part of the English force was made up of commoners.

Thus, in these (again from the English point of view) great confrontations, a motley crew of lords and commoners stood shoulder to shoulder and fought for the greater good of England. In addition, the English had the luck to find, in Shakespeare, a poetic voice capable of putting into stirring words the patriotic feeling engendered by these feats. For example, here, according to Shakespeare, is Henry V addressing his troops before the battle of Agincourt.

We few, we happy few, we band of brothers.
For he today that sheds his blood with me
Shall be my brother; be he ne'er so vile,
This day shall gentle his condition.
And gentlemen in England now abed
Shall think themselves accursed they were not here,
And hold their manhoods cheap whiles speaks
That fought with us upon Saint Crispin's day.

And the French, of course, had Joan of Arc. In 1429, at the nadir of France's fortunes, the Maid of Domremy, (significantly enough) sprung from peasant stock, appeared, raised the siege of Orleans, and carved a path through the English to Rheims, where the Dauphin was crowned King Charles VII of France after the manner of his ancestors. Joan commanded the French troops for just one year before she was taken prisoner and, ultimately, burned at the stake by the English as a heretic. The reaction of an English soldier, who was present, was, "We are lost. We have burnt a saint."

Truer words were never spoken. Her splendor forever undimmed, Jeanne d'Arc rides indomitably down the corridors of time to take her post beside every soldier of France, wherever entrenched, and stands ready, when the trumpet sounds, to raise the banner of the Fleur de Lis and lead France to her greater glory.

From a strictly historical perspective, Joan presents a problem. Here we have a peasant girl, who, until she appeared at the

Joan Weeps *for the soldiers slain in the attack on the English bastion of Saint-Loup, the first of the battles to raise the siege of Orleans. From an illustration by Maurice Boutet de Monvel for his book* Jeanne d'Arc *published in Paris in 1896. The book was republished in 1980 by Viking, now a subsidiary of Penguin. A copy of the original book can be found in The Pierpont Morgan Library in New York.*

Dauphin's court, had ostensibly spent her life in a small, remote, provincial village, where she tended her parents' garden and livestock, and listened to the voices of saints in her father's garden.

Shortly thereafter, she entered the French line, where she not only exhibited her competence in handling a war-horse and the weapons of war but also demonstrated a professional understanding of the strategy and tactics of the battlefield. How did she come by these skills?

The Hundred Years War saw no abatement in the development of the English Constitution. And in at least one respect, this evolution was speeded by the demands of the war.

Since we're used to thinking of a country's constitution as a document making up the supreme law of the land and spelling out the structure and function of the government, it might pay to pause here and note that such isn't the case with England. Instead, for England, it makes more sense to say that the supreme law of the land *is* the Constitution. In England, the Constitution just grew and consists of the common law (made up of judicial decisions), statute law (law passed by the legislature), and convention, in as much as they all three bear on the state's power and its restraint in the form of the rights of the people. For England, its constitution is a concept, both intangible and real, unwritten, and strongly felt. Again, like common law, it's a matter of things being the way they ought to be.

During the reign of Edward III, a new court, the chancery, was set up to try the civil cases referred to the king's council by the court of common pleas.

In 1387, Richard II, the grandson and successor of Edward III, initiated the practice of creating peers by letters patent. It was these peers who became the lords invited to attend Parliament. In the early Parliaments, the gentry tended to associate with the lords. But when the peerage shut the gentry out, they discovered the common interest they had with the burghers, which was that, when taxes were instituted, they fell most heavily on the burghers and the gentry. As a result, by the end of the 14th century, the separation of Parliament into the House of Lords and the House of Commons was complete.

The Commons exploited the demand for money that the war made on the king. Again and again, Parliament was called to consent to taxation. Before giving consent, Commons would present the king with petitions for the reform of grievances.

Frequently, these petitions were converted into statutes by the king and given the force of law. The Commons was learning how to legislate.

Thus, not only did the English nation arise out of the Hundred Years War, it did so as one well on the way to a constitutional monarchy in which a legislature expressed the will of (at least, some of) the people.

No similar development occurred in France. Like other feudal kings, the kings of France used a Great Council to get consent to their decisions on state matters. And Philip the Fair created the precedent of including burgher representatives as well as the lords in these councils. As time passed, these councils came to be known as the States General (Etats Generaux), which was divided into three groups, one each for the three estates that were represented in the States General: the clergy, the lords, and the burghers, who were known as the Third Estate. The States General voted by estate.

The first part of the Hundred Years War laid France low. The losses at Crecy and Poitiers were minor when contrasted with the ruin of the northern and western parts of France. As a matter of military principle, the English army methodically devastated the land wherever it went. And both armies, English and French, lived off the land in time of both truce and war. To all this was added a level of taxation much greater than France had ever before experienced. Over and over, the king summoned the States General to consent to taxes. But the people were dissatisfied, and the States General grew bolder. In the year of Poitiers, the States General, led by Etienne Marcel (president of the Third Estate and provost of the Parisian merchants (essentially, he was the mayor of Paris)) and Robert le Coq (president of the clergy and bishop of Laon), refused consent except on conditions that gave the States General practical control of the government, which was unacceptable to the king. The stalemate continued until 1358, by which time Marcel, backed by armed citizens of Paris, was in virtual control of the city. At this point, Navarre was in league with the English. Marcel was about to open the gates of Paris to the Navarrese when he was slain by Jean Maillart, the leader of the royalist party that was developing in Paris in reaction to the disarray into which France was falling. Support for the king then continued to grow. The outcome of this rebellion was that the States General fell into disrepute and was seldom called.

As a result, when the nation of France emerged from the Hundred Years War, the States General was looked on, rightly or wrongly, as a failed institution, and in France, the way was paved for an absolute monarchy. For France, the king was the state.

Compounding the problems of the Hundred Years War was the Black Death, possibly some type of bubonic plague, which swept over Europe in 1348 through 1350. Perhaps as much as a third of the population died. Obviously, all peoples felt the pain, but in England, which had a much smaller population base than France (four million versus 21 million), the outcome was a second agricultural revolution. There wasn't enough labor left to do the work, and the price of labor rose correspondingly. Landlords found that they could no longer afford to hire agricultural labor. As a consequence, they resorted to leasing large portions of their landholdings to free peasant families.

The causes that led to the end of the Hundred Years War were multiple. In 1422, Henry VI, the son of Henry V, ascended to the throne. His was a weak government. The French developed artillery, for by now, gunpowder had found its way into war's arsenal. A 22 inch caliber cannon fired huge stone balls at the many castles still controlled by the English in France. Under such bombardment, fortresses that previously could have been taken only by extended siege were now invested in days. In general, the French were just more enterprising than the English in applying the developing tools of war. Inspired by Joan, the French nobles began to close ranks behind the king. And the king finally succeeded in establishing a standing army.

The Hundred Years War had no sooner ended than England was engulfed by the War of the Roses (1455 - 1485), a dispute over the crown between the House of York (the badge of which, according to tradition, was the white rose) and the House of Lancaster (with which the red rose has been incorrectly associated (the red rose was the emblem of the Tudors)). There was no dispute over principles in this quarrel, and the general populace wasn't involved. It was strictly an internal fight between factions

Spain in 1469

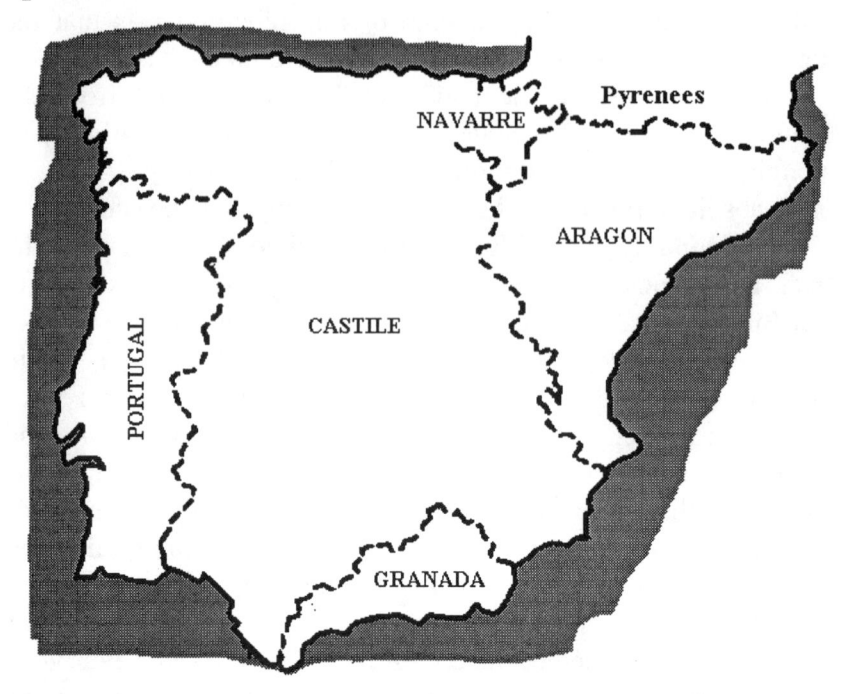

[Map of the Iberian Peninsula showing Portugal, Castile, Navarre, Aragon, and Granada, with the Pyrenees labeled.]

of the royal family and the lords who supported them. As a result, the significant outcome of the war was the elimination of the old nobility. Each battle took its toll, and each change of fortune in the quarrel resulted in increasingly bloody executions of the members of the losing faction. Confiscation of noble estates was another feature of this conflict, which enriched the crown. English serfdom had already disappeared. The War of the Roses wiped out the last vestiges of feudalism in England.

During this period, one other European nation emerged. This was Spain. Separated from the rest of Europe by the forbidding Pyrenees, it developed in its own way according to its own timetable. Since 1034, the Christian kingdoms in the north of Spain had been striving to drive the Moslems, whom they called Moors, out of the peninsula. By 1248, after a 200 year struggle, the Moors had been pushed into a southern pocket of the peninsula called Granada. The rest of Spain was divided into four Christian realms: Portugal, occupying essentially the space it does today; Navarre, a small kingdom stuffed up against the western edge of the Pyrenees; and Castile and Aragon, which divided the rest of the peninsula between them.

This state of affairs continued until 1469, when Ferdinand of Aragon married Isabella of Castile. When these monarchs came to power in their respective kingdoms a few years later (Isabella in 1474 and Ferdinand in 1479), the two kingdoms were combined into one. The royal couple then proceeded to convert the Iberian peninsula, excluding Portugal, into the most absolute monarchy in Europe. They started by reestablishing law and order through the creation of a force of mounted police, drawn from the common people and named the Hermandad, or Holy Brotherhood. With the encouragement of the people, they then relieved the feudal lords and crusading orders of Spain of their authority and brought them under the control of the throne. Next was the Spanish church. They received from Pope Sixtus IV the power to name the top church officials in Spain, which they used to staff the church with unimpeachable men committed to orthodoxy and unswervingly loyal to the crown. The Spanish Inquisition, which had been established in 1478, was employed to wipe out all forms of heresy. In 1483, Ferdinand and Isabella appointed Torquemada, whose name has become a synonym for cruelty, as head of the Spanish Inquisition.

In 1492, Ferdinand and Isabella conquered Granada. Banishment of the Moors and Jews from Spain added to the religious and racial uniformity of the kingdom. Both Aragon and Castile had a Cortes, similar to the French States General. Ferdinand and Isabella diluted the power of these councils by not calling them. They quickly became irrelevant. After Isabella died in 1504, there were uprisings in Castile. Ferdinand put them down. In 1512, Ferdinand took Navarre. Formation of the Spanish nation was complete.

The States of the Church. *Also known as The Donation of Pepin. There were several Pepin's. This Pepin, known as Pepin the Short (a misnomer), was the son of Charles Martel and the father of Charlemagne.*

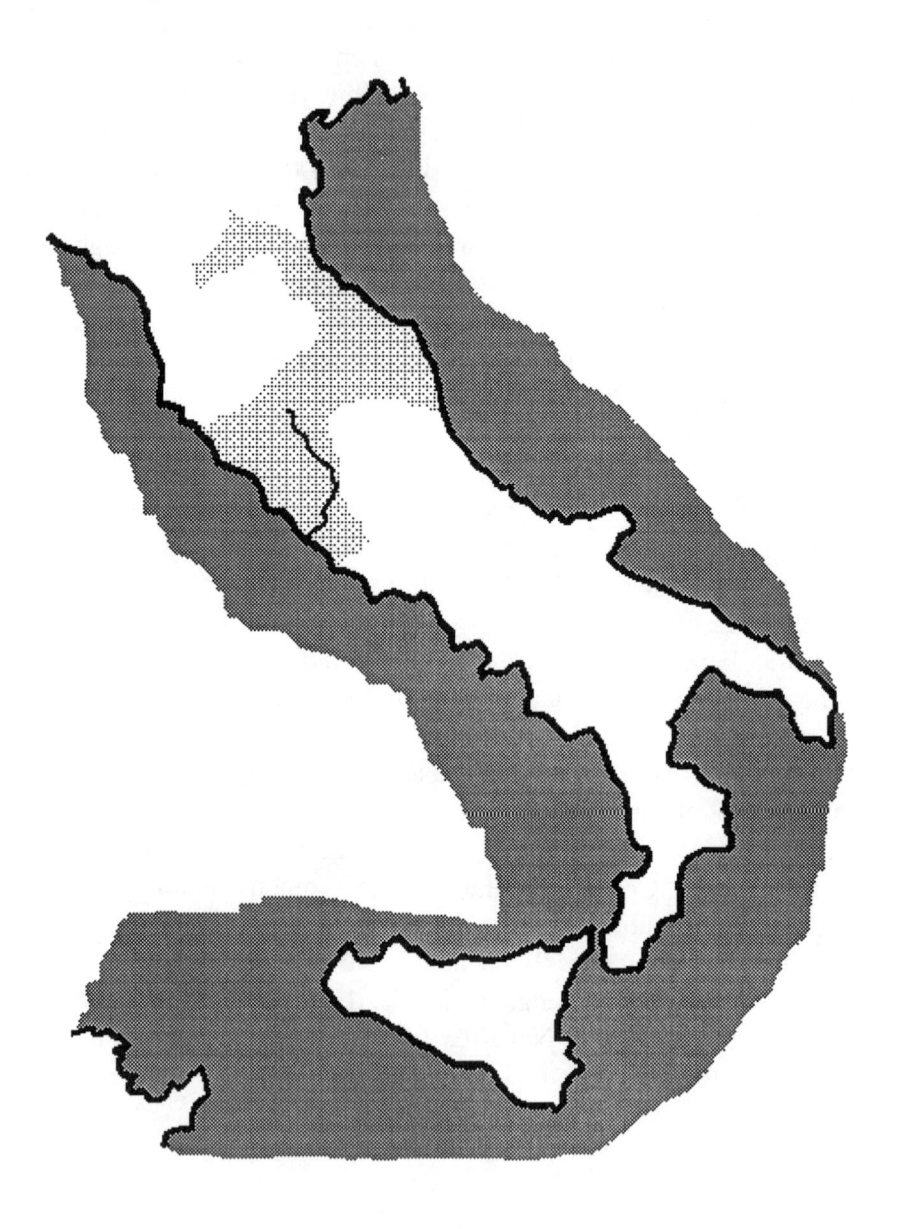

CHAPTER NINE

The Reformation

In 1522, the breakaway of Protestant sects from the Roman church began. Historians refer to this schism as the Reformation.

Why did the Reformation occur?

First, the Roman church was corrupt. The administrators of the church were worldly. They practiced:

1. Pluralism, the accumulation of multiple offices and livings by one official
2. Nonresidence, accepting offices in places where they didn't live, so that they could accumulate the benefices of the offices even though they were absentee and, therefore, nonperforming officials
3. Simony, the sale of church offices (the name comes from Simon Magus, who, as described in the Bible (Acts 8: 18, 19), offered money to the Apostles in return for being given the power to confer the Holy Ghost on other people)
4. Nepotism, for their families and even for their children, for they were anything but celibate (for example, the infamous Borgia's, Cesare and Lucrezia, were the children of Pope Alexander VI)

Church officials were wealthy and ostentatious.

From 1309 through 1377, the popes lived, not in Rome, but in Avignon, just outside the southern border of France. During this time, almost all of the popes and cardinals were French. The papacy was essentially an arm of the French government.

Then came the Great Schism (1378 -1417), when there was one pope in Rome and another in Avignon.

Also, the papacy owned large tracts of land in Italy. To protect them, it took part in Italian politics. It hired mercenaries and practiced local warfare just as any other feudal lord.

And here, we've just touched the highlights of the church's venality.

But the Roman church had been corrupt for centuries. Its corruption may have been sufficient to create and nurture a propensity for the Reformation. But by itself, it wasn't enough to

The Geography of Luther's Life

result in such a change. To see what new factors added the weight necessary to precipitate the Reformation, let's look at the man whose actions resulted in this transformation — Martin Luther.

Luther was of peasant stock. His grandfather was a farmer. But his father was a miner, first as a laborer and then, eventually, as a mine owner. As a consequence, Luther's father was well enough off to send Luther to the university at Erfurt. In 1505, Luther received the degree of master of arts and entered on the study of law.

Luther's childhood indoctrination led him to think of God as a strict, implacable judge. He was tormented by the fear that nothing he could do would be sufficient to merit salvation. He subscribed to the church doctrine that, to be saved, one had to be dedicated to performing good works, such as prayer, giving alms, fasting, making a pilgrimage, or to really be sure, adopting the ascetic life of a monk. After two months in the study of law, Luther withdrew and became a monk. But though he gave himself up to extreme asceticism, he had no confidence that he had earned salvation. His reading of Saint Augustine exposed him to the Pauline concept of predestination. "For the children being not yet born, neither having done any good or evil, that the purpose of God according to election might stand, not of works, but of him that calleth." (Romans, 9:11) For a person in doubt, the idea that nothing he can do can either save or damn him (and that many more are predestined to be damned than are elected to be saved) must have been terrifying.

In 1508, Luther was appointed to the post of instructor at Wittenberg. Around 1515, while preparing for a lecture, he read the sentence, "The just shall live by faith." (Romans, 1:17) He had read this sentence often. But now he saw it in a new light: that a person was saved by faith and by faith alone. It took Luther a while to puzzle out the details of his theology, but ultimately, he came to the conclusion that, if faith alone led to salvation, then good works were unnecessary. Moreover, each person was able to act as his own intermediary before God. Neither pope nor the hierarchy of the church was necessary to his salvation. The place to look for religious truth was in the Bible, not Rome. Every person was free to read and interpret the Scriptures according to his own light. The Bible said nothing about popes, monasteries, adoration of saints, ecclesiastic courts, sacraments other than baptism and communion, celibacy of priests, purgatory, and

Martin Luther. *From a painting by Cranach the Elder. The painting now resides in the Bristol Museums & Art Gallery.*

worship of Mary. In particular, it said nothing about church ownership of property. In fact, it was emphatic on the point that the apostles should be anything but concerned about their wherewithal. Therefore, all should go.

Moreover, Luther's thinking continued, if a person was a member of the elect (elected by God to be saved), then it would be possible for him to hold to a strong faith in God. Thus, the fact wasn't father to the conviction. Instead, the conviction was father to the fact. If one's faith was strong, then he was a member of the elect. And although faith alone saves, for those who were strong in the faith, good works follow. As Luther said, "The tree bears fruit, the fruit does not bear the tree." To Luther, the ideal Christian wasn't the ascetic monk or the crusading knight held up as exemplars by the Roman church. He was, instead, the good citizen — the devout commoner who was a loving husband and father, upright, diligent and frugal.

For years, despite the discrepancy between his beliefs and the practices of the church, Luther kept his peace. The event that caused him to speak out was the indulgence of 1517. Briefly, and with some simplification, the idea of an indulgence is as follows. The clergy can absolve a penitent from the guilt of his sins and, consequently, remove the punishment that otherwise awaited him after death. But the sinner still has to do penance, either on earth or else in purgatory, for his sins. Only then can he go to his reward. Penance consists of doing good works. But an alternative was to make a contribution to the church, in return for which the church would grant the sinner an indulgence, which was the remission of all or part of his penance.

From a dispassionate point of view, such a contribution might have a more positive social effect than, for example, saying prayers. But the fact that the contribution was of money soon led to the idea of buying an indulgence, of paying one's way out of the consequences of sin. Johann Tetzel, a monk and the agent (of the indulgence of 1517) whom Luther took on, is alleged to have said, "Drop a coin in the box and all your sins fly away." Tetzel was also accused of selling sealed letters stating that the sins a person was intending to commit would be forgiven. Luther was particularly distressed by the tendency of indulgences to make people think in the accounting terms of so much for an indulgence, so much penance taken care of. This type of mechanical thinking, thought Luther, distracted the people from the message of the gospel (the good news) that, by accepting Christ as one's lord, one could gain eternal life.

In 1517, Pope Leo X offered indulgence to all who would contribute to the payment of the cost of completing the massive new basilica of St. Peter's. Despite his misgivings, Luther remained quiet. He did develop his 95 theses on indulgences, but he kept them to himself. A thesis is a point its proposer is willing to defend in debate, not because he's necessarily convinced that it's true, but because he feels that discussion of the point will provide insight into the issues to which it's related.

The aspect of the indulgence of 1517 that triggered Luther into action was the prohibition of all other sermons while the indulgence was being preached. Luther wrote to the Archbishop of Mainz to protest this prohibition. Luther enclosed his 95 theses in his letter. He then passed out his theses to his friends. Ultimately, they fell into the hands of the printers. In fact, until one printer numbered them, there weren't 95 theses; there were just Luther's theses on indulgences. Despite the legend, it's unlikely that Luther posted his theses on the main door of the Castle Church of Wittenberg.

Luther didn't consider his theses heretical, and they probably weren't. But they did stand in opposition to both the intent of the church and the then current ecclesiastic practices. In fact, after publication of the theses, sales of indulgences fell off. As a consequence, Luther was repeatedly challenged by champions of the church. In each of these confrontations, conducted both in debates and in pamphlets, Luther revealed more of his convictions, which in turn, led to further challenges. Once he got started, Luther almost seemed to revel in astounding his critics. He ultimately got around to referring to the pope as the Antichrist.

Finally, in 1521, Luther was invited by Charles V, the Holy Roman emperor, to attend the Diet of Worms under safe conduct and testify concerning his teachings, which he had incorporated into a number of books.

The Diet was the Great Council of the princes of the principalities making up what would ultimately become Germany. At least theoretically, they were vassals of the Holy Roman emperor. The history of the Holy Roman empire is tortured.

Although not used until the 12th century, its name harks back to the times of the Carolingian empire, where as we saw, there was an ecclesiastic belief that the spiritual empire of the church should be accompanied by a secular Roman empire. When the Carolingian empire fell apart, the popes, nevertheless, continued in their belief that a Holy Roman empire existed; that there should be an emperor at the head of it; and that it was their prerogative to elect that emperor, which in fact, they did, by picking, sometimes under duress by an aspiring emperor, the most acceptable of the available rulers whenever the current emperor passed on.

But by Luther's time, the Holy Roman empire had metamorphosed into a feudal organization of principalities, primarily German, centered in what would ultimately become Austria. The emperor of the Holy Roman empire was still elected, but instead of being elected by the pope, he was now elected by a number of electors, all German ecclesiastics or princes. By Luther's time, there were seven such electors. Thus as Voltaire correctly observed, the Holy Roman empire was neither Roman nor an empire. He maintained that it wasn't holy either. But that may be more an opinion than an observation.

At the diet, Luther was asked if he would repudiate his books. He agreed to retract any of his doctrines that proved contrary to Scripture. This, of course, was unacceptable to the church, since the church considered its own authority and traditions, rather than the Bible, as the source of true faith. Luther then gave his historic response.

> ... my conscience is captive to the word of God. I cannot and I will not recant anything, for to go against my conscience is neither right nor safe.

Whether he then continued, "Here I stand, I can do no other." isn't known. The words aren't in the transcript of the diet and made their appearance in the first published version of his reply.

After this testimony, Charles told Luther that Luther might return to Wittenberg under Charles's safe conduct but without preaching. Charles then proclaimed that he would proceed against Luther as a notorious heretic. Frederick, the elector of Saxony, in which Wittenberg was located, had Luther taken secretly to the castle of the Wartburg in Eisenach for concealment. Frederick was one of the seven electors who elected the Holy Roman emperor. Luther stayed at the Wartburg for almost a year.

To this point, Luther's experience parallels that of two other reformers, John Wyclif (1320 - 1384) of England and John Huss (1369 - 1415) of Bohemia (in the western part of the modern Czech republic). The doctrines of the three were essentially the same. Yet they came to different ends. Wyclif, like Luther, had the protection of people in high places. When the church would no longer tolerate him, he was able to retire as a parish priest at Lutterworth. Huss wasn't as fortunate. He appeared before the general council at Constance (at which the Great Schism was ended and the papacy was restored to Rome), which declared him a heretic, and despite having a safe conduct, he was burned alive. In 100 years, what had changed that allowed Luther to succeed where Wyclif and Huss had failed?

For one, printing and the production of paper had moved from China to Europe. In 1456, Gutenberg had printed his Bible. So in contrast to Wyclif and Huss, who also committed their doctrines to writing, Luther was able to get his books and pamphlets published and distributed to the public at an affordable price. In fact, publishers clamored to get at Luther's works, for they knew that Luther's writings would sell. Luther would provide the manuscript and oversee the publication. After that, it was in the hands of the publisher. Luther never asked for, nor received, a cent for his writings.

Second, the burghers, as a segment of the population, had continued to grow. And the Reformation concept of the ideal Christian was more congenial to this rising class than that of the Roman church.

But the telling factor was the growth of national feeling. In France and Spain, what were essentially national churches already existed. These countries, with their considerable political power, had already been granted, by the Roman church, the right to both nominate all their higher ecclesiastic officers and retain a good portion of the funds, collected by the church within their borders, for the support of the national Roman churches. But in northern

Europe, where the relatively small nation of England and the various German principalities weren't able to face Rome with comparable bargaining power, most of the monies collected flowed directly to Rome. By embracing Protestant doctrine, these states were not only able to cut off this enervating outflow of funds but were also able to close down the monasteries within their borders and confiscate the property and considerable wealth thereof.

When Luther became the head of a state church, he modified his doctrine that every person was free to read and interpret the Scriptures according to his own reason. Luther's position had been that anyone who studied the Bible seriously would come to the same conclusions that Luther had. When it became evident to him that this wasn't the case, he saw to it that the doctrines of the Lutheran church became orthodox. Dissenting opinion was persecuted. For example, Luther and Ulrich Zwingli, another reformer, disagreed on the interpretation of the Eucharist. Zwingli maintained that it was just a symbol of the body and blood of Christ. Luther's position was consubstantiation: no priest could change bread and wine into the body and blood of Christ (transubstantiation), but to the fervent communicant, Christ came spiritually and physically by His own will and power. In consequence of this disagreement, Luther admonished Duke Albrecht of Prussia not to allow any Zwinglian in his territory on pain of everlasting damnation.

Of course, Luther was no worse than the head of any other state church. Between 1542 and 1564, John Calvin, yet another reformer, was head of what amounted to a reformed theocracy in Geneva. In the first four years of Calvin's theocracy, 58 people were put to death for heresy against Calvin's teachings, and this out of a total population of just 16,000.

In 1526, a diet met at Speyer, Charles V (the Holy Roman emperor) being absent, and issued the Recess (Decision) of Speyer, which sanctioned the religious autonomy of each German principality. In 1529, Charles ordered the Diet of Speyer reconvened and repealed the Recess of 1526. The Lutheran minority in the diet published a Protest against the decree, which is how reformers acquired the name Protestant.

Luther Translating the Bible. *From an illustration by Steele Savage for the book* Martin Luther *written by Harry Emerson Fosdick and published by Random House in 1956.*

In 1534, Luther published his German translation of the Bible, a work of over ten years. In addition to being a poet and composer (his most famous work is probably the hymn, *Ein Feste Burg Ist Unser Gott (A Mighty Fortress Is Our God)*), Luther, as a son of the people, spoke the common vernacular. Consequently, he produced a translation that had the same effect and prestige in the Germanic tongue as the King James version did a century later in England. It remains the greatest prose work in German literature.

In 1501, Arthur, the eldest son of Henry VII of England, married Catherine of Aragon, daughter of Ferdinand and Isabella of Spain. In 1502, Arthur died. Catherine brought with her a rich dowry and represented an important political liaison, neither of which England wanted to lose. The proposal was that Arthur's brother, Prince Henry, marry Catherine. Leviticus 20:21 declared such a marriage unclean and condemned it to childlessness. But the pope granted a dispensation, and in 1509, six weeks after Prince Henry's accession to the crown as Henry VIII, the marriage was publicly celebrated.

With the exception of one girl, all the offspring of this union died. Henry was haunted by the Biblical curse; he was concerned about the succession; and sometime between 1525 and 1527, he fell in love with Anne Boleyn, the sister of his favorite mistress and a lady in waiting to the queen. Henry wanted to solve his problems by getting a papal pronouncement that the dispensation allowing him to marry Catherine was in error; that consequently, the marriage was invalid; and that, therefore, he was free to marry Anne. Left to his own devices, the pope, Clement VII, would probably have accommodated Henry. But he was, at the time, the virtual prisoner of Charles V, the Holy Roman emperor (and also the nephew and strong upholder of Catherine), and wasn't in a position to do anything. Consequently, Henry turned to Parliament.

In 1533, Parliament passed the Act in Restraint of Appeals, which allowed the Archbishop of Canterbury to annul the marriage with Catherine. Later in the same year, Parliament produced the First Succession Act, which declared that succession to the throne was to be in the children of Henry's marriage to Anne. Finally, in November 1534, the Act of Supremacy was passed, which proclaimed Henry as the "supreme head" of the Church of England. As in the other states that adopted a non-Roman state church, England gobbled up its Roman monasteries.

It's in England that the relation between nationalism and the Reformation can be most clearly seen. Here was England, a sovereign nation, concerned about the succession to its throne and being prevented from taking action because the head of its church was in the power of a foreign state. Neither Henry nor England was unhappy with the structure and practices of the English church, so they weren't changed. The only modification was in its allegiance, which was switched from the pope to the English king.

By casting out all aspects of the Roman church in which its corruption had found fertile soil, the Protestant sects did reform the church. The period of the Protestant breakaway from the Roman church, in this sense, deserves the name Reformation. Indeed, with the exception of the Lutheran church, all Protestant sects of the time were referred to as reformed churches.

The misleading aspect of the name Reformation is that the emphasis on the Roman church's corruption and its reformation by the breakaway Protestant sects masks the fact that the Protestant revolution got its start as a nationalistic act of adopting a state church loyal to the state alone.

What was the effect of the Reformation?

Nietzsche felt that, once orthodoxy was questioned, the end result would be atheism. He couldn't have been more wrong, and a reason for this will be proposed shortly. Today, there may be more people willing to profess atheism than there were in the past. But again, this has no direct relation to the questioning of orthodoxy. Instead, it's a function of the increasing religious tolerance experienced over time.

In 1904, Max Weber put forth the proposition that the Protestant ethic was one of the prime motors behind capitalism. According to Weber, Protestants believed that material wealth in this life was a sign of election. Consequently, they worked hard to assure that they were among the elect. There have been attempts to test Weber's thesis. The results have been, at best, dubious. Catholics seem to be able to accumulate capital as readily as Protestants.

In any case, as time passed, the Protestant sects abandoned the principle of predestination. In contrast, the principle of salvation by faith alone was given increasing emphasis, particularly in the more evangelical sects, which show all the signs of growing patronage. The explanation appears to be that, if one can be strong in the faith (born again, as the current usage has it), then salvation is assured. Consequently, despite one's station in this life and the vicissitudes that one is heir to, eternal glory awaits all true believers after death. For those who feel that they've been unfairly treated by life, which includes many of us, this doctrine has strong appeal. It certainly outweighs any cold Nietzschean logic arguing for atheism.

But the most important outcome of the Reformation flowed from the inseparable sectarian aspect of Protestantism. If every person was able to interpret the Bible as he saw fit, the door to new interpretation could never be closed. The resulting multiplication of sects produced irresistible pressure for religious toleration. The end result was the separation of church and state. Religious choice was the first action recognized as off-limits to state interference. It was the opening wedge of the concept of limited government — the idea that there are aspects of a person's life in which the government has no right to interfere.

And now a footnote on the continuing development of constitutional government in England. Within England, Henry VIII was one of the most powerful of men. He was viewed with wonder and awe, was the physical manifestation of national ambitions, and enjoyed the confidence of his people. Even so, he recognized that he was most effective as King in Parliament — that is, when the King, Lords and Commons worked together to enact law. The management of Commons by Henry, aided by his secretary, Thomas Cromwell, was crude and outrageous. But it demonstrated that Commons was worth taking the trouble to manage. Under this tutelage, Commons made great strides. During Henry's reign, Commons passed as many statutes as all prior Commons combined.

In the council of Henry VII, there had been a group closer than others to the king. While Thomas Wolsey, Cromwell's predecessor, was Henry VIII's minister, this inner group was dispensed with, because Wolsey didn't care for rivals. However, under Cromwell, it reappeared and was called the Privy Council. Members of the Privy Council who weren't peers frequently sought election to Commons. When elected, these privy councilors became spokesmen for the king in Commons. The Privy Council was a proto-cabinet.

Europe, Asia and Africa

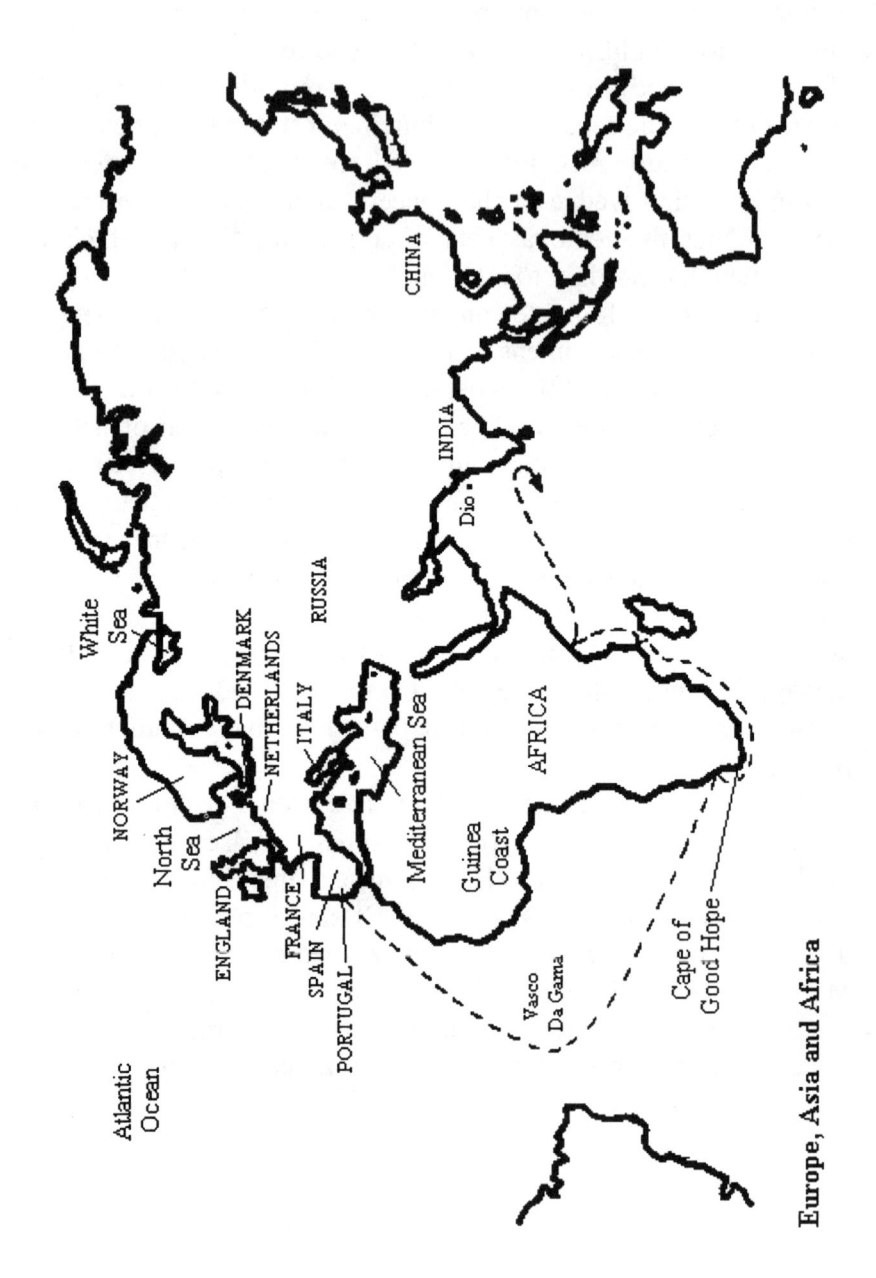

CHAPTER TEN

The New World

For centuries, the pepper, nutmeg, cinnamon, and other spices (in demand because alternative methods of preserving food were rare), together with the dyes, fragrant woods, jewels, silks, tapestries, and rugs (luxury goods that carried a high price in relation to their size and weight), of Asia were sought by Europe. Until the 16th century, the only land and water routes to Asia were through the Middle East, which was under Moslem control. Consequently, the typical route taken by Asian products to northwestern Europe was over the Alps from the trading cities of Venice, Genoa and Pisa, which in turn, dealt with Moslem middlemen. When the memoirs of Marco Polo, who served for 20 years in the court of Kublai Khan in China (or Cathay, as the Europeans called it), were published in 1298, the appetites of the Europeans were further whetted. Even if only some of what "Marco of the millions" said was true, here lay a land of unbelievable wealth peopled by a race dedicated to peace. The very thought of it was almost more than the poor and warlike Europeans could stand. Since the Italian city-states were doing well enough in their role as middlemen, it was the nations on the Atlantic seaboard that took the lead in the quest for a new route to Cathay.

The compass had reached Europe in the 13th century, and sailing beyond the sight of land became standard practice in the Mediterranean, where navigators used charts, called portolans, to set their courses. These portolans showed coasts, harbors, landmarks, and compass bearings, but the techniques used in their construction weren't adequate for mapping the broader reaches of the Atlantic. They employed neither longitude nor latitude. Moreover, ships that served in the Mediterranean were inadequate to the challenge to survival presented by the stormy Atlantic seas.

It was Prince Henry of Portugal, the Navigator, who for over 40 years before he died in 1460, dedicated himself to solving these problems. He brought to Portugal some of the most outstanding

An Early Atlantic Ship. *From photographs owned by Rebecca E. Marvil and reproduced in the book* Columbus and the Age of Discovery *written by Zvi Dor-Ner and published by William Morrow in 1991. The photographs are of a "reconstruction" of Columbus's flagship, the Santa Maria. "Reconstruction" is in quotes because nobody knows just how the Santa Maria looked. We know it was a* nao *(a small, round bellied vessel), and we know what sails it carried. Beyond that, everything is speculation, based on the characteristics of other ships of the period.*

mathematicians and astronomers of Europe, who developed the astronomical instruments and trigonometric tables that allowed the determination of the latitudes necessary to map the African coast. The Portuguese also designed seaworthy ships. They narrowed the width of the hull and added multiple masts and multiple, small sails on each mast. While increasing maneuverability, these enhancements also permitted the construction of larger and sturdier ships. Not only could these ships withstand the Atlantic storms, they also proved to be excellent platforms for cannon.

Prince Henry's investments paid off. At first, exploration of the African coast was done in the traditional way. The Portuguese sea captains inched their way down the coast and, before Henry's death, had set up regular trade with the Guinea coast. The profitability of this trade dampened further exploration, but in 1486, Bartolomeo Diaz finally rounded the southern tip of Africa. Just 11 years later, Vasco da Gama set out for India. The route he selected was to sail southwest into the Atlantic until he reached the right latitude, at which point he changed course and sailed southeast toward the Cape of Good Hope. In this way, he avoided coastal currents and took advantage of the prevailing winds. He was out of sight of land for 96 days, covered around 4500 miles between landfalls (compared to 36 days and 2600 miles for Columbus's first voyage), and must have nearly reached Brazil. He missed the cape by around 130 miles, a tour de force of navigation in light of the tools then available.

In 1509, the Portuguese engaged the Moslems outside of the Indian port of Diu. In this contest for control of the Indian ocean, the Portuguese were able to sit outside of the reach of the Moslem fleet and use it as a gunnery target. The Moslems were still practicing the heretofore standard naval strategies: ramming and closing with, grappling, and boarding the enemy. The idea of an artillery duel at sea was foreign to them. All this was true because the Portuguese had the ships that could accommodate the cannon necessary for artillery warfare and the Moslems didn't.

Of course, Columbus, sailing under a Spanish charter, touched the New World in 1492. The New World was named America after Amerigo Vespucci, who sailed somewhat after Columbus but was a better promoter. Mystery clouds the whole affair; the only

The Latin New World

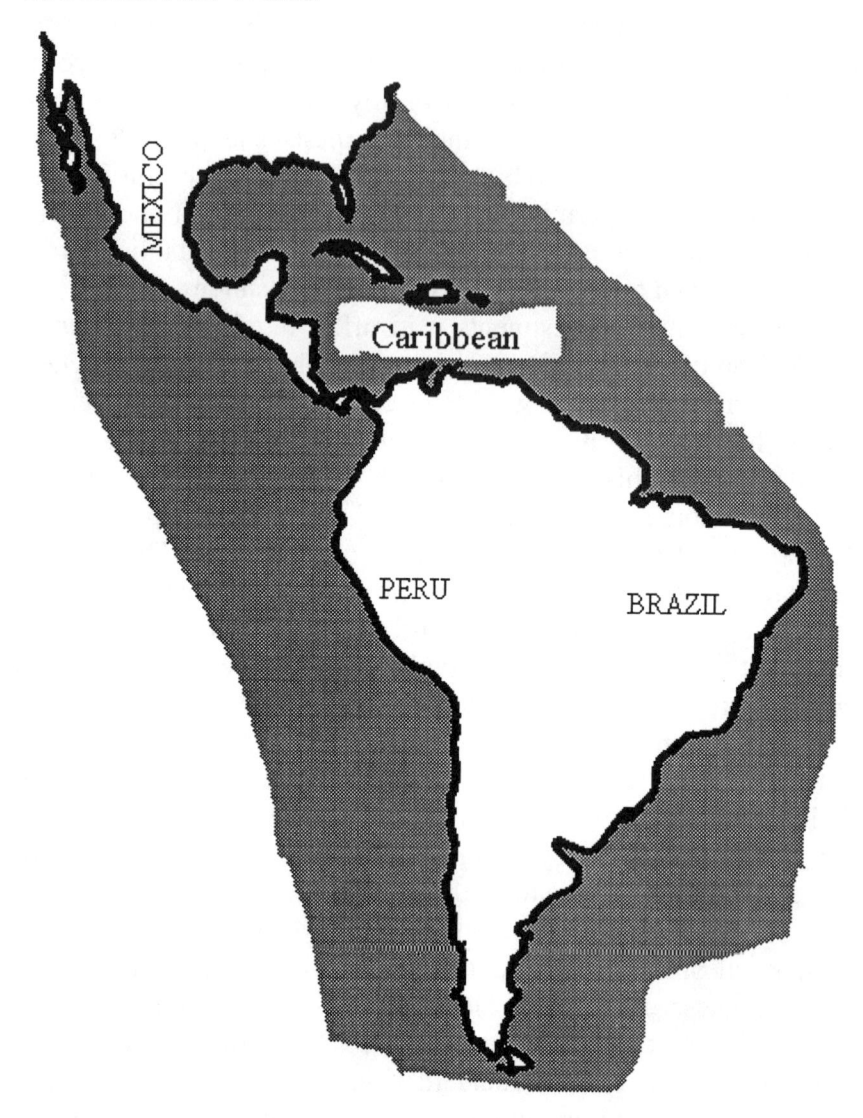

documentation of Vespucci's voyages are his own accounts. Vespucci also either coined or made popular the term, New World.

Columbus's discovery turned out not to be Cathay. But the Spanish began a program of settlement anyhow. Then in 1519, Cortez discovered in Mexico more gold and silver than had ever before been known to Europeans. Not many years later, Pizarro took from the Incas in Peru amounts of gold and silver that dwarfed the riches of Mexico. For a while, these instant riches pumped life into Spanish industry and commerce. But in the long run, there was just too much gold. Spanish prices outdistanced those in other countries, so that Spain purchased more than it sold. As a consequence, Spain's suppliers, rather than Spain, reaped the long-term positive effects of the new wealth. Moreover, the windfall encouraged the bellicose nature of the Spaniards to the detriment of what little taste for work they had. And finally, the wars conducted by Charles V, to whose Holy Roman empire Spain belonged, and Philip II, Charles' son and king of Spain, also contributed to the flow of gold from Spain. It took about two generations to run through the treasure. When it was gone, it was hard to tell that it had ever been there. Spain went into a decline from which it has yet to recover.

Henry VIII of England recognized that, if he could defend his coasts, he didn't need a standing army. This contrasted with France, which had to maintain a large standing army to protect its borders. Consequently, Henry routed the funds he could spare, from England's meager resources, to constructing a navy. However, after Henry's death, the fleet fell into such disrepair that, when Queen Elizabeth I came to the throne, she found herself with only the shadow of a navy.

Elizabeth's navy was rebuilt by John Hawkins, originally a merchant trading with the Spanish colonists until, in 1567, the Spanish cut off this commerce. Basically, Hawkins was a slaver. He was the first to put a slave ship in Spanish Caribbean waters. Hawkins became a member of the navy board in 1578 and applied his advanced ideas to the English fleet. He lengthened ships even further, so more guns could be brought to bear; constructed a gun deck, used only for guns, over the cargo deck; and shrunk the castles, which made the ships faster, more stable, and capable of sailing closer to the wind. By 1587, when Hawkins retired, the queen had 18 large galleons and seven smaller ones.

When Spain cut off English access to the Spanish colonies, the English merchants became armed smugglers and pirates. English ships looted the Spanish Main (the Caribbean coast of South America), seized treasure ships, and attacked Spanish commerce.

From the North Sea to the Caribbean, English privateers harassed Spanish shipping. Even the coast of Spain wasn't immune. As a result, Philip decided that England had to be put down, and in 1588, the Spanish Armada set sail. Its purpose was ill conceived and, in all probability, impossible of execution. The object was to sail from Spain to the Netherlands, where an army would be embarked for an invasion of England. The Spanish never even got the army on board.

The English navy was smaller than the Armada. But it was more maneuverable and had more telling firepower, on which the English sea captains capitalized. The Armada, severely mauled, was driven into the North Sea, from where it managed to limp back to Spain by circumnavigating the British isles. The defeat marked the beginning of Spain's decline.

Under Queen Elizabeth, the growth of constitutional government continued. The queen generally made her decisions on the basis of the counsel of a few favored advisers. She chose not to sit with her Privy Council. However, the Privy Council, made up of some 12 to 20 officials, was essential to Elizabeth's rule. Its members carried out the administration of the kingdom. In effect, they were the crown in action.

Commons remained rather disorganized. By now, it was an elected body. But it wasn't always in session and its membership kept changing. Under these circumstances, continuity and leadership were provided by the privy councilors who were members of the Commons. They sat near the speaker and provided an approximation of ministerial leadership.

The opening of the New World accentuated an economic trend already present. Long distance commerce between the Italian city-states and the Middle East generally involved sizable amounts of goods, which called for the investment of substantial funds and offered the possibility of significant profit. The possession of wealth as a means of making money thus became apparent. As time passed, other large-scale demands for goods arose. Nations needed to equip and supply their armed forces. Burgeoning cities constituted concentrated markets for massive amounts of consumer and commercial goods. And the opening of new passages to

Africa, India, China, and the New World created the most remunerative trade ever.

Double-entry bookkeeping was invented in Italy in the 15th century and, by the beginning of the 16th century, was in use all over Europe. Double-entry bookkeeping was codified by Luca Pacioli, a monk, who incorporated, into one of his books, the practices being followed by traders in Venice.

Double-entry bookkeeping made clear the underlying function of money in all enterprise and also allowed bankers to create clearing systems, so trade could take place without the inefficient transfer of coin. It could no longer be denied that money made money, which justified paying interest on debt and broke the strangling hold that the church proscription of usury had maintained on dealing in money. The age of capitalism had begun.

Capitalism had an advantage over the guild system, with which it grew to compete. It was flexible. It could flow from product to product and location to location as change dictated. Capital was accumulated in various ways. There were family houses, partnerships, and joint-stock companies. Joint-stock companies were generally established only when it was desired to take on particularly risky ventures, such as opening trade to new lands; the charter for the company was issued by the government; and a grant of monopoly was typically involved. The joint-stock company was father to our present-day corporation and involved similarities, such as purchase of stock by passive investors and management of the enterprise by company officers. But they also retained features of partnerships. For example, each stockholder remained liable for all company obligations. The first English joint-stock company was the Muscovy Company, set up in 1553 to take advantage of the just discovered route to Russia through the White sea.

Capitalism replaced the guilds in two basic ways. The first took place when a series of guilds worked one after another on a product, which was then distributed by a merchant guild. A good example was cloth-making. Wool moved from weavers to dyers to fullers to shearmen, and only then was it ready to be sold as cloth. From the craftsmen's point of view, the only ready market for their output was the merchants. As a consequence, the merchants were in an excellent position to control prices through collusion. By the end of the 13th century, this process was well under way. The next step in the transformation was for the merchants to purchase the wool and contract with the craft guilds to make up the cloth. The transformation became complete when the merchants began to hire their own, non-guild employees to do the work. By the 16th century, this method of production had taken over the English cloth industry.

The other way guilds were replaced was when the masters of a guild decided that they wouldn't allow anyone else to become a master. These masters then threw off the old restraints on how many apprentices and journeymen a master could use. In effect, the masters became capitalist employers and all other members of the guild ended their careers as journeymen.

In either case, the character of employment changed. Under the guild system, the distinction between journeyman and master was small, since each journeyman eventually became a master, and each master did no more than make a living. But under capitalism, the employer (master) was a person who had invested his capital in his business with the intent of making his capital grow. The employee (journeyman) worked for a wage. If he wanted to become an employer, he had to accumulate capital and enter an industry in the face of existing competition with no aid or support from a paternalistic guild. It became a more individualistic, uncaring economic world, but also one that held out high incentive for those who discovered new markets, new products, and more efficient production techniques. The stagnation of the guild system had been traded in for the productive potential of capitalism.

England was particularly adept at encouraging new enterprise. With its parliamentary form of government, there was a direct information channel flowing from entrepreneurs to politicians, who were always willing to foster new business, increasing, as it did, tax revenue.

During the emergence of Europe from the chrysalis of the Middle Ages, interest in mathematics and the physical sciences reappeared and grew. Copernicus revived the idea of the sun as the center of the solar system. Kepler reinforced this idea by discovering that the orbits of the planets were elliptical rather than circular. Galileo introduced the use of the telescope in studying astronomical phenomena, set an example for preciseness in the measurement of physical data, developed empirical evidence in support of the theory of a heliocentric solar system, and encouraged the idea of trying to fit mathematical formulae to observational data. Descartes invented analytical geometry, which was to lead to the development of calculus.

It was, indeed, a new world, new in many ways.

Oliver Cromwell *with two members of the New Model Army, a cavalryman and a musketeer. From an illustration by Victor Ambrus for the book* The Story of Britain *written by R. J. Unstead and published by Thomas Nelson & Sons Ltd. in 1970.*

CHAPTER ELEVEN

The English Revolutions

Good Queen Bess was the last of the Tudor line. To find a successor, it was necessary to go back to the progenitor of the House of Tutor, Henry VII. His daughter, Margaret, had wed James IV, king of Scotland. James IV was succeeded by his son, James V. The daughter of James V was Mary Queen of Scots. Mary was Catholic and had been Queen of France. When her husband died, she returned to Scotland at the age of 19. She married Henry Stuart and had a son. The Protestant Scots revolted, and Mary was forced to abdicate in favor of her infant son, who became James VI. She fled to England, where she became Elizabeth's prisoner until she was ultimately executed for plotting against Elizabeth. It was her son, James VI of Scotland, who succeeded to the English throne as James I, the first in the Stuart line of English kings.

James' experience in Scotland was poor preparation for his English reign. The Scottish lords were feudal chieftains who didn't view the king as sovereign. To prevent them from pursuing their wild, independent ways, James reigned as a tyrant. He was also put upon by the ministers of the Scottish church, or Kirk, who felt that they, as God's clergy, had the right and duty to guide the king on all moral matters and were continuously trying to get involved in James' conduct of state affairs. The Kirk was Presbyterian and, as a Calvinist sect, didn't believe in a church hierarchy. But James controlled it in the same despotic way he handled his nobility — he set up bishops, loyal to him, over the pretentious ministers. To justify his tyranny, James cited the divine right of kings. But this was no political expedient. He was sincerely and deeply committed to the principle. He was unfamiliar with anything like Parliament and couldn't understand its function.

One aspect of English culture that James found congenial was the English church. Its ceremonies, the control the bishops exercised over the church, and its acknowledgment that the king was its unquestioned head all appealed to him.

The people who were unhappy with the English church had come to be known as Puritans. The Puritans weren't a sect. The label covered a range of opinion on religious theory and practice. However, the Puritans held in common the idea that the English church retained too many characteristics of the Roman church. They wanted to "purify" it.

On his journey from Scotland to England in 1603, James was presented with a Puritan petition asking for certain changes in church practice. James declined comment but agreed to a future discussion of the matter with the combined attendance of Puritans and Anglicans. As a consequence, in January 1604, James, backed by Anglican bishops, entertained a deputation of four Puritans, headed by Dr. Reynolds of Oxford. In one of his presentations, Reynolds had the misfortune to use the word presbytery. James interpreted this to mean that the Puritans were Presbyterians and that, consequently, one of their goals was abolition of the bishoprics. He dismissed the delegation with a diatribe that included his famous summary, "No bishop, no king."

Elizabeth had looked the other way when Puritan ministers didn't conform to all the regulations of the English church. "I seek not to carve windows into men's souls," she said. But now, all who wouldn't comply were removed from their posts. In 1607, a small congregation in the town of Scrooby in Nottinghamshire moved with their expelled ministers and William Brewster, the bailiff of the archbishop of York, to Leyden in the Netherlands. In 1620, they made their way in the Mayflower to Plymouth, Massachusetts.

During James' reign, the lawyer, Sir Edward Coke, tried to establish, in the Bonham case, the concept of judicial supremacy. His position was that "when an act of Parliament is against common right and reason or repugnant or impossible to be performed, the common law will control it and adjudge such act to be void." This principle, critical to the concept of limited government, was never accepted in England. Coke also tied his daughter to a bedpost and beat her unmercifully until she agreed to marry a man who would advance Coke's fortunes, a not uncommon practice of the time.

James was responsible for organizing the group of scholars who produced the King James translation of the Bible, one of the monuments of English literature. Interestingly enough, James had gotten the idea from Reynolds, who, at his conference with the king in 1604, had asked, apparently on an impulse, if a new translation of the Bible could be made.

However, in general, James' English reign was a disaster. As could be expected of a king dedicated to the principle of divine right, he quarreled with Parliament and treated it with disrespect. To compound the problem, at this point in time, Parliaments were intent on increasing their control of policy. A clash was inevitable. Parliament presented James with many petitions for the reform of grievances, many related to the royal prerogative, the power of the king to act on his own authority. Under a ruler with whom it didn't identify, Parliament questioned features of royal government that it had accepted without demur under the beloved Elizabeth. Consequently, it never got around to voting supply for James, until in exasperation, he would dissolve it. Without funds and without a Parliament to vote them in, he would then turn to various expedients to raise money, each of which alienated some segment of the populace. Strapped for financing, James was impotent in the realm of foreign policy. He was unable to make good on either his threats or his promises. When he died in 1625, he left his son, Charles I, a dissatisfied populace, an empty treasury, and a threatening international situation.

Charles was no improvement on his father. In addition to the dissatisfaction that he had inherited from his father, he generated antagonisms of his own. He, also, was an advocate of the divine right of kings. He believed in the unity of church and state. In his mind, the Church of England was inseparable from his divine right to rule. Charles favored the High Anglican school of churchmen and made one of them, William Laud, the archbishop of Canterbury. In Laud's view, the focus of worship was the altar and the sacrament, not the preacher and the pulpit. Consequently, he imposed a rigid control on the church and persecuted the Puritans.

His goal was to suppress all but High Anglican services, hold the clergy to strict conformity, and stifle criticism of the church.

Because of the divine right of kings, Charles felt that to resist his will was to sin. As a consequence, if the people were so evil that they would compel him to make commitments in which he wasn't in sympathy, he was under no compulsion to honor these commitments. He was, therefore, considered duplicitous and untrustworthy.

Charles continued his father's battle with Parliament and, when he couldn't get supply from it, resorted to questionable means for raising funds, just as his father had done, which further alienated the people. Out of these skirmishes, several acts defining civil rights emerged. One was the Petition of Right, which was brought into being in direct response to several inflammatory actions of Charles'. It was made up of four points.

1. No man should be forced to pay the government any gift, loan, or tax without its prior endorsement by Parliament. Charles had tried to raise money by compelling the people to loan the government money.
2. No man should be held without reason. People who refused to submit to Charles' forced loan had been confined without being told why. No reason could be given, of course, since a person couldn't be confined for refusing to loan money.
3. Soldiers and sailors shouldn't be billeted in private homes without the consent of the homeowners. To save money, Charles had done exactly that.
4. Martial law shouldn't be declared. To enforce his billeting of soldiers in private homes, Charles had taken just such action. In later generations, this point had to be modified, since there are situations in which a government does have to be able to declare martial law.

Commons didn't incorporate these principles in legislation, since passage of such laws would imply that the principles weren't previously in force. Instead, they were expressed in the form of a petition to the king to stop breaking the law.

Charles ultimately and reluctantly agreed to abide by the Petition. Commons then voted him supply. However, he and

Commons continued to disagree, and he ultimately dismissed it. For the next 11 years, he avoided calling Parliament.

During this period, Charles decided that the liturgy of the Scottish church, which was Presbyterian, should be based on the English Book of Common Prayer. He was, of course, the king of Scotland as well as the king of England. The result was a Scottish revolt. To meet this challenge, Charles was forced to call Parliament to finance military preparations. Instead of voting supply, Commons began work on a compilation of grievances. In response, Charles dissolved Parliament.

The Scots crossed the border and occupied two northern counties. They then called a halt, since they felt that they had obtained enough of a bargaining chip to force England to stop interfering in their religious practices. For the English, occupation of its countryside was intolerable, and irresistible pressure built up for Charles to fortify England by once more calling Parliament, which he ultimately did.

One of the first thing that this Parliament did was to pass the Triennial Act, which specified that no more than three years should separate the end of one Parliament and the beginning of the next. Parliament also abolished the prerogative courts (most notably, the Star Chamber), leaving the courts of common law uncontested. In addition, Parliament passed a bill declaring that it couldn't be dissolved without its own consent. To all these laws, Charles reluctantly agreed.

Nevertheless, contention between Charles and Commons continued. Angry mobs gathered outside the king's palace. Commons did little to disperse them. Goaded on by his queen, who was forever urging him to behave in a firm and resolute manner (she was a French princess), Charles had impeachment papers drawn up against five of the chief Puritans in Commons. When Commons wouldn't give up the five, Charles, together with several hundred troopers, entered the House of Commons to take the five. The five, however, having been warned, had left. The king observed, "I see that the birds are flown," gave some polite reassurances, and left.

The invasion of the House of Commons was Charles' ultimate act of indiscretion. It so outraged the London mobs that, within the

A Cavalier. *From an illustration by J. C. B. Knight for the book* Looking at History *written by R. J. Unstead and published by Macmillan in 1957. A cavalier was a horse soldier of noble birth. This illustration creates an image that tends to reinforce the myth that the English Civil Wars were fought between the Cavaliers and the "Roundheads", a name applied to Puritans, who were supposed to have cropped their hair short. In fact, only a small part of the forces of Charles I was made up of Cavaliers, and many Cavaliers didn't support the king. Moreover, Cromwell and many of his men wore their hair long.*

week, Charles was forced to abandon London and send his queen to France. With him went the majority of the lords and the royalist minority in Commons.

There were now two seats of government in England, one with the king, the other with the Puritans in what remained of Commons. Commons began to recruit its own army. On August 22, 1642, Charles raised his standard at Nottingham and summoned his people to his aid. What was known as the First English Civil War had begun.

The war lasted four years. In return for Scottish help, Commons agreed that, at the war's end, Presbyterianism would be established as the state religion of England. But the telling element in the conflict was the New Model Army, established midway in the war, recruited from the more devout Puritans, and organized by Oliver Cromwell. Well armed, superbly trained, and kept under a strict military and moral discipline, the New Model was the most effective part of the Parliamentary army. Despite the fact that Cromwell was tireless in drilling his army to a razor's edge of perfection and exhibited a fine sense of strategy and tactics, he invariably and sincerely attributed his army's successes unilaterally to God. His apocryphal advice to his troopers exemplifies Cromwell's approach to battle. "Put your trust in God, my boys," it went, quickly followed by the practical admonition, " ... and keep your powder dry." This most common version of the quotation is from *Oliver Cromwell's Advice*, a poem by Valentine Blacker, written in 1834. According to Edward Hayes, in whose collection of ballads (of Ireland, no less; the poem is appropriately identified as an Orange ballad) the poem appears, the source of the line is the following "well-authenticated" anecdote. Cromwell addressed his troops before they were to cross a river to attack the enemy, and he concluded with the words, " ... put your trust in God; but mind to keep your powder dry."

At the war's end, Commons was victorious, and Charles was its prisoner. The army was at odds with Commons over the idea of a state religion, Presbyterian or otherwise. Subscribing to a variety of sects, the soldiers were bound together by the idea that each person should have the freedom to believe and worship as he wished. As a result, they were known as Independents.

The Independents also believed that state sovereignty lay in the people. Just as a congregation chose its pastor, so the people should choose their governors. Commons should be kept responsive to the people by frequent election.

The Presbyterians were in the majority in Commons, and in the spring of 1647, it decided to disband the army without back pay. The army mutinied. In June, it took Charles. Charles' seizure gives insight into his character. Cornet Joyce (Cornet was a title, not a name), with almost 400 troopers, was commanded by Cromwell to seize Charles, who was staying at Holmby House, where he had been lodged by Commons while it tried to decide what to do with him. When Joyce appeared, Charles asked him where his commission (written orders) was. Joyce hesitated a minute and then pointed to his troopers. "Indeed," replied the king, "It is one I can read without spelling; as handsome and proper a company of gentlemen as I have seen this many a day ... Where next, Mr. Joyce?"

In August, the army entered London. In March 1648, the Second Civil War began with scattered uprisings of Royalists followed by an invasion from Scotland. The uprisings were soon quelled, and Cromwell defeated the Scots. It then became apparent that the reason for the Royalist and Scottish action was because Charles had come to a secret agreement with the Scots to restore him to the throne in return for abolishing Episcopacy and establishing Presbyterianism in England.

The army removed the Presbyterian members from Commons. Charles was tried and convicted, by a court set up by the remaining Rump Parliament, of treason against the nation, primarily for colluding with the Scots. Up to this point, treason had been a crime that could only be committed against the king.

Charles was executed. The Rump Parliament abolished the House of Lords and decreed that England would now "be governed as a Commonwealth ... by ... the representatives of the people in Parliament."

In fact, the Commonwealth was the continued rule of the Rump Parliament, since only Parliament, as the sole remaining vestige of government, could dissolve itself, and this it refused to do. The Rump Parliament represented only those Independents who had favored Charles' execution, a constituency that made up a small minority of the population. It was, therefore, unpopular. In addition, international threats to England remained. To protect its interests, the Rump Parliament maintained a standing army of 44,000. It was at this time that the redcoat of the English soldier was introduced.

The army was, however, a mixed blessing, in that it favored frequent election and, thus, was also critical of the Rump Parliament. It was, therefore, necessary for the Rump Parliament to keep this army occupied. Ireland presented an opportunity. In 1641, the Irish had revolted against the English gentry (landowners) and Protestants in Ireland. The insurrection had been put down. But tales of atrocities committed by the Irish, probably both having a basis in truth and, at the same time, being exaggerated, returned to English ears. As a result, the Independents viewed the Catholic Irish as wild beasts to be killed on sight, much as, in later times, whites were to characterize the native Indians of the US.

By 1649, the Catholic lands in Ireland had come to represent a potential base for the invasion of England by its continental enemies. Consequently, Parliament sent Cromwell, with 12,000 men, to pacify Ireland. The Irish had no army and depended on walled towns for its defense. Cromwell's first target was Drogheda, which put up resistance. Cromwell captured the town, and urged on by hate for both the Irish and Catholics, he took advantage of the age old principle of siege warfare to massacre the inhabitants. Wexford suffered the same fate. By 1652, a third of the Irish population had died, and Ireland had been subdued.

As frightful as they were, Cromwell's atrocities in Ireland were no worse than those committed before or since and would probably have been written off as no more than normal acts of war. But at the war's end, the Irish were treated by the English the same way the Indians were treated by the US. The land of all Catholics who had participated in the rebellion was seized and awarded either to the Englishmen who put up the money for the campaign or to Cromwell's soldiers as compensation for arrears in pay. The great Irish landowners were now Protestant. The Irish were reduced to laborers on the lands of the new owners. Catholicism was virtually proscribed. The result was the apparently undying enmity that the

Irish Catholic holds for the English, which has come to be known as the curse of Cromwell.

Despite the continuing demands of the army, the Rump Parliament refused to dissolve itself and call for elections. Finally, on April 20, 1653, Cromwell, together with 30 troopers, went to the House, where he took his seat. He was a member of Commons. In fact, he was an unusual member. According to the Self-denying Ordinance, passed in 1644, no member of Parliament could hold any command, civil or military. However, Cromwell was so important to the Parliamentary cause that he was made an exception.

Cromwell listened to the debate for a while. Then, standing up, he started to berate the Parliament. The more he talked, the more upset he got. Finally, he said, "Come, come. I will put an end to your prating. You are no Parliament." His troopers then escorted the Parliament out of the House and locked the doors. With this act, the last shred of legal government disappeared. What was left was Cromwell at the head of the army.

From then until Cromwell's death in 1658, attempts were made at various forms of government. In 1654, a written constitution was tried. Despite intensive effort to control their composition, Cromwell was no better able to work with his Parliaments than had been Charles before him, and they were soon dissolved. In 1655, Cromwell partitioned the nation into 12 districts and put a major general in charge of each of them. This worked in terms of security, but it brought military rule to the citizen's doorstep and increased his dislike for it. In 1657, Cromwell became a hereditary "Protector" — that is, a king in all but name. Basically, Cromwell ruled as a military dictator.

After Cromwell's death, his son, Richard, assumed the position of power but was unequal to the task. The army deserted him. At this point, General George Monk, the army commander in Scotland, took control. He recalled the Rump Parliament and restored to it the Presbyterian members expelled in 1648. This reconstituted Parliament dissolved itself. A new Parliament was then elected, the House of Lords was restored, and the new Parliament invited Charles II, the son of Charles I, to come back to England as king. The government of king and Parliament had been restored (1660). But it was a monarchy tempered by the legislation passed by Parliament under Charles I. The royal prerogative, and the principle of the divine right of kings that supported it, were gone.

So now, Cromwell must be evaluated. He had his faults. But his contribution was clear. The breakdown of the government under James and Charles I was almost inevitable. In the potential chaos of the interregnum, Cromwell held England together so that, when the return to normalcy was possible, England was there to take advantage of it.

Under Charles II, the Commons was divided, as it had been at the beginning of the century, into a Court party, which usually supported the king, and a Country party, which typically opposed him. Thomas Osborne, the Earl of Derby, who was Charles' principal minister from 1674 through 1678, went out of his way to encourage the support of the Court party. In response to such partisanship, the Earl of Shaftesbury formally organized the opposition Country party. One of Shaftesbury's supporters was John Locke.

This formalization of political alignments was the beginning of political parties. Later under Charles, the names Tory and Whig began to be used. Both names, when first introduced to refer to political positions, were pejoratives. Neither was new. Tory was the name that had been used to identify an Irish Catholic bandit, Whig the name that had been used to refer to a Scottish Covenanting zealot. The Tories supported the English church and the king's rights. The Whigs were for restricting the prerogatives of the crown and for religious toleration except for Catholics.

Charles II died in February 1685. His brother, James II, succeeded him. James was a Catholic. His first wife bore him two daughters, Mary and Anne, both of whom were brought up Anglican. His second wife was Mary of Modena, also a Catholic. James tried to make England Catholic by both legal and extralegal means. The English people confined their resistance to legal channels until 1688, when Mary of Modena delivered a boy. The specter of an unending succession of Catholic kings was too much to bear. A group of Whig and Tory leaders invited William III of the Netherlands (grandson of Charles I by his daughter Mary and husband of Mary, daughter of James II) to invade England with an army around which the people could gather in revolt against James. On November 5, William and his army disembarked at Torbay in Devon. James ran away but was apprehended by English fishermen and returned to England. William didn't want to create a martyr. He left James unguarded, James ran away again, and this time he reached France.

William summoned a duly elected Parliament, which had to establish the legalities of the matter. Both William and Mary insisted that William be king. Consequently, the Commons decided that James, having broken laws and left the nation, had abdicated. It then declared William and Mary joint sovereigns with administration being William's responsibility (1689).

In the next few years, Parliament passed several acts that, together, made up the revolutionary settlement. In so doing, it was influenced by a number of political thinkers, the most outstanding of which was Locke. Locke held that man possessed rights, such as religious liberty and equality before the law, with which the state couldn't interfere. The preservation of life, liberty and property was the prime function of the state. Governments must be subject to restraint to keep them from degenerating into despotism. This restraint was effected by dividing the government into executive, legislative and judicial branches with checks and balances between them. If a government failed to carry out its function, it could be justly overthrown.

The Bill of Rights was passed in 1689. Among other things, it established that the king couldn't be Catholic, that a standing army in peacetime was legal only if agreed to by Parliament, that excessive bail and cruel and unusual punishments were illegal, that members of Parliament could exercise free speech, and that Parliament should be called frequently. The Bill of Rights also outlawed the king's suspending and dispensing powers. His dispensing power had permitted him to except people from laws on a discretionary basis. His suspending power had allowed him to void a law or "interrupt an activity". Dismissing an official, who had been duly appointed to his position, would be an example of interrupting an activity.

The Toleration Act, also of 1689, gave the right of public worship to Protestant nonconformists (Protestant sects other than the Anglican). Even though Catholics weren't covered by the act, after 1689 they were generally left to practice their religion as they pleased.

Beginning in 1689, Parliament met every year.

In 1694, the Bank of England was founded. The subscribers to a government loan of 1,200,000 pounds were incorporated by Parliament as a joint-stock bank with the right to issue notes and discount bills. Since the government didn't have to repay this loan as long as it paid the interest on the loan, this arrangement was the beginning of the national debt.

Also in 1694, Queen Mary died. In 1701, the Act of Settlement was passed. It declared that, if William and Anne, his sister-in-law, died without issue, the crown would pass, not to the Stuart line, but to Sophia (granddaughter of James I by his daughter Elizabeth), Electress Dowager of Hanover, or her heirs. It also stated that judges could be removed from office only for offense against good behavior demonstrated to the satisfaction of Parliament. The separation of the judiciary from the crown was now complete.

In 1695, censorship of the press was allowed to lapse.

William died in 1702 and was succeeded by Anne. During most of Anne's reign, England was at war with France. In 1703, Portugal joined England and its allies after requirements Portugal had set up were met. One was a commercial treaty with England under which English cloth entered Portugal and Portuguese port wine entered England at low custom rates. This treaty resulted in a switch in English taste from claret to port.

These years also saw the growth of science. In 1662, the creation of The Royal Society of London for Improving Natural Knowledge formally recognized weekly meetings to cultivate physics and mathematics, which had been going on since 1645. Robert Boyle, who stated the physical law governing the expansion of gases, was a member. Newton was president of the society for 24 years. The most notable immediate impact of the work of these scientists was the decline of superstition. When an alleged witch was brought to trial in the time of Queen Anne for flying from

London to Oxford on a broomstick, the judge dismissed the case with the observation that be knew of no law against such an act.

In 1714, Queen Anne died, and George I, Sophia's son and the Elector of Hanover, ascended to the throne, thus marking the beginning of the Hanoverian dynasty. The king was the hereditary head of the executive branch of the government. It was his responsibility to see that government was effective. To carry out this duty, he presumably had the right to choose his ministers as he saw fit. But by the time of George I, it had become clear that, while Parliament couldn't dictate whom the king could appoint as ministers, it could and did dictate whom he couldn't. For unless the king's ministers and Commons were able to work with each other, the machinery of government broke down.

By 1720, the national debt had grown to about 51 million pounds. The government wanted to shrink it. In return for interest payments over a period of years, the South Sea Company offered to take over the debt. The government agreed. The company called in the government bonds in return for new shares of company stock. Speculation in the company's shares then began. Share price went from 150 pounds to 1000 in a short time. In September, the crash occurred, people lost large amounts, and protest against the government took place. One victim of this crash was Newton. He had invested in South Sea stock, and anticipating a crash, he had sold out. However, the price of the stock kept rising, and he bought in again. This time he was caught.

Robert Walpole got the East India Company and the Bank of England to buy in excess of 18 billion pounds of South Sea Company stock. This put public credit back on a sounder footing and let the South Sea Company stockholders get out from under with at least a part of their original investment.

Walpole was a hero. In April 1721, he was appointed First Lord of the Treasury and Chancellor of the Exchequer. This put him in control of the government, a position he maintained for the next 21 years. To all intents and purposes, he was England's first prime minister, although in his time the title didn't exist. He was the trusted minister of the king in Commons and the trusted minister of Commons in the king's administration.

Despite the achievement of the English people in creating a parliamentary government, it should be recognized that Commons was only an approximation of a representative government. A number of the boroughs, from which members of Commons were elected, had almost no eligible voters. Rotten boroughs, they were called. These rotten boroughs were dominated by men of wealth and position (who frequently didn't even live in the boroughs), which gave them considerable control over the activity in Commons. At the same time, a number of heavily populated areas had grown up since the boroughs had been established, and these areas had no representation. During this period, a significant factor in maintaining a prime ministership was the dispensing of patronage, in the form of sinecures and pensions, a skill at which Walpole excelled.

The Southern Colonies

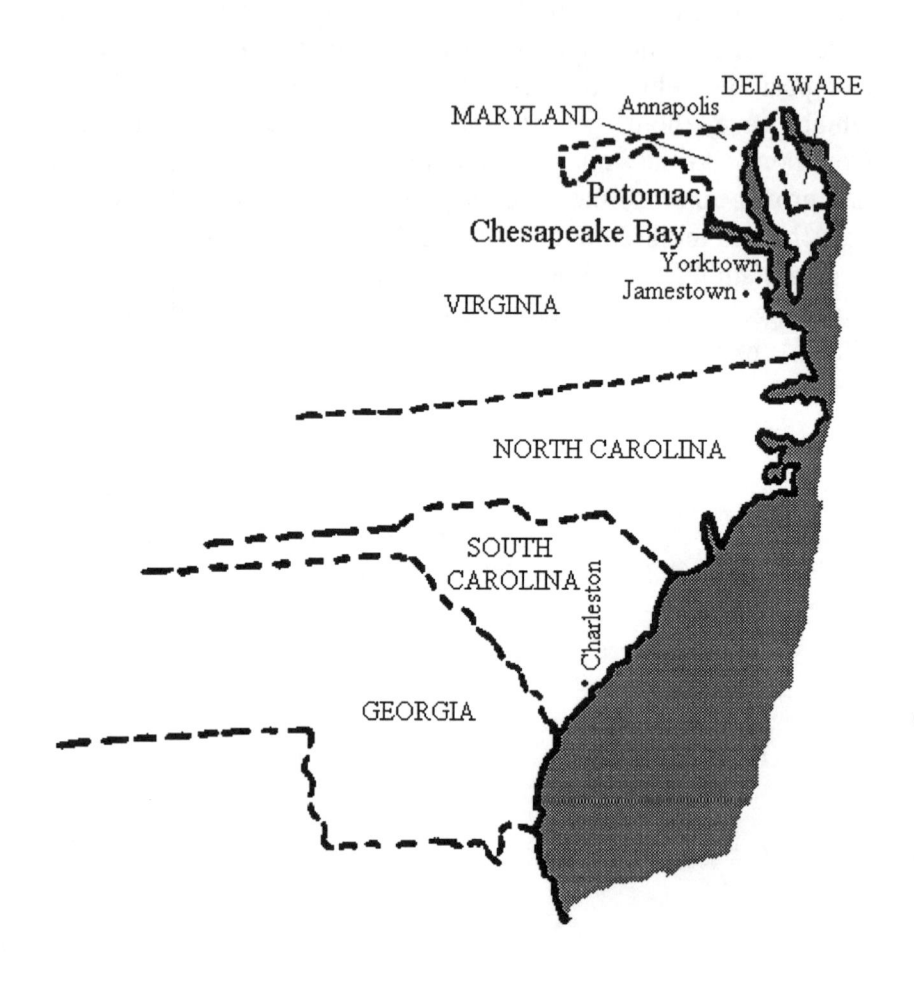

CHAPTER TWELVE

The American Revolution

In 1606, a group of English speculators was given a royal charter for the Virginia Company, named after England's virgin queen, Elizabeth. In May 1607, the company established its first colony at Jamestown on the Virginia coast of Chesapeake bay. Unlike previous attempts at English settlement, this one took. A significant factor in the colony's survival was one of the settlers, Captain John Smith. A soldier of fortune, Smith was confined for mutiny during the voyage to America, not by the ship's officers but by his fellow colonists. However, on arrival in America, when the colony's sealed orders were opened, it was discovered that the company had made Smith a member of the council that was to govern the colony. The rest of the council excluded Smith from membership by not permitting him to take his oath of office. However, deteriorating conditions at the colony ultimately resulted in Smith being elected president of the settlement.

Smith was captured by Indians and saved from execution by Pocahontas. The only documentation for this event is Smith's writings. But investigation of Smith's description of others of his adventures, improbable as they were, supports their veracity.

When Smith got back to the settlement after this adventure, he was greeted with the sight of a group of the inhabitants preparing to leave the colony by sea. Smith aborted this mutiny by threatening to sink the mutineers' boat with cannon fire. This was the third time he had put down such a revolt. In the aftermath of one of the previous uprisings, he had executed one of the mutineers. This time he just dispatched the chief mutineers to England as felons. Smith dealt with malingerers by vowing to exile into the wild all who wouldn't work. In general, Smith's willingness to provide responsible leadership, combined with his insight into the reality that, if the colony was to survive, it must be peopled with good laborers and men adept with tools, was instrumental to the settlement's success.

A second factor influencing the colony's viability was the fact that the Virginia Company kept pumping settlers into Virginia, because it was necessary to "season" them, as the colonists termed it. Attrition, from disease and desertion back to England, was high. Of the 105 original settlers who made it to Virginia (41 died at sea), only 38 survived to the end of the year. The rest had died, primarily from disease. But by 1628, there were an estimated 3000 Virginians.

The third factor contributing to the survival of the Virginia settlement was tobacco. In addition to supporting themselves on the land, the colonists had to produce a commodity that could be traded for English products, which represented almost everything the colonists needed to raise their living above a subsistence level. The colony was also supposed to generate income for the company's stockholders.

There was no gold or silver to be found. After experimenting unsuccessfully with other goods such as silk, glass, soap, lumber, grain and wine, the colonists discovered that tobacco was a viable commercial product. Demand for tobacco was already heavy and continued to increase. Large profits could be made. Tobacco cultivation started in 1612. At one point, even the streets of Jamestown were planted with tobacco.

In 1618, the head of the company, Sir Thomas Smythe, was replaced by Sir Edwin Sandys. In the six remaining years of the company's life, Sandys introduced two significant reforms. The first was the headright system of land allotment, which contrasted with the previous company monopoly of the land. Under the headright system, a settler got 50 acres for himself and another 50 for each member of his family or servant who came with him. This policy spoke to the basic yearning driving settlers to the New World, which was to escape the misfortunes of the Old. In the 17th century, this escape took the form of land ownership. Subsequently, headright allotment of land became the standard way of attracting colonists to the English New World.

Sandys' other reform was to set up a general assembly for the colony, in which representatives, called burgesses, of the settlers met, beginning in 1619, to discuss and legislate on the problems they faced.

However, Sandys wasn't an effective manager. In 1624, the company failed, and Virginia became a crown colony.

The most profitable cultivation of tobacco required great plantations with lots of inexpensive labor. Initially, indentured servants were used, but disease continued to make inroads on the population, and there weren't enough servants to go around. In 1619, Dutch merchants introduced African slaves to Virginia. For two generations, growth in the slave population was slow. The Virginians managed their slaves as if they were indentured servants and were known to allot land to them at the end of a term of slavery. However, by 1660, importation of slaves had begun to increase, and their status in the life of the colony as subhuman chattel became fixed.

In 1629, the Massachusetts Bay Company was formed. In 1630, the company sponsored 11 ships with 700 colonists, 240 cows, 60 horses, and the royal charter of the company. John Winthrop, the governor of the colony, located his settlement on the Charles river. This settlement ultimately grew to be the city of Boston. By 1640, Archbishop Laud's persecution of the Puritans had driven around 20,000 people across the Atlantic to the Massachusetts colony. Some died. Some gave up and went back to England. But by 1640, there were 14,000 colonists in Massachusetts.

The charter of the company was unique among its type, since it didn't require that company headquarters be in London. The Puritans in Massachusetts held a general court of the company and moved the company headquarters to Massachusetts. In effect, this made Massachusetts a self-governing colony. However, the event was more a historical oddity than a significant fact. The reality of the situation was that all of the colonies quickly became self-governing whether they had the right to do so or not.

The Massachusetts colony was no more tolerant of religious diversity than were the Anglicans, and efforts were made to see that colonists conformed to local practice. When a group could no longer put up with this treatment, it would leave to establish a colony of its own. In this way, in 1635, the town of Hartford was founded in the Connecticut river valley. These colonists were joined by others from England. The result was the settlement of

The Northern Colonies

River Towns, ultimately to become the colony of Connecticut.

Roger Williams had been expelled from Cambridge by Archbishop Laud. Williams emigrated to Massachusetts but found the colonists there as tyrannical as the Anglicans. He organized a group that objected to this religious discrimination. The administration of the Massachusetts colony concluded that Williams was a disturbance and decided to return him to England. Forewarned (by the former and again-to-be governor of the colony, John Winthrop), Williams ran away and established the town of Providence. In 1636, others of his persuasion from Massachusetts joined him. In this way, the colony of Rhode Island was formed.

This colony was the first political organization to practice the separation of church and state. It owed its viability to the distillation and sale of liquor.

On March 9, 1622, James I made a grant to John Mason, who came from the county of Hampshire in England. Mason named his grant New Hampshire. Subsequently, it was discovered that, because of geographic confusion, the New Hampshire grant was contained within the Massachusetts grant. The Mason family pursued its claim, and on September 18, 1679, New Hampshire was split off from Massachusetts and became an independent colony.

In 1632, George Calvert, Lord Baltimore, a Catholic courtier, requested a patent authorizing a colony near Virginia. After he died, the patent was given to his son, Cecilius, under whose direction the colony was established. It was called Maryland in honor of the queen of Charles I, Henrietta Maria. You remember her. She was the French princess who got Charles into all of his trouble.

North Carolina was settled by colonists from Virginia and became independent in 1660. South Carolina was created by the same charter that gave birth to North Carolina, but it wasn't settled until 1670. Both the Carolinas were named after Charles I. We've already seen that, in Latin, Charles is Carolius.

The Dutch of New Amsterdam extinguished New Sweden. In 1664, the English conquered New Amsterdam and converted it into the colony of New York, which was named after the Duke of York, who led the campaign against New Amsterdam and who ultimately became James II.

While the expedition to take New Amsterdam was still at sea, the Duke of York ceded a portion of his colony to Sir George Carteret and Lord Berkeley, because when Carteret was governor of the Isle of Jersey, he gave sanctuary to Charles II when he was still a prince in exile. Carteret named his colony New Jersey.

In 1681, the Quaker, William Penn, founded Pennsylvania as a refuge from religious persecution. Quaker friends from England joined him in this new colony. However, Penn hadn't founded a colony for Quakers, but for any who wished to escape religious prejudice. He had his promotional pamphlets translated into

German. The Rhineland sectarians, who had been oppressed by the German princes, responded in great numbers. The Peace of Westphalia (1648) had given each German prince the choice of Lutheranism, Calvinism or Catholicism as the exclusive religion of his principality.

By 1775, there were about 100,000 Germans in Pennsylvania. Irish Protestants also added to the colony's population. In 1775, Philadelphia had 40,000 residents and may have been the second largest city in the English empire. London was the largest, and the other contenders were Dublin and Edinburgh.

Originally, the colony of New York included both the land that became Pennsylvania and the former colony of New Sweden. When Penn founded Pennsylvania, the colony of New Sweden became part of Pennsylvania. But the Swedes and Pennsylvania Quakers didn't get along, and in the 1690's, Penn granted the Swedes the right to their own deputy governor. In this way, the colony of New Sweden became the colony of Delaware. The name comes from Lord De La Warr, an early governor of Virginia. It was first applied to the river, then to the Indian tribe, and finally, to the state.

The last of the 13 colonies was Georgia, founded in 1732 partly as a place of rehabilitation for people imprisoned for debt in England, partly as a plantation for the cultivation of silk, but primarily as a buffer against the Spanish in Florida and the French in Louisiana. It was named for King George II, who succeeded his father, George I, in 1727.

England was a careless parent to its colonies. During their formative years, its attention was demanded by its Civil and Revolutionary Wars and their attendant problems as well as with international relations in Europe. It expected its colonies to be a source of income and not an object of expense or trouble. It trusted that they would take care of themselves, and indeed, they did. When England finally looked to America with other than peripheral concern, it was faced with a set of colonies peopled primarily by native-born Americans, self-reliant, self-supporting and self-governing. Locke's ideas found even more fertile soil in the New World than the Old.

The situation varied from colony to colony, but basically, the colonies were chartered bodies subject to the crown. The king appointed a governor for each colony. As a matter of fact, the colonies served as a kind of dumping ground for England's superannuated politicians. But it made little difference. The governor was paid by the general assembly of the colony. As always, money talked. In each colony, political power sat in the assembly.

The colonies were happy with the state of affairs as it existed. In particular, they wanted no quarrel with England, for they were aware of the French menace to their own well-being, and they had only to England to look for their defenses.

In 1756, the Seven Years War began. In America, it was known as the French and Indian War. On one side were England and the Prussia of Frederick the Great, on the other France and the Austrians. In the beginning, things didn't go well for England. In June 1757, William Pitt the Elder (later Earl of Chatham) became Secretary of State and, in effect, prime minister. Pitt directed a war which was fought over an area running from India in the East to America in the West.

In October 1760, George II died and was succeeded by George III, his grandson by his son Frederick. In March 1761, France made clear that it wanted to end the war. Negotiations began. But Pitt kept on with the war. He felt that France's ability to make trouble had not yet been destroyed. Pitt then discovered that Spain had secretly agreed to enter the war on France's side. Pitt was for striking Spain. But the rest of the king's council disagreed. In October, Pitt resigned. Thomas Newcastle, First Lord of the Treasury, took over. In 1762, Spain entered the war and Newcastle resigned because the council had opposed him on the amount of the subsidy to be granted Prussia. George appointed Lord Bute, his onetime tutor, as First Lord of the Treasury and George Grenville, a brother-in-law of but disowned by Pitt, as Secretary of State. Lord Bute was in charge and continued negotiations for peace.

In 1763, the Peace of Paris was signed. Pitt was distressed. "... we have given her (France) the means of recovering her prodigious losses and of becoming once more formidable to us ...", he said. Notwithstanding, the terms of the peace treaty benefited England. It acquired Canada, France gave Louisiana to Spain in payment for Spanish losses, and as a consequence, France disappeared as a presence in the New World. In April 1763, Bute resigned and Grenville became head of the government's administration.

From the point of view of the colonies, the outcome of the war was twofold. First, it removed France as a threat, which strengthened the colonists' feeling that they were capable of looking out for themselves. Second, it brought the colonies to the English government's attention. Part of the war had been fought in America, and England decided that, in the future, the colonies should bear some of the cost of their defense. To this end, Grenville pushed through Parliament the Stamp Act of 1765, which required documents to have placed on them a stamp for which the person concerned had to reimburse the English government. Covered by this act were legal documents, commercial documents (liquor licenses, mortgages, insurance policies, custom clearances, etc.), pamphlets, almanacs, and newspapers. The effect on the colonies was electric.

Until 1765, conservatives, partial to England, had dominated the corridors of power in the colonies. The Stamp Act pulled the rug out from under the feet of these conservatives and led to the rise of radicals in the colonies. Patrick Henry and his coterie stampeded the Virginia assembly into enacting a number of anti-Stamp resolutions, the nub of which was the principle of no taxation without representation. The resolutions were passed at the end of the assembly session after most of the members had gone home.

Mobs burned the stamp distributors in effigy and pulled down the houses of conservatives. The distributors got the message and resigned. On October 7, the Stamp Act Congress met in New York. Only nine of the colonies were represented. Of these, three sent only unofficial or irregularly chosen delegates. The resolutions adopted were measured but resolutely endorsed the principle of no taxation without representation.

The significance of the congress was that, for the first time, an inter-colonial assembly produced what amounted to legislation welcomed by all of the colonies. By the New Year, the Stamp Act had been reduced to nothing. With the exception of Georgia, and there for a short while only, not a stamp had been sold; the Sons of Liberty, as the radicals called themselves, had, in effect, become the administration in the colonies; and life was continuing in its usual, unstamped way.

George had dismissed Grenville in July 1765. The new ministry, led by the Marquess of Rockingham, decided that the Stamp Act had to go. On March 18, 1766, Parliament repealed it.

In July 1766, Rockingham was succeeded by Pitt. In March 1767, Pitt went mad and secluded himself yet stayed in office. As a consequence, Charles Townshend, Chancellor of the Exchequer, was able, for a few months, to control the administration. He sponsored a Revenue Act that placed duties on the glass, lead, painter's colors, paper, and tea imported into the colonies from England. The previously passed Navigation Acts prohibited direct import of products from other countries. The revenue from the duties was to be used to establish a colonial civil list, which would allow England to reimburse colonial governors and customs and other officials rather than have the colonies provide for these costs. Townshend then contracted a "fever" (quotes because the illness was never more precisely identified) and died.

Here again was taxation without representation coupled with a threat to colonial self-government. As was typical, Massachusetts colonists were first to react to the Revenue Act. They adopted a boycott of imported English goods — loaf sugar, cordage, anchors, coaches, men's and women's hats, shoes, snuff, mustard, and glue, among others.

Although Pitt didn't resign until October 1768, the ministry had been reconstituted the winter before with the Duke of Grafton now in charge. In August 1768, New York joined Massachusetts in the boycott. In March 1769, Pennsylvania signed on. In January 1770, the Duke of Grafton was succeeded by Frederick, Lord North. By the beginning of 1770, all the southern colonies had joined the boycott. By the spring of 1770, only New Hampshire wasn't participating. On March 5, 1770, North initiated the repeal of the Revenue Act with the exception of the import duty on tea.

In 1772, the revenue schooner HMS Gaspee ran aground. American smugglers from Newport, Rhode Island then boarded the Gaspee and burned it. The reason they gave for their action was that its commander had impressed men from Rhode Island; stolen sheep, hogs and poultry; and felled fruit trees for firewood. He had also been uncommonly diligent in combating smuggling.

The Gaspee incident forced an English response, which was ineffective. The colonists refused to testify against each other, so no culprits were found and no inditements were returned. But the charge to the commission, set up to investigate the incident, directed that those taken into custody as a consequence of the commission's findings were to be sent to England for trial, which violated the right to a trial by a jury of one's peers. As a result, the Virginia general assembly, known as the House of Burgesses, recommended that inter-colonial committees of correspondence be set up to coordinate responses to any such future "acts of aggression".

By September 1772, the East India Company was close to bankruptcy. The English government had to get involved in order to avoid a financial disaster. North sponsored the Tea Act, which allowed the company to both ship tea to the colonies without paying the import tax and sell directly to the public. The effect was twofold: American smugglers would have to accept a smaller profit in order to compete, and the American retail distribution system would be bypassed by all the tea sold by the company. This was enough to justify a negative reaction. But the fact that the company didn't have to pay duty on its tea emphasized to the colonists that they were still being taxed without having a say in the matter. It was on this violation of liberty that they chose to focus.

The reaction of the colonies to the Tea Act was to decide not to allow any East India Company tea to be unloaded at their ports. The first company tea ship arrived in Boston on November 28, 1773. For almost three weeks, the tea remained aboard. Sam Adams, perhaps the leading Son of Liberty in Massachusetts, said that the tea should be shipped to England. But this couldn't be done without the approval of the governor, which he refused to give. He thought he was in command of the situation.

Reexportation required that an export duty be paid. If it wasn't paid on the first tea ship by December 17, the tea could be legally taken over by customs and sold. By December 16, there were four tea ships in the harbor. That night these tea ships were boarded by a mob thinly disguised as Indians. All the tea chests were brought on deck, opened and emptied into the harbor. Ten days later, Philadelphia sent its tea ships to England. Tea was debarked at Charleston but found no buyers. On March 9, 1774, Boston destroyed 30 more chests of tea. On April 22, New York had its own tea party.

In response, North passed the Coercive Acts, known in the colonies as the Intolerable Acts. They closed the port of Boston, suspended the Massachusetts assembly, gave the Massachusetts governor control of the colony and made him answerable only to the king, put Massachusetts judges and other officers of the law under the direction of the governor, and gave the governor the right to quarter English troops in whatever way he found necessary.

The reaction of the colonies was predictable. Thomas Jefferson put their feelings into words when he described the Intolerable Acts as "a deliberate and systematic plan of reducing us to slavery." On September 5, 1774, the First Continental Congress met in Philadelphia. This time only Georgia declined to attend. It was being attacked by Indians and didn't want to do anything to discourage England from defending it.

The other colonies sent their most prominent sons. The congress decided to ignore the Intolerable Acts and not conduct any trade with England. North's reply was the Restraining Act, which outlawed all commerce between any New England colony and any English dominion and prohibited the New England colonies from entering the Newfoundland fishing banks. Thus, in contrast with previous confrontations with England, defiance on the part of the colonists failed to result in an English retreat.

It was now April 1775. There was an increased English military presence in Boston, and the colonies were preparing to meet force with force. On April 18, General Thomas Gage, the newly appointed Massachusetts governor. dispatched some 800 infantrymen on a nominally secret mission to destroy a cache of arms that the colonists had stored at Concord. But word got out.

Washington at Valley Forge. *From the painting* March to Valley Forge *painted by William B. T. Trego in 1883. The original now hangs in the Valley Forge Historical Society building in Valley Forge, Pennsylvania.*

Night-riders preceded the troops to alert the countryside to the approaching infantrymen. At 5 am, the local militia of Lexington, somewhat less than 70 in number, drew up on the village green to resist the English. When the confrontation occurred, a shot was fired, from which side nobody knows. The English then opened general fire and dispersed the militia. Eight colonists were killed, nine wounded. The shot heard round the world had been fired, and the American Revolution began. Actually, the expression "the shot heard round the world" comes from a poem written by Emerson to commemorate the battle of Concord. But the first shots of the American Revolution were fired at Lexington.

The English continued on to Concord but failed in their mission, for the arms had been moved. At noon, the English began their return march to Charlestown, which they reached at sundown. The march was one continuing conflict along what came to be known as Battle Road. By the time the English had reached their destination, the colonists had over 2000 men in the field. These colonists were led by their militia commanders, primarily men who had fought together in the Seven Years War and who were used to coordinating their commands. In addition to the continuous skirmishing, there were several confrontations between large formations of troops. Just before reaching Lexington, the English forces were saved from annihilation by the appearance of relief forces from Boston. The English lost 65 dead, 180 wounded, and 27 missing; the colonists, 50 dead, 39 wounded, and 5 missing.

On May 10, Fort Ticonderoga was taken by Ethan Allen and Benedict Arnold, thus cutting off any possible movement of English troops from Canada. On the same day, the Second Continental Congress convened in Philadelphia. One of its first tasks was to select a commander in chief for the American army that was already forming in New England. It should, Congress thought for purposes of solidarity, be a Southerner. George Washington was the obvious candidate. He was from the right colony and had had at least some military experience. Washington considered himself unqualified and accepted the commission only as an obligation. He said to Patrick Henry, "From the day I enter upon the command of the American armies, I date my fall, and the ruin of my reputation." He was, of course, wrong.

Washington was an essential factor in the American victory. The colonists had just one army led personally by Washington. To defeat the colonies militarily, all England had to do was crush this army. How England would have fared under the resulting guerrilla resistance is another question, but not one pertinent to the point here.

However, the Continental army was never destroyed. The English commander, General William Howe, never followed up his victories with a vigorous pursuit of the defeated colonial army. Various hypotheses have been offered to explain his actions. Howe was a Whig and, for the first few years of the war, hoped for a reconciliation. One hypothesis put forward is that these feelings influenced his actions. Another proposed explanation is that Howe felt that the forces at his disposal were all that he was going to get and that, consequently, he had to husband these resources. Therefore, he wasn't disposed to expose his men to enemy fire. Sometimes this second explanation is embellished with the idea that Howe, who was in charge of the English forces at Bunker Hill, had been so pummeled in that engagement that he had no desire to confront the Continental army.

In any case, the Continental army suffered more at the hands of the Americans than those of the English. The colonies could claim around 280,000 able-bodied men. But the largest the Continental army ever got was 25,000. Underpaid (when paid at all) in the constantly inflating Continental paper money (the worthlessness of which became proverbial), underfed, unsheltered, and unequipped by unfeeling civilians, the regular Continental soldier found desertion tempting. Of sound judgment, tenacious, dignified, conscientious, and always at his post, Washington set the example that prevented the Continental army from completely melting away.

On July 17, 1775, the battle of Bunker Hill was fought. It was actually fought on Breed's Hill. Both Bunker and Breed's Hill had been fortified, Breed's as a preliminary defense for Bunker. When the colonists were driven from Breed's Hill, they also abandoned Bunker Hill. They were running low on ammunition.

Although the colonists were forced to retreat at the battle of Bunker Hill, they inflicted such heavy losses on the English (2200 English soldiers attacked the hill and 1054 died) that the battle has always been thought of as an American victory. Shortly after, Washington took over command and set about to bring discipline to the army and put Boston under siege. By early March 1776, the English recognized that their position was indefensible and retreated to Halifax, Nova Scotia (New Scotland). Halifax was named after George Dunk, the Earl of Halifax, who established the settlement.

Congress made one final attempt to resolve differences, the Olive Branch Petition. The English rejected it. Congress then decided that too much had already been invested in defense of America's liberty to return to the state of affairs before the war and resolved to declare the independence of the United Colonies. Thomas Jefferson was chosen to draft this Declaration of Independence.

In many ways, the Declaration is an unremarkable document. For the most part, it consists of a list of 28 grievances against the English king, some of which aren't very compelling. However, it begins with a preamble that makes the Declaration deathless. From 13 colonies still suspicious of one another, to a young nation facing an untamed frontier, through the soul racking struggle of a Civil War, to its emergence as a world power and its need to resist the threat of totalitarian empire, the US has never ceased to be faced with the question of its identity. And at every point, the Declaration has provided the timeless answer.

> We hold these truths to be self-evident, that all men are created equal, that they are endowed by their Creator with certain inalienable Rights, that among these are Life, Liberty and the pursuit of Happiness. That to secure these rights, Governments are instituted among men, deriving their just powers from the consent of the governed.

Congress adopted the Articles of Confederation as the basis for governing the new Union of States. The states adopted constitutions and took the occasion to liberalize their political environments. Except in New England, established churches (churches supported by the state) were abolished; bills of rights were adopted; land was redistributed (at the expense of emigre Loyalists); and New England, Pennsylvania, and Delaware made slave trade illegal. In April 1776, Congress had already decreed that, as a war measure, no more slaves were to be imported.

The Americans won the war. The reasons were multiple. One, already cited, was the good fortune of having Washington as commander in chief and the sound judgment of Congress in leaving him at that post throughout the vicissitudes of the war.

A second factor was the stake the combatants had in the conflict. For America, it was win or become servants. From England's point of view, loss of its American colonies wasn't desirable. But such a setback wasn't the end of everything. The English empire would still go on.

Third, although England pursued a sound strategy throughout the war, it was made nugatory by the steady series of tactical blunders with which it was carried out.

Finally, America was conducting a rebellion against England, pure and simple, and it could devote its efforts to this task. For England, the American rebellion was just one aspect of one of the interminable continental wars in which it was forever engaged. France, eager to get back at England for its defeat in the Seven Years War, had been shipping arms to the colonies almost since the start of the war. When General Horatio Gates and his militiamen defeated Gentleman Johnny Burgoyne and his 7000 regulars at Saratoga on October 17, 1777 and kept the road from Canada blocked, France became convinced that the English could be beaten. In the next year, she declared war on England, an act soon copied by her ally, Spain. From this point on, sea power became the telling military factor in the struggle. England mauled the French fleet. Nevertheless, the French fleet proved decisive in the American cause. In 1781, it participated in the siege at Yorktown that resulted in the surrender of General Charles Cornwallis.

Throughout the war, the strength of the patriot cause grew. The considered opinion is that, when the war began, there was a substantial patriot party, a smaller Loyalist party, and a majority that was neutral. The war, the Declaration of Independence, and the durability of the American cause encouraged patriot support. In addition, whenever the English were victorious, the local Loyalists would rally to them. The English would then leave, and their supporters would have to run for their lives. Almost all of them (about 80,000) settled north of Lake Erie and founded English-speaking Canada. This dispora left the patriots in control.

The battle between the patriots and Loyalists was most pronounced in the South, where Banastre Tarleton organized a Loyalist force. Tarleton's tactics were barbaric and included midnight raids, ambushes, and murders. The result was outrage that fed the patriot cause. Loyalists were driven from their jobs and property.

When the news of Yorktown reached North, he exclaimed, "Oh God! It is all over." His government was replaced by a ministry led by Rockingham and, after Rockingham died, by William Shelburne. On September 3, 1783, Shelburne agreed to a new Treaty of Paris. American independence was acknowledged, concessions were made to American fishermen in Canadian waters, and the Great Lakes and the Mississippi were established as the northern and western borders of the new nation.

Early in 1783, it had become apparent that peace would soon be established. The army hadn't been paid, and a movement to set up military rule in the colonies began. Washington's officers called a mass meeting for March 11. Washington expressed "disapprobation of such disorderly proceedings" and called his own substitute meeting to be held on March 15. As a consequence, the March 11 meeting was canceled. On March 15, Washington gave his prepared speech, in which he pleaded with his officers to not interfere with the civil government and stated his belief that, in the end, the government would "act justly". When he was finished, he saw, from the expression on his officers' faces, that they hadn't been convinced. He then remembered a reassuring letter, from a congressman, that he had brought with him. He withdrew the paper from his pocket and then hesitated. Finally, he produced a pair of eyeglasses, something he had, until this point, hidden from all but his closest friends. "Gentlemen," he said, "you will permit me to put on my spectacles, for I have not only grown gray but almost blind in the service of my country." That was all it took. As Jefferson later said, "The moderation and virtue of a single character probably prevented this Revolution from being closed, as most others have been, by a subversion of that liberty it was intended to establish."

Unfortunately, Washington was a better example than he was a forecaster. The army was mustered out without pay. Washington

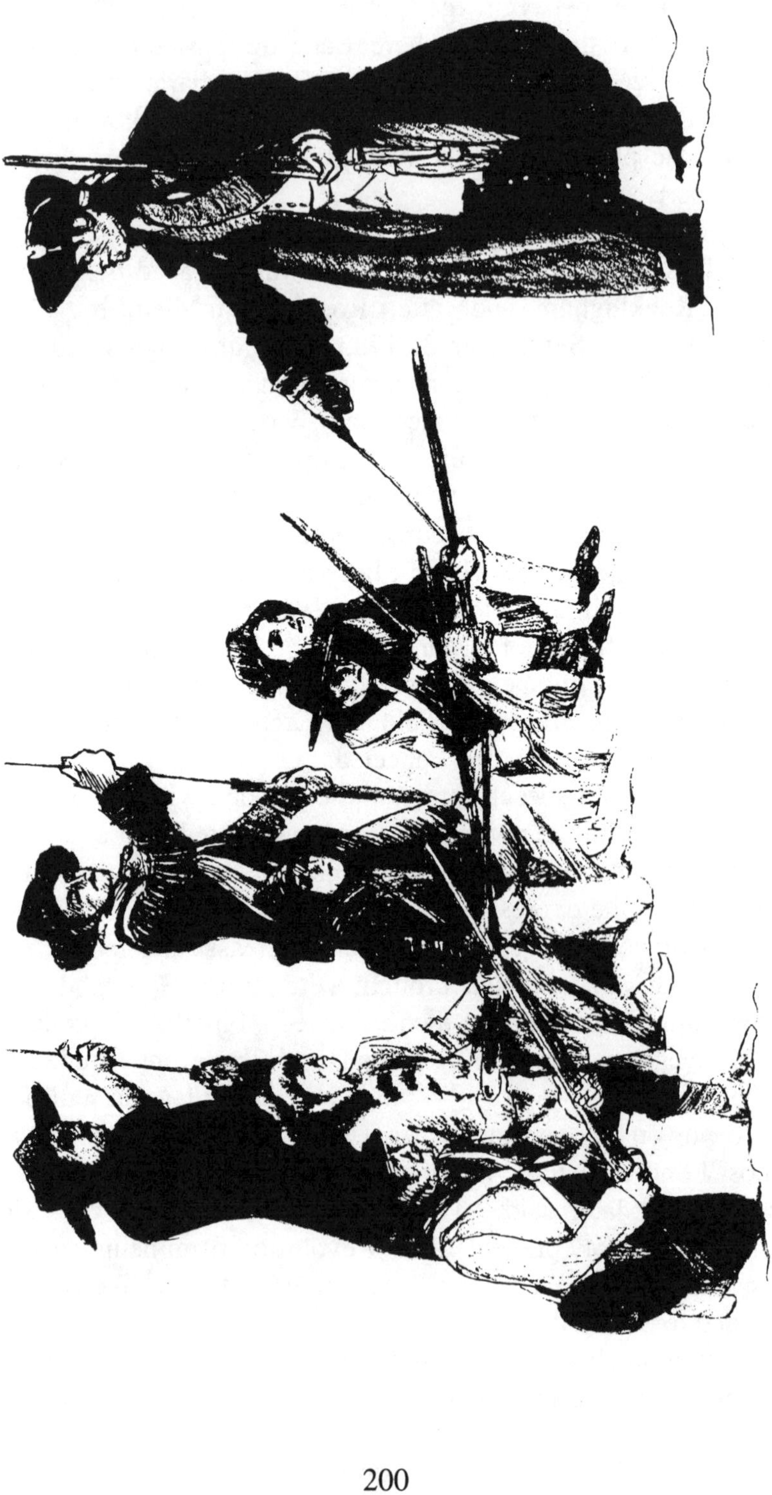

Von Steuben Drills Continental Soldiers at Valley Forge.

From a mural by Edwin Austin Abbey. By permission of the Commonwealth o Pennsylvania. The mural is in the Senate Chambers at the State Capitol in Harrisburg. During the winter of Valley Forge, Baron von Steuben joined the Continental forces. He advertised himself as instrumental to Frederick the Great and made reference to the estate in Swabia that he had earned in recognition of his services. In fact, he was a soldier of fortune. He had served in Frederick's army but owned no property and was down on his luck. However, he presented two desirable assets to Congress. He was willing to serve for no pay, just expenses, and he unequivocally accepted Washington as his superior. At Valley Forge, he undertook to drill the army on how to maneuver and fire in formation. He used an interpreter to communicate with the troops, since his only English consisted of curses, which he used liberally when things went wrong. This made the soldiers laugh. Von Steuben would goodnaturedly join in the laughter, which endeared him to them. He was successful in training the men because he was willing not only to tell them what to do, but also why they should do it. The soldiers' demand that they understand what they were doing made a deep impression on von Steuben. It wasn't something that he was used to. As a result of von Steuben's training the army that emerged from Valley Forge the next spring consisted of, not only marksmen who were deadly when defending an entrenched position or skirmishing, but also a disciplined corps that could hold its own on European-style battlefields.

The US in 1783

had the torment of watching his veterans dispersed like a "set of beggars".

Congressional government under the Articles of Confederation wasn't without achievement. It had conducted a victorious war and negotiated a favorable peace treaty. It had convinced the colonies, with charter claims to the west (Massachusetts, Connecticut, Virginia, the Carolinas, and Georgia had charter claims that extended to the Mississippi river), that they should give up these claims and let Congress administer the territory between the Appalachians and the Mississippi and between the Great Lakes and Spanish Florida. And it had enacted the Northwest Ordinance, which set up the rules for the political development of the Northwest Territory. The Ordinance stated that, when any part of the territory could boast of at least 60,000 residents, it could become a state and that the territory would be divided into, at least, three, at most, five states.

However, the Congress had no diplomatic or military power. Its financing was wishful thinking. It had to make requests to the states for allocations of funds. It never received the amounts needed to provide leadership at the national level.

In the meantime, the states began to grow away from one another. In particular, they set up tariff barriers and taxed each other's trade.

The men who had struggled for American independence viewed these developments with misgivings and abhorred the drift toward "anarchy and confusion". Sentiment for overhauling the national government began to grow.

James Madison had arranged a meeting between Maryland and Virginia to resolve difficulties involving use of the Potomac river, which constituted their common border. In this meeting, Maryland and Virginia did reach a mutually satisfactory compromise. The success of this meeting reinforced the feeling that a conference involving all of the states might be of help in resolving the Union's commercial problems. As a consequence, Virginia issued an invitation for all of the states to meet at Annapolis, Maryland in September 1786 for this purpose. Only five states (New York, New Jersey, Pennsylvania, Delaware and Virginia) sent delegations. But Alexander Hamilton was there. He wrote a report to all of the states in which he proposed that the Union's commercial relations could never be developed peacefully while the Articles of Confederation remained as they were. The report recommended that a convention be convened in Philadelphia on the second Monday in May 1787 to consider amendments to the Articles. The report was signed by all of the delegates to the conference. Total attendance, including Hamilton: 12.

All of the states but Rhode Island agreed to send delegates to the meeting, the purpose of which Congress endorsed. In May 1787, the convention began its deliberations. By May 14, the official opening day, only a few delegates had arrived in Philadelphia. The remainder drifted in over the course of the rest of the month.

The delegates were the pick of the revolutionary leadership. Their goal was to assure that their revolution didn't end in failure. They had been molded by their service in the army, Congress, state assemblies, and diplomatic posts and recognized that what they came up with must fit both the American experience with self-government and the hopes of the American people for the future. As a consequence, they were, in the main, of one mind. They quickly agreed on basic principles and spent their time thrashing out details. What they settled on, after almost four months of discussion, had been tempered in argument by men who were, in aggregate, a microcosm of the diversity that made up America. The convention was, indeed, wiser than any of its members. It produced a written Constitution, the first in the world. It incorporated the best principles of just government forged in the English experience of the previous seven centuries as seen through the prism of the American perspective.

The delegates quickly concurred that the principle drawback of the Articles of Confederation was that Congress had been defined as a government of states. They were also of one accord that the corrective was a national government that related to citizens rather than states. In this way, a fundamental principle of government was recognized. A government of states is nothing more than an alliance, since each state remains sovereign and, if the alliance wants to control the actions of a state that has decided to go its own way, the only method available is war. A government of people, however, is something to which every citizen has an allegiance, the constitution of such a government is the supreme law of the land, and deviant political behavior by an individual or a group is action against the nation and can be dealt with in its courts. Politicians like to refer to their state of origin as "the sovereign state of …", particularly at national political conventions. But if the states of the Union had ever been sovereign, it was a sovereignty relinquished with the ratification of the Constitution. The Founding Fathers agreed that the states had rights. Indeed, they were so convinced of this fact that they felt it was superfluous to include them in the Constitution. They got added later when the Bill of Rights was ratified. But secession wasn't such a right — it ran counter to the very concept of a nation.

The convention delegates were also of one mind that the national government should consist of an executive, a legislative, and a judicial branch, in accordance with Locke's principle and English practice. They substituted an elected president for England's executive, which consisted of a hereditary king, soon to become purely symbolic, and a prime minister, who was the leader of the dominant party in Parliament. The idea of a Parliamentary prime minister didn't strike the Americans as an adequate separation of the executive and legislative functions.

The delegates decided that the legislature should be made up of two chambers, a lower House of Representatives and an upper house, or Senate, because that's what they were used to in Parliament and their own state governments. However, a difficulty then arose. The large states maintained that, to be representative of the people, both houses should be constituted so that each member was elected by residents of a district of approximately the same population as every other district, initially set at 40,000 with each slave counting as three fifths of a person. The small states were willing to abandon some of the uniform treatment they had been accorded under the Articles. But they were adamant that some recognition be given to their interests as states.

Through June and the first half of July the controversy ran on, until the delegates began to doubt that agreement would ever be reached. Ultimately, the large states compromised: the House would embody proportional representation of the people while the Senate would allow each state an equal vote. This compromise was essential at the time if a Constitution were to be accepted. Yet as it turned out, the problem it addressed has never been relevant. The US has never split on an issue that pitted the large and small states against each other. As James Madison predicted, intranational conflicts have been between regions, such as the North and South.

The next difficulty surfaced near the end of August. It was less clear cut and more portentous. New England insisted that Congress be allowed to enact a navigation act by a majority vote. Navigation act was a term of the time for legislation having to do with what goods could be shipped where in what bottoms.

The right navigation act might give US merchants, who were based in New England, an edge in their competition with their English counterparts. Not so incidentally, it might also put the South at the mercy of the New England merchants when it came to shipping the staples, such as rice, tobacco and cotton, on which the Southern economy depended. As a consequence, the South in general, and the Carolinas and Georgia in particular, wanted a two-thirds majority to pass a navigation act.

At the same time, Virginia and Pennsylvania, maintaining that continued importation of slaves was only adding to an already formidable problem, proposed that the wartime proscription on such importation be reconstituted. This South Carolina and Georgia also resisted.

Virginia's concern here was less than disinterested. It's tobacco lands were becoming depleted. As a consequence, it's revenues from the sale of tobacco were going down. But it had a surplus of slaves, the sale of which helped offset the decline in its tobacco revenues. Cutting off other sources for slaves could only enhance the price that Virginia's slaves would bring.

The compromise was that slave importation would continue and a navigation act could be passed by a majority. Congress was granted the right to outlaw slave importation after 1807. Such importation was forbidden as soon as possible, in 1808.

On September 17, 1787, the convention delegates endorsed the Constitution. It now remained for the states to ratify. Nine had to do so to bring the Constitution into force. Delaware was first (December 7), Pennsylvania second (December 12). New Jersey (December 18), Georgia (January 2, 1788), and Connecticut (January 9) followed. On February 6, Massachusetts ratified. Maryland was next (April 26). Then came South Carolina (May 12). And finally, New Hampshire (June 21).

Technically, the Constitution was now in place. But 40 percent of the colonists weren't yet covered by it. Still to ratify were both

New York and Virginia, states without the support of which the Union would be inoperable. On June 25, Virginia ratified, after Madison agreed that, when the new government convened, he would work on having a bill of rights enacted as a Constitutional amendment. New York ratified on July 26 after New York city and several adjoining counties threatened to secede from New York state and join the Union as a separate state. Only North Carolina and Rhode Island held back. Eventually they also ratified, North Carolina on November 21, 1789 and Rhode Island on May 29, 1790.

The campaign for ratification of the Constitution was carried out in publications and speeches. One set of such publications, *The Federalist Papers,* written under the pen name of Publius, was at one and the same time an authoritative documentation of the intentions of the Founding Fathers and a classic of political theory, since the authors were really Hamilton, Madison, and John Jay, the Confederation's foreign secretary.

One question with respect to the Constitution remained: Who decides what the Constitution says? The answer is judicial supremacy — that is, the Constitution is what the Supreme Court says it is. The Constitution says nothing about judicial supremacy. The most it commits itself to is that it and the treaties made under it are "the supreme law of the land". The forefather of US law is English common law, which is essentially judge-made law. Thus, the tendency toward judicial supremacy existed in common law. As we've already seen, Coke was logical enough to enunciate the principle, although it was never accepted in England. Hamilton argued for it in *The Federalist Papers.* But it took John Marshall, appointed Chief Justice of the Supreme Court by John Adams, to exercise the principle in the case of Marbury versus Madison, thus establishing the right of the Supreme Court to declare laws unconstitutional.

The Constitution contained one monumental flaw. It recognized slavery, which was in conflict with the principles stated in the Declaration of Independence. At the time, the choice was between a constitution that recognized slavery or no constitution at all. But the fact that it was inevitable that the Constitution recognize slavery didn't remove the eventual travail that this situation would cause.

At the time of the ratification of the Constitution, slavery was a fact of life in all of the colonies. Shortly thereafter, the Northern states began to abolish slavery. In Massachusetts, New Hampshire, and Vermont, freedom was unqualifiedly granted. But in the other Northern states, only those slaves born after a specified future date were to be freed and, then, only after having attained maturity. When the Civil War began, there were still slaves north of the Mason-Dixon line.

CHAPTER THIRTEEN

The French Revolution

There's no evidence that, when told that the people had no bread, Marie-Antoinette, queen of France at the time of the French Revolution, said, "Let them eat cake." Given her personality and the unbelievably venomous campaign of slander conducted against her, it's unlikely that she did. She was born and brought up a Habsburg princess and was spoiled, stubborn and simpleminded. She was also a dutiful, if inattentive, mother and a faithful, supporting wife. It was not infrequently said that she was more a king than her husband.

Nevertheless, bread was a significant factor in the Revolution. In a figurative sense, bread stood for the necessities of life. But it also had a literal meaning. A four-pound loaf was the staple of three quarters of all French men and women, it took two of these loaves each day to feed a family of four, and it had come to be expected that purchase of this bread should consume no more than half of a person's income. Doubling of bread prices was seen as both a disaster and an unconscionable state of affairs.

This was the case because holdovers from feudalism were still prominent in France. The idea of a just price remained prevalent. In the riots that occurred during the Revolution, shops weren't looted. Instead, the mobs forced the retailers to trade at what was considered to be the just price. Before the Revolution, the people looked to their King-Father to see that the necessities of life were available in sufficient quantities at the just price. After the Revolution, they transferred this expectation to the government that replaced the king. Inadequate supplies and unjust prices could be the result of only one thing: enemies of the people — speculators, greedy processors and retailers, and corrupt government officials — were creating crises from which they could reap extortionate returns at the expense of the people. As a consequence, shortages not only led to privation, they also encouraged the idea that the nation harbored within it a selfish, unpatriotic nest of conspirators that needed to be excised.

Like the English and American Revolutions, the French Revolution had an ideological base. But unlike its predecessors, which looked to Locke for their philosophical direction, the French Revolution was inspired by the writings of Jean-Jacques Rousseau. Both Locke and Rousseau were concerned with the "social contract" under which people lived together.

The idea of a social contract was one that had been developing for the last century or so. It had to do with the question that wouldn't go away: What justifies the right of those in authority to rule? Since the ascendancy of Christianity in the Western world, the answer had been the divine right of kings: the king ruled absolutely because he had been granted this right by God. In the 17th century, this concept began to lose currency. People started casting about for a substitute rationale, specifically, one that would justify the right to govern on a human, rather than a divine, basis.

The first to make a significant contribution in this area was Thomas Hobbes, whose treatise, *The Leviathan,* was published in 1651. Hobbes' position was that, in a state of nature, man's lot was unenviable. He described this state as one of "No arts, no letters, no society, and, which is worst of all, continual fear and danger of violent death, and the life of man solitary, poor, nasty, brutish, and short." Hobbes maintained that, to avoid this human tragedy and enjoy the benefits of civilization, man entered into a social compact in which the monarch (the leviathan) was given the absolute power to rule and, thus, save man from his own worst inclinations.

Locke wasn't so concerned with man's state of nature as such. But he agreed that, when left to his own devices, man tended to be stubborn, selfish and quarrelsome, and that man's best chance for the good life was to put himself under the impartial control of a political organization. For Locke, the function of government was to prevent depredations by man against man.

In contrast, Rousseau's position was that the nature of man was good. As a consequence, if citizens weren't as well off as they should be, the fault lay with distortions in the social contract that they had with their government. Once the government was reformed so that the will of the people, which Rousseau capitalized as the General Will, could be expressed, the evils of society would disappear. Such a line of thought led irrefutably to the conclusion that, as long as evils persisted, there must be enemies of the people in the government. Once more, the idea of a conspiracy was reinforced.

In addition, the concept of man as innately virtuous injected into the argument an unavoidable dichotomy. It was we virtuous ones against those corrupt, conspiring others. And neutrality wasn't a possibility. If you weren't with us, you were against us. Throughout the Revolution, its leaders were mesmerized by the goal of having only men of unimpeachable integrity in the government. Since this goal was unattainable, these leaders were continually faced with what to them were enemies of the Revolution in positions of power. These foes had to be destroyed if the Revolution were ever to be brought to a successful conclusion.

The hallmark of a government is its ability to impose its will on its people, whether that will be that of a tyrant or laws duly passed by a representative legislature and in conformance with the country's constitution. By definition, an insurrection is a breakdown in this central monopoly on force. But when the fighting is over, normalization requires that this central authority be reestablished. In the French Revolution, this never happened. As a result of the unrealistic expectation that, under normal circumstances, society would be beneficial for all, the existence of conspiracies preventing this desirable situation became self-evident. As a consequence, the Revolution exhibited a never-ending ability to create a new insurrectionary movement as soon as the previous one had either taken over the reins of government or been destroyed.

Almost ceaseless warfare had placed heavy demands on the French economy. When the latest round of conflict ended with the Treaty of Paris in 1783, the French treasury was in a precarious, but not impossible, state. However, peacetime extravagance at the French court coupled with corrupt tax collection created the situation where, in December 1785, it became impossible for the French government to secure new financing. Anticipation of future taxes had been used up by outstanding loans. If the government were to continue its present practices, it had to establish new taxes,

Revolutionary France

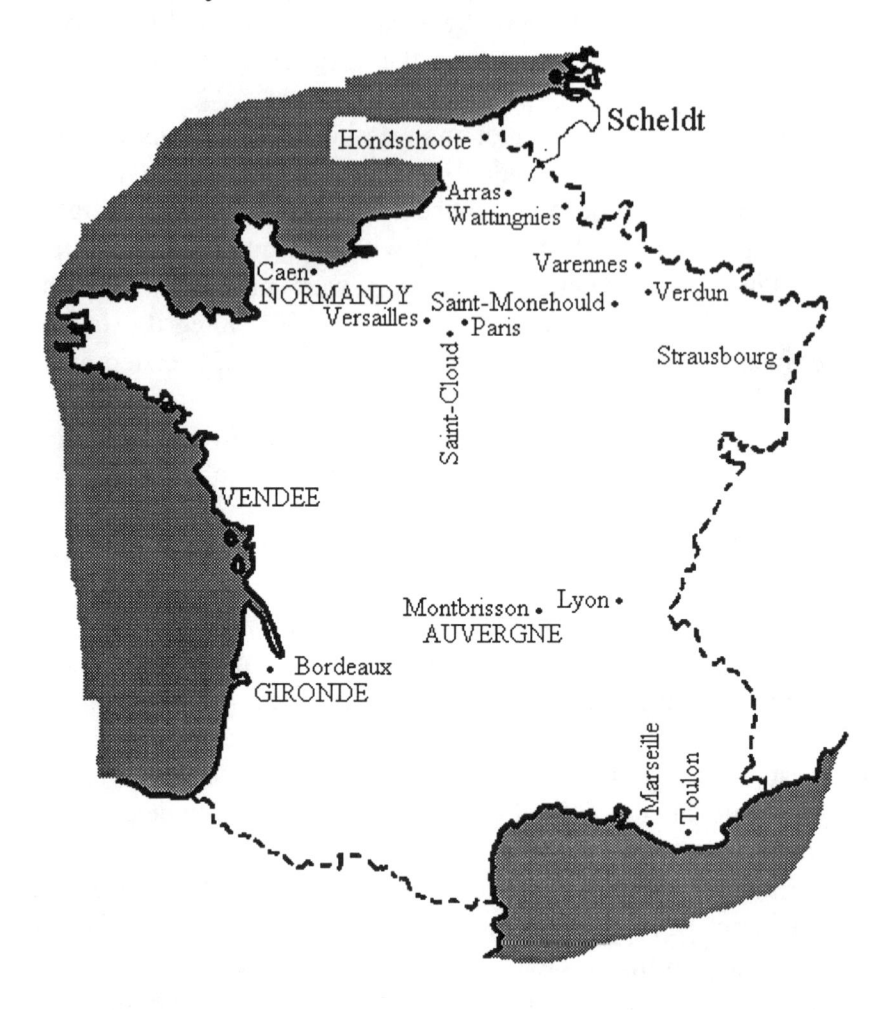

not so much for their revenue value in and of itself as for their ability to serve as collateral.

Under Louis XV, new taxes would have been imposed by the royal command: "Le roi le veult" (The king so wishes it). This was a command that had to be obeyed. But in 1785, it wasn't Louis XV sitting on the throne; it was his grandson and successor, Louis XVI. And Louis XVI didn't want to command; he wanted to be loved. So he cast about for some way to get his people to approve new taxes. First he tried an Assembly of the Notables, a hand-picked gathering of the elite. Their opinion, surprisingly liberal for such a group, was that only the States General could approve taxation. Louis then tried to force through taxation. But the Parlement of Paris, basically a court of law in which the king's decrees had to be registered to become law, agreed with the Notables that only the States General could authorize taxation. The battle was protracted, but on August 8, 1788, Louis capitulated and announced that the States General, which hadn't met for 175 years, would convene on May 1, 1789 at the royal court, Versailles.

Before the end of the month, the current controller-general (finance minister) resigned, and Louis reappointed a previous controller-general, Jacques Necker. Necker was popular with the people, for not only did he see to revenues, he also cut expenses at the court and reduced corruption in the collection of taxes.

The next question was how the States General should be constituted. The Third Estate (the commoners) maintained that, if it were to be fairly represented, its number of members should be twice the number of each of the other two estates and that the three estates should assemble as one body and vote on issues by the head rather than each estate having just one vote. On December 27, 1788, a government edict decreed that the Third Estate would have double representation. But the practice of meeting and voting by estate was to be retained.

On the opening day of the States General (May 5, 1789), the three estates met at the Salle des Menus Plaisirs in Versailles to be addressed by the king. The fifth deputy of the Third Estate for Arras was Maximilien Robespierre, a lawyer. He had been a judge but had resigned because he couldn't bring himself to pronounce a sentence of death. The last deputy from Paris was Emmanuel Joseph Sieyes, an abbe.

After the opening ceremonies, the Third Estate continued to meet in the Salle des Menus Plaisirs while the other two estates met individually elsewhere. As a consequence, the members of the Third Estate could have sat wherever they wanted. But they pointedly left the benches of the other two estates empty in anticipation of the day when all three estates would deliberate in common.

On June 10, at the initiation of Sieyes, the Third Estate began the daily roll call in the Salle des Menus Plaisirs as if all three estates were meeting together. On June 13, three of the clergy responded to the call. On the 17th, those meeting in the Salle des Menus Plaisirs decided to call themselves the National Assembly. In response, Louis resolved to once more address the united States General to command the estates to resume their sessions in separate chambers. As a consequence, the Salle des Menus Plaisirs was closed so carpenters could prepare the room for the king's address. In this way, the National Assembly found itself locked out of its meeting place, in heavy rain, no less.

It was then that Dr. Joseph Ignace Guillotin, also a deputy for the Third Estate, remembered a tennis court (in those days, tennis was exclusively an indoor thing) owned by a friend of his in the Rue de Vieux Versailles. Dr. Guillotin is an interesting character. An ex-Jesuit, he published a tract that was instrumental in the Third Estate's battle for double representation. In December 1789, he presented, to the National Assembly, the argument that, since all French citizens were equal, beheading, a relatively humane form of execution previously reserved for the nobility, should be extended to all. This argument included a rather detailed description of a machine that could be used to carry out these executions. At the time, Guillotin's proposal wasn't adopted. It was, in fact, met with laughter. Consequently, Guillotin dropped the matter. But Dr. Antoine Louis, the perpetual secretary of the Academy of Surgeons, ultimately produced a memorandum to the effect that the machine would, in fact, produce instantaneous death. In one week in April 1792, Tobias Schmidt, a piano maker by trade, created a prototype, which claimed its first victim on April 25. Guillotin resented the fact that the machine that he had described was named after him.

It was to this tennis court, suggested by Guillotin, that the National Assembly repaired, where they affirmed that, wherever they met, they were the National Assembly. They continued to meet at the tennis court, where their numbers now included 47 nobles and over 150 clergy. One of the king's brothers rented the tennis court to break up the meetings, but the Assembly met instead at the Church of Saint-Louis, where it decided to convene in the Salle des Menus Plaisirs immediately after the king's address.

On June 23, when Louis had completed his presentation and dismissed the States General, he and his court left the hall. Carpenters then entered to dismantle the dais and platforms built for the event only to discover the National Assembly remaining in its seats. The master of ceremonies for the address repeated to the Assembly the king's command to leave. At this point, one of the members of the Assembly, Honore-Gabriel Mirabeau, claimed he replied, "Go tell those who have sent you that we are here at the will of the people and that we will not be dispersed except at the point of bayonets." When informed of the situation, Louis uttered the less dramatic but perhaps more portentous words, "Oh well, let them stay."

By now the National Assembly had taken the position that it represented the nation and that, if anyone claimed authority on the basis of belonging to one of the first two estates, they must be something other than citizens, concerned with vested interests, selfish, unpatriotic, parasitic, and heedless of the common people. On June 27, at Necker's urging, Louis wrote to the deputies of the first two estates "engaging" them to unite with the Third Estate "to achieve my paternal goals", thus in effect, dissolving the States General and recognizing the National Assembly.

The Assembly decided that, before any new taxes were authorized, a far-reaching governmental reform should be made. It was to this task that the Assembly addressed itself.

Sometimes, conspiracy theories are right. There was a royal plan to get rid of Necker and the National Assembly. Thousands of troops were being concentrated in and around Paris. More than a third of them spoke no French. On Saturday, July 11, at 3 pm, the king told Necker to leave France. The king and his advisers thought a Sunday would be the optimum time for Necker's exile to become public, since the National Assembly didn't meet on Sundays and, thus, wouldn't be able to take immediate action. However, for the unofficial center of the opposition, the Palais-Royal, it was ideal. Once the gardens of Cardinal Richelieu, the Palais-Royal had been converted by the Duc de Chartres into an

The Severed Head of the Governor of the Bastille, *stuck on a pitchfork. From a sketch in the Bibliotheque National de France in Paris.*

arcade of cafes, theaters and shops. It was also renowned for its prostitutes.

The Palais-Royal was packed. By about 3 pm, a crowd of about 6000 had congregated around Camille Desmoulins, who was standing on a table in front of a cafe and urging the crowd to resist the treachery that had resulted in the dismissal of Necker. A mob formed, units of the gardes francaises (the Paris militia) joined the mob, and by 1 am of the 13th, royal troops had abandoned the center of Paris. Gunsmiths and armorers were forced to deliver muskets, sabers, pistols, and shoulder belts to the rebels. On the morning of the 14th, a force, estimated at about 80,000, moved on the Invalides, where armament was stored. It took over, more than 30,000 muskets were passed out, and cannon was requisitioned. The last remaining necessity was powder. This was locked away in the Bastille.

At the Bastille, a battle occurred. The fortress was taken around 5 pm. Eighty-three members of the citizen's army died in the fight. In revenge, the governor of the fortress was executed. His was the first head to be cut off and raised on a pike.

On the 15th, the king, accompanied only by his two brothers, appeared before the National Assembly, confirmed the withdrawal of his troops, and denied any plot against the Assembly. On the 16th, Louis invited Necker to return. On the evening of the same day, the king's younger brother and his followers became the first of the emigres to cross French borders for two purposes, their safety and to enlist foreign powers in the battle against the Revolution.

Newspapers that relied on abusive language to gain readership began publication in the summer of 1789. One was *L'Ami du People,* put out by Jean-Paul Marat, which characterized politicians of whom it disapproved as "blood-sucking" and worthy only of quick excision from the body politic.

The police force that the rebels developed was the National Guard. It was headed by Lafayette, who served under Washington during the American Revolution, and incorporated large parts of the gardes francaises. One of the captains of the Guard was George Danton, a lawyer by training. For the Guard's badge, Lafayette created the tricolor cockade by adding the white of the Bourbons to the red and blue of Paris.

On October 4, a market woman, in haranguing a crowd, put the blame on the queen for their lack of bread and importuned them to march on Versailles to seek redress. On the 5th, the tocsin was rung from the Church of Sainte-Marguerite, and led by a woman beating a drum, a mass of women chanting the title of the recent pamphlet, *When Will We Have Bread?*, marched toward the Hotel de Ville (City Hall). As they moved, they were joined by other women carrying cudgels, sticks and knives. By the time they reached the Hotel de Ville, the crowd numbered about six or seven thousand. Seven hundred muskets and two cannon were confiscated, and the crowd threatened to pillage the building and burn its papers. They were diverted from this action by a captain of the National Guard, who agreed to lead a march on Versailles. Shortly thereafter, the crowd set out in a rain storm.

Paris was in turmoil. It wasn't until two hours later (about 11 am) that Lafayette was able to reach the Hotel de Ville. The women had already left, and the National Guard had decided to make their own march to Versailles. After arguing vainly against the idea for hours, Lafayette finally agreed to lead the march with the idea that, if he were present, he might be able to keep things under control.

At the end of a six hour march, the women arrived at Versailles. The National Guard got there around midnight. Both had come to the conclusion that the king should move his residence to Paris. At about 5:30 the next morning, an armed crowd entered the palace. The queen managed to avoid them by abandoning her apartment and rushing to the king's quarters. The National Guard then rescued the royal family, after which Louis agreed to move to Paris.

Three hours later, an assemblage, which Lafayette estimated numbered 60,000, left Versailles. In the van and bringing up the rear were the National Guard. Following the leading soldiers were the royal carriage accompanied by Lafayette, the members of Necker's ministry, the National Assembly, and what remained of the court. Behind them were wagons carrying flour from the palace bins. Women rode astride cannons, carried bread loaves at the ends of their pikes, and sang that they were bringing "the baker, the baker's wife, and the baker's lad to Paris." After numerous ceremonies to greet the king, the royal family finally reached their new home, the Tuileries, at 8 pm. The National Assembly took up residence in the Manege, a former royal riding school next to the Tuileries.

An antimonarchist faction began to develop in the National Assembly. Since they sat on the left of the hall, they were referred to as being "of the left", the first use of such terminology. Following the move of the National Assembly to Paris, these antimonarchists rented the refectory of the Jacobin monastery, in the Rue Saint-Honore, in which to hold their meetings. Consequently, they were called Jacobins. The Jacobins encouraged the public to join their group. By August 1790, the Paris chapter of the Jacobins had 1200 members. A year later, they had over 400 affiliates in the provinces.

In 1791, the royal family decided to spend the Holy Week in Saint-Cloud, a retreat just outside of Paris where the king had a palace. They were prevented from doing so by an angry crowd, motivated by hunger and anticlericalism, at the palace gates. Lafayette tried to separate the crowd so that the royal carriage could move out, but his men defied him and refused to help. For an hour and three quarters the king and queen were confined in their immobile coach and subjected to the crowd's invective. Finally, they resigned themselves to returning to the palace. It was this event that convinced Louis that he must leave France.

At 2 am on June 21, a carriage carrying "Baronne Korff" (actually the royal governess) left Paris. With her were her governess and valet (actually the queen and king), her children (actually the royal children), and a nurse (actually the king's sister). They were recognized in Sainte-Menehould and were forced to stop in Varennes, where they had arrived at 11 pm. They were just 30 miles from the border.

The aborted escape attempt enraged the Paris crowds. It also damaged Lafayette's credibility, since he was responsible for the king's care. But its most corrosive impact was the destruction, among the more moderate members of the National Assembly, of confidence in the viability of a constitutional monarchy. Emigration increased.

In September 1971, the National Assembly produced a constitution for France. On the next to last day of the existence of the National Assembly, a law (to ban the political clubs, such as the Jacobins, that had become such powerful factors on the political scene) was proposed. The rationale for the law was that, with the adoption of the constitution, the Revolution was over and the political clubs, therefore, were now superfluous. Robespierre spoke against the bill. During his term in the National Assembly, he had risen to a position of influence because of his unwavering insistence that only men of unimpeachable integrity be allowed to govern.

Robespierre's argument was that the proposed law went counter to principles endorsed in the constitution: the right to assemble peacefully and speak freely on public matters. He then attacked the idea that the Revolution was over. To believe this, Robespierre proposed, was to assume that the constitution had been put in place and wasn't going to be dislodged. Yet he saw opponents everywhere "fighting less for the Revolution than for their own domination under the name of the monarch."

The law passed but was never enforced. On the next day, September 30, the National Assembly dissolved itself. When Robespierre appeared outside the Manege, he was greeted with acclaim. He then started a newspaper, *La Defenseur de la Constitution,* to serve as the vehicle for his public communications, for the delegates of the National Assembly had disqualified themselves from membership in the Legislative Assembly set up by the constitution.

In October, Lafayette ran for mayor of Paris and was trounced. He then resigned from his post in the National Guard and moved to his estates in the Auvergne.

The Legislative Assembly replaced the National Assembly in the Manege. There arose, in the Legislative Assembly, a group known as the Girondins, because three of the leaders of the group came from the Gironde, an area in southwest France. They were committed to passing legislation in the Assembly that the king would veto, thus revealing himself as an enemy of the nation.

In August 1791, Leopold of Austria, Marie-Antoinette's brother, and the Prussian king, Frederick William, issued a threatening declaration pressing for restoration of the French king. In the byzantine reasoning of the then current diplomacy, the purpose of this declaration was to encourage the French to give constitutional monarchy a chance. But to the literal minds of the Assembly members, it was an insult to the sovereignty of the people. The response of Louis' foreign minister to this declaration was weak, which enraged the Assembly. It decided to impeach the minister.

For about a week, Louis struggled with the situation. Then he decided to try and disarm his opponents by appointing a Girondin ministry. Austria saw this switch in ministers as a surrender to the mob. By the second week of April 1792, 50,000 Austrian troops had been massed on the Belgian border. At the time, Belgium was part of the Netherlands, which in turn, was part of the Austrian empire. In the Assembly, war was declared. Lafayette was appointed commander of one of the three theaters of war.

Five days after the declaration of war, a dinner was held for the Strasbourg garrison. At the dinner, Rouget de Lisle, a young army engineer who had made a minor reputation in Paris as a composer, was importuned to write a song for the departing armies. On April 16, he produced *La Marseillaise,* originally titled *Chant de Guerre de l'Armee du Rhin (War Song of the Rhine Army).*

The war started out badly for France, and the conflict between Louis and the Girondins intensified. Finally, Louis dismissed the Girondins ministry. On June 20, a demonstration was organized by the leaders of the political clubs. The stated purpose of the demonstration was to plant a liberty tree on the grounds of the Tuileries to protest the gs' dismissal. After planting the tree, the people crowded around the palace grounds. The Val-de-Grace regiment, which had accompanied the demonstrators, brought up cannon; the press against the palace gates was such that, to avoid their collapse, they were opened; and the crowd entered the palace and confronted the king. All afternoon, Louis responded with dignity to the crowd's jeers and refused to budge from his position. Finally, at 6 pm, the mayor of Paris appeared. He said that he had just been made aware of the king's circumstances. "That is astonishing," replied Louis, "Since this has been continuing for some hours." After lengthy argument, the mayor convinced the crowd that it should leave, and at 8, the king was released. After this indignity to the king, Assembly deputies, anxious for their safety, began to leave Paris.

On June 28, Lafayette appeared before the Assembly and asked that the law against political clubs be enforced. His request was turned down.

Paris was becoming an armed camp. National Guards from the countryside poured in. On July 30, 500 Guards from Marseille arrived singing de Lisle's anthem, which is how it got its name.

By now, the Prussians had entered the war against France, and their commander issued a manifesto written by an emigre. It asked the French people to rebel against the "odious schemes of their oppressors" and threatened with the "rigors of war" any who resisted.

This manifesto called out an extreme response. An "Insurrectionary Commune" was formed. It replaced the council at the Hotel de Ville and took over command of the National Guard. This Commune included Robespierre, Marat and Danton. By now, the Assembly was a quarter of its original size.

On August 10, the revolution against the king reached its culmination. Insurrectionary forces moved against the government, 600 royal troopers were killed in what was more a massacre than a battle, and Louis and his family were taken prisoner.

Lafayette's commission was revoked. Disillusioned with the Revolution, he crossed the line of battle, surrendered to the Austrians, and spent the next seven years in prison.

The Commune had demanded and gotten from the Assembly the power to question and imprison suspects without due process, and control of Paris shifted from the Assembly to the Commune. During the two weeks following August 17, over 1000 people were incarcerated. On August 28, Danton instituted "domiciliary visits". These came late at night, when everyone was home. A number of men would bang on the door of the chosen house. When the door was opened, they would enter brandishing sabers, pikes and guns. A search would then be conducted for suspects and compromising papers.

Verdun was attacked by the Prussians. If it fell, the road to Paris was open. Volunteers left for the front. With the departure of these fighting men, concern began to surface that there was now no local force to deter the counterrevolutionaries, just imprisoned, from making common cause with the criminals whose accommodations they shared, breaking out, and falling on the populace.

On September 2, rumor of the fall of Verdun reached Paris. In response, a mob massacred the prisoners. They were mostly hacked to death with knives, axes, hatchets and sabers. Those who got off easiest were the ones shot. What began as an execution of political prisoners soon spread to the slaughter of all inmates: criminals, beggars, and persons, including children, held on request by their families. Authorities at some prisons participated in the massacre. The others turned their heads. More than 1400 people were killed. The Commune took no action against the killers. The message was clear. In the next two weeks, a number of executions occurred in the provinces.

A National Convention was elected to create a new constitution. Robespierre, Sieyes, Marat and Danton were members of the Convention, which opened on September 20. Among its first acts was to try Louis. The charge against him was that, while he expressed support for the Revolution, his actions demonstrated that he was really a counter-revolutionary. With this there was little quarrel. He was convicted and, on January 21, 1793, executed.

In addition to being at war with Austria and Prussia, France got into a dispute with England over navigation on the river Scheldt. The river was closed to commercial traffic by international agreements, and France wanted it opened. On February 1, the Convention declared war on England.

For administrative purposes, the revolutionists had divided France into units called departments. On March 10, a counterrevolutionary uprising began in the department of the Vendee. Government troops were able to subdue the large towns but were ineffectual in the countryside, where ambush was an ever-present possibility and combatants were indistinguishable from villagers. In both the degree to which the enemy was denounced as subhuman and the brutality to which it was subjected, the Vendee became the model for other counter-revolutionary uprisings.

The Convention now set about to consolidate power. On March 6, it sent 80 of its members, called (beginning in April) representatives on mission, to the departments, to guarantee obedience to the Convention's decrees. They were royal intendants brought up to date, traveling representatives of the central government. Richelieu had introduced royal intendants to impose royal government on the provinces.

On March 11, a Revolutionary Tribunal was set up in Paris to try suspects accused of counter-revolutionary acts. On April 6, the nine member Committee of Public Safety was established to coordinate the various committees of the Convention. Robespierre joined the committee in July. The committee became the executive arm of the Revolutionary government.

The Revolutionary government had been financing itself through the sale of confiscated church properties. As this source of revenue dried up, the government printed more and more assignats, paper money, which resulted in inflation, although the term, inflation, hadn't yet been coined. The rising prices presented a danger to the government. As a solution to the problem, a form of egalitarianism began to take shape. On December 2, Robespierre identified a "right of subsistence", to which property rights were subordinate. Only the surplus over that needed to support the people could be used for commercial purposes. Those who made money by exploiting the people were criminals.

The Jacobins weren't ready to adopt this egalitarianism. As a result, they were upstaged by a group known as the *enrages*. To the *enrages*, it was time to take action against exploiters. Monopolists and speculators should be executed. If the government wouldn't do the job, then the people should strike down these "blood-suckers". The seat of power of the *enrages* was the Commune. One of the most vituperous of the *enrages* was Jacques Rene Hebert, editor of the newspaper *Le Pere Duchesne*.

The *enrages* program appealed to the sans-culottes. At its height, the sans-culottes "movement" represented, at most, two or three thousand men. Its leaders were mostly lawyers and revolutionary nobles, rather than laborers. The name, sans-culottes, came from the fact that these leaders, like the working people whom they claimed to represent, wore trousers rather than the tight breeches and stockings espoused by the "aristocracy". The breeches were the culottes. Thus, sans-culottes was "without breeches". Incidentally, Robespierre wore breeches and stockings to the day he died.

The sans-culottes accused the Girondins of causing the current national difficulties.

By April, the Jacobins had accepted egalitarianism as a Revolutionary goal. On May 2, the Convention decided to regulate grain trade, which the Girondins opposed. The Revolution was moving full circle, back to the paternalism that existed under the monarchy.

On May 10, the Convention moved from the Manege to the Tuileries. At a meeting of the Jacobins on the 26th, Robespierre encouraged "the people to place themselves in insurrection against the corrupt deputies." On June 2, an armed mob, estimated at 80,000, surrounded the Tuileries, where the Convention was meeting. With sans-culottes, armed with pikes and muskets, stationed in the aisles, the Convention voted to expel the Girondins, after which the Girondins were put under house arrest. Girondin supporters left Paris determined to incite the provinces against the capital.

There was considerable reaction to this Jacobin extremism. Revolts occurred in Bordeaux, Marseille, Toulon, Montbrison and Lyon. On June 10, a Girondin group appeared in Caen in the department of the Calvados. On July 7, they paraded on the Grande Cour of Caen to recruit volunteers. A 25 year old woman, Charlotte Corday, was a spectator. She detested the Jacobins, whom she believed had betrayed the Revolution. She was convinced that Marat was the root of the problem, and that, if he could be eliminated, the Revolution would be saved. She decided that destroying Marat was her responsibility.

On July 9, Corday left for Paris. On the morning of July 13, she bought a kitchen knife with a five inch blade, which she hid in her dress. That evening at 7 pm, she was outside Marat's house. Marat was suffering from a disorder that turned his skin into a

A Sans-Cullote. *From an illustration by Hablot L. Browne for* A Tale of Two Cities *by Charles Dickens. The book was republished in 1949 by the Oxford University Press. By permission of Oxford University Press.*

mass of flakes and sores. He alleviated his discomfort with cool baths laced with kaolin solution. He would sit in his shoe-shaped tub with a wet cloth tied around his head and write on a box set on end by his side.

Corday had made her way to the top of Marat's stairs when she was confronted by Simonne Evrard, Marat's fiancee. Corday raised her voice so Marat could hear her inform Evrard that she wanted to tell him about some traitors in Normandy. "Let her in," called Marat. Corday sat down in a chair beside the bath. When Evrard left to get some more kaolin solution, Corday stabbed Marat once in the chest. It killed him.

At Corday's trial, the Jacobins tried to connect her to the Girondins. She insisted that she had acted alone. When told that she must have had instruction, since any blow to the chest other than the one she had struck wouldn't have been fatal, her response was that she was lucky. She was, of course, convicted and executed.

On July 26, the Convention approved the death penalty for hoarders of "goods of the first necessity" — bread, salt, wine, butter, meat, vegetables, soap, sugar, hemp, wool, oil and vinegar. On August 9, silos were established throughout the country to store grain during years of good harvest for use in years of poor.

Also in the summer of 1793, a new constitution was adopted. On August 11, a day after the celebration of the adoption, the Convention, in defiance of the constitution, refused to dissolve itself and remained in power.

On August 23, a national conscript army was created. All bachelors and childless widowers between 18 and 25 were called.

On September 5, the news reached Paris that Toulon had opened its harbor to the English fleet. On the same day, the Convention authorized the armee revolutionnaire, basically sans-culottes, to go into the countryside and collect food for Paris. On September 11, a price ceiling was put on grain. On the 29th, the ceiling was extended to 40 grocery and household items.

On September 17, the Convention passed the Law of Suspects, which put into effect what came to be known as the Terror. The law empowered the Committee of Public Safety to arrest and punish people espousing broadly defined counter-revolutionary plans. Arrest was so arbitrary under the Law of Suspects that, by the beginning of December, there were 7000 people in prison.

In mid-autumn, the Revolutionary government introduced a program of total mobilization. Factories were converted to produce cannon, muskets, ball and shot. Church bells from all parts of France were melted down to feed this production. By the spring of 1794, 3000 laborers were fabricating 700 guns a day, and 6000 mills were producing powder.

As this war effort grew, the tide began to turn. On August 25, Marseille was retaken. The English were stopped at Hondschoote on September 8. On October 9, Lyon was recaptured. And the Austrians were repulsed at Wattingnies on October 16.

At first, the Jacobins had some difficulty finding the right men. But once sufficiently enthusiastic leaders were appointed, terrible vengeance was taken on the Girondins. For example, in Lyons, 1905 people were executed, most by being tied together with rope and fired at by cannon. Those who survived were stabbed or bayoneted.

In October 1793, the Girondin leaders were brought to trial on the charge that they had done their best to support the king. This was hard to prove, since it wasn't true. When Antoine Quentin Forquier-Tinville, the public prosecutor and a relative of Camille Desmoulins (last seen in this narrative when he was haranguing the crowds in the Palais-Royal at the time of Necker's dismissal), found that the defense was beginning to make an impression on the jury, he asked the jury, as was his right, if they "had heard enough to be illuminated" and, thus, were able to deliver a verdict. The answer to this question was invariably yes. The Girondins were found guilty. On October 31, they went to the guillotine. The executioner, Charles Henri Sanson, now practiced, decapitated the 22 prisoners in 36 minutes. Charles was the seventh generation of Sanson's to serve as the executioner of Paris.

In August, Toulon was brought under siege. Only two days into the siege, the artillery commander was wounded. His place was taken by Captain Napoleon Bonaparte. Napoleon played an important part in the siege and was promoted to acting Lieutenant Colonel. He early recognized the strategic role that Fort Eguillette, which dominated the Toulon harbor, played in the ability to hold

Toulon. But it was four months before he could acquire sufficient forces to carry out his plans. The attack of the fort began on December 14. By December 18, the English recognized that the fort was going to fall and that, as a consequence, their ships were going to become targets for cannon in the fort. The fleet left Toulon, the city was retaken, and Napoleon became a Brigadier General.

On March 4, Hebert, leader of the *enrages*, decided that it was time to make his move. He covered with a cloth the bust of Liberty at the Cordeliers, a political club with minimal dues to attract working class members who could give credibility to its claim to represent the people. This veiling was the ritual call to insurrection. But the government had done its job in consolidating power. The rising failed due to lack of both informal and Commune support. Hebert and 19 of his supporters were arrested and, on March 24, went to the guillotine. The Jacobins had eliminated the rival *enrages*. There remained one other dissident group, the *Indulgents*, led by Danton and Desmoulins.

The *Indulgents* felt that, now that France's military position had improved, it was time to relax the Terror. Unfortunately, some of the *Indulgents*, assigned to liquidate the colonial trading monopoly, the Company of the Indies, were stripping its assets for their own gain, and Robespierre had proof of this theft. Even though Danton and Desmoulins weren't involved, they refused to give up their friends. As a consequence, they were all arrested together and brought to trial on April 2. Danton, with his bull head and thundering voice, was a potent manipulator of the public. As the trial progressed, the people became so supportive of Danton that Louis Antoine Saint-Just, a protege of Robespierre, testified that the defendants were plotting revolt and that Desmoulins' wife was part of a cabal planning to kill members of the Committee of Public Safety. As ridiculous as it was, this testimony gave Fouquier the opportunity to adopt his standard practice of "asking" the jury if they had been sufficiently "enlightened". They had. On April 5, Danton, Desmoulins, and the other *Indulgents* went to the guillotine.

Augustin Robespierre, Maximilien's brother and a fellow deputy in the Convention, had been impressed by Napoleon.

Under Augustin's sponsorship, Napoleon was appointed as the operational planner for the Army of Italy. Italy wasn't yet a nation. The states of which it was eventually to be made up were pawns in the war with Austria.

By mid-April 1794, the pacification of the Vendee was more or less complete. Guerrilla warfare continued. But the area was, as the French generals promised, a desert, its farmland burned, its herds slaughtered, its villages razed and depopulated. Those executed were estimated to have been just under a quarter million.

On June 10, the Law of Prairial was passed. The law was named after the month, in the revolutionary calendar adopted by the Convention, in which the law was enacted. It decreed that anyone "slandering patriotism", "seeking to inspire discouragement", "spreading false news", or "depraving morals, corrupting the public conscience and impairing the purity and energy of the revolutionary government" could be brought before the Revolutionary Tribunal. In such cases, this court was restricted to one of two actions: acquit or condemn to death. No witnesses could be called, and there was no counsel for the defense. The position was that the jury, good citizens all, would produce correct verdicts. As a consequence, the pace of executions increased. In just under six weeks, the rate went from 17 a day to 26.

Little by little, during the last weeks of July, an anti-Jacobin coalition began to form. Those whom the Jacobins had already denounced as criminals and those who thought it was only a matter of time before they were singled out made common cause. This group was called the Thermidorians, since their action against the Jacobins took place in the month of that name in the Convention's revolutionary calendar. On July 27, the Convention arrested the leading Jacobins. But the Commune refused to let any of its prisons be used to jail these men and began to organize an insurrection. However, of the 48 Paris *sections*, only 13 responded to the call. This was enough to liberate those arrested. But the Thermidorians were able to muster a counterforce from the other *sections*. The Thermidorians declared Robespierre and his associates hors de la loi (outlaws), which meant that they could be executed as soon as they were captured.

By 2 the next morning, the insurrectionary force has dispersed. The Thermidorians moved on the Hotel de Ville to retake the freed prisoners. As they approached, the dead body of Augustin Robespierre dropped from a window. Inside, they found other suicides. Maximilien Robespierre's jaw was smashed, apparently from a failed attempt to kill himself.

After daylight, 17 Jacobins were executed. When Robespierre's turn came, Sanson pushed him onto the plank of the guillotine, which smeared blood on his neatly maintained coat and nankeen breeches. To remove any obstacle to the blade's free fall, Sanson ripped away the paper bandage holding Robespierre's jaw together. His screams of pain ended quickly with his decapitation. On the next two days, 83 others followed the first 17 to their fate. Fouquier was tried. He pleaded that he had only done his job. In May 1795, he went to his death primarily concerned that he was leaving his wife and children destitute and shunned by society.

The end of the Terror didn't mean the end of the killing. The Counter-Terror was more informal but just as lethal. In the morning, Counter-Terrorists would congregate at an inn as if for a holiday and then set out to hunt down their chosen victims for the day. The Counter-Terror accounted for about as many deaths as the Terror (somewhere around 20,000).

The fall of the Jacobins left Napoleon vulnerable. He was, after all, a protege of Augustin Robespierre. Napoleon was arrested on August 9, 1794. However, after two weeks of investigation, he was cleared of suspicion. He then returned to his planning position for the Army of Italy.

Early in 1795, Napoleon was put in charge of an infantry brigade in the Vendee. He thought that, if he accepted this appointment, it would be the end of his career. Consequently, on arriving in Paris on the way to the Vendee, he feigned illness. He was then assigned to the Topographical Bureau of the Committee of Public Safety until he recovered.

In August, the Convention came up with a new constitution. It provided for a two-chamber legislature, the Council of the Elders and the Council of the Five Hundred, and a five person executive committee, called the Directory and chosen by the legislature from its members. To prevent any resurgence of Jacobins or royalists, the Convention decreed that two thirds of the first legislature must be made up of Convention members. A referendum approved the new constitution handily. But the royalists, who had, by now, accumulated considerable power in the Paris *sections* and the National Guard, objected to the two-thirds rule and initiated another insurrection. The Convention put one of its deputies, Paul Barras, in charge of the government forces. Barras had led the Thermidorian troops that had apprehended Robespierre and the other Jacobins at the Hotel de Ville.

Barras, who had observed Napoleon at work at Toulon, asked for Napoleon to be appointed as second in command. Once named, Napoleon quickly took over and dispersed the insurgents by firing on them with cannon. He referred to his method of mob control as giving the rabble a "whiff of grapeshot". He was made a Major General and, soon after, took command of the Army of the Interior.

The two-thirds rule wasn't the last time the Thermidorians tampered with the operation of the new constitution. It called for elections each year, and whenever the royalists or Jacobins won a significant number of legislative seats, the Thermidorians would annul their election.

On March 11, 1796, Napoleon was given command of the Army of Italy. His campaign was a series of successes, which paid off for both him and the government. Large "indemnities" were levied on conquered territories. This self-financing expansion simplified France's financial problems. In 1798, the government further simplified its financial difficulties by defaulting on two thirds of its debt.

For Napoleon, unbroken victory gave him the confidence of his troops. He increased his hold over them by using some of the "indemnities" to give them half of their pay in silver rather than in paper money.

In May 1799, Sieyes became a director. By then, the Directory was in difficulty both at home and abroad. A number of factions were vying for power, one of which was Sieyes, who wanted to install himself as dictator but needed a general to whom to delegate the defense of the country. Napoleon had just returned from Egypt. Of the factions involved, Napoleon found Sieyes the most acceptable, even though he had little respect for Sieyes. He made clear to Sieyes that, as a result of the coup d'etat that they intended to bring off, the executive arm of the government must be made up of three Consuls, of which Napoleon must be one. On November 11, Napoleon dispersed the Council of the Five Hundred with the Council's own guards. The Council of the Elders then decreed an executive of three Consuls, and a rump of the Five Hundred, probably less than one hundred members, ratified the decree.

Another constitution was now in the making. In it, one of the three Consuls was to be the First Consul, the other two being "consultative". Eventually, Napoleon became First Consul. But from the start, he controlled the government.

Like the many marcher lords before him, Napoleon's political power flowed most directly from the loyalty of his troops. In addition, in a patriotic nation where military success was at a premium, Napoleon's many victories gave him, at least temporarily, the support of the public. But if he were to remain in command, Napoleon had to consolidate his power in the political arena. Despite a tendency toward pronouncements that, in the mouth of some other man, would have led to suspicion of insanity (for example, "Remember that I march accompanied by the god of victory and the god of fortune."), Napoleon proved to be as adept a politician as he was a general.

When the government needed finances, Napoleon forced the leading war contractor to disgorge and contribute part of his profits to the state treasury. He created a Council of State, a kind of cabinet, and appointed to it the best people he could find, whether they were royalist, Jacobin, or what have you. He negotiated a concordat (agreement) with the pope. Although neither side was satisfied with the results, it defused the religious conflict that had disrupted the nation since the start of the Revolution. He created the beginning of a civil service with his auditeurs. They were called auditeurs because they could attend sessions of the Council of State but couldn't speak. He established a national education system independent of the church. He instituted a uniform system of taxation from which no one was exempt. And it was at his initiative that the Code Napoleon, which standardized French law, was developed.

In 1802, the constitution was modified so that Consuls held their office for life. Even so, continuing fear of a resurgence of the Jacobins or royalists resulted in the establishment, in May 1804, of a hereditary French empire with Napoleon as the first of a Bonaparte dynasty.

Thus ended the French Revolution. If the goal of revolution is progress toward constitutional, representative government under a rule of law recognizing the citizen's right to pursue his life with a minimum of government interference, then unlike the English and American Revolutions, the French Revolution has to be judged a failure. Why did it fail?

One factor contributing to this failure, which we've already recognized, was the unrealistically high level of idealism woven into French revolutionary thinking. The unattainability of the goals called for by this sort of ethos led unavoidably to a kind of devil theory to explain the failure of behavior to come up to expectation. In the rhetoric of such fanaticism, the enemies of virtue were brutally dehumanized and, as a consequence, became fit objects for extermination. The flip side of unbending morality was a ceaseless flow of blood. An unrealistic world view has to either be abandoned or enforced with unbending coercion.

The other factor contributing to the failure of the French Revolution was the lack, on the part of the French, of any experience with constitutional government. It took England 700 years to develop its constitution. Its revolutions were essentially stopgaps to prevent the clock from turning back too far on the slow and fitful evolution of constitutional monarchy. The American colonies had England's example before it as well as a personal experience with self-government that, in the case of some colonies, extended over more than a century. The colonists produced just one constitution, and it has now lasted over 200 years.

Not only did France not have such a basis on which to build, it explicitly rejected all the historical tradition it did have. At the time of the formation of the States General in 1789, the lawyer Constantin Volney wrote, "What does it matter to us what our fathers have done or how and why they have done it ... ? The essential rights of man, his natural relations to his fellows in the state of society — these are the eternal bases of every form of government." Given these Rousseauian first principles, the framers of the French constitution were determined to create what reason alone said was right. As a result, they produced some beautiful prose, of which the Declaration of the Rights of Man and of the Citizen is perhaps the outstanding example. But their governments were arbitrary and repugnant. As Thomas Carlyle said in his history of the Revolution, "France was long a despotism tempered by epigrams."

In nine years, the French produced four constitutions. The first three were dead letters from the start; those in power simply ignored them. The fourth just endorsed the already existing fact of Napoleon's dictatorship. The sobering conclusion seems to be that, even in a civilized nation with a long history, establishment of a constitutional, republican, limited government is a job demanding much more than just being familiar with some philosophy about government and putting words to paper.

Given the above analysis, one would have to conclude that the English and American Revolutions were exceptions rather than the rule. Unfortunately, history bears out this line of reasoning. It was the French Revolution, with the seeds of disaster built in, that became the model for subsequent revolutions, most notably the Russian.

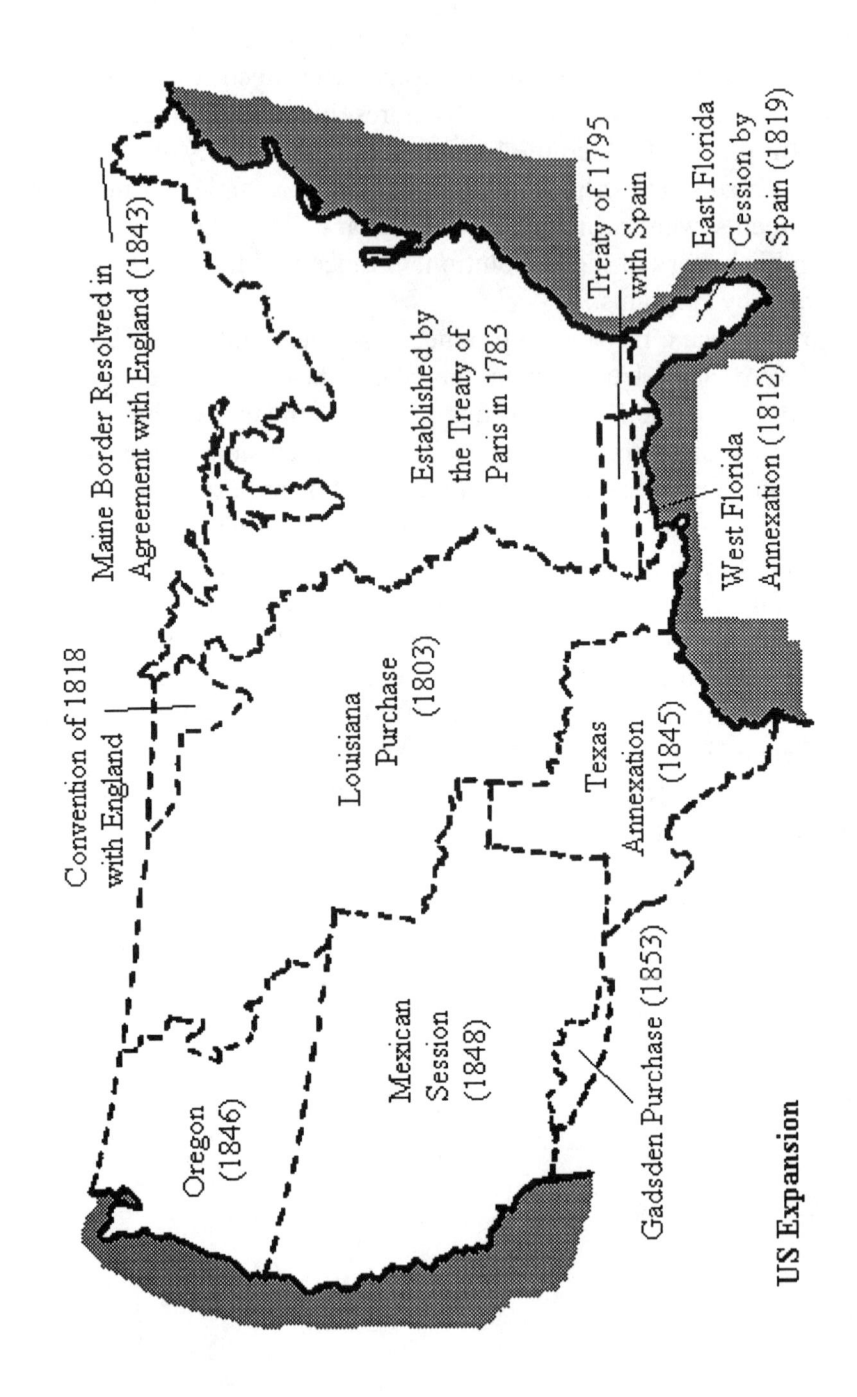

Maine Border Resolved in Agreement with England (1843)

Treaty of 1795 with Spain

East Florida Cession by Spain (1819)

Established by the Treaty of Paris 1783

West Florida Annexation (1812)

Convention of 1818 with England

Louisiana Purchase (1803)

Texas Annexation (1845)

Oregon (1846)

Mexican Session (1848)

Gadsden Purchase (1853)

US Expansion

CHAPTER FOURTEEN

The US Expands

We left off in our history of the US with the ratification of the Constitution. The Constitution called for a federal government. Those in favor of the Constitution were known as Federalists. Prominent among the Federalists were the people who had attended the Constitutional Convention and the subsequent state ratifying conventions. To achieve their objectives, the Federalists knew that the Constitution not only had to be ratified, it also had to be implemented. Fearful that the anti-Federalists, if they got into power, might subvert the progress made so far, the Federalists campaigned actively for office.

The efforts of the Federalists were met with overwhelming success. Washington received the unanimous endorsement of the electors, 11 of the Senators and nine of the Representatives elected had been members of the Constitutional Convention, another 24 of the members of Congress had been members of state ratifying conventions, and all but seven members of Congress were Federalists. John Adams, Washington's vice president, began his term under somewhat of a cloud. He garnered only 34 out of the 69 available electoral college votes. However, by the end of his term as vice president (eight years), Adams was recognized as a Federalist second only to Hamilton.

Initially, provision had been made for 26 Senators and 65 Representatives. However, at the time of the first elections, neither North Carolina (five Representatives) nor Rhode Island (one Representative) had yet ratified the Constitution. Therefore, they weren't represented when the first Congress convened. As a consequence, initially, the first Congress was made up of 22 Senators and 59 Representatives. This meant that the total possible representation in the electoral college was 81. New York never got around to choosing the eight electors to which it was entitled, and two electors each from Maryland and Virginia never made it to the meeting of the electoral college on the day set for it to conduct its vote. Poor traveling conditions and illness were some of the reasons given. So the electoral college cast 138 votes, two each by the 69 electors present. Of these votes, Washington got 69. The other 69 were split between Adams and the other candidates.

All the appointees to the Supreme Court were Federalists. The Chief Justice, John Jay, was one of the authors of *The Federalist Papers*. Of the other four appointees to the Supreme Court, three had been members of the Constitutional Convention, and all had been members of state ratifying conventions. The determination of the number of judges on the Supreme Court was left by the Constitution to Congress. As indicated, this number was originally established at five and was increased from time to time until, in 1863, it was set at nine.

In addition to the Supreme Court, 13 district courts and three circuit courts were set up. All the appointees to these courts were also Federalists.

The Constitution didn't call for a cabinet for the President. Instead, it specified that one of the President's powers was to appoint the principal officer in each of the executive departments, these departments to be established by Congress. From the beginning, these "principal officers" were known collectively as the cabinet. Soon after the organization of Congress, provision was made for a Department of Foreign Affairs (the name of which was soon changed to the Department of State), the Department of War, the Department of the Treasury, an Attorney General, and a Postmaster General. Washington appointed Hamilton, the "giant of federalism", as Secretary of the Treasury; General Henry Knox, another fervent Federalist and Washington's chief of artillery during the Revolution, as Secretary of War; and Edmund Randolph of Virginia, a Federalist convert, as Attorney General.

For Secretary of State and Postmaster General, Washington selected men who didn't fit the Federalist stereotype described above. Jefferson became Secretary of State. He had been Minister to France while the Constitution was being drafted and ratified. Nevertheless, he was in favor of the Constitution. Samuel Osgood became Postmaster General. He had been active in government at the national level under the Articles. He had originally opposed adoption of the Constitution but had ultimately come to accept it.

The term Federalist quickly devolved in meaning from one in favor of the Constitution to a designation for a collection of particular political attitudes espoused by a faction, which we know as a political party. In this sense, Washington wasn't a Federalist. He detested political parties and publicly warned against them.

In the political party sense, Hamilton was the quintessential Federalist. He believed in an aristocracy of wealthy men — merchants, financiers and manufacturers, who would benefit themselves, the nation, and all citizens with their energy and foresight. He thought giving political power to the populace would be to the nation's detriment. Hamilton believed in a strong central government that would take whatever steps were necessary to optimize the activity of the aristocrats and that would cooperate with them in attaining their ends.

Such an extreme position begged for opposition, which was soon forthcoming. These anti-Federalists called themselves Republicans, which from clarity's point of view is unfortunate, since the Republicans of Hamilton's day have nothing to do with the Republican party as we know it today. The leader of the Republicans was Jefferson, whom the Democratic party considers its forefather, just as the current Republican party claims Abraham Lincoln as its progenitor.

Jefferson's view of the ideal nation was agrarian. The model citizen was the independent farmer, prosperous and civilized, living in a nation without populations huddled in great cities and free of a wealthy class that would bring about a concentration of political power antithetical to free citizens. Jefferson believed in the judgment of the common man. Strangely enough for the father of the Democratic party, he was in favor of as little government as possible.

Our present experience makes it hard for us to believe, but until the advent of Franklin Roosevelt, the Democratic party was the avowed advocate of minimal government. It was the Federalists and the Republican party that emerged from the Civil War that believed in government intervention at the federal level. Since Reconstruction, the two political parties have been more similar than different. At most, they offer a difference in emphasis.

Eventually, such personal animosity developed between Hamilton and Jefferson that they found it impossible to stay in each other's presence. But until that point was reached, they both served faithfully and effectively in Washington's cabinet. It's a credit to Washington's administrative ability that he was able to contain, within one cabinet, such capable but incompatible men and see to it that the nation benefited from the best contributions the two had to offer. Jefferson devoted himself to establishing the country's foreign relations, and Hamilton set up the financial underpinnings of the nation.

Hamilton's first goal was to make the nation creditworthy. The American colonies had financed their revolution in two ways: they had issued fiat money and they had borrowed. In the summer of 1776, the Continental Congress had begun issuing bills of credit, noninterest-bearing notes (the infamous "continentals") to pay troops and domestic military suppliers. By November 1779, over $241 million, in face value, of these continentals had been issued. The amounts by year were 1775 — $6 million, 1776 — $19 million, 1777 — $13 million, 1778 — $63 million, and 1779 — $140,052,480. The colonies were jointly responsible for redeeming these continentals in stated amounts between 1779 and 1782, a responsibility they never fulfilled. The colonies also issued their own paper notes in the total amount of $290,524,776.

The result of the issue of all this fiat money was inevitable. The money depreciated. Ultimately, it became worthless. No one would accept it in payment of debt. In effect, it became a tax that fell most heavily on those who had made the greatest commitment to the revolution, the soldiers and the people who supplied them. To show their disdain for this fiat money, barbers papered their shop walls with it and sailors had clothes made from it.

By the beginning of 1790, the nation's domestic debt amounted to about $41 million. It was made up of three categories. There were loan certificates, representing money lent to the government by citizens. These loan certificates amounted to about $11 million. Interest had been paid on them until 1782. Another category of debt was final settlement certificates, issued in 1783 to soldiers being mustered out and to individuals for supplies and services during the war. These certificates amounted to about $17 million.

Finally, there were indents, certificates for accrued interest, totaling about $13 million. All this debt paper traded actively on a market in New York, which eventually became the New York Stock Exchange. Loan certificates characteristically traded for about 25 cents on the dollar, final settlement certificates for 15 cents on the dollar, and indents for 10 cents on the dollar.

In addition to this domestic debt, the nation had borrowed about $12 million from foreigners. In total, individual state debts amounted to about another $20 million.

To make the nation creditworthy, Hamilton proposed that all this debt, federal and state, of about $72 million, be called in and replaced by a standard federal debt issue, to be paid off in specie — that is, coin, or as they say, hard money, since in those days, coins were made of gold and silver.

Hamilton was insistent that the exchange, of the standard federal debt issue for outstanding debt, be made with the current debt holders. The objection to this approach was that it would reward speculators who had bought up the debt certificates from hard-hit farmers and veterans. However, this was no furtive operation. As already pointed out, there was an active public market for these certificates. Hamilton was firm on the point that only if current holders were paid would the nation's credit be established. His bill was passed in 1790. Twenty nine members of the House held certificates that the bill would fund. Hamilton held none.

The $20 million of state debt presented a different problem. Some Southern states had already paid their debts; the remaining Southern debt, in proportion to the population, was much less than that of the Northern states; and Hamilton was from the North. Hamilton got around these difficulties by arranging to have the national capital located on the Potomac rather than in Philadelphia, thus enlisting the support of Virginia for his plan, which was enough to carry the day.

Hamilton was right when he maintained that funding the debt would establish the creditworthiness of the nation. Foreign purchase of US debt went from $2.7 million in 1788 to $33 million in 1801.

In the Coinage Act of 1792, Hamilton defined the basic monetary unit of the nation and provided for its supply. The act defined the dollar as 371.25 grains of pure silver and called for a ten dollar gold coin, termed an eagle, made up of 247.50 grains of pure gold. Small silver and gold coins as well as copper cents and half cents were also defined. The act established a mint that would coin gold and silver presented to it without charge in unlimited quantities.

The choice of bimetallism created a problem. As the price of gold and silver varied on the world market, one metal coin would drive the other out. At times, nothing but silver coins would circulate. At other times, nothing but gold coins would be in use. Finally, in 1873, the silver content of coins for less than one dollar was reduced to a value substantially below the amount stamped on the coin. This created small coins of fiat value only, the silver dollar and small gold coins went out of circulation, and bimetallism was effectively abolished.

Until the Civil War, government-issued money consisted of specie. Paper money was created by banks. For example, suppose a storekeeper wanted to add to his inventory. In return for a commitment to pay the bank $500 in six months, the bank might give the storekeeper $485 in bank notes today. The difference of $15, the "discount", was the bank's charge for this service. Once issued, the bank notes would be used as money until someone returned them to the bank to be redeemed in specie or to make a deposit.

One might ask: Why didn't the storekeeper issue his own notes? Of course, he could, if he could get his suppliers to accept them. But the storekeeper's notes would have been a sometime thing. His business was keeping store, not banking. The bank, on the other hand, issued notes all the time. It was part of the bank's business. And if the bank always redeemed its notes on request, they would get a reputation for being as useful as specie for money.

Since only a fraction of the notes a bank issued was ever presented for redemption, the bank didn't have to have specie to redeem all the notes it issued. And since the more notes it issued, the more money it made, a bank was encouraged to engage in fractional reserve banking — that is, issuing notes the total value of which was some multiple of the specie the bank held in its vaults. Of course, in times of speculative fever, things sometimes got out of hand, and when a bank became overextended in its note issue, a "bank run" — a large number of people presenting notes for redemption — might force a bank to suspend redemption. However, it's important to realize that a bank run could force even a conservative bank into suspension, since all banks practiced fractional reserve banking. Some were just more speculative than others in that, given a specific specie base, they issued more notes than did their more conservative counterparts.

When a bank suspended redemption, panic over the value of the bank's notes would then occur — that is, their value as a unit of exchange would become uncertain and diminish. Loss of faith in the money supply would, in turn, inhibit commerce and industry. The result was economic depression, where prices dropped, firms failed, and people were thrown out of work.

A third program of Hamilton's was establishing a national bank. In Hamilton's mind, the national bank would be like any other bank except that it would be bigger and serve as a repository for government funds. Thus, it would accept deposits and issue bank notes. Hamilton thought that this second function was the most crucial, since it would augment the nation's money supply, which in turn, would stimulate trade and investment. The bank began operation in December 1791 and was chartered for 20 years. As it happened, the most important function of the national bank turned out to be to act as a constraint on excessive bank note issue. Since the national bank received all payments due the government and followed conservative lending policies, it tended to accumulate notes issued by other banks. It promptly returned these notes to the issuing banks for redemption, thus reducing the specie reserves on which these banks could issue notes.

Hamilton was in sympathy with the idea that the bulk of the revenues needed to support the federal government should come from import tariffs. In fact, in good mercantilist fashion, he thought tariffs should be set high enough to protect embryo manufacturing and allow it to grow. However, the tariff of 1789 had little or no protectionist features and probably made sense from a revenue raising point of view. Internal taxes were unpopular and would have been difficult to collect. Tariffs, on the other hand, could be relatively easily collected at seaports. And although they were really a tax on citizens, they gave the appearance of being a tax on foreign producers. Until the Civil War, about seven-eighths of federal revenue came from custom duties. Most of the rest came from the sale of public land. After the War of 1812, tariffs started to increase toward protectionist levels, both as a result of increased nationalism and the pressures of manufacturing interests that had grown up under hothouse conditions during the trade restriction caused by the war.

Unfortunately, the Tariff of 1789 failed to provide enough revenue to meet interest payments on the newly issued bonds now representing the national debt. To correct this deficiency, Hamilton proposed an excise tax on liquor, the first in a long line of taxes on sin. This proposal was embodied in the Excise Tax of 1791. Eastern distillers shifted the tax to consumers. However, because poor transportation prevented shipment of grain to Eastern markets, Western farmers distilled their grain into whiskey for local use in barter trade and were unable to pass the tax on to their customers. So to them, the excise tax was a direct tax. Many of them refused to pay it. In 1794, when a US marshal tried to serve warrants on those indicted for refusing to pay, an insurrection, known as the Whiskey Rebellion, occurred. Washington and Hamilton headed up an army detachment to suppress the insurrection, in the face of which resistance disappeared. Hamilton had been Washington's chief of staff during the Revolutionary War.

The leaders of the insurrection were tried in Philadelphia. Only two were found guilty, and Washington pardoned them.

Hamilton maintained that his programs would benefit all citizens. His feeling was that even farmers would profit from business expansion. But the farmers didn't see it that way. They viewed the debt refunding as a reward for speculators. The bias of the government toward hard money restricted the money supply, and for farmers, money was already hard enough to get. They also conceived of the national bank as an establishment for the benefit of moneyed interests only. The tariff raised prices on the imports on which the farmers relied for manufactured goods. And of course, the excise tax on liquor was a direct tax aimed at them alone.

In 1791, Vermont (Verd Mont, French for green mountain) joined the Union. It was made up of land contested by New York and New Hampshire. Ethan Allen, a real estate speculator, was on the New Hampshire side. The Green Mountain Boys, the troop with which he took Fort Ticonderoga at the beginning of the Revolutionary War, was originally formed to resist the attempt of New York to eject New Hampshire settlers from the area.

As already noted, in February 1793, France declared war on England. England demolished most of France's merchant marine. To compensate, France eliminated its trade restrictions so that ships of any nation could carry goods to and from France. This was an opportunity for the US. But the door on it was rapidly slammed shut by England. England decreed that all neutral ships transporting French goods were subject to seizure, and in June, England began a program of capturing all ships with cargoes of grain or flour bound for France. In a short time, England has taken over about 300 US ships. In addition, England impressed English seamen serving on US ships and was none too careful about how it was done. As a result, many US citizens ended up in the English navy.

England's arbitrary actions in defiance of US interests raised demands for countermeasures. For many reasons, the Federalists didn't want to have trouble with England. The federal government was still in its infancy and not in a condition to take a threatening stance on issues. England accounted for 90 percent of US imports. Cutoff of this trade would make the federal government insolvent. English investment made trade on a credit basis possible and financed government bonds. But most importantly, the Federalists appreciated that England's actions were forced on it. England's viability was a function of its control of the seas. Attempts to circumvent this control naturally stimulated an extreme response. As a consequence, in May 1794, Jay was sent to England to negotiate a treaty for the US.

When the treaty Jay negotiated became public, Jay was burned in effigy. Hamilton, while trying to defend the treaty, was hissed and stoned. Nevertheless, the Jay Treaty was to the benefit of the

US. Most importantly, the US stayed neutral. But also in keeping with the treaty's terms, the English evacuated its forts in the Northwest, something it had agreed to do but hadn't done at the end of the Revolutionary War, which finally made US dominion in the area a fact.

The Jay Treaty also underscored some of the prevailing characteristics of US citizens. Though viewed, perhaps primarily by themselves, as a fiercely independent people ready to fight for their rights at the drop of a hat, and though, through their freedom of speech, such attitudes have been given frequent public expression, in fact, US leaders have rather consistently chosen appeasement over confrontation. Such hardheaded acknowledgment of the inevitable has undoubtedly saved the US from much otherwise unavoidable travail. Secondly, US citizens seem to be a kind of reincarnation of their democratic forefathers, the Greeks, in their propensity to expose themselves to danger by placing sectional interests above those of the nation and have risen above these difficulties only by means of their determination to endure.

The 1783 Treaty of Paris, in which England ceded East and West Florida to Spain, left the boundary between the US and West Florida undefined. The US maintained that the boundary was the 31st latitude. Spain insisted that it was 32 28'. The reason for this disagreement was as follows. In the 1763 Treaty of Paris, Spain had ceded East and West Florida to England. This treaty had set the northern boundary of West Florida at the 31st latitude. However, when England organized the civil government of West Florida, it set the northern boundary at 32 28'. In 1795, a treaty between the US and Spain finally set the boundary at the 31st latitude.

After two terms, Washington stepped down. As a result, the election of 1796 was the first pitting the two political parties against each other. The Federalists ran John Adams for president and Thomas Pinckney for vice president. The Republican candidates were Jefferson and Aaron Burr. However, because of the way the Constitution was written, the electoral college voted for these people without regard to slate, each elector voted for two people, the person with the most votes became president, and the person with the next most votes vice president. Adams won the presidency with the most electoral votes. But Hamilton, spiteful over the fact that Adams, rather than he, had been selected as the Federalist candidate, had championed Pinckney as the presidential candidate in the campaign. Alienated by this action, some of the electors, who had given their first vote to Adams, cast their second for Jefferson rather than for Pinckney. Consequently, Jefferson became Adams' vice president.

No sooner had Adams assumed the presidency than he was faced with another international crisis precipitated by the continuing English-French conflict. This time it was the French that outraged the US. Many Federalists, who balked at going to war with England, were all for taking on France. The army and navy were built up, and an undeclared naval war was carried on. However, even though he was a Federalist, Adams refused to become a party to the effort to impel the US into a war. When the commission he sent got to France, they found Napoleon, rather than the Directory, at the government's helm. With Napoleon, the Convention of 1800 was executed. Once more, war had been avoided. And the Convention released the US from its commitment (in the treaties of 1778) to ally itself with France.

During the agitation over the French, the more extreme Federalists persuaded Congress, in 1798, to pass the Alien and Sedition Acts. The Alien Acts were never put into action. But under the Sedition Act, 24 Republican editors were jailed. US citizens were incensed by this departure from the spirit of US law. Taking advantage of the situation, the Republicans defeated the Federalists in the election of 1800.

In 1800, it was again Jefferson and Burr, this time against Adams and Charles Cotesworth Pinckney. Jefferson garnered 73 electoral votes, Adams 65. In an unusual manifestation of party unity, Burr also received 73 votes. Therefore, under the Constitution as it stood, Jefferson and Burr were tied for the presidency. The election was, consequently, thrown into the House of Representatives. Despite his animosity toward Jefferson, Hamilton considered Burr an unprincipled opportunist. Even though a number of Federalists preferred Burr, Hamilton finally prevailed. On the 36th ballot, Jefferson became the nation's third president. Burr became vice president. And in 1804, the Constitution was amended so that the electoral college first voted for president and then, on a second ballot, voted for vice president.

Although the Republicans were now in control, no attempt was made to alter the financial arrangements Hamilton had put in place. They worked too well. However, in keeping with his principle that the best government was the least government, Jefferson did everything he could to reduce federal expenditures. He was in favor of no navy and practically no army. Imports continued to increase. With the added revenue, Jefferson decreased the national debt from $80 million in 1801 to $47 million in 1809. He pardoned those imprisoned under the Sedition Act, which like the Alien Acts, had expired. And Congress repealed the whiskey tax.

In 1800, Napoleon forced Spain to restore Louisiana to France. However, his military problems in Europe prevented him from defending Louisiana against possible English incursion. Consequently, in 1803, he sold it to the US for $11,250,000 in bonds, which was possible only because of the solid US credit established by Hamilton.

In 1804, New Jersey became the last Northern state to abolish slavery. But it was a creeping kind of abolition. Slaves born after 1804 became free on attaining a prescribed age, 25 for males, 21 for females.

Jefferson responded less to his stated principles than to his interests. He was a strict constructionist of the Constitution, and since it didn't say that the US could buy land, he thought the Louisiana purchase was unconstitutional. But he also believed it was good for the farmers. Consequently, he went along with it. He was opposed to spending government funds, presumably on principle, although he also thought federal expenditures benefited the business classes to the detriment of the farmers. However, when Western farmers complained that they couldn't get their produce to Eastern markets, he had federal funds appropriated to construct a road to the West.

But if the Republicans resembled their opponents, the Federalists, by being ruled by their interests rather than by their principles, the Republicans failed in their need to be pragmatic in the international arena, where the continuing conflict between

England and France caused both combatants to give short shrift to US interests. Both England and France interfered with US trade, and England continued to impress seamen. Jefferson refused to come to any agreement with England that didn't prohibit impressment. Consequently, for reasons already stated, no agreement was forthcoming. Frontiermen in the Northwest were in repeated conflict with Indians and maintained that the Indians were incited, supplied and abetted by the English. But the attitude of these Westerners was hardly disinterested, since their expansionist plans included taking over Canada. New Englanders were just as driven by their concerns. Trade with England was profitable to them. They wanted to avoid war with England.

In 1808, Jefferson was followed to the presidency by Madison, whom Jefferson had chosen to succeed him. Madison had cooperated with Hamilton in developing *The Federalist Papers*. But he was an agrarian. After the Constitution had been ratified, he had left the Federalists and joined the Republicans.

US settlers continued to pour into West Florida. In 1810, they revolted against Spain and petitioned for admission into the US. On October 10, Madison issued a proclamation in which he declared that West Florida was part of the Louisiana Purchase. In 1812, Congress passed an act formally annexing West Florida.

In the continuing disruption of US trade caused by the English-French conflict, the most vocal of the agrarian Congressmen advocating war with England were known as the War Hawks and were led by Henry Clay of Kentucky and John Calhoun of South Carolina. On June 1, 1812, Madison finally gave in to the importunings of the War Hawks and asked Congress to declare war on England.

The War of 1812 was a strange war. England was enmeshed in a European conflict with Napoleon. At the beginning of the war, there were only 5000 English troopers in Canada. The population of Canada amounted to 500,000 as against eight million in the US. Yet despite repeated attempts, the US was unable to make any headway in Canada. Reluctance of militiamen to fight away from their home soil was apparently a factor. New England remained opposed to the war. Throughout the war, New England sold large amounts of food and other supplies to the English fleet off the US coast and to the English armies in Canada. In return, England didn't blockade New England.

During most of the war, negotiations for peace went on, since England was really interested in fighting in Europe, not America, and the US knew it was in a losing war. The Treaty of Ghent, which ended the war, was signed on December 24, 1814 and simply returned the combatants to the state that they were in before the war. Communications were so bad that, on January 9, 1815, English forces, unaware of the treaty, invaded New Orleans and were decimated by US militiamen shooting from behind bales of cotton. It was the biggest battle of the war. About 5000 men were engaged on each side. The battle helped propel the US commander, Andrew Jackson, on the path of public adulation that finally ended in the White House. The story could have been different, for Jackson failed to defend his flank. However, the English obligingly attacked him head on.

The Federalists were discredited by their reluctance to support the War of 1812. Their candidate for president in the 1816 election, Rufus King, garnered only 34 electoral votes as against 183 cast for the Republican candidate, James Monroe, Madison's Secretary of State. The poor showing signaled the demise of the Federalist party. It disappeared from the political scene, and the US entered the so-called Era of Good Feeling, where everyone was nominally a Republican.

As an indication of the extent to which the Republicans had been won over by Hamilton's financial policies, in 1816, the second national bank was established, also with a charter of 20 years. The charter of the first national bank had run out in 1811. The second national bank was established to act as a restraining influence on the note issue undertaken by the state banks that had proliferated since 1811.

The Harrison Land Act of 1800 had been designed to meet the needs of Western settlers and included a deferred payment plan. Taking advantage of this plan, speculators bought immense tracts on credit that they then disposed of, also on credit. But in 1817, the government announced that, in the future, it would accept payment, under the act, in specie only. At the time, outstanding debt to the government was in the millions of dollars. The debtors, who had been operating almost exclusively on credit, had difficulty meeting their payments. After the War of 1812, English manufacturers dumped their pent-up supply of products in the US, which put pressure on US manufacturers. With the defeat of Napoleon at Waterloo in 1815, peace at last came to Europe, and with it came increased European agricultural production. As a consequence, foreign markets for grain and other agricultural products grown by US farmers began to fade away. In 1818, the national bank took action that compelled state banks to reduce the amount of notes in circulation. Many of the Western state banks were shaky and pressed their debtors. Mortgages were foreclosed, produce prices fell, and land values declined. The result of all these factors was the Panic of 1819, which put many small banks and weaker merchants out of business. Recovery finally set in in 1824. Rightly or wrongly, the experience strengthened the idea that the national bank was opposed to the common people.

In a convention with England in 1818, it was agreed that the boundary between Canada and the US, from the Great Lakes to the Rocky Mountains, would be the 49th parallel. In 1819, Spain ceded East Florida to the US as compensation for damages to US commerce during the Napoleonic wars.

In 1820, Monroe was reelected. He got all the electoral votes but one. The dissenting vote was cast so that no one but Washington would have been elected unanimously.

However, in 1824, sectional splits began to show among the Republicans. The Republican caucus chose William Crawford for its candidate. The practice of using party conventions to nominate candidates had not yet begun.

But Crawford failed to satisfy several sectional interests. As a consequence, a number of state legislatures put up candidates. Tennessee nominated Jackson; Kentucky, Clay; and Massachusetts, John Quincy Adams, son of John Adams. Jackson got the most electoral votes, 99. But it wasn't a majority. Consequently, once more, the election had to be decided in the House. Clay had faired the worst of the four candidates. He instructed his supporters to vote for Adams, which gave Adams the election. Adams made Clay Secretary of State. The Jacksonians charged the two with a "corrupt bargain". Then Adams offered, as the administration's program, Clay's so-called American System, which was developed to appeal to the Northeast and the Middle West. It promoted the idea of activities at the federal level to encourage nationwide commerce. It advocated a national bank, road-building supported by the federal government, and tariffs to protect infant industries. The Democratic party was formed to oppose this program. The party was made up of the Western supporters of Jackson, the Southern followers of Calhoun, and Martin Van Buren's New York state machine.

By 1827, most religious and property barriers to voting rights had disappeared. Universal suffrage for men had become the rule.

By continuously bringing attention to the "corrupt bargain" that put Adams in office, the Democrats planted the idea that Jackson, who had received the largest popular vote, had been swindled out of the presidency by a minority representing vested interests. Jackson was as aristocratic as Adams. But in the election of 1828, he presented himself as a man of the people. He decisively defeated Adams.

Jackson is apparently always going to be identified with the spoils system. However, he didn't create it. It went back to the formation of the nation. The victorious party in an election filled the appointive offices with their own kind, especially those who had been particularly zealous in supporting the party. In this way, partisan support was rewarded and encouraged. But Jackson publicly embraced the spoils system and maintained that it was for the good of the people. After all, it increased the control of the majority over the levers of government, didn't it?

In addition to the general attitude of the Democrats that the national bank was the creature of those defeated in the election, Jackson supporters also felt that it had worked actively for the opposition. In 1832, just before his election for a second term, Jackson vetoed a bill to extend the bank's charter. Jackson considered his reelection to be a mandate to continue his war on the national bank. He instructed his Secretary of the Treasury to withdraw the government's deposits from the bank. When he met resistance, he just kept changing Secretaries of the Treasury until he found one who would cooperate. It was his third appointee, Roger Taney, who complied. This was the Taney, who later, as

Supreme Court Chief Justice, handed down the infamous Dred Scott decision. His appointment as Chief Justice was his reward for complying with Jackson's wishes.

Jackson then put the government's funds in state banks, "pet banks" his adversaries called them, which implied that Jackson was extending the spoils system by rewarding the banks that had supported him.

In 1834, the Republicans changed their name to the Whig party to emphasize their opposition to the "reign of King Andrew".

In 1836, the charter of the second national bank ran out. Ever since Jackson had emasculated the national bank, state banks had begun to appear, many with minimal specie. Note circulation increased. With it went speculation in Western land. Concerned about the quality of the bank notes that the government was getting for the sale of public land, on July 11, 1836, Jackson issued his Specie Circular, which called for all public land to be paid for in specie. This action didn't do much to dampen land speculation, but it led people to doubt the soundness of bank notes. English creditors stepped up requirements for payment. On May 10, 1837, the New York banks stopped redeeming bank notes in specie. Shortly afterward, every large city bank followed suit. By the end of May, all banks had suspended note redemption. The Panic of 1837 was on. Stores, factories and banks closed. Men were thrown out of work. The price of land and agricultural products fell dramatically. Recovery finally came in 1844.

In 1844, James Polk was elected on the Democratic ticket. Polk was dedicated to expansionism in keeping with the principle of Manifest Destiny, the belief that the US was destined to expand. How far this expansion was destined to go varied with the person to whom you were talking.

The first item on Polk's expansionary program was Texas. Texas was originally part of Mexico but had been settled by US citizens. It seceded from Mexico in 1835. In 1845, it was annexed by the US and became a state. At the time, a good portion of the territory claimed by Texas was also claimed by Mexico.

The next item on Polk's agenda was the Oregon territory. The US and England had competing claims on Oregon. Being unable to resolve their differences, they had agreed in 1818 to joint occupation. In Polk's annual message of 1845, he asked Congress to perfect US claims by informing England that the US would recognize joint occupation for just one more year. However, Polk didn't want war with England. He had his eye on the Mexican territories of California and New Mexico. The English were overwhelmed with internal difficulties and also had no desire for war. As a consequence, on June 15, 1846, a treaty was executed that made the 49th parallel the boundary from the Rockies to the Pacific, with England keeping all of Vancouver island.

In 1836, the then newly elected president, Van Buren, recommended, as a substitute for a national bank, an Independent Treasury into which all monies due the government were to be paid in specie. However, it wasn't until 1846 that the Independent Treasury was established on a permanent basis. It then remained the government's financial arm until 1914, when it was absorbed into the Federal Reserve System.

In 1846, the US also went to war with Mexico. The Mexican War was one of the two wars that the US entered enthusiastically. The other was the Spanish American War in 1898.

The fervor of Manifest Destiny swept all before it. US forces were outnumbered in the field and hindered by the tepid support given by Polk. The generals conducting the war were Zachary Taylor and Winfield Scott, both Whigs. Although Polk wanted them to win victories, he didn't want them to win glory. Nevertheless, the US overwhelmed the Mexicans. The peace treaty was signed at Guadeloupe Hidalgo on February 2, 1848. In it, Mexico gave up New Mexico and California to the US. The Mexican War also resolved the territorial dispute between Texas and Mexico, in favor of Texas, of course. A portion of this disputed land became part of the state of Texas. The rest was purchased by the US from Texas in 1850 and became unorganized territory.

The Gila river valley wasn't part of the territory ceded by Mexico to the US. But in 1853, as a result of negotiations conducted by James Gadsden, a South Carolina railroad president and minister to Mexico, it was purchased for $10 million. With the Gadsden Purchase, the continental boundaries of the US were established.

By the 1850's, stock trading on the New York Stock Exchange had become active. To facilitate this trading, New York banks created the call loan. Here funds were loaned to stock traders, the securities purchased with the funds serving as collateral. To maximize the funds available for call loans, the New York banks paid small banks, all over the US, interest on demand deposits made in the New York banks. The easy money stimulated industry. But many of the projects proved to be overly optimistic. When they didn't make a profit, stock prices dropped. Banks began to call in their call loans. In many cases, stocks couldn't be sold quickly enough to meet the call. As the New York banks weakened, the out of town banks withdrew their deposits. By October, most banks had suspended specie payments. The Panic of 1857 was on. Much of the nation's business was paralyzed. Over 5000 firms, representing liabilities of almost $300 million, failed. Hundreds of thousands were unemployed. In terms of economic impact, the panic was probably the worst the country had experienced up to this point. But it was short. By early 1858, most banks had once more begun to redeem notes in specie. Commerce and industry then picked up.

The expansion of the nation, from 13 states on the East coast to a continent wide country, was accompanied by a similar growth in transportation, industry, commerce and farming. Stimulus for this economic activity came from private, state and federal sources. The state and federal governments pitched in with financial help. The federal government also made land grants. Nevertheless, the size of the government's presence in the nation's economy was small. Federal spending on all government activity before the Civil War was only one or two percent of national income. Government spending on all levels probably amounted to not much more than five percent of national income.

Transportation between the East coast and the interior varied between poor and nonexistent. The initial response to this problem was road building, which occurred first in Pennsylvania. In 1792, the Philadelphia and Lancaster Turnpike Company was established. In two years, it had completed the 62 mile Lancaster Pike at a cost of $465,000. The road was the favored route of those moving into the Ohio country. And Philadelphia merchants

Some Principal Rivers, Lakes, Cities, Roads and Canals in 1860

profited from being able to do business with one of the most productive agricultural areas in the country. So much was collected in tolls that the company was able to pay a dividend of as much as 15 percent a year.

The success of the Lancaster Pike was widely broadcast. For the next 30 years, turnpike building was brisk. The turnpike companies were financed by stock subscription, state aid, lotteries, and local aid from counties and towns.

Although several turnpikes ran west, none reached the trans-Allegheny (the land to the west of the Allegheny mountains in the Appalachian range). As a result, Western farmers were unable to share in the English importation of US foodstuffs during the Napoleonic wars. They demanded that the federal government do something to rectify the situation. In response to this agitation, the government built the Cumberland Road, running from Baltimore west. It was called the Cumberland Road because, when construction began in 1811, its Eastern terminus was Cumberland, Maryland. Soon after, it was extended east to Baltimore.

By 1818, the Cumberland Road had reached the Ohio river, and in 1833, Columbus, Ohio. It was first opened for traffic in 1817. For 20 years, it was the main road for settlers into the trans-Allegheny and for farm products out of the region. Ultimately, the Cumberland Road became the National Old Trails Road, running from Washington DC to Los Angeles and following the Sante Fe Trail. It was the only national highway built exclusively by the federal government and was turned over to state control in 1837.

The success of the Cumberland Road stimulated the formation of companies planning interstate undertakings and looking for federal financial assistance, which was forthcoming to many. Granting federal aid for road building came to an end when Jackson vetoed the Maysville Road bill. Like a good Democrat of the times, Jackson had campaigned in opposition to all such federal expenditures.

Thereafter, only military roads were financed by the federal government. Our current interstate system of roads was federally financed. But it was built at the initiation of Eisenhower as a military preparedness measure.

States, counties and towns continued to make government monies available to road builders. But these funds were limited. With the advent of the steamboat and railroad, private toll companies became unprofitable.

The first successful steamboat was built by Robert Fulton. In August 1807, the Clermont, a 160 ton side-wheeler, took just 62 hours to make the round trip between Albany and New York. But Fulton wasn't only good at building steamboats. He was

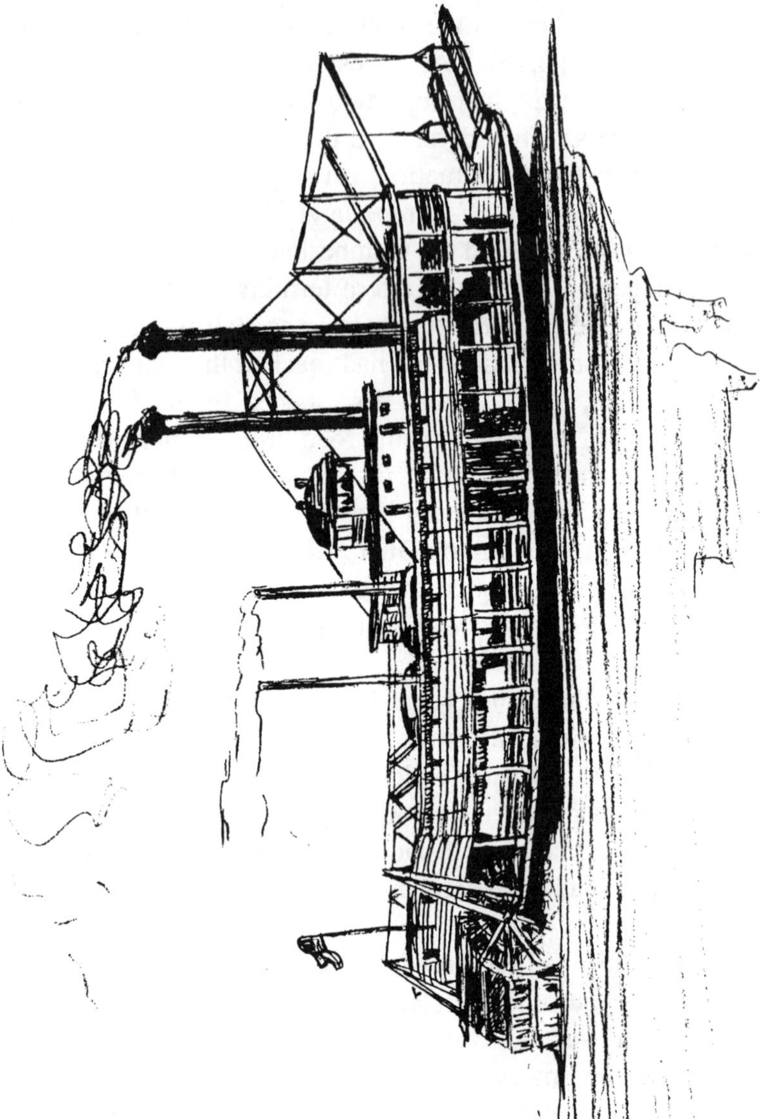

A Mississippi Stern Wheeler.

From an illustration by Edwin Tunis for his book Oars, Sails and Steam published by Thomas Y. Crowell in 1952. These steamships were designed by Henry Shreeve to navigate the waters of the Mississippi and Missouri rivers. Because the water in these rivers was sometimes shallow, the stern wheel was constructed so that it could be raised out of the water and, to minimize draft, the engines were seated on the deck. Consequently, for the convenience of the passengers, a second deck, the "texas", was built above the engine deck. Because there was a scarcity of wharves, the ships were designed so that they could be run up onto the bank of the river, after which the suspended gangplanks at the bow of the boat would be lowered to rest on the land.

The Erie Canal. *From a drawing in the Library of Congress.*

also clever enough to get grants of exclusive use of the navigable waters of New York state from that state and the lower Mississippi from the New Orleans territory. The subsequent battle over these monopolies reached the Supreme Court in 1824, where Marshall struck them down on the ground that the Constitution gave to Congress the authority to regulate interstate commerce. The case against Fulton was argued before the Court by Daniel Webster.

With the destruction of Fulton's monopolies, steamboat activity expanded. Steamboats operated on all the navigable rivers emptying into the Atlantic. Steamboat building in Pittsburgh, Wheeling and Cincinnati stimulated the growth of these cities. Steamboats on the Mississippi and its tributaries grew from 60 in 1820 to more than 1000 in 1860. However, traffic on this waterway was hazardous, because of submerged obstacles, shoals, strong currents, and continuously changing channels. Between 1822 and 1860, the federal government subsidized steamboat service on the Mississippi in the amount of $3 million for improving traffic conditions.

With the construction of Western roads originating in Philadelphia and Baltimore, and with steamboats plying the Mississippi, New York city, despite its favorable harbor, began to see its role, as an international trade terminus, decline. Plans to build a waterway connecting the Hudson with Lake Erie had been discussed as early as 1784. But until 1817, it was all talk and no action. In that year, New York state, under the governorship of DeWitt Clinton, decided to take on the job. By 1825, the Erie Canal was complete. It was 363 miles long and cost somewhat less than $8 million to build. In operation, it resembled two long lines of barges moving in opposite directions. During its first year in business, which was less than a full season, 13,000 barges moved between Albany and Buffalo, and tolls returned one seventh of its cost.

The Erie Canal converted New York city from a market town into the leading metropolis in the US. By 1850, New York had passed Boston, Philadelphia and Baltimore in both population and wealth. The canal also stimulated trade on the Great Lakes. Again by 1850, Cleveland, Detroit, Milwaukee and Chicago were contending with Pittsburgh, Cincinnati, St. Louis, and New Orleans for control of trade in the West. By 1850, 3200 miles of canals had been built, the construction being financed primarily by the states, although the federal government helped with land grants.

In 1826, a three-mile tramway was constructed to run from the granite quarries in Quincy, Massachusetts to the Neponset river. This tramway was a gravity railroad. The loaded cars coasted from the quarry to the river under the influence of gravity. The empty cars were then drawn back up the tracks to the mines by mules. From this modest start, by 1840, there were 2818 miles of track in the US, almost all of it serving local needs. Canal interests hampered railroad growth. In 1833, the New York legislature forbade railroads from carrying freight in the state. Pennsylvania and Maryland threw up similar roadblocks. This resistance began to crumble around 1850. For the next ten years, substantial progress was made in both laying track and combining short lines into interstate arteries.

The railroads were built and operated by private firms. But they got significant help from all levels of government in the form of gifts of money and land, and guarantees of railroad securities. Once it became clear that railroads were profitable, bankers bought large quantities of stock. By 1860, a network of over 30,000 miles of track, more than existed in the rest of the world combined, crisscrossed the nation, primarily in the North. The East coast was connected by rail with St. Louis, New Orleans, Memphis, and Milwaukee. Chicago, junction point for over a dozen lines, had become the hub of the nation's rail traffic. Both canal and railroad construction were stunted in the South, since it had a more satisfactory arrangement of natural waterways for transportation.

In 1790, the US wasn't a manufacturing nation. What manufacturing existed was done on a handicraft basis. But the US was aware of the machine production going on in England, particularly in the textile trade. England, which profited from its production techniques, guarded them jealously. Nevertheless, knowledge of the techniques did reach the US. In 1789, Samuel Slater, who was responsible for constructing equipment for an English cotton factory, came to the US. He got in touch with Moses Brown, a member of a commercial family in Providence, who provided him with financing. He then built, from memory, two carding machines and a water frame of 24 spindles. In 1790, his cotton mill, the first in the US, went into business.

Other Englishmen followed in Slater's footsteps. But the foreign demand for US produce made it more profitable to import manufactured goods than fabricate them. In 1800, there were only 15 mills in operation, all in New England.

However, as the Napoleonic wars made inroads on international trade, the US was thrown back on its own resources for manufactured goods. This development culminated during the War of 1812. For example, in 1816, there were almost 150 textile mills in Rhode Island. But just one year later, renewed importation resulted in the closing of all but one of these mills, as it happened, the old Slater mill.

Nevertheless, neither foreign competition nor the panic of 1819 could hold back Yankee inventiveness for long. In 1824, Samuel Batchelder built a loom that wove patterned fabrics. John Goulding's inventions facilitated woolen manufacture. Chemical bleaching and cylinder machines for fabric printing went into use long before 1860. And in 1846, Elias Howe invented the sewing machine.

Advances were also made in the production of metals and fabrication of metal products. In 1830, Frederick Geisenhainer, a clergyman, successfully melted iron ore by using anthracite coal. Around 1840, the hot blast furnace was introduced. By 1851, about 600,000 tons of iron were being turned out each year. Machines for producing nails, tacks, bolts, files, wire, screws, chains, firearms, and other metal products were created. Eli Whitney and Simeon North simplified clock, firearms and machinery production by introducing interchangeable parts. In both variety and effectiveness, US machine tools became preeminent.

By 1860, there were over 140,000 manufacturing firms with over a billion dollars of capital invested, employing over 1,300,000 people and producing almost $2 billion in annual sales.

Agricultural production in the West expanded on the basis of a continuing introduction of new and improved tools. In 1834, Cyrus H. McCormick patented his reaping machine. By 1851, he was producing over a thousand reapers a year in his Chicago plant. In 1837, John Deere produced the first plow made completely of steel. Ten years later, he established a factory in Moline, Illinois, which by 1858 was turning out more than 13,000 plows a year. Grain drills and seeders, cultivators, mowers, hay-rakes, harvesters, binders, and threshers were invented, improved, and in wide use.

The West's agricultural expansion, combined with the transportation facilities that had grown up to move its grain and meat, usurped a number of Northeastern markets formerly supplied by local farmers. As a result, the local farmers turned to truck gardening, fruit raising, and dairy farming. They were helped in this specialization by the ubiquitousness of the rail network that allowed them to speed their products to the metropolitan areas.

The US in 1860

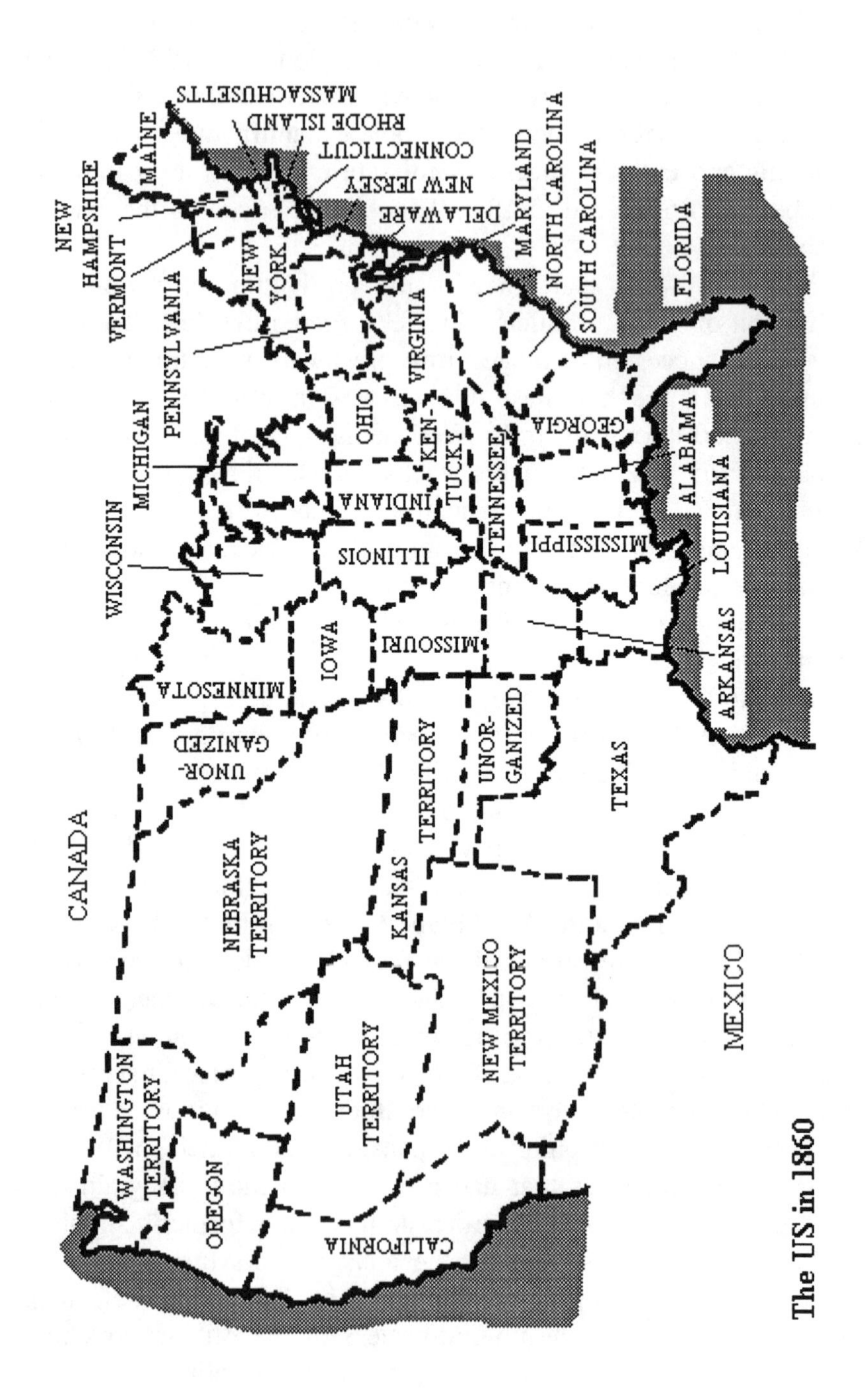

The South was an overwhelmingly agrarian society given over to the production of commercial staples — tobacco, rice, sugar cane, and cotton — that were shipped outside the South for use. There were small farms, some dedicated to subsistence farming, some engaged in producing staples. But the vast majority of the South's staples were produced on a relatively small number of large plantations, the political and social institutions of the South were controlled by the heads of these plantations, and plantation labor was almost totally slave.

Lincoln. *From a photograph made by Mathew B. Brady on February 9, 1864. The photograph appears in the book* The Photographs of Abraham Lincoln *published by Harcourt Brace & Company in 1944. This is the most familiar portrait of Lincoln, since Brady's photograph was used as the model for the engraving on the $5 bill.*

CHAPTER FIFTEEN

The Civil War

By 1860, the US was a continent-wide country containing 33 states, two (California and Oregon) on the West coast and the rest in the East. The intervening area was made up of territories not yet organized into states. The Eastern states were divided into two regions, the North and the South. The North was where grain, meat and produce were grown, where manufacturing, invention, and the use of labor-saving devices took place, and where a free-labor economy existed. The South was an agrarian society given over to the production of commercial staples — tobacco, rice, sugar cane, and cotton — that were shipped outside the South for use and that were grown with slave labor.

The Deep South (South Carolina, Georgia, Alabama, Mississippi, Louisiana, and Florida) was firmly committed to slavery. Slavery was significant, but not so prominent, in the next tier of Southern states — Arkansas, Tennessee, North Carolina, and Virginia. It was also legal but even less prevalent in Kentucky, Maryland and Delaware. Further north, laws had been passed to prevent its growth and assure its death, but in 1860, there were still slaves north of the Mason-Dixon line.

For some time, there had been, in the North, growing agitation to abolish slavery. In response, firebrands in the Deep South maintained that slavery was the South's business and was also best for the welfare of blacks, and that abolitionists should mind their own business. There was no effort on the federal level to abolish slavery, but there were attempts to confine it to the states where it already existed. Such limiting actions were also resisted in the Deep South, and as a result, the issue remained open.

If the situation had been static, there might not have been a problem. But such wasn't the case. The nation was growing. And with the addition of each state to the Union, the political mix in Washington changed. Neither the North nor the South wanted to see its opponent gain the edge at the federal level. As a consequence, the potential emergence of one new state after another increasingly focused the nation's attention on the question that seemed like it wouldn't go away: Would the next state to join the Union be slave or free? Whether slavery, if left alone, would have either died a natural death or remained restricted to the Southern territories amenable to plantation farming are questions that have been heatedly debated. My personal opinion is that slavery would have spread just as far as it was given the opportunity to do so.

In 1853, Stephen A. Douglas was chairman of the Senate committee on territories. Douglas was the beneficiary of a substantial increase in the value of his Chicago real estate investments (which were considerable) due to his ability to see that federal land was granted for the construction of a railroad from Chicago to Mobile. Douglas's investments eventually made him a multimillionaire, no mean feat in those days.

By 1853, the idea of a transcontinental railroad had become a dream of entrepreneurs, politicians and frontiersmen. If it were to run from Chicago, the value of Douglas's holdings would be further increased. But for this to happen, the remaining portion of the Louisiana Purchase would have to be organized into a territory. So Douglas and the chairman of the House committee on territories, William A. Richardson (like Douglas, an Illinois Democrat), introduced bills to organize the Nebraska territory. The bill got through the Senate. But to get it enacted in the House, the help of some Southern representatives was required. To get this support, the interest of these representatives in slavery had to be addressed. So Douglas included in his bill an article making the Missouri Compromise (which banned slavery north of the latitude 36 30' in the Louisiana Territory) inoperative in the territories to be organized and called for the organization of two territories, Nebraska, west of Iowa (a free state), and Kansas, west of Missouri (a slave state).

Implicit in the bill was a compromise: Nebraska would become a free territory, Kansas a slave one. Douglas's bill was passed. But contention over the measure destroyed the Whig party. Northern Whigs voted against the bill 50 - 0. In the face of this unanimous rejection of their interests, Southern Whigs joined the

Democrats, who were more congenial to slavery. In the North, an antislavery coalition emerged as the Republican party.

In the 1854 campaign for congressional and state offices, Douglas actively supported the Democrats. Also involved was Abraham Lincoln, who still considered himself a Whig. Lincoln, "aroused ... as he had never been before" by the Kansas-Nebraska Act, campaigned for candidates for the Illinois legislature who were opposed to the provisions of the Act. His hope was that their election would create a bloc in the legislature that would name him to the Senate. In those days, senators weren't elected. Instead, they were appointed by state legislatures. It took the Seventeenth Amendment, which became effective on May 31, 1913, to make senator an elective office.

In this 1854 campaign, Lincoln admitted flatly that, with respect to the existence of slavery in the South, "If all earthly powers were given me, I should not know what to do ..." But on one point he was firm. The expansion of slavery must stop.

In the election of 1860, the Democratic party, the only remaining national party, split. The Southerners bolted the convention and chose to run John C. Breckinridge, the current vice president. The remaining rump nominated Douglas.

The Republican convention was held in Chicago. The Republicans, strictly a Northern party, were united and had a plethora of candidates, each with some political flaw. The perfect candidate turned out to be Lincoln, at the time a relative unknown. To the roar of 10,000 spectators, most of them supporting Lincoln, Lincoln was nominated on the third ballot. Lincoln won the presidency on electoral votes and would have done so even if his opposition had been united. But he was a minority president, since he garnered only 40 percent of the popular vote.

To the Deep South, the election of a Republican president, who made no bones about his opposition to the expansion of slavery, was the signal that its battle, within the nation, was lost. In December 1860, South Carolina seceded, followed closely by Mississippi, Florida, Alabama, Georgia, Louisiana and Texas. Delegates from the six states of the Deep South convened on February 4, 1861 to form the Confederacy.

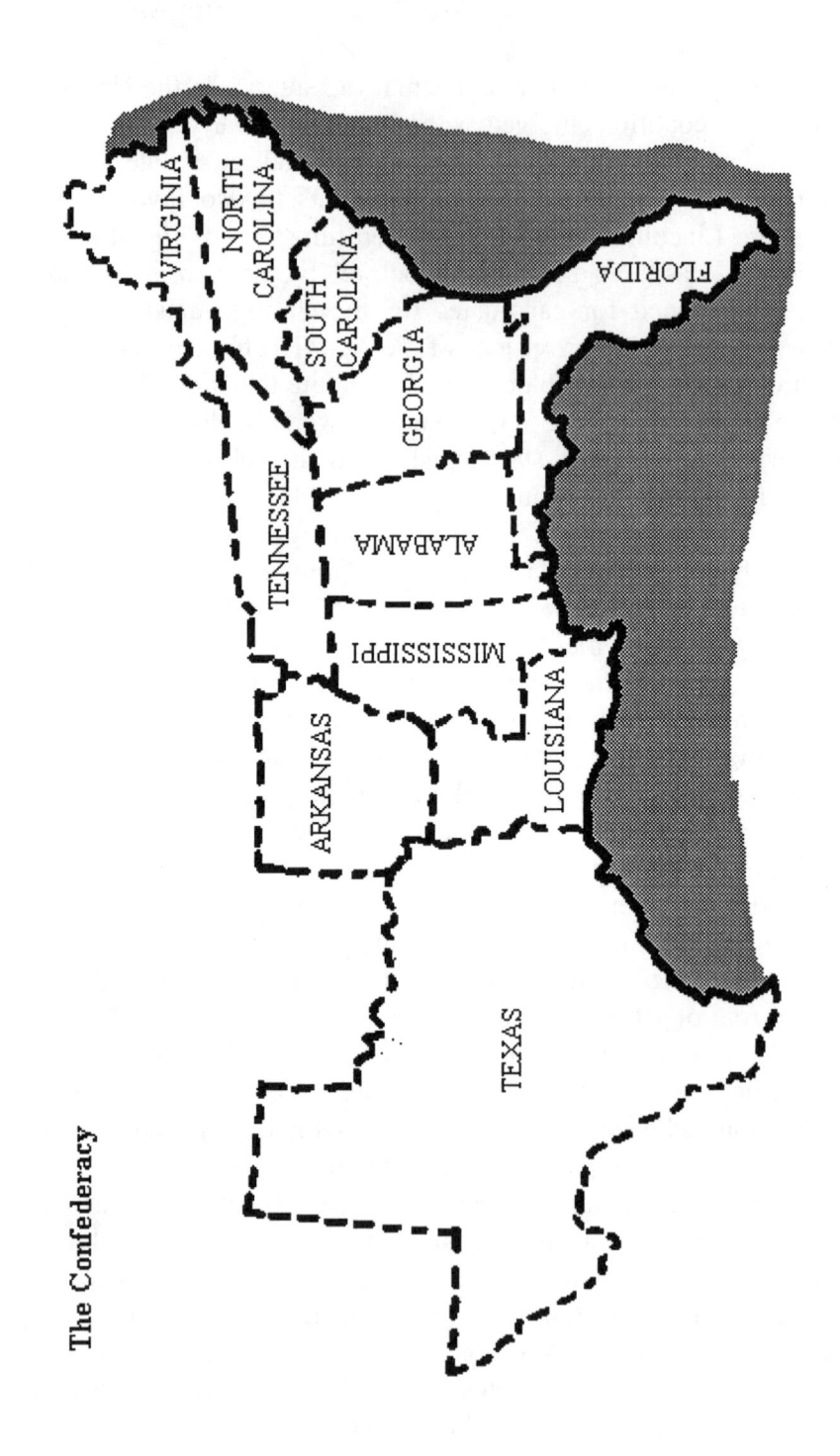

The Confederacy

VIRGINIA
NORTH CAROLINA
SOUTH CAROLINA
GEORGIA
FLORIDA
TENNESSEE
ALABAMA
MISSISSIPPI
ARKANSAS
LOUISIANA
TEXAS

The South felt safe in its secession because it was convinced that "Cotton is King". The South practically monopolized the world's cotton production. Without its cotton, went the South's reasoning, enough of the North's industry would be so paralyzed that war would be impossible. And even if war came, England and France, also dependent on the South's cotton, would recognize the South as a separate nation and come to its aid.

There then occurred the time of "masterly inactivity", where the federal government was, in William H. Seward's words, "conciliatory, forbearing and patient", to give unionists in the Deep South an opportunity to begin a "voluntary reconstruction" of their states. Seward was a founder of the Republican party and would become Lincoln's Secretary of State. Lincoln approved of this approach as long as no extension of slavery were permitted.

By the time of Lincoln's inauguration, the only Union properties in the Deep South not held by the Confederates were Fort Taylor at Key West, Fort Jefferson in the Dry Tortugas, Fort Pickens on an island in Pensacola bay, and Fort Sumter on an island in Charleston harbor, a major outlet for Southern staples. On April 12, at 4:30 am, the Confederates fired on Fort Sumter. On April 15, Lincoln called 75,000 militiamen into national service to suppress the rebellion. As a result, Virginia, Arkansas, North Carolina, and Tennessee joined the Confederacy. The other four slave states didn't secede. The loyalty of Delaware was never in doubt, but the way in which the other three states were kept in the Union was irregular.

In Maryland, Lincoln prevented secession by sealing off Frederick, where the legislature was in session, and jailing, under a suspension of the writ of habeas corpus, 31 secessionist legislators. They remained under arrest until a new legislature was elected in November, one that turned out to be overwhelmingly Unionist.

In Missouri, the governor, Claiborne Jackson, and most of the legislature were for secession. However, a convention, elected to consider secession, voted to stay in the Union. Jackson took steps to join the Confederacy, but Captain Nathaniel Lyons, commander of the arsenal in St. Louis, organized a fighting force and drove Jackson's militia into the southwest corner of the state. The majority of Missouri was now under Union control, but the governor and most of the legislature had left the capital. A rump of the state convention that had rejected secession was reconvened. It chose a new governor and governed Missouri until January 1865, when a new administration was put into office under a freshly drawn, free-state constitution. The Confederacy recognized Jackson and his legislature, which voted to become the 12th state of the Confederacy. But soon afterward, Jackson and his entourage were forced out of Missouri and served only as a government in exile for the remainder of the war.

Kentucky decided to "occupy a position of strict neutrality" in the Civil War. Such a stand made little sense, since a state was either in the Union or out of it. But Lincoln didn't want to lose Kentucky to the Confederacy. Consequently, he accepted the situation even to the extent of letting the Confederacy conduct a large amount of trade in war materials with the North through the state. Ultimately, the Confederacy invaded Kentucky, rapidly followed by Union forces. However, by moving first, the Confederacy became the aggressor. The legislature voted to go with the Union. The governor, the now Senator Breckinridge, and other Kentuckians went with the Confederacy. They formed a provisional government, which was accepted as a Confederate state. By the end of 1861, the southwest corner of the state was in Confederate hands, the rest being occupied by the Union.

Finally, West Virginia broke away from Virginia with the intent of coming back into the Union. The difficulty here was that, to create a new state from the territory of one already in being, the Constitution called for the agreement of the existing state, and Virginia wasn't about to go along. This impediment was rather creatively circumvented. A convention met in Wheeling on June 11, 1861, declared that, since the heretofore Virginian government had seceded, the offices of the Virginia government were open, formed the "reorganized" government of Virginia, named Francis H. Pierpont governor, and provided for the election of a legislature and other officials. Subsequently, a popular vote overwhelmingly supported an "ordinance of dismemberment". In 1862, a constitution for the new state of West Virginia was adopted. The "restored" Virginia government agreed to the creation of the new state. On June 30, 1863, Congress accepted

West Virginia into the Union. All this was possible because, during the proceedings, the Union was in military control of West Virginia. In 1864, the Pierpont government of Virginia left Wheeling and established itself in Alexandria.

The Union won the war. One factor in its favor was the good fortune of having Lincoln as president.

Lincoln was a consummate politician. He dealt in the realm of the possible and wasn't above currying political favor. When he was a postmaster, he was known to have used his franking privileges for his friends.

At the Republican convention in Chicago in 1860, the galleries were jammed with thousands of vocal Lincoln supporters who had gained admission through the use of counterfeit tickets. The spoils system was still in place during Lincoln's administration, and he made full use of it.

Notice has already been made of Lincoln's willingness to go to almost any extreme to keep Maryland, Missouri and Kentucky in the Union. With his characteristic sense of humor, Lincoln had observed that, "while I hope to have God on my side, I must have Kentucky."

Maryland wasn't the only place Lincoln used the suspension of the writ of habeas corpus. He employed it to silence many voices that he considered dangerous to his cause.

Union soldiers were heavily pro-Republican. Consequently, where state laws prohibited absentee balloting, Lincoln saw to it that soldiers were furloughed so that they could vote.

When Lincoln began to suspect that some of the officers in McClellan's army, perhaps even McClellan (who was commander of the Union forces in the East), didn't sympathize with Lincoln's goals, he dismissed, as an example, Major John J. Key (the son of Francis Scott Key, the composer of the Star Spangled Banner) and ruined his career. Key's offense was to state, in a private conversation, in answer to the question of why the Union hadn't bagged the rebels after the battle of Sharpsburg, that it was "not the game" to destroy the rebel army but to bring about a settlement that would allow the perpetuation of slavery. Sharpsburg was one of the many instances where McClellan's caution led him to miss opportunities to inflict damage on the Confederate army.

We think our current politicians are corrupt. But they're pussycats compared to the politicians of Lincoln's day. Yet despite the fact that Lincoln swam in these waters and demonstrated over and over that he was a politician extrordinaire, he was a man of unquestioned personal integrity. He never took an action for his own personal benefit. All his efforts were directed to the attainment of those fundamental goals to which he was personally and deeply committed.

One of those goals was the preservation of the Union. At the time of the secession, he said that the "central idea" of the Union position "is the necessity of proving that popular government is not an absurdity." From this position he never wavered. His unswerving dedication to Union preservation was a pillar of strength during the many dark days of the Civil War.

On slavery, the other insistent question of the Civil War, Lincoln's attitude was more suspect. We know he was opposed to the extension of slavery. We also know he personally abhorred slavery.

Lincoln did issue the Emancipation Proclamation. But it was a military measure carried out under "war powers". He knew it would have little legal force once the war ended. Moreover, as a military measure, it was concerned with the seizure of enemy resources. Its intent was to warn the Confederate states that, if they didn't return to the Union, then as the Union forces advanced, the slaves in the conquered territories would be freed. As Lincoln expressed it, "We wanted the Army to strike more vigorous blows. The Administration must set an example, and strike at the heart of the rebellion." Emancipation was a means to victory, not an end in itself. It would allow the enlistment of freed slaves into the Northern army and, in Lincoln's words, "... help us in Europe, and convince them that we are incited by something more than ambition."

In an open letter to Horace Greeley's *New York Tribune* on August 22, 1862, Lincoln said, "My paramount object in the struggle *is* to save the Union, and is *not* either to save or destroy slavery. If I could save the Union without freeing *any* slave I would do it, and if I could save it by freeing *all* the slaves I would do it; and if I could save it by freeing some and leaving others alone, I would also do that." It's the case that, in response to one peace feeler, Lincoln authorized Greeley to bring to him under safe conduct "any person anywhere professing to have any proposition of Jefferson Davis in writing, for peace, embracing restoration of the Union and abandonment of slavery." On the other hand, on August 17, 1864, he wrote, to a War Democrat (the Republicans were the war party; the Democratic party was split; those opposed to the war were known as Peace Democrats, those that supported the war as War Democrats), an unsent letter in which he stated, "If Jefferson Davis ... wishes to know what I would do if he were to offer peace and re-union, saying nothing about slavery, let him try me." Nevertheless, by the time Lincoln was ready to run for reelection, he had decided that his terms for the end of the war were union *and* emancipation.

Lincoln took the standard Republican stance with respect to the Dred Scott decision. The opinion of the court was that, even though Scott had lived in Illinois, a free state, for two years, he remained his master's property. The Republican position was that this decision made slavery possible in all states. To the Republicans, for a state to be free it must offer freedom to any slave brought by his master within its borders, no matter for how short a time.

With respect to equality, as opposed to freedom, Lincoln's posture would have been unacceptable today. In the Lincoln Douglas debates, Lincoln was at pains to spell out his position. "I am not, nor ever have been in favor of bringing about in any way the social and political equality of the white and black races ... I am not nor never have been in favor of making voters or jurors of negroes, nor of qualifying them to hold office, nor to intermarry with white people, and I will say in addition to this that there is a physical difference between the races which I believe will for ever forbid the two races living together on terms of social and political equality." Lincoln never again addressed himself to this subject in such broad terms. At the end of the war, he did make a statement on black suffrage, which indicated that he had modified his position somewhat. But what he said makes it clear that he was still basically of the same mind. He made the statement on April 11, 1865, in what has come to be known as his last speech, although of course, at the time, he didn't know that it would be his last. What he said was, "I would myself prefer that (the vote) were now conferred on the very intelligent and on those who serve our cause as soldiers."

Lincoln's standard solution to what to do with the free black was colonization — emigration of blacks to another land where "they would have better opportunities." Whether this was a genuine attitude or a political ploy to dull apprehension over emancipation we'll never know. It was an unfeasible position to assume, although Lincoln was hardly alone in espousing it. A person of Lincoln's intelligence and reasonableness should have recognized it as such. As one Republican said: As a practical matter, colonization "is a damn humbug. But it will take with the people." On the other hand, it should also be kept in mind that Lincoln arrived at his positions with great difficulty. He worked at them laboriously until he was sure he had reached the right conclusion. As a result, even though he typically began from a very conservative position, over time, Lincoln's attitudes grew. His remarks concerning the franchise in his last speech indicate that his position was changing and that he might not any longer consider colonization a viable option. But if he were mulling over alternatives, we have no indication of what they might be.

Lincoln was one of those rare people who combined a dedication to the rights of the people in general with a genuine sympathy and respect for the individual. But for the sake of the Union, he was willing, for more than four years, to preside over the bloodiest war in US history. Over 620,000 soldiers died, 360,000 Yankees and at least 260,000 Confederates. The number of Southern civilians who died as a result of the war has never been determined. But the total loss of lives in the war was as large as in all other US wars, including Vietnam, combined.

To some extent, the magnitude of these casualties was a result of the military strategy that Lincoln promoted. Whatever other advantages the North had over the South, Lincoln recognized that perhaps the most crucial was numeric superiority. Lincoln was convinced that maneuvering for position would never win the war. The winning strategy was to destroy the South's ability to fight. To accomplish this, Union forces must continuously confront the rebel armies, and whenever the military position promised at least equal casualties, the enemy must be attacked until he was ground down to impotence. Lincoln keep changing generals until he found one who agreed with him. That general was Ulysses S. Grant. When Grant took command, Union casualties began to mount. But so did the Confederacy's. And if the count in the North's win column didn't go up, the count in the loss column did stop its climb.

In addition to Lincoln and numeric superiority, another factor favoring the North was its strength in any category you want to name. At the end of the war, the South was devastated. In contrast, the North came out of the war stronger than it went in. As a result, the Union army was the best fed, best clothed, best armed, and best supplied that the world had yet seen.

But this superiority in numbers and supplies can't account for the North's victory. There have been many cases where outnumbered and under-supplied peoples have nevertheless bested their enemies. On the South's side of the ledger, it must be recorded that the general military opinion of the time was that the Confederate soldier was the most effective, efficient and dedicated fighting man the world had yet known. The Southern soldier's drawback was that his dedication was local, to his commander or his state rather than to his nation or a cause. In addition, the South was a confederacy. It wasn't unknown for a Southern state governor to ignore the Confederacy's call for troops on the basis that they were needed to protect the home state.

The fact of the matter was that, despite draft riots and evasion, peace movements, endless desertions, anti-black demonstrations, and incompetent military leadership that led to year after year of defeat and missed opportunities to inflict punishment on the enemy, the Northern man was just more willing to continue to shoulder arms for the Union than was his Southern counterpart to persevere in his support of the Confederacy. Sherman's terrible march of destruction through the South ("We cannot change the hearts of those people in the South," he said, "But we can make war so terrible … that generations would pass away before they would again appeal to it.") and the Confederacy's inability to stop him marked the end of the South's willingness to fight.

Grant. *From a photograph taken by Mathew Brady at Cold Harbor, Virginia in 1864 during the siege of Petersburg. The photograph is in the Mathew Brady Collection at the National Archives in College Park, Maryland.*

On top of the South's other woes, its cotton policy was also a failure. The Confederacy never embargoed cotton. But the planters voluntarily enforced an embargo on themselves. However, England had already built up a cotton surplus. A shortage wasn't experienced until the summer of 1862. By then, increasing prices had expanded cotton growing in Eygpt and India. For the rest of the war, the bulk of Europe's cotton was supplied by these alternate sources. In addition, the South had underestimated both England's abhorrence of slavery and its disinclination to break the North's blockade of the South, when respect for a blockade was such an essential part of England's defense strategy. France would have recognized the South if England had led the way, but this England never did.

Blacks participated actively and with dedication in the war. By the end of the conflict, there were almost 200,000 blacks in the Union military. They made up one eighth of the Union army and one seventh of the Union navy. They fought with distinction in several battles and earned 21 Congressional Medals of Honor.

Northern victory in the Civil War saved the Union. But the government that fought the war created precedents for a plethora of actions heretofore considered forbidden.

The government started printing paper money (the famous "greenbacks"), fiat money that was legal tender for all debts, public or private. It levied taxes on liquor, tobacco, playing cards, carriages, yachts, billiard tables, and jewelry. It established license taxes on almost all professions but the clergy, stamp taxes, taxes on the gross receipts of corporations, taxes on dividends and interest paid to investors, inheritance taxes, and individual income taxes. It created the Bureau of Internal Revenue to administer these taxes. In the 1900's, the name of this bureau was changed, in characteristic government doublespeak, to the Internal Revenue Service.

The Lincoln administration was the first US government to institute a draft. And it established the Freedmen's Bureau. Catering to special interests was, of course, nothing new to the federal government. What was new here was the creation of a national bureaucracy to carry out a social program. The Jeffersonian idea that the best government was the least government had been seriously flouted. Nevertheless, in all fairness, it must be noted that the Freedmen's Bureau was a bureaucracy dedicated to eliminating itself and ended its involvement in every responsibility assigned to it as soon as it could find another means that it thought would achieve the objective.

The Civil War also introduced dramatic innovations in the art of warfare. It was the backdrop for the first battle between ironclad ships. The Union ironclad, the Monitor, was the precursor of the modern naval vessel: it had a low profile, speed and maneuverability, revolving gun turrets, and a few guns of heavy caliber rather than broadsides of cannon. The age of the wooden ship had passed.

Ground warfare was also revolutionized. Until the Civil War, soldiers carried muskets into combat. These weapons had a effective range of about 80 yards, and to make up for their inaccuracy, infantry had to maintain close order and fire in volleys. Tactics emphasized the offensive. Artillery could move forward with advancing troops because, at ranges of a couple of hundred yards, cannoneers and horses, needed to drag the cannon, were relatively safe from enemy musket fire. These field guns would blast holes in the enemy ranks through which the infantry that they supported would then pour. Such frontal attacks succeeded because double-timing infantry with bayonets fixed could cover the last 80 yards of a charge in the 25 seconds it took defenders to reload.

But by 1855, a practical rifle (from the German, riffeln, to groove) for large-scale army use had been developed. It was Jefferson Davis, the future president of the Confederacy but the then Secretary of War, who converted the US army to the rifle. With an effective range of 300 to 400 yards, the rifle allowed defenders to reduce an attacking force before it could come close enough for hand to hand combat. It also kept artillery too far back to be useful in close fighting. Finally, rifles became deadly weapons in the hands of sharpshooters, who could pick off the enemy with relative impunity. This led to the construction of earthworks whenever a position was assumed. By the end of the conflict, the trench warfare characteristic of World War I was well developed.

The physical principle on which the rifle is based is the fact that a spinning projectile is more accurate than one that doesn't spin. A useful analogy here is that a spinning football can be thrown more accurately than a wobbling or tumbling one. To impart the necessary spin, the inside of the rifle barrel is scored with a series of spiral grooves. The function of the projections, called lans, created by this grooving inside the barrel, is to grip the projectile as it moves through the barrel and give it the required spin. The problem with the muzzle-loading rifle was how to ram a large enough projectile down the barrel of the gun so that it would be affected by the rifling. The ultimate solution to this problem was to avoid it entirely through the use of ammunition encased in cartridges and loaded through the breech of the gun. However, before breech-loading rifles were invented, the first practical solution to this problem was the "minnie ball", named after Captain Minie of the French army who invented it. The minnie "ball" wasn't really a ball. It was more of a cylinder, and it had a cavity at its base. When the gun was fired, the explosion of the powder expanded the edges of the cavity so that the rifling could grip these edges and impart a spin to the bullet.

The rifle existed long before the Civil War and was carried by many Continental soldiers. Their solution to the problem of getting a projectile, down the muzzle of a rifle, that would be affected by the rifling was to wrap the ball in a moist patch of deerskin. The deerskin made the package flexible enough for it to be rammed down the barrel and, yet, was also firm enough so that the rifling could grip it and give the encapsulated ball the necessary spin. The moist deerskin, when rammed down the muzzle, also tended to clear the residue left from the previous firing, which if allowed to accumulate, would otherwise have soon fouled the rifling and made it nugatory. The English soldiers, on their retreat from Concord, marveled at the colonists' ability to deliver such deadly fire from such long distances.

Finally, the need to order uniforms in bulk led the Quartermaster Bureau to provide clothing manufacturers with a graduated series of standard measurements for uniforms, which was, thereafter, used for men's civilian wear.

CHAPTER SIXTEEN

Reconstruction

Reconstruction is a funny word. Andrew Johnson, the man who succeeded to the presidency on Lincoln's assassination, preferred the word restoration. Nevertheless, Reconstruction is the word that history and historians have given us. Even so, it's definition is elusive. From a process point of view, Reconstruction had two goals: bringing the Southern states back into the Union and seeing that all bars to political and civil equality for blacks were removed. Once Reconstruction is defined in these terms without further qualification, it's clear that Reconstruction didn't end until the civil rights activities, begun in the 1950's, had come to fruition.

But historians don't use the term Reconstruction in this way. To see how they use the word, it's necessary to add to its definition by observing that the term was employed to describe a policy pursued by the Republican party. In this more restrictive sense, Reconstruction ended in 1877 with what the historian C. Vann Woodward termed the Compromise of 1877, in which the Republican party abandoned its policy of Reconstruction.

Lincoln began Reconstruction on December 8, 1863 with his Proclamation of Amnesty and Reconstruction. In this proclamation, Lincoln offered forgiveness and resumption of rights "except as to slaves" to anyone, other than those who occupied the top levels of Confederate officialdom (both civilian and military), who swore an oath of loyalty. When at least ten percent of a state's residents, as measured by the number of those who had voted in the 1860 presidential election, had taken this oath, this loyal group could set up a new state government, the constitution of which had to abolish slavery. The state could then seek representation in the federal government, although Lincoln emphasized that Congress reserved the right to pass on the acceptability of those that endeavored to join it. Louisiana, Tennessee and Arkansas followed Lincoln's directions, and Lincoln recognized Pierpont's Virginia government in Alexandria as legitimate. However,

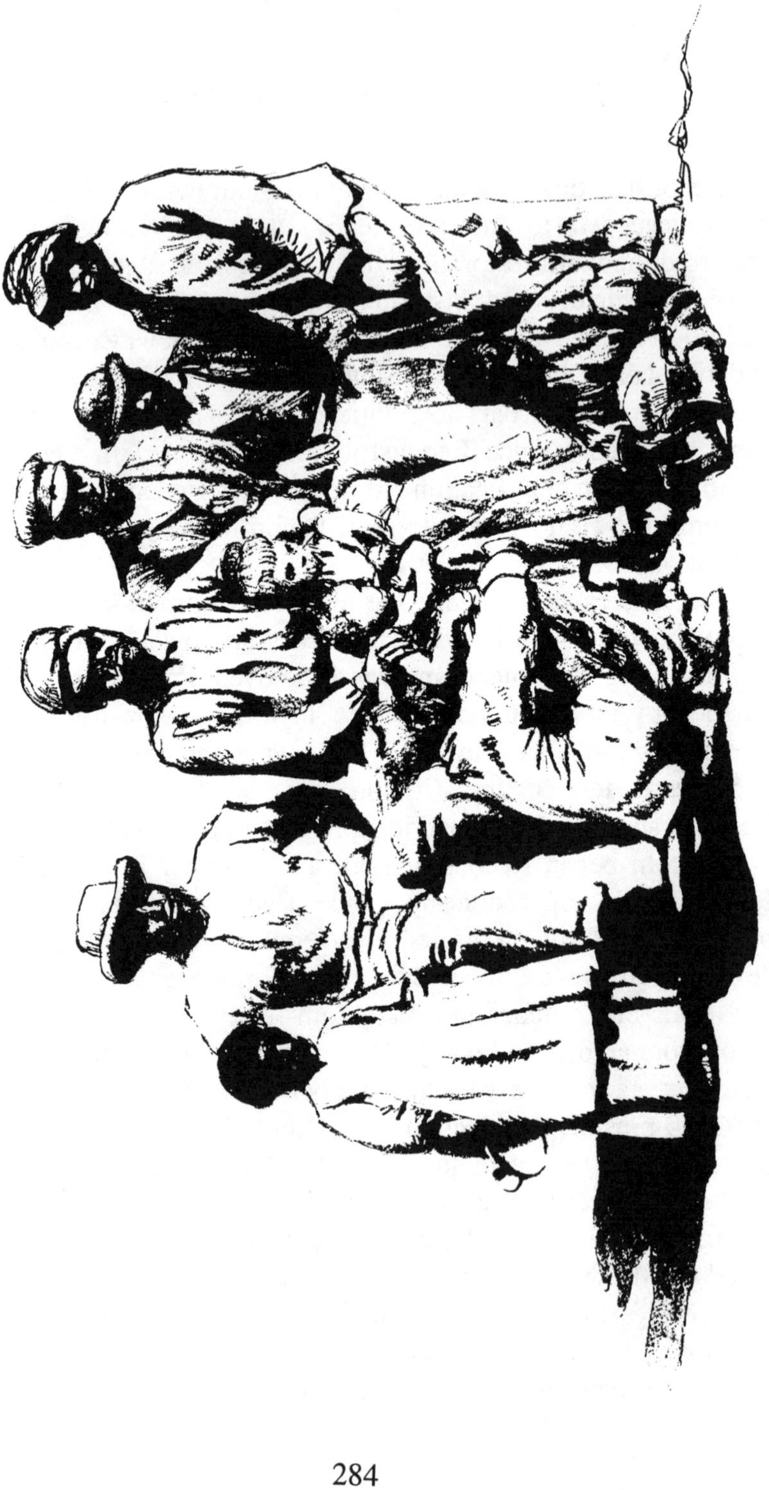

Congress declined to accept the members these four "reconstructed" states sent to Washington.

On January 31, 1865, the Thirteenth Amendment, abolishing slavery, passed Congress. It was ratified in the same year.

In March, the Freedmen's Bureau was created. It was accountable for, among other things, determining how free labor was going to work in the South; setting up schools for freedmen; helping the destitute, aged, ill and insane, both black and white; resolving differences between the races; and seeing that blacks and white Unionists were granted the same protection under state and local law as that enjoyed by the other residents. The bureau's commissioner was General Otis Oliver Howard, a Civil War veteran after whom Howard University in Washington DC was named. Howard University was established in 1867 by the US government for the higher education of primarily freedmen, largely because of Howard's urgings.

In the beginning, Congress didn't allocate any funds to the Freedmen's Bureau. Howard used army personnel to carry out the bureau's activities. Maximum employment at the bureau was 900. It ceased operation in 1872.

On April 14, 1865, Lincoln was assassinated. Johnson became president. Johnson had been a Democrat all his life. Lincoln had selected him for vice president because, as a Democrat from a border state (Tennessee), he might help in the election of 1864, in which the Republican party chose to refer to itself as the Union party.

Historians like to knock Johnson, particularly by comparing him to Lincoln. Certainly the men were different. Lincoln had a sense of humor, skill in the political arena, and an empathy for others. Johnson had almost no friends and took no one into his confidence. He was intolerant of opinions other than his own and seemed incapable of compromise. Equally certainly, he failed to administer a successful Reconstruction policy. Whether Lincoln could have done better we'll never know.

A Group of Freedmen Shortly After the End of the Civil War.
From a photograph in the William Loren Katz Collection in New York city.

In any case, Johnson's Reconstruction policy was indistinguishable from Lincoln's. He recognized the governments of Arkansas, Louisiana, Tennessee and Virginia created under Lincoln's administration. He then issued his plan of Reconstruction on May 29, 1865. In general, rebels who swore Union loyalty and endorsed emancipation were pardoned and given all their property rights except for slavery. However, 14 classes had to appeal individually for presidential pardons. These classes included major Confederate officials and owners of more than $20,000 of taxable property. State conventions were to be held to create governments. All those pardoned and meeting ante bellum voter qualifications could vote for convention delegates. The conventions must renounce state debts related to the rebellion (the Confederate debt had already been repudiated, since it had been contracted for by an illegal organization that no longer existed), nullify secession, and accept the Thirteenth Amendment. Once these conditions had been met and the states were operating as "republican forms of government" under their new constitutions, their Reconstruction would be complete.

In the beginning, Johnson issued pardons sparingly. But by September, they were being granted in large numbers, as many as hundreds in a day. By 1866, more than 7000 Southerners excluded because of property ownership had been pardoned.

The Southern states more or less met Johnson's requirements. From the Southern point of view, secession had now been repealed and slavery abolished, so the obligations to the conquering union had been satisfied. The next job was to restore the South's viability. And this meant getting back to plantation production as soon as possible.

Slavery had provided the labor for this economy. But slavery was no more. A new labor force had to be found. The assumption was that the blacks would continue to constitute this labor force. As the Southerners saw it, the job was to make use of this labor feasible. The result was the Black Codes. Freedmen were to be paid wages. But they were required to hire out by the year under written labor contracts. Once entering such a contract, freedmen couldn't strike or leave their jobs. If a freedman broke his contract, he forfeited his wages and could be fined. Any freedman without a home or a labor contract was a vagrant and was fined. If he couldn't pay the fine, he was hired out. Freedmen were prohibited from possessing firearms, ammunition or knives. Disturbing the peace, preaching without a license, and selling liquor were punishable by heavy fines. Freedmen could travel only with written permission of their employers. Blacks under 18 who were orphans or whose family couldn't provide for them were apprenticed to white men. Once an apprentice, the black remained bound to the white until he was 21 if he were male, 18 if female.

From the Southerners' point of view, the Black Codes may have been nothing more than what they felt was necessary to get work out of what they considered to be inferior, inefficient blacks. Either the Southerners were too insensitive to realize it or bold enough to think that they could get away with it (their later actions indicate that the second motive may have been the applicable one), but they apparently never took into consideration the North's reaction to the Black Codes. To the North, they represented the return to the content, if not the form, of slavery.

When the Thirty Ninth Congress assembled, a Joint Committee on Reconstruction, made up of six senators and nine representatives, was established to develop a Reconstruction plan. The resolution setting up the committee also stated that, until the plan was created, no Southerner could join Congress. Without disparaging the intentions of the Republicans (who enacted this resolution) to do right by the freedman, it must nevertheless be noted that the 11 states, seeking re-admission to Congress, were uniformly Democratic. To have seated the men elected by these Southern states would have been to destroy the Republican hold on Congress.

On June 13, 1866, Congress passed the Fourteenth Amendment. It, for the first time, provided a definition of a US citizen (any person born or naturalized in the US) and enjoined the states from restricting his "privileges and immunities", depriving him of life, liberty or property without "due process of law", or preventing him from enjoying "equal protection under the laws". It was a national guarantee of equality before the law.

In the congressional elections of 1866, Republicans ended up with more than the two thirds majority needed to pass bills over a

Carpetbaggers. *From a painting by N. C. Wyeth for the cover of the book* The Pike County Ballads, *a collection of poems by John Hay. The painting is now owned by the Diamond M Foundation and currently hangs in The Texas Technical University Museum in Lubbock.*

presidential veto. For the next two years, the Republican Congress was going to dictate federal policy.

On March 2, 1867, Congress passed the Reconstruction Act. Alone of the Southern states, Tennessee had ratified the Fourteenth Amendment and had been brought back into the Union. The remaining ten rebel states were partitioned into five military districts with troops in each to back up the authority of the district commanding officer, since "adequate protection for life and property" wasn't present in the Southern states. Because this arrangement put control in the hands of the president, who was commander in chief of the armed forces, Congress passed a series of acts to prevent Johnson from interfering in its Reconstruction plans. It located the headquarters of the general of the army (Grant) in Washington where it could keep track of what was going on, and it decreed that all executive orders concerning military operations must be promulgated by the general of the army. Presidential Reconstruction was swept away.

The district commanding officers under this new, so-called "Radical Reconstruction" had the duty of enrolling qualified voters (now all males 21 years or older, resident for at least a year, and not guilty of any crime or participation in the rebellion) to elect delegates to new constitutional conventions. The conventions would set up new state governments and preside over the first elections under the new constitutions. When the new governments had ratified the Fourteenth Amendment and Congress had approved the new constitutions, the reconstructed states would be re-admitted to Congress and the military regimes would be dissolved. By 1870, the necessary steps had been taken and all Southern states were again participating in the federal government.

The solid support of blacks, carpetbaggers (Northerners who had come South after the war) and scalawags (Southerners who supported Radical Reconstruction), who constituted the mass of eligible voters (700,000 out of a male population of around four million), gave the Republicans control in the majority of the South.

In 1868, at the federal level, Grant became president. On March 30, 1870, the Fifteenth Amendment, specifying that "the right of citizens of the United States to vote shall not be denied or abridged by the United States or by any State on account of race, color, or previous condition of servitude", was added to the Constitution. It was the last act of the radical reconstructionists. Grant's slogan was, "Let Us Have Peace." By 1871, only Arkansas still based voter eligibility on nonparticipation in the rebellion.

Ultimately, the South's determination to establish white supremacy, which it referred to as the "redemption" of Southern society, outlasted the Republicans' dedication to reforming the South. Several factors were involved.

One was the use of violence. Among other vehicles employed to carry out this intimidation was the Ku Klux Klan, originally founded in 1866 as a social club. But the Klan quickly changed its spots. By 1867, it was systematically using savage methods (whipping and murdering) to achieve its goals, which were to destroy the Republican party and return the black to his second class position in the South. The Klansmen operated at night and tried to hide their identity with robes and masks. But undisguised vigilantes carried out their work of bloody intimidation in daylight with justified faith that they wouldn't pay for their crimes.

A second factor was the charge of corruption in Southern Republican government. Carpetbaggers and scalawags were anathema in the South. Consequently, if they weren't successful enough to make themselves financially independent, and (like many other Southerners) they frequently weren't, they had just two options, leave the South or go into politics, for the South closed all other avenues of livelihood to them. Many chose politics. And when they got into positions of power, a good number decided to do as well for themselves as they could. Republican politicians (carpetbagger, scalawag and black) did tend to be corrupt. Mitigating this situation was the fact that, under Grant, politics everywhere was venal. Nevertheless, corruption was a strong stick with which to beat Republican stewardship in the South.

And finally, the radical reconstructionists died out, and no one stepped forward to take their place.

Not so slowly and very surely the black was deprived of his political and civil rights. As W. E. B. DuBois said, "The slave went free, stood a brief moment in the sun; then moved back again toward slavery."

With industrialization in the North and the whole expanding West in which to invest, few financiers were interested in putting their money into the violent and unstable South. As a consequence, the South was cash poor and ran on credit. Most planters were able to hold onto their land. But they were destitute. The system of labor that evolved to farm the plantations was sharecropping. A family, generally black, was given responsibility for a plot of land. It shared the crop produced with the land owner. This system had appeal for both the land owner and the sharecropper. The black sharecropper was removed from direct white supervision. And unlike a wage system, which attracted only men, sharecropping gave each man's family an incentive to go into the fields and work.

The difficulty was that neither the land owner nor the sharecropper had any cash on which to subsist until the crop came in. Consequently, they both had to depend on credit for their necessities. Credit was available only on the basis of reliable collateral. In the South, the only crop that constituted reliable collateral was cotton. Consequently, all factors moved the South toward a one crop (cotton) economy. Increasingly, the South began to resemble a banana republic.

By 1876, all the Southern states but Florida, South Carolina, and Louisiana had been redeemed — that is, the Democratic party was in firm control and white supremacy had been unquestionably established. In the presidential election, Rutherford B. Hayes, the Republican, ran against Samuel J. Tilden, the Democrat. Tilden chalked up an impressive lead in the popular vote. But as the returns rolled in, the Republicans noticed that, if Hayes were able to carry Florida, South Carolina, and Louisiana, he would win the presidency by one electoral vote. The Republicans controlled the election machinery in these three states. The election boards in these states invalidated enough votes to deliver the electoral votes of these states to Hayes. The Democrats won the state house in Florida. But in South Carolina and Louisiana, the state elections were contested. Federal troops, which still occupied South Carolina and Louisiana, were dispatched to guard the state houses, so that the Republican candidates could make good their claim to the state offices.

The Democrats challenged the presidential results. Congress established a commission to investigate the situation. In a straight party line vote, the commission awarded the disputed electoral votes to Hayes. The Democrats were outraged and vowed to tie up the House so that the electoral votes couldn't be officially counted, which would make an inauguration on March 4 impossible.

The impasse was resolved by the Compromise of 1877, put together at Wormley House, a hotel in Washington (interestingly enough, owned by a black), in February. What was agreed on no one knows. But the results were clear. The Democrats called off their dilatory tactics; Hayes was elected president; Hayes directed the federal troops, guarding the South Carolina and Louisiana state houses, back to their barracks; the Democrats assumed the governorship in both states; and Hayes and the Republicans turned their backs on any further Reconstruction efforts in the South. The South was now completely redeemed, and Reconstruction was no more.

Thus, in terms of justice for the black, Reconstruction was a failure. But the outcome was also a tragedy for the whole South. It became a land of nostalgia and provincialism with a defective economic system. The only Americans with a less promising future than the Southern whites were the Southern blacks.

What remained were the Fourteenth and Fifteenth Amendments. They provided a firm foundation for the slow climb toward equality that exploded into the civil rights movements of the 1950's and 60's.

CHAPTER SEVENTEEN

The Industrial Revolution

The US that fought the Civil War was rural. According to the 1860 census, five sixths of all US citizens lived in bucolic surroundings. Between the end of the Civil War and the beginning of World War I, this rural country was wrenchingly transformed into a wealthy, productive, densely populated, city dwelling, industrialized nation. It was an Industrial Revolution.

As we've already noted, the Industrial Revolution wasn't a new thing. It began in England and Scotland in the 18th century, and it wasn't long before the ingenuity and industriousness of the Yankee enabled the US to outstrip the old country in the production of textiles, metal products, and farm machinery. Note has also been taken of the favorable impact of turnpikes, canals and railroads on commerce in allowing new markets to be opened up and penetrated.

However, by the end of the Civil War, there was a vast area of the US still outside the transportation network centered in the Northeast. By then, the railroad had been established as the most flexible, economic means of transportation for the times. The US threw itself into railroad construction without restraint. In 1916, railroad track mileage peaked at 254,037.

Not only did the railroad open up the country to commerce and employ thousands upon thousands of people. It was also made up of steel rails and rolling stock, and ran on coal, which resulted in the creation and development of a host of other industries: new coal and iron mines, new coking, iron and steel plants, and new workshops to build and maintain engines and passenger and freight cars. Not only did the needs of the railroads call forth these other industries, the railroads made these other industries possible by providing the volume transportation necessary to deliver the coal and iron ore to the steel mills and the steel to the plants that shaped it into the required products.

Besides the railroad, another impetus to industry was the discovery of a new lubricant and fuel, petroleum. The first refinery

A Steam Engine *trails its train and a plume of smoke across the Western plains. From a photograph in the collection of Lucius Beebe as reproduced in his book* Hear the Train Blow *written with Charles Clegg and published by Dutton in 1952.*

began operation in 1859 at Oil Creek, Pennsylvania. Initially, petroleum was used primarily in the form of kerosene as a fuel for lamps.

As we've already observed from time to time, in addition to material and labor, the third factor needed by industry was capital. The industrial explosion that occurred at the end of the 19th century created an unusually heavy demand for capital at the same time that the mechanisms for making capital available were in their infancy. As a result, the ability to manage capital — to accumulate, use and maintain it — became the most rewarded skill of the times, and the men who were unusually proficient in this area — men such as Andrew Carnegie, Jay Cooke, Henry Clay Frick, Jay Gould, Edward Harriman, James Hill, J. Pierpont Morgan, John D. Rockefeller, and Cornelius Vanderbilt — were lionized as captains of industry and held up as models for emulation. They were also castigated as robber barons, an epithet coined by Matthew Josephson, which he used as the title for a book that he authored. Like other muckrakers, Josephson wrote to correct what he thought was the unsubstantiated exaltation of these men.

For better or worse, the balance seems to have tipped in favor of seeing these men as robber barons, thanks to the forceful, entertaining style in which the muckrakers wrote. In a sense, this is unfortunate. The early capitalists were unbridled competitors, and they did engage in excess. They took on each other in law courts at the same time as they fought pitched battles with what amounted to private armies. But they lived in new times with no precedents to guide them. And they have been given a bad press.

To take one example, Vanderbilt's statement, "The public be damned," is generally cited as evidence of the lack of concern with which the capitalists viewed the source of their revenue. But the saying has been torn out of context. First of all, it wasn't the rough, tough, fabulous Cornelius who made the remark, but his less colorful and more plodding son, William. There are two versions of how Vanderbilt came to make this statement. According to Josephson, the occasion for the comment was the cancellation of the fast extra-fare mail train between New York and Chicago, because it wasn't making money. A reporter wanted to know why the action was being taken when the public found the train both useful and convenient. Couldn't accommodation be made? "The public be damned," exploded Vanderbilt, "If the public want the train why don't they pay for it?"

According to Albro Martin, the occasion for the remark was the institution of limited trains (express trains for which intermediate stops were limited) between Chicago and New York by the Pennsylvania railroad. The reporters asked Vanderbilt if the New York Central (Vanderbilt's railroad) was going to introduce such limited service, since it served the public's need for better passenger service. "The public be damned," exploded Vanderbilt,

A Vat of Molten Steel *being poured into a mold at the Jones and Laughlin Steel company in Pittsburgh, Pennsylvania, in the late 1800's. From a photograph in the National Archives in College Park, Maryland.*

"We will run limited trains because the Pennsylvania runs limited trains."

Either way, far from being a display of indifference, the remark exhibited only the most basic kind of economic sense. Martin points out that reporters of the day were frequently less than ethical, and there's a good chance that Vanderbilt never made the remark. In any case, the fact of the matter was that, during this period, most industries were continually short of funds and assiduously courted the public, since that's where the money was.

The early capitalists have also been accused of being wasteful. The example usually cited was the building of parallel railroad lines, which was done to prevent competitors from obtaining a dominant market position. But was it so wasteful? Today in transportation, the railroad plays second fiddle to trucking, and we've been more accustomed to seeing track torn up than laid. It's inappropriate to compare the conditions of today's railroads with the vitality they showed in the late 1800's. But some of their lassitude has to be attributed to the intense regulation under which they ultimately came, in part to prevent the alleged wastefulness previously lamented. This deadening regulation was relaxed in 1980, and US railroads now show indications that they may revive.

A better basis for comparison might be AT&T, which until recently, was a highly regulated monopoly (because we felt we couldn't afford parallel communications lines) that recognized its public responsibility and took special pains to see that it was served. Nevertheless, AT&T's monopoly was broken. We now have a plethora of parallel communications systems. Is this wasteful? If the jury is out on this question, there's no doubt that the resulting competition has yielded significantly less expensive communications facilities.

Finally, let's look at the predatory pricing that Rockefeller was said to have practiced so effectively to drive out other producers. The idea was to set prices so low that his competitors couldn't make a profit. When they were financially exhausted and had to retire, Rockefeller would then remain as a monopoly and be able to manage his prices without competitive restraint. There's no doubt that Rockefeller put his competitors under price pressure. "A good sweating will be healthy for them," he said. He early recognized that refining was the choke point of the petroleum industry, and he set out to dominate it. But price cutting was only one of his weapons, and a minor one at that. Most of Rockefeller's competitors ended up by joining the Standard Oil Company on generous terms and became loyal members of the organization.

Economists are generally agreed that predatory pricing is poor policy. It drains resources while being practiced, and no sooner does the surviving monopolist begin to enjoy his unique position than new competitors arise to take the place of those driven out. And so it was with Rockefeller. By 1898, Standard was refining 83.7 percent of all the oil produced in the US. Yet those independent refiners continued to crop up. The first gusher at Spindletop, Texas in 1901 was the crushing blow, occurring long before the Standard trust was dissolved in 1911 under the Sherman Anti-Trust Act. This breakup was more apparent than real. Thirty eight companies were created out of the old Standard. But Rockefeller had a large stake in all of them, most of the officers of these companies had been developed by him, and these managers took few actions without first consulting with John D.

The Sherman Anti-Trust Act was passed in 1890. Initially, it was used primarily against labor unions, a not unreasonable target, since the act was designed to prohibit combinations in restraint of trade. Theodore Roosevelt is generally characterized as the "trust buster". He did use the Sherman Act to break up J. P. Morgan's railroad trust, the Northern Securities Company. Morgan was finally vindicated in 1970, when the railroads making up his trust were merged to form the Burlington Northern.

In any case, trusts were stronger when Roosevelt left office than they were when he entered. There was little love lost between Roosevelt and Morgan. When Roosevelt went on his African safari, Morgan said, "We expect the first lion Roosevelt meets to do his duty." Nevertheless, when Roosevelt and Morgan came together, which they did frequently, they more often acted in concert than contention.

Roosevelt's hand-picked successor, William Taft, was more active in the antitrust arena than Roosevelt. It was under Taft that both US Steel and Standard Oil were sued for being in violation of antitrust law.

In another note on the rising importance of capitalism, in 1867, Karl Marx published the first volume of his work, *Das Kapital*. In fact, it was Marx who coined the word capitalism.

By 1900, the US was the world's leading industrial nation. It produced more coal and pig iron, and processed more raw cotton, than its nearest competitor, England, produced more iron ore and steel than Germany, more gold than Australia, and nearly as much silver as Mexico, more tobacco and cotton than India, and more wheat than Russia. The telephone and electric light bulb had been invented and were being perfected. The steam engine, the steam turbine, the dynamo, and the internal combustion engine were all proven. Use of the telegraph was widespread. Bridge building and the production of iron pipe and steel wire were mechanized. Cereal and sugar processing, brewing, and distilling were done in plants.

Gasoline driven cars became commercially available in 1896. Ten years later, Henry Ford introduced mass production into the industry. By 1915, almost a million cars and trucks were being turned out each year. The automobile stimulated the steel, rubber, glass, copper, leather, textile and petroleum businesses. It also led to a new round of road, bridge and tunnel construction.

The tin can introduced a fundamental change in fruit, vegetable and fish processing. New machinery raised cotton and silk production to hitherto unimagined levels. In 1907, Leo H. Baekeland transformed phenol and formaldehyde into the first plastic, which he called Bakelite. In 1910, the mechanical fabrication of an artificial textile, rayon, became commercially feasible.

In addition to the markets that all these industries and innovations created, the emergence of a nationwide market free of trade restrictions also served as a powerful stimulus to business activity. It was during this period that invention was converted from an individual to a corporate activity, which resulted in the founding and growth of research laboratories devoted to the deliberate creation of new products.

However, it shouldn't be thought that all this industrial advance was accomplished without pain. The period following the Civil War saw burgeoning railroad building financed by debt. By the end of the war, tariff walls had been raised to such a protectionist level that all sorts of inefficient manufacturing became possible. Prices for agricultural products were good, which encouraged farmers to borrow so that they could extend their land holdings. The air went out of this inflated boom when, on September 18, 1873, Jay Cooke went bankrupt. Cooke had marketed the government's bonds during the Civil War and was the financier of the Northern Pacific railway. The stock market immediately broke. By now, banks loans came in the form of demand deposits set up by banks and against which borrowers could write checks, rather than in the form of bank notes. Correspondingly, bank suspension of redemption now took the form of refusing to cash checks rather than refusing to exchange specie for notes. By the end of September, most banks were refusing to cash checks.

By the end of the year, the financial crisis was over. But this Panic of 1873 had revealed the incredible weakness of the financial structure of the railroads and had dealt a sharp blow to the confidence of the population. Railroad construction came to a halt, which brought the steel industry to its knees. Business failure and unemployment became endemic. Recovery finally took hold in 1878.

In the early 1890's, the US experienced a continuing outflow of gold, which led to concern over whether it could remain on the gold standard. This concern led to a sharp drop on the stock market in the first half of 1893. The Panic of 1893 was on. Banks once more resorted to refusing to cash checks. By fall, business failures were numbered in the thousands, among them many prominent railroads. These hard times continued for three more years. Almost one fourth of railroad capitalization went through bankruptcy proceedings. Agricultural prices collapsed. An estimated three million people were unemployed. It wasn't until 1897 that the economy recovered.

It's estimated that, between 1830 and 1910, about 35 million people immigrated to the US. This migration occurred in three waves. The first began in the 1830's and reached a high-water mark of 427,833 in 1854. The second, starting in the 1870's, crested at 788,992 in 1882. The third brought in about a million a year during the first decade of the 20th century. A fourth wave of immigration is now occurring. In the 1980's, over ten million immigrants entered the US. Despite this influx, the highest the percentage of foreign born in the US has ever gotten was 15 percent, which was attained in 1890.

The impediments to immigration were formidable. The only affordable transportation was steerage, where lack of space prohibited privacy, ventilation was poor, and living conditions were far from healthy. When the harrowing trip was over, the immigrants were faced with the rigors of the New World. Lowlife lay in wait to grab the immigrants' luggage and, for a fee, lead them to ill kept lodging houses. There they were overcharged until their money ran out, at which point they were unceremoniously thrown out. The fortunate were met at the boat by friends or relatives who would guide them through their indoctrination into the New World. Even so, their housing and working conditions were abominable. Young and old, men labored for a pittance in unsafe jobs, and women sat at home in overcrowded tenements where they spent their days and much of their nights cutting and sewing.

And still, they came. They were driven by intolerable conditions at home. Famine, epidemic, the collapse of economies, the pressure of population on land, and political, religious and racial persecution impelled them across their borders. In addition, the demand of US enterprise for labor lured them on. Foreigners were actively recruited by US industry.

Labor organizations have been present in the US since its inception. However, for one reason or another, most of these organizations have had fleeting lives. Their impact hasn't been so much in what they did as it was in the programs that they developed that were adopted and put in place by the major political parties. Such programs include prohibition of child labor, work-place safety, lien laws, abolishment of imprisonment for debt, and the eight-hour day.

The first labor organization to become a permanent feature on the US scene was the American Federation of Labor (AFL), which grew out of an organization formed in 1881 under the name of the Federation of Organized Trades and Labor Unions of the United States and Canada. Like its successor, it was partial to the crafts and had little to offer the unskilled. For representation, this group had to wait for the formation of the Congress of Industrial Organizations (CIO), which split off from the AFL in 1936.

The AFL owed its longevity to its program. The union members were interested in personal betterment. They saw the union as an instrument to further that quest. Strikes were permissible if directed toward a pragmatic objective. But collaboration with the bosses was generally a more productive way of attaining the membership's goals.

US unions recognized that economic life wasn't compartmentalized from politics and have been politically active. But more extreme commitments, particularly to socialism, which maintained that capitalism was the root of the workingman's troubles and that the means of production had to be nationalized, was something espoused by only shorter lived groups on the fringes of the labor movement.

A part of the US population, weighted toward farmers, had always been in debt. These debtors were interested in measures that would alleviate their condition. As a consequence, the country has been more or less continuously treated to efforts aimed at "soft money" (an increase in the money supply, which would inflate away at least part of the debt burden), making loans available at lower than normal rates, and debt suspension. One manifestation of this tendency was the populist movement that began in the 1870's, one of the planks of which was support for continued availability of "greenbacks", the paper currency issued during the Civil War, when the government's supply of specie proved inadequate to cover obligations incurred in support of the war. In effect, the populists wanted fiat money (valued because the government would say it was good for payment of all debts, public or private, and would back up its proclamation with the force of law) instead of "hard money", currency backed by the government's willingness to exchange it at face value for gold coin. Today, fiat money is what we have. To keep a curb on inflation, the volume of this money available in the economy is restrained by the actions of the Federal Reserve System.

The greenbackers were shoved aside by the mania for silver that swept the West and South in the eighties. The goal here was silver coinage, pushed heavily by the silver mining concerns in the West.

The greenbackers rightly, although vainly, stressed that a shift in financial politics to free silver fatally undermined the program they were trying to promote. Nevertheless, the greenbackers were preempted by the silverites, memorialized in William Jennings Bryan's speech to the Democratic convention in 1896. In expressing his opposition to continuing the gold standard, he said, "You shall not press down upon the brow of labor this crown of thorns, you shall not crucify mankind upon a cross of gold." In 1892, he had said that he did not "know anything about free silver" but "the people of Nebraska are for free silver and I am for free silver. I will look up the arguments later."

In any case, Bryan lost the election; William McKinley became the nation's 25th president; the gold standard, which had been adopted in 1879, was retained; and the People's party, the political manifestation of the populist movement, disappeared from the public scene. In the longer perspective, the US went off the gold standard in 1933, and the nation now has the fiat money for which the populists had worked so hard and unavailingly. But the populist voice hasn't been stilled. The cry for soft money and subsidized loans continues to be heard.

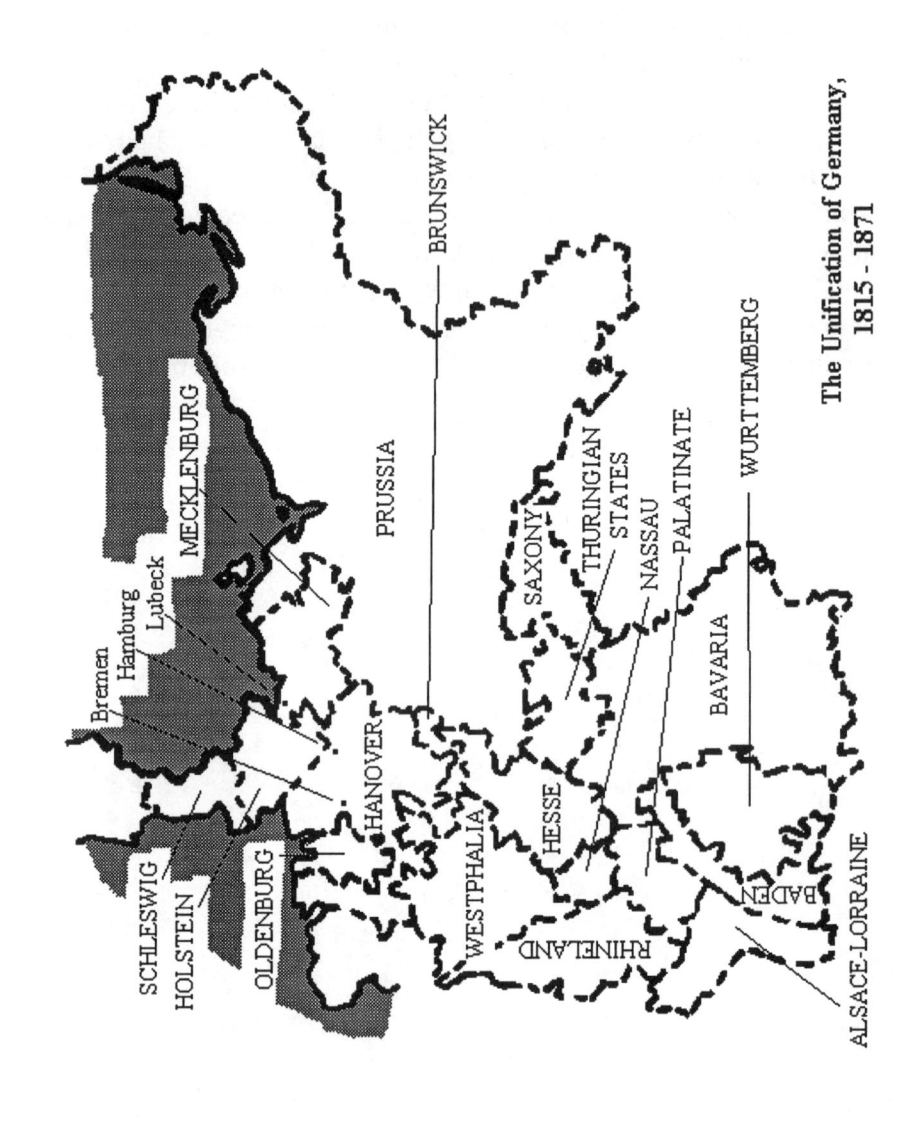

The Unification of Germany, 1815 - 1871

CHAPTER EIGHTEEN

The First World War

In 1870, the German states, under the leadership of Otto von Bismarck of Prussia, responded to a French declaration of war by handing France a decisive defeat at Sedan on September 1 and capturing the Emperor Napoleon III. On January 28, 1871, Paris capitulated, and an armistice was concluded. In the wave of enthusiasm for collective action that followed this military victory, on April 14, the representatives of the German states met in the Hall of Mirrors at Versailles and proclaimed the formation of the nation of Germany. It was composed of 25 states: the four kingdoms of Prussia, Bavaria, Saxony and Wurttemberg; five grand duchies; 13 duchies and principalities; and the three free cities of Hamburg, Bremen and Lubeck. In the peace treaty ending the Franco-German war, signed at Frankfurt-on-Main on May 10, France ceded the region of Alsace-Lorraine to Germany and agreed to pay a war indemnity of five billion francs.

In 1879, after extended negotiation, an Austro-German Alliance was signed. It made sense. Germany felt threatened by France. Austria felt threatened by all the countries on her borders, including Germany. After the Alliance, the Germanic flavor of the Habsburg monarchy no longer constituted a lure to German aggression. Instead, it caused each country to look on the well being of the other as inseparable from its own. The Austrians committed themselves to coming to the aid of Germany if Germany became the object of French aggression. Germany's reciprocal commitment came into play if Russia advanced on Austria.

Germany had designs on Russia. One of the things holding Germany back from advancing on its eastern neighbor was the presence of France to its rear. Germany considered France a mortal enemy. It seemed that, sooner or later, Germany must do battle with this foe. If Germany were to succeed in knocking out France, Russia would then be left to face Germany alone. In an analogous way, France wasn't enamored of taking on Germany by

Europe in 1914

itself. So these two otherwise unlikely candidates, the republic of France and the Russian autocracy, were, willy-nilly, drawn together out of mutual self-interest. Ultimately, a Franco-Russian Alliance was signed in 1894, in which the parties committed themselves to come to each other's aid if attacked by Germany or one of her allies.

In 1871, Germany had demonstrated its military prowess. By 1914, it dominated Europe industrially. It was also at the forefront in terms of organizational effectiveness, education, medicine, social legislation, and population growth. Its achievements engendered an increasing pride of accomplishment, which led to thoughts of a race destined for greatness. Territorial expansion was a necessary concomitant of such a future. So sooner or later, to the German mind, military action was probably inevitable. The Franco-Russian Alliance made a two front war equally unavoidable, and that's what the German military planned for.

On Sunday, June 28, 1914, the Archduke Francis Ferdinand, heir to the Austrian throne, and his wife, the Duchess of Hohenburg, were assassinated in Serajevo, Bosnia. The assassin was a consumptive 19 year old, Gavrilo Princip, a Bosnian by birth.

In 1878, at the Congress of Berlin, the European powers had redrawn a part of the map of the Balkans to give Russia some compensation for having just defeated Turkey but to prevent it from assuming the more dominant position in the area that it had been conceded by its treaty with Turkey. Russia agreed to this renegotiation in response to threatening moves by England. As a part of this territorial rearrangement, the province of Bosnia continued to be part of Turkey but was to be garrisoned and administered by Austria. In effect, Austria had the say in all of Bosnia's military and political affairs. In the summer of 1908, a coup occurred in Turkey. Austria was fearful that the new government might try to reassert its dominion in Bosnia, so in 1909, Austria annexed Bosnia. Thus, technically, Princip was an Austrian subject.

However, Princip was involved with the Black Hand, a Serbian terrorist organization dedicated to detaching the southwestern provinces of Austria, which were Slavic, from Austria and joining them to Serbia. In the South Slavic language, "South Slav" is Yugoslav.

Nevertheless, no tie has ever been made between the Black Hand or Princip and the Serbian government.

In those days, there was a Serbian nation. Not only did the country exist, but it had recently expanded its borders at the expense of Turkey, the "sick man of Europe" (so-called because it was expected to collapse any day), which had been defeated in 1912 by a coalition of Bulgaria, Greece, Montenegro and Serbia.

The phrase, sick man of Europe, was coined by Russia, which suggested to England that they had better carve up this sick man between them before he fell apart, certainly an innovation in the annals of medical treatment.

The Austria of the Habsburgs was more a relic of the Middle Ages than a modern nation. It was what remained of the Holy Roman empire. It was made up of a number of ethnic groups that presented it with multiple volatile threats to its unity; it was unable to establish an effective rapport with its diverse populace; as a consequence, it maintained its unity by keeping its minorities in thrall; and it felt that, to maintain internal stability and prevent Serbia from becoming a lodestar for its south Slav minorities, it had to take strong action against Serbia, even without unquestioned proof that the Serbian government was party to the archduke's assassination.

However, before doing anything, Austria checked to be certain it had Germany's backing. Germany recognized that Austria's proposed action might lead to war between Austria and Russia, which in turn, would drag both Germany and France into the conflict. But then, sooner or later, war was inevitable, and now might be better than later, since with the passage of time, it looked like Russia could only grow stronger. Consequently, Germany assured Austria that it was behind Austria.

As a result, at 6 pm on July 23, Austria delivered a note to Serbia in which Serbia was accused of, among other things, encouraging the growth of a subversive movement in Austrian territory. The note ended with ten demands, several impinging on Serbia's sovereignty. Unconditional acceptance within 48 hours was called for.

The Serbian reply essentially agreed to the dictates. Only Austria's insistence, that its judges conduct the trials of the accessories to the plot to assassinate the archduke, was questioned. But even this Serbia was willing to submit for review by either the International Tribunal at the Hague or a meeting of the great powers.

The reply was delivered to the Austrian minister in Belgrade, the Serbian capital, at 6 pm on July 25. Since the reply wasn't unconditional acceptance of Austria's demands, the minister signed and dispatched a previously prepared note breaking off diplomatic relations and caught the 6:30 train for Austria. On July 28, Austria declared war on Serbia. On July 29, Belgrade was shelled by Austrian artillery stationed on the Austrian side of the Danube. On July 30, Austria began to mobilize.

When Sergei D. Sazonov, the Russian foreign minister, heard of the shelling, he decided that the time had come for his country to get involved. In keeping with the principles of pan-Slavism (the idea that there existed a bond between all Slavic peoples), Russia had routinely presented itself as a protector of the Balkan states, one of which was Serbia. But Sazonov's decision to act had more than altruistic motives. Russia's desire for access to a warm water port dictated a continuing interest in seeing that developments in the Balkans were in its favor.

At Sazonov's urging, Tsar Nicholas II approved an order for general mobilization. A few hours later, the tsar revoked the general mobilization in favor of a partial mobilization against Austria alone.

To understand what was happening here, it's necessary to appreciate the significance that the term, mobilization, had in 1914. Mobilization referred to a deliberate act on a nation's part. Not only were the nation's armies marshaled for action, but a complex set of initiatives, that placed the whole nation on a war footing, was put into effect. Among thousands of other measures, reserves were called up, leaves were canceled, troops were transferred to battle stations, martial law was declared in frontier areas, fortresses were manned, and rail transport was taken over. Mobilization took, at a minimum, days to take place. For a country such as Russia, with an inadequate rail system and other inefficiencies, the time required ran into weeks.

There were two unavoidable consequences of this state of affairs. One was that, to carry out mobilization, detailed plans had to be prepared far in advance of the actual act of mobilization. The complexity of these plans were such that it was felt, at least by the military (who laid them out and were responsible for implementing them), that they couldn't be modified on short notice without creating chaos. As a result, to the military mind, mobilization was an all or none affair: you either initiated it in toto or you didn't do it all.

The other inevitable consequence of a world made up of countries, each with a mobilization plan, was that, if a nation's neighbor began to mobilize, the nation had just two options, either remain passive in the face of a potential enemy preparing for all out military action or mobilize yourself. You can imagine what the typical choice was.

Understandably then, the Russian military reacted violently against the idea of trying to mobilize against Austria alone. By late afternoon on July 30, the tsar was persuaded, and the orders for general mobilization were reissued. As a consequence, Russia began to mobilize, not only on her Austrian border, but also on her German frontier.

In response, on July 31, Germany issued an ultimatum to Russia to demobilize within 12 hours and make "a distinct declaration to that effect." At noon on Saturday, August 1, the ultimatum ran out without being responded to. Less than an hour later, a telegram was sent to the German ambassador in St. Petersburg in which he was directed to declare war by 5 that afternoon. At 5 pm, Germany decreed general mobilization.

German mobilization was just the first step in its "two front" strategy, which it felt it was forced into by the Franco-Russian Alliance. The strategy had been formulated by Count Alfred von Schlieffen, chief of the German general staff from 1891 to 1906. He completed this "Schlieffen plan" in 1906. It had remained virtually unchanged since then. The essence of the plan was that Germany must deal with its opponents one at a time. This meant that either France or Russia had to be taken out quickly, so that Germany could then concentrate on its remaining foe. Russia couldn't be this first target, since its expanse would allow it to frustrate a rapid victory simply by staged retreat.

The estimate was that it would take Russia six weeks to complete mobilization. By that time, France could be conquered. However, it couldn't be defeated by an attack on the Franco-German border. There France had fortified itself, and Germany didn't have the time that it would take to conquer this frontier by siege. The alternative was to sweep through Belgium, attack the French armies from the rear, and demolish them.

At 7 pm on August 1, the first border was breached. A German company moved into Luxembourg to take over a railroad station and telegraph office where the lines from Germany and Belgium intersected. The place the Germans violated the border was named Trois Vierges. These three virgins were supposed to be faith, hope and charity. But in the world's eyes, they soon came to represent Luxembourg, Belgium and France.

In the early evening of August 3, the German declaration of war was delivered to France. Later that same day, Sir Edward Grey, the English foreign secretary, standing at a window in Whitehall with a friend and watching the street lamps being lit, was inspired, by some reverse image of what he was physically watching, to make the remark that has, ever since, epitomized the First World War, "The lamps are going out all over Europe; we shall not see them lit again in our lifetime."

At two minutes past 8 in the morning of August 4, the Germans crossed the Belgian border at Gemmenich. In 1839, Belgian neutrality had been guaranteed in perpetuity by the five major European powers, one of which was Germany's predecessor, Prussia. The others were Austria, England, France and Russia.

At noon on August 4, King Albert of Belgium appealed for "concerted and common" action by the guarantors of his country's neutrality. England felt that it now no longer had any choice. An ultimatum had been prepared in which it was stated that England felt bound "to uphold the neutrality of Belgium and the observance of the treaty to which Germany is as much a party as ourselves." When there was no longer any question that Belgium had been invaded, the ultimatum was presented by the English ambassador to the German chancellor, Theobold von Bethmann-Hollweg, and "a satisfactory reply" was demanded by midnight. In response, Bethmann delivered a tirade in which he placed on England the responsibility for all the dreadful events that might follow, and "all for just a word, 'neutrality', just for a scrap of paper … " In this offhand way, and probably without even noticing it, Bethmann thus uttered the phrase that was to reverberate throughout the world.

Midnight in Berlin was 11 pm in London, and when this

Belgium and Luxembourg

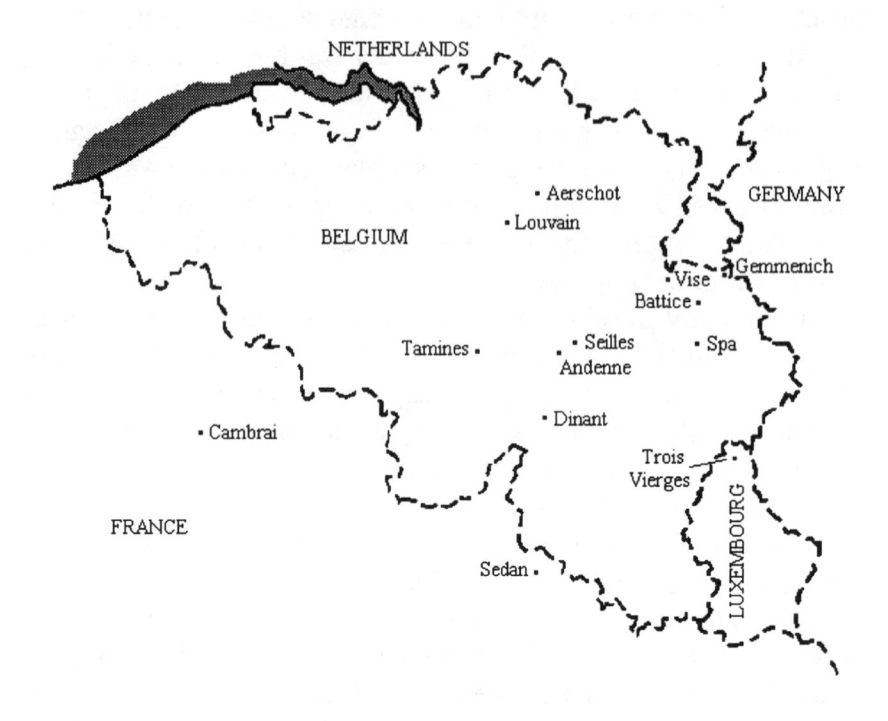

moment arrived with no reply from Germany, England declared war.

As they marched through Belgium, the Germans solidified their reputation as Huns, on which they had begun work in 1870 after Sedan. In the civilian population, the Germans saw guerrillas. To suppress guerrilla tactics, real and imagined, they took and executed hostages, and sacked and burned towns. Battice, Aerschot, Andenne, Seilles, Tamines, Vise, Dinant, Louvain ... each name represented untold atrocities, the details of which accumulated into an overflowing mountain of horror to which the world reacted with irrepressible revulsion.

And still the German juggernaut rolled on. The French pleaded with the Russians to take action soon, before the French army was overwhelmed. In response, Russia went on the offensive before the organization of its supply lines for its armies was complete. Preliminary action took place on August 12, and the general advance began on August 17. Waxing and waning, the battle finally drew to a close on August 30. The Russians were hampered by a shortage of artillery shells and inadequate communication facilities. Toward the end of the battle, literally starving Russian soldiers stumbled through swamps crisscrossed by causeways where Germans manned machine guns at every intersection. It's estimated that the Russians lost over 30,000 men, dead or missing, and an additional 92,000 were taken prisoner. When the French expressed their condolences to the Russian commander in chief, the Grand Duke Nicholas, a member of the royal family, he replied that, "We are happy to have made such sacrifices for our Allies."

The Russian offensive did get the Germans' attention. On August 25, two German corps were transferred from the Western to the Eastern Front.

Whether the missing two corps were the decisive factor is one of those historical imponderables, but on November 11, the French, with some help from England, finally brought the German advance to a halt along the Marne. The conflict then sank into trench warfare, where it remained for over three years and voraciously sucked up material, munitions, money and men. It's estimated that, in the war as a whole, Russia and Germany lost a million and three quarters men each, England just under a million, France and Austria over a million each, and the US 126,000. In total, the number of deaths was about eight and one half million. England, in particular, yielded up the flower of her youth to death's embrace. These young men were inspired by high hopes for the world that might emerge at the war's end and enlisted in large numbers. In those days, people spoke of honor and glory with sincere openness.

On February 1, 1917, Germany embarked on a policy of unrestricted submarine warfare: all vessels, Allied or neutral, in the war zone around England and France would henceforth be torpedoed without warning. The object was to drive all shipping, which formed a vital supply line to the Allies, off the high seas.

The US refused to end its merchant shipping in the war zone and began to lose vessels to German submarines. President Woodrow Wilson, reelected on the slogan, "He kept us out of war", and deeply pacifist, finally bowed to the inevitable and on April 2, 1917, asked a joint session of Congress for a declaration of

The Western Front

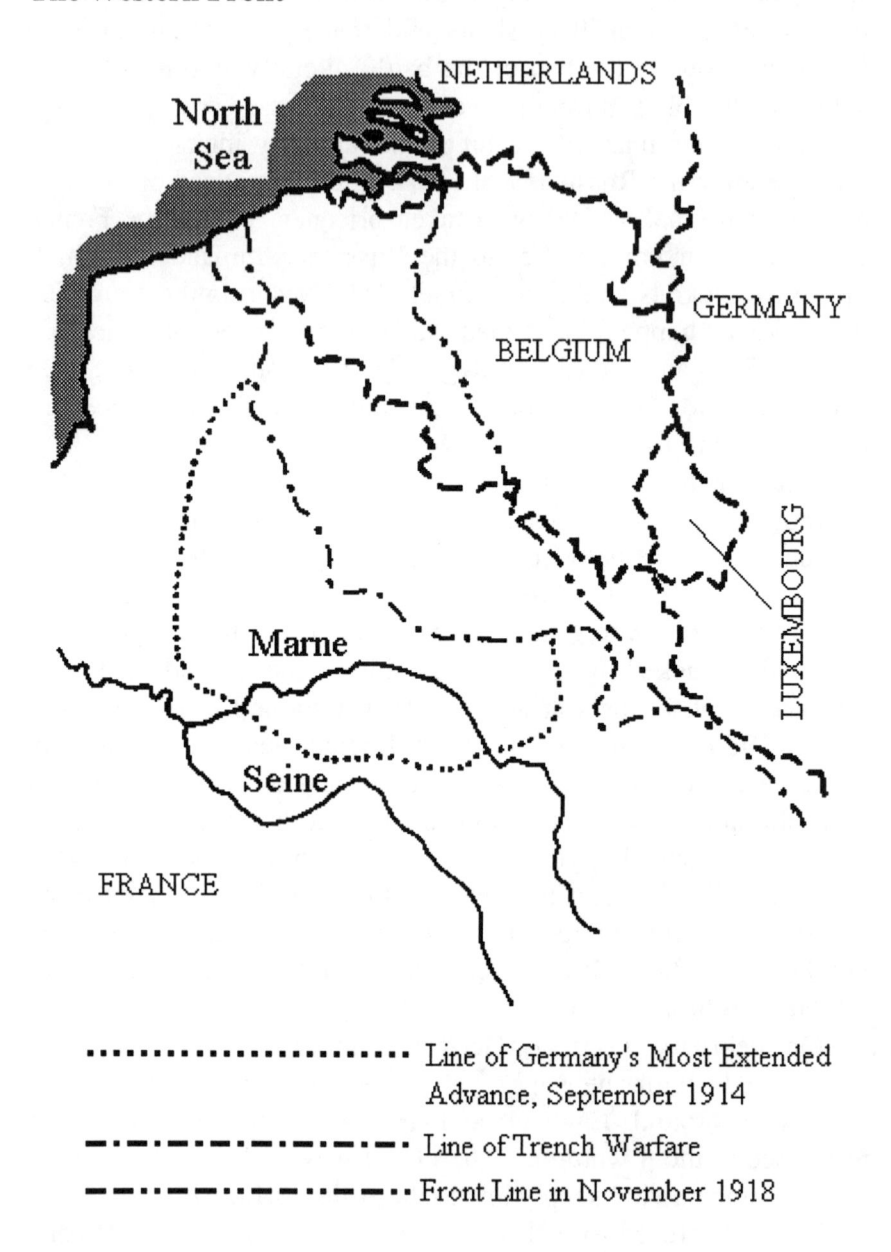

.... Line of Germany's Most Extended Advance, September 1914

—·—·—·—·—·—·—·— Line of Trench Warfare

—··—··—··—··—··—·· Front Line in November 1918

war. "The world must be made safe for democracy," he said. War was declared on April 6.

Although unrestricted submarine warfare brought the US into the war, it can't be said to have been an unsound policy. It was the result of an unflinching stare into the reality that, at bottom, the war was one of supply. The object was to throttle England and France before they choked off Germany. And it nearly succeeded. When Vice Admiral William Snowden Sims of the US navy arrived in London on April 9 (to confer with the English admiralty), Sir John Jellicoe, First Lord of the Admiralty, confessed that, "It is impossible to go on with the war if losses like these continue."

Fortunately, an on-the-spot, successful defense against the submarine was developed. It was the convoy. By August, an encompassing network of Atlantic convoys had been formed. Shipping losses continued. But now they were low enough to be more than offset by new construction. The supply line to Europe held. England and France were saved. As a result, the Allied blockade of Germany continued to gain strength. The doom of Germany became inevitable. At 5 am on November 11, 1918, the Germans agreed to the terms of an armistice.

The First World War saw many advances in war machines and methods. Two new tools, the submarine and machine gun, were well established at the war's beginning. The other innovations took place during the war. The development of convoy tactics has already been noted. The English invented the tank, although its use in concentration didn't take place until the battle of Cambrai, which began on November 20, 1917 and lasted until December 4. Like most of the other battles on the Western Front, it ended as more or less of a draw. But it foreshadowed the battle tactics of the future. Instead of the usual sustained artillery barrage followed by an infantry advance, the Allies initiated the battle of Cambrai with the release of waves of tanks and infantry concurrently with the opening of artillery fire.

At the beginning of the war, the airplane was used almost exclusively for observation, a contribution that, in and of itself, shouldn't be underrated. Armament, if any, consisted of a rifle or pistol carried by flight personnel. By the end of the war, the

Two German Infantrymen Seek Shelter from Artillery. *From a photograph in the Library of Congress.*

airplane, although still in its infancy as a weapon, was a recognized battle factor, so much so that, on April 1, 1918, the English organized the Royal Air Force (RAF), a fighting arm coequal with the army and navy.

One of casualties of the war was Wilson. He wanted the peace treaty to be the basis for world peace. To see that this objective was attained, be headed the US delegation to the peace conference in Paris. He remained in Europe, with one short trip home, for more than six months. To Wilson's mind, the way to world peace was to establish a League of Nations. He insisted that the League Covenant be written into the treaty. The Senate was leery of the

A US Soldier Caught in Barbed Wire *became an easy target for the Germans. From a photograph in the Library of Congress.*

League. But Wilson was adamant. He undertook a personal sweep of the country to galvanize the support of the people. Worn out by his efforts, he was overcome in Pueblo, Colorado. He was quickly returned to Washington, where he had a stroke. The treaty was repudiated in its entirety by the Senate. Although Wilson lived longer than his successor, Warren G. Harding, he spent the rest of his life a physically and spiritually broken man.

The question that begs for an answer is: Were the Germans barbarians? There's no clear answer. In the strict sense, the answer is, "No." The day when enclaves of civilization were surrounded by marches to insulate them from the barbarian hordes who roved the hinterlands had long since passed. But in a larger sense, Germany was a Johnny-come-lately, have-not nation living cheek to jowl with two international empires, England and France, and it felt that it deserved better. The Treaty of Versailles just aggravated this situation. The English and French expanded their empires. Germany lost the overseas possessions it had,

Alsace-Lorraine was returned to France, other territory was given to Belgium and Denmark, sections of what it considered its homeland were taken over to make way for the resurrection of Poland, and it was forced to assume the responsibility for starting the war and subjected to reparations, the amount of which was initially left undefined but which was ultimately set at $33 billion in April 1921. The Treaty of Versailles was an instrument of vindictive punishment for Germany and planted the seeds of World War II.

The horrors of the Western Front left the Allies with a deep distaste for war of any kind, which bred in them an inclination to try to negotiate their way out of conflicts. Some would call it a policy of appeasement.

The German psyche, on the other hand, still colored by the tinge of Prussian militarism and deeply resentful of what was considered misunderstanding during the war and mistreatment afterward, remained impervious to such appeals. Far from being a war to end all wars, the First World War was a sacrificial offering of monumental proportions the hoped for outcome of which was dashed on the rocks of nationalism and retribution. The phrase "the war to end war" was coined by H. G. Wells.

CHAPTER NINETEEN

The Great Depression

The Great Depression was the name given to the deepest economic downturn ever experienced by the US. According to one student of the period, it began during the waning days of October 1929 and ended on December 7, 1941. This, of course, is hyperbole. The economy showed signs of strain long before the stock market crash. Between 1925 and 1929, the price of almost all agricultural commodities dropped in world markets. Bank failures in the 20's were common. The coal and textile industries were less than vibrant. In 1926, sale of new housing began to weaken. By the spring of 1929, general unemployment had become significant. The Federal Reserve indices of industrial activity and factory production reached a peak in June. By fall, all the more respected indicators of manufacturing output had turned down. However, it was the dramatic price drop on the New York Stock Exchange that brought the great depression to center stage.

From then on, the depression remained the focus of attention until it was upstaged by the entry of the US into World War II. Nevertheless, it was 1943 before average annual unemployment fell to less than its predepression level.

Economic downturns weren't unusual in US history. To the contrary, one might say they were almost a characteristic feature of the national scene. There were scores of minor downturns in addition to the major ones that started in 1819, 1837, 1857, 1873 and 1893.

In terms of its duration, which was more than double the length of any of its predecessors, the great depression deserves the modifier, great. But in another sense, the adjective is redundant, because the US has had only one depression. Although the term, depression, wasn't new in 1929, prior to that time, the term generally used to identify an economic downturn was panic. As part of his program to manage the nation's way out of the 1929 downturn, Herbert Hoover, the incumbent president, chose to refer to the downturn as a depression. He thought that, by so doing, he

Howard Street in San Francisco during the Depression. *From a photograph in the Franklin D. Roosevelt library in Hyde Park.*

could prevent the populace from adopting the mindset associated with the word panic. In other words, Hoover's subliminal message was, "Keep up your confidence. This isn't another panic. It's just a depression." The devastation of what Hoover dubbed a depression was such that no administration since has dared to use the term. When the economy now turns down, what we have is a recession. Alfred Kahn, Jimmy Carter's chief inflation fighter, had the temerity, at one point in his public career, to use the term, depression. He was so severely reprimanded for his offense by his political superiors that he pledged thereafter to always substitute the word banana.

But the depression was no joke. From 1929 to the nadir of the depression in 1933, gross domestic product dropped 29 percent, consumption expenditures by 18 percent, construction by 78, and investment by 98. By 1933, unemployment was in the neighborhood of 25 percent of the work force. Hunger was extensive. Perhaps the worst consequence of the depression was the lack of self-confidence bred by the inability to find a job. By the time a job was found, such an undermining of the spirit often led to a nervousness that inhibited the ability to perform, which resulted in an early dismissal. The continual presence of an unemployed, despondent man in the house also placed unusual demands on family relationships.

On the other hand, the situation shouldn't be overdramatized. At all times during the depression, at least 75 percent of those who wanted to work were able to do so. Starvation did occur. But it was rare. The long-term trend toward longer life continued unabated throughout the depression. And the primary impact of the depression on the family was to intensify trends already in existence. Weak families broke up. Strong relationships became even more supportive.

The depression not only differed from its predecessors in its duration, it was also the first to be managed. The classic approach to a panic had always been that it was a normal event about which not much could be done. The proper policy was to let the natural forces work themselves out until the economy recovered. Grover Cleveland, the president who presided over the Panic of 1893, put this policy into words when he said, "Though the people support the Government the Government should not support the people." To be fair to Cleveland, it must be pointed out that he made this remark, not during the Panic of 1893, but six years earlier when he vetoed the appropriation of $10,000 to provide seed grain to Texan farmers. Nevertheless, a point is being made, and Cleveland essentially repeated these words in his 1893 inaugural address.

As we've already observed, the first time the federal government encroached on the workings of the nation was during the Civil War. At the time, everyone involved agreed that it was

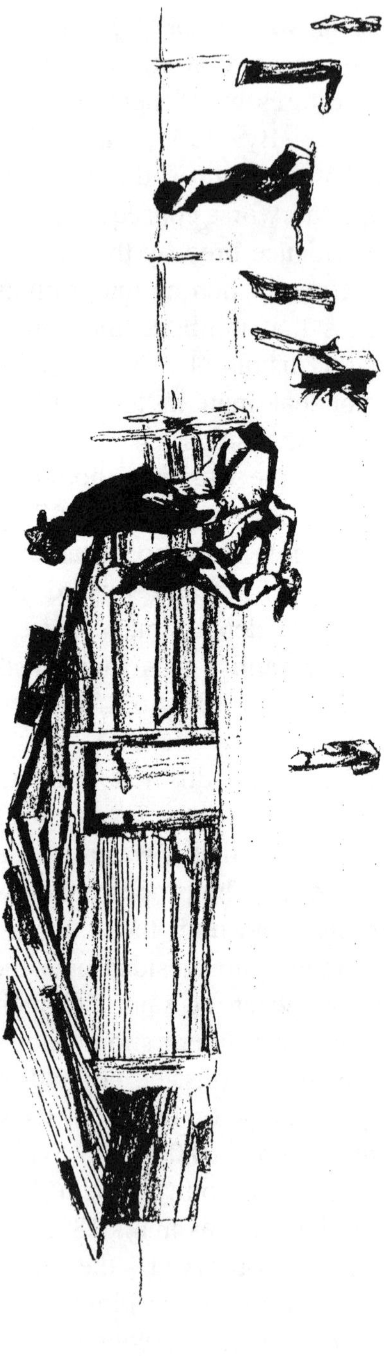

the only way to get on with the war. But the public attitude remained that a federal bureaucracy was an undesirable, if not abnormal, state of affairs. Consequently, the bureaucracy built up during the Civil War was dismantled as soon after the war's end as possible, and the government returned to its policy of noninterference in the affairs of its citizens.

The First World War was the country's second experience with coordination on a grand scale at the federal level. Early in 1918, Bernard Baruch, a Wall Street financier, was placed in charge of the War Industries Board, which directed all manufacturing in the interest of the war effort. The railroads were nationalized. Fuel use was strictly regulated. And the National War Labor Board arbitrated differences between labor. and management.

In the middle of this national management was none other than Hoover. When the war began, more than 150,000 US citizens were stranded in Europe because travel agencies refused to accept US traveler's checks, personal checks, or letters of credit. Hoover and a group of engineer friends located in Europe pooled their resources to help these people return home by personally extending credit to them. The occupation of Belgium and northern France by German troops left about seven and one half million Belgians and two and a half million French — men, women and children — threatened with starvation. Hoover organized the Commission for Relief in Belgium and arranged with the Germans for the passage, through their blockade, of food and clothing for these people. He appealed to the charity of the world for funds. Over four years, the Commission supported these people, isolated behind enemy lines, with about five million tons of food and clothing. When the US entered the war, Wilson appointed Hoover the US food

---

An Oncoming Dust Storm. *An Oklahoma farmer and his sons move toward shelter. From a photograph by Margaret Bourke-White. The photograph is in the Library of Congress and is, perhaps, the best known photograph to come out of the depression. It was in the mid 30's that the farms of the Great Plains became a dust bowl. It was a tragedy in and of itself and was complicated by occurring during the depression. But it wasn't a necessary part of the depression.*

administrator. He boosted farm production to unheard of heights and tripled exports to the Allied countries. After the armistice, he became director general of the American Relief Administration, whose activities saved over 100 million lives in the ten new and resurrected states in Europe.

With the onset of the depression only 11 years after the end of the war, those in positions of power had personal recollections of what the government could do in times of crisis. If the national economy could be managed to contribute to the defeat of the country's enemies, why couldn't it be managed to combat an economic downturn?

The received wisdom depicting Hoover as a conservative do-nothing and his successor, Franklin Delano Roosevelt, as an infallible activist argues with the facts. The contrast between the two was of manner rather than approach. Both were determined to take whatever action was necessary to turn the economy around at the same time as neither knew how to do it.

Hoover's overwhelming inclinations were for rapidly getting involved. After all, he wasn't called "the great engineer" for nothing. When the depression came, he quickly went into gear. Less than a month after the stock market crash, he had initiated the first of a number of conferences with business and labor leaders to reverse the usual reaction to a panic. He appealed to the business leaders to not lower prices or wages and to not reduce the size of their labor force.

Because he believed that government actions should provide a "balance wheel" for the economy, Hoover inaugurated new federal public works on a broad scale. He created the Reconstruction Finance Corporation to make loans to businesses in trouble, an agency Roosevelt saw fit to continue and rely on during his administration. He sponsored a $25 million loan to the Department of Agriculture to supply seed and feed to indigent farmers. All these actions anticipated Roosevelt's policies. It's probable that, if Hoover had been able to retain the presidency, his ultimate actions would have either paralleled or exceeded the ones actually taken by Roosevelt.

But of course, such a succession was impossible. For one thing, the depression happened on Hoover's watch, and the US electorate believes in rejecting such unlucky officers of the day, even when they have no responsibility for what has developed. In addition, Roosevelt was a politician, and Hoover wasn't. Hoover evidenced little feeling for or empathy with individual sufferers. In an attempt to build public confidence, he said things that gave the impression that he was either insensitive, or unwilling to or incapable of facing the facts. He resented criticism and found working with Congress difficult. In sum, he was unable to create the aura of friendship and trust that Roosevelt's unflappable affability projected.

So in 1933, Roosevelt assumed the presidency, a position he retained for the rest of the depression. His approach to the depression, which was termed the New Deal, was consistently political. The object was to keep a majority of the people on his side. His administration was characterized by ambiguity. Actions were taken, first to meet one set of interests and then to meet another, with contradictory and spotty results. But the approach was effective in keeping his administration in office. And through it all, Roosevelt successfully masked the failures of and intramural infighting in his retinue and, to an astounding degree, convinced his constituency that he was both wise and dedicated. His typical approach to a problem was to listen to advocates on all sides of the issue and then tell them to shut themselves in a room, iron out their differences, and bring him a bill on which they could agree.

The goal of many of the New Deal programs was to force supply back into balance with demand by reducing supply and, thus, maintain the existing price level. Again, this approach echoed the acts of Hoover, who had implored business to maintain wages and prices.

The first efforts of this policy were rather gross. In agriculture, the hungry nation was treated to the spectacle of the destruction of six million piglets and 200,000 sows. Ultimately, the Agricultural Adjustment Administration brought far more benefits to the large-scale farmers than to the small. When land was taken out of production to qualify the owner for government support, it was frequently the tenant and sharecropper land that went into the land bank.

Under the National Recovery Administration (NRA), industry was invited, through its trade associations, to administer prices and limit production. The effort failed, and in 1935, the Supreme Court declared the NRA unconstitutional, not because it encouraged collusion, but because it constituted an unwarranted delegation of legislative power to the executive. The death of the NRA probably came as a relief to Roosevelt. "You know," he said, "The whole thing is a mess. It has been an awful headache ... "

The New Deal's work programs (the Civil Works Administration, the Public Works Administration, the Works Progress Administration, the National Youth Administration, and the Civilian Conservation Corps) can also be seen as efforts to reduce supply, in this case, the supply of labor. However, the work programs also had more beneficial effects. They provided relief to the unemployed, and they provided it in return for work. As such, the humiliation of a handout was avoided, and those involved could engage in constructive work. All these programs added significantly to the economic, cultural and environmental infrastructure of the US.

The New Deal also reacted to specific problems and responded to special pleas. The Farm Credit Administration and the Home Owners' Loan Corporation refinanced farm and home mortgages, at least some of which would have otherwise been foreclosed. In an attempt to prop up the faltering bank system, the Federal Deposit Insurance Corporation was instituted to guarantee bank deposits, a program that, later expanded to deposits in savings and loan associations, ultimately resulted in the savings and loan debacle and bank problems of the late 1980's, which cost the US taxpayer over $160 billion to clean up. After all, how cautious would you be in making investments if your assets were guaranteed against loss? Roosevelt wasn't in favor of this program. Like several other aspects of the New Deal, it was forced on him by Congress.

The Rural Electrification Administration brought electricity to most farms. But having served its purpose, it (like other bureaucracies) refused to retire and turned to such functions as providing electricity to ski slopes.

A Silver Purchase Act was passed, presumably in response to pressure for remonitizing silver, although this never happened. It conferred riches on the owners of silver mines and provided employment for a few thousand miners, but otherwise, it had no discernible effect in the US. However, for countries, like China, that were on the silver standard, the results were devastating.

It's even less easy to see the relation between the battle to reduce unemployment and some of the other New Deal programs. Roosevelt wasn't in favor of the Wagner National Labor Relations Act and couldn't see how it would speed economic recovery. But Congressional support was so overwhelming that it was going to pass no matter what he did, and labor was an important part of the New Deal coalition, so he put it on his "must" list of legislation.

A minimum wage was also legislated, primarily at Roosevelt's insistence. It established a precedent that has never been repudiated and continues to be a deterrent to the hiring of unskilled, especially teenage, labor.

The Tennessee Valley Authority was part of Roosevelt's visionary plan for transplanting work and workers in rural areas. It was the New Deal's one foray into socialism, the ownership of production facilities by the government. It still exists today and provides, to those within its grid, below cost power service, compliments of the US taxpayer.

The Social Security Act was the result of opportunism. The idea of social insurance has appeal to the have not's, and during the depression, there were a lot of have not's. But a scheme that had nothing to offer those in the greatest need and reduced employees' paychecks during hard times can scarcely be called responsible legislation. Nevertheless, Roosevelt was delighted with the Social Security Act. " ... no damn politician can ever scrap my social security program," he exulted. On that point, he certainly was right. Despite the fact that social security taxes have become a burden on the US worker and that the plan is marvelously inefficient, it remains a political shibboleth. Not even such a frank and principled (or if you prefer, reactionary and insensitive) a president as Ronald Reagan, at the height of his popularity, dared to speak out against it. However, there is now some indication that, someday, enough political courage may be mustered to deal with this monster.

Mostly, the depression leaves us with a lot of unanswered questions. No one knows what caused it or why it lasted so long.

There's the fact that it was the first managed panic. Would it have been shorter if, like previous panics, it had been subjected to the hitherto standard policy of benign neglect? To counterbalance the conservative tilt of this question is the fact that, since the Second World War, the US has never experienced an economic downturn anything like the depression. Can it be that the US has actually taken some steps in the right direction as far as mitigating economic hardship? Or could another depression occur?

And if it really was the significant step-up of spending to support US effort in the Second World War that brought about the end of the depression, couldn't the US have spent itself out of the depression in other ways sooner? Granted that defeating the totalitarian, racist, expansionist nations of Germany and Japan was a worthy objective, it still remains true that, in and of themselves, there are few more useless objects on which to spend money than arms and armament. On the other hand, the government did throw a lot of money at the depression before the Second World War, and this action had little curative effect. Maybe the even greater spending during the Second World War and the end of the depression were nothing more than concurrent events, the end of the depression being the result of one or more other, unidentified causes.

Then, on a slightly different tangent, there's the general impression that economic downturns seem to be preceded by some kind of speculative excess. This leads to the idea that the downturn is an unavoidable drying out period that must be gone through to purge the speculative poisons from the economic body. But if this is the case, couldn't excessive speculation be avoided in the first place? And if so, how?

You want my opinion? I think the cause of the depression was no different than the cause of any other panic experienced by the US or any other country. When a new profit opportunity opens up, it's pursued by making investments in the real and financial goods related to the opportunity. As this investment continues, demand for these goods tends to outstrip supply. The result is a price increase.

At this point, things can continue in a rational way. Or a sense of euphoria, fed by greed, can begin to build up and encourage overtrading, where the real goods related to the profit opportunity are bought for resale rather than for use and the financial goods related to the opportunity are purchased in anticipation of capital gains rather than income. These goods are then termed the objects of overtrading.

Credit expands to fund and encourage the overtrading, and euphoria excalates into mania. Distress occurs when people involved in the overtrading begin to recognize that a bubble is being created where there isn't enough money for everyone to sell out at the top.

Eventually, the bubble bursts, and panic begins. There's a flight from goods to money, and the price of the objects of overtrading drop. The panic then begins to feed on itself. The price drop signals a shortage of money. As a consequence, selling picks up, prices fall further, and loans are called. There's a revulsion with the objects of overtrading, people dump them as fast as they can, and they're no longer accepted as collateral for loans.

The fear that feeds the revulsion spreads from the overtraders to the population in general. Spending is reduced to bare necessities, which exacerbates the economic distress that follows a panic. Sales fall off, inventories build up, plants close, firms fail, and unemployment spreads. The distress continues until enough confidence in the economy is generated to dispel the fear feeding the distress.

In the case of the depression, the object of overtrading was stock, the source of credit expansion was the call loans that banks and corporations made to allow stock to be bought on margin, and the circumstances restoring confidence was the success in the prosecution of the Second World War.

So, could a depression happen again? Absolutely. And how can we avoid it? Unless we can change human nature, I don't think that we can.

Finally, there's inflation. The country did experience inflation during the Civil War. But over the 19th century as a whole, no inflation occurred. It wasn't until the 1930's that inflation became a permanent feature of the economic scene. So the depression, or some other concurrent action, related or unrelated, has injected an element into the nation's economy that wasn't there before. The gold bugs maintain that, in going off the gold standard in 1933, the restraint imposed on the money supply by the available supply of gold had been removed and that, with the loss of this restraint, politicians were free to inflate the money supply. The gold bugs may have a point in explaining why inflation now seems to be unavoidable. But their solution to this problem (return to the gold standard) is as bad as the problem, since the gold standard didn't provide a uniform commodity value for money either.

The New Deal has left one other legacy, a federal bureaucracy, the growth of which was speeded up during the Second World War and which has yet to be brought under control. This is a dangerous situation. Some bureaucracy is needed to run a government. But excessive bureaucracy breeds corruption, hide-bound routines, impractical zeal, and an accumulation of stupidity in high places.

CHAPTER TWENTY

The Second World War

In the year in which Roosevelt became the president of the US, Adolph Hitler was appointed chancellor (the chief minister of state) of Germany. To explain how he was able to rise to this position of power, it's necessary to go back to the closing days of World War I.

Because of political unrest in Germany, on September 30, 1918, the kaiser (emperor) dismissed his ministers and established a parliamentary government. The parliament in Germany was the Reichstag. For chancellor, the kaiser named his cousin, Prince Max von Baden, in response to the unanimous recommendation of the parties in the Reichstag.

On October 2, the German generals reported that the military situation was hopeless and urged the government to seek an armistice. As a consequence, on October 4, Prince Max formally requested negotiations for an armistice from Wilson. Throughout the rest of October, Wilson sporadically issued the demands that would have to be met for armistice negotiations to begin. Finally, on October 23, Wilson declared that, if he had to work "with the military masters and monarchical autocrats of Germany", he must insist not on negotiations, but surrender. In response, General Erich Ludendorff, nominally second in command to Field Marshall Paul von Hindenburg but, in fact, all but dictator of Germany, a position he had maintained for the previous two years, called for a mass conscription to carry on the war. Prince Max refused to consider such a step. As a consequence, on October 26, Ludendorff resigned.

Ludendorff's resignation eliminated one obstacle to negotiating with Wilson. To remove the other, Prince Max, supported by the Reichstag, called on the kaiser to abdicate. To remove the kaiser from pressures to bow to the government's will, his followers convinced him that he should move to his military headquarters at Spa in Belgium, which he did on October 29.

On November 3, Admiral Reinhard von Scheer ordered the German fleet in the North Sea to move against the enemy — "Vanquish or perish honorably," the admiral commanded. In response, crews at Kiel and Wilhelmshaven murdered their officers and flew red flags from the gaffs of their ships. The sailors then boarded trains going south to spread the revolution.

With the country disintegrating and indications that the Allies were preparing a massive offensive to begin on November 14, time for negotiations was running out. On November 6, the government decided that an armistice delegation must leave Berlin that same day. From Spa, the kaiser indicated that he agreed with this decision. A civilian, Matthais Erzberger, was chosen to head the delegation. The highest ranking army officer in the delegation was a divisional general, low enough in the pecking order so that the officer caste could consider itself not involved in the negotiations. On November 7, the German delegation began deliberations with an Allied team headed by Marshall Ferdinand Foch in a train coach on a railroad siding in the Compiegne forest. Although the delegation had "full power" to negotiate, any agreement remained subject to the ratification of the German government.

On November 8, Brunswick and Munich went Red. On November 9, most of the other major cities, the rail centers, and the supply depots were taken over by the revolutionaries. Despite repeated attempts, Prince Max had failed to convince the kaiser that he must abdicate. On November 9, on his own initiative, Prince Max announced that the kaiser had renounced the throne. Prince Max then resigned. Friedrich Ebert, the leader of the Social Democratic party, which held the majority in the Reichstag, became effective chancellor.

At 2 in the afternoon of November 9, Philipp Scheidemann, a colleague of Ebert's, sat down to a lunch of watery potato soup in the restaurant of the Reichstag building. The Koenigplatz outside the building was swarming with people and red banners. Scheidemann's lunch was interrupted with the news that the Spartacists, led by the Left Socialists Rosa Luxemburg and Karl Liebknecht, had taken over the Imperial Castle and were about to proclaim a soviet republic. Scheidemann hurried to the reading room balcony, which overlooked the square, and proclaimed "the great German Republic!" At 4, Liebknecht tacitly seconded this proclamation by issuing a proclamation of his own for the "Free Socialist Republic of Germany", not a soviet republic. At 7:40 pm, the kaiser boarded a train in Spa that was to take him, the next day, to refuge on the neutral soil of the Netherlands.

On November 10, the Ebert government authorized the Erzberger delegation to conclude an armistice, which amounted to accepting an Allied dictat. The armistice agreement was signed at 5 in the morning on November 11. The armistice went into effect on the eleventh hour of the eleventh day of the eleventh month of the year.

Thus, although relentlessly urged on by the German high command, all the steps leading to the armistice (the request for negotiations and the actions resulting in Ludendorff's resignation and the kaiser's abdication) and the signing of the armistice were actions of a civilian government. This led to the myth that the German army had been "stabbed in the back" by a cowardly civilian government that had given up in a war the military could have won. The words "stabbed in the back" were supplied by Ludendorff, via the English Major General Malcolm, who (when Ludendorff was explaining to him how the civilian government had betrayed the army through lack of support) asked Ludendorff, "Do you mean, General, that you were stabbed in the back?" "Stabbed in the back?" replied Ludendorff, "Yes, that's it exactly. We were stabbed in the back." Hitler was to later use this argument to highlight the futility of a democratic government, justify establishing a dictatorship, and appeal to the army for support.

On January 19, 1919, a National Assembly was elected to draft a new constitution. The assembly met in Weimar on February 6 and, on July 31, produced the Weimar Constitution, one of the most democratic ever written.

The only way in which the Weimar Republic could have realized the dream depicted in its constitution was if it undertook drastic housecleaning. The constitution stood for democracy, but all the institutions in Germany were rooted in the country's authoritarian tradition. To eliminate this chancre, the Weimar government would have had to destroy the industrial monopolies

The Geography of Hitler's Ancestors and Youth

and cartels that controlled the country's capital plant, break up the feudal Junker estates, purge the Prussian officer caste from the army, and remove the authoritarians from the civil service, police, universities, and the judiciary — particularly, the judiciary. No matter what the crime, even assassination or treason, if it was committed by a person with authoritarian commitments, his judicial treatment was light. But if the offender supported the republic, the laws were ruthlessly applied. For example, hundreds of Germans were given lengthy terms in prison for treason because they objected to the army's persistent violation of the Versailles Treaty.

Whether the Weimar Republic could have stood up to these institutional forces and bent them to its will is problematic. In any event, it didn't even try. So Germany became a country with a government that its power structures abhorred. It was into this vacuum that Hitler stepped.

For generations, Hitler's forebears lived in the Waldviertel, a district of Austria between the Danube and the Czech provinces of Bohemia and Moravia. In 1842, Adolf's grandfather, Johann Hitler, a wandering miller, married a peasant woman named Maria Schicklgruber. Five years before, Maria had borne an illegitimate son, whom she named Alois. Maria died in 1847. Johann then dropped from sight. Thirty years later, he surfaced in the town of Weitra and testified that he was Alois' father. So on November 23,

1876, the parish priest at Doellersheim crossed out the name of Alois Schicklgruber in the baptismal registry and substituted the name of Alois Hitler.

Adolph was born to Alois on April 20, 1889 in the town of Braunau am Inn, just across the border from Bavaria, a state of Germany. So Hitler was born an Austrian but of German stock. And although Hitler's father carried the name of Schicklgruber for 39 years, Hitler was never named Schicklgruber. It's true that, while down and out in Vienna (1909 - 1913), he drew and painted pictures of local landmarks, which he sold to trades people for various uses (for example, to fill up frames offered for sale), and he made commercial posters for shopkeepers. But he was never a house painter or paper hanger. In fact, he went to some lengths to avoid any sort of regular work.

Hitler was a high school dropout. He was also a teetotaler, a nonsmoker, and a vegetarian. By the time he was 16, he was consumed by politics. He was repulsed by the Habsburg monarchy and the non-Germans in Austria. At the same time, he acquired an admiration for anything German. He was an omnivorous reader. His favorite books were on German history and mythology. He expressed a desire to be a painter or an architect. But the Vienna Academy of Fine Arts twice rejected him for lack of talent, and he never applied to the academy's School of Architecture.

In December 1908, Hitler's mother died. His father had preceded her by six years. After his mother's burial, Hitler left for Vienna, where he lived for the next four years. He supported himself by doing odd jobs, such as shoveling snow, beating carpets, and carrying bags at the railroad station. He lived in flophouses and ate at charity soup kitchens. And he continued his prodigious reading. It was during this period that a number of his ideas were formed. He studied the activities of the political parties in Austria and developed what he saw as the necessary conditions for political success.

1. The use of terror, both physical and what he called "spiritual" — the unleashing of a barrage of lies and slanders against the adversary.
2. The necessity to arouse the masses, and rhetorical exhortation as the only way to achieve this end.

3. The support of long-established institutions, such as the army and big business.

There are indications that Hitler was an anti-Semite before he went to Vienna. In any case, his experiences in Vienna either developed or intensified these feelings.

In May 1913, Hitler moved from Vienna to Munich, probably to avoid military service, because he didn't want to associate with the Jews, Slavs, and other minorities that would be found in the Austrian army. In Munich, his life followed the pattern set in Vienna. Then in 1914, the war began. Hitler petitioned King Ludwig III of Bavaria for permission to join a Bavarian regiment. His request was granted.

Hitler served with valor during the war. He received two decorations for bravery. He was also wounded twice. The end of the war found him in a military hospital where he was recovering from an English gas attack.

When Hitler left the hospital, he returned to Munich. His first political activity was to give information to a commission of inquiry established by the army to look into the short-lived soviet republic that workers had set up in Munich in early 1919 and that the army had overturned. He apparently made an impression on the army, because it then gave him a position in the Press and News Bureau of the Political Department of the army's district command.

In his new post, Hitler attended a course of "political instruction" that the army gave its soldiers. When some good things were said about Jews, Hitler interrupted the lecture and delivered an anti-Semite tirade, which so impressed his officers that he was made an educational officer of a Munich regiment. An educational officer's primary job was to combat subversive ideas, such as pacifism, socialism and democracy.

In this new role, Hitler came into contact with Anton Drexler, who had founded a political party, the German Workers' party, and who gave Hitler a booklet. Hitler read the booklet, found that it contained a number of the ideas that he embraced, and ended up joining the party. He became the seventh member of the party's committee, which also constituted the party's membership. Army captain Ernst Roehm was a member of the party when Hitler joined in 1919.

Hitler assumed the responsibility for the party's propaganda and began to organize meetings to spread the word. On April 1, 1920, the name of the party was changed to the National Socialist (Nazi) German Workers' party. In the summer of 1920, the emblem of a black swastika set in a white circle against a red background was adopted by the Nazis.

By 1921, Hitler was the Nazi's major orator, organizer and propagandist. Some of the other members of the committee that ran the party felt that Hitler was becoming too dictatorial. Hitler offered to resign, but the committee decided that this would be fatal to the party. So Hitler got to dictate his terms — the committee was abolished and Hitler did assume dictatorial powers.

The next step was to develop a strong-arm unit to quash dissent. In the beginning, ex-servicemen were used to deal with hecklers at meetings. These brawlers were then organized into squads that, on October 5, 1921, were named the Sturmabteilung, SA for short, and were given brown uniforms. The activity of the SA was soon broadened from maintaining order at Nazi meetings to breaking up the meetings of other political parties.

Hermann Goering was one of Germany's war heroes. He was the last commander of the Richthofen Fighter Squadron and holder of the Pour le Merite, the highest war decoration in Germany. He came to Munich to pursue economics at the university but soon fell under Hitler's spell. He joined the Nazis in 1921, gave lavishly to the party treasury, and helped Roehm organize the SA. In 1922, Paul Goebbels joined the party.

Ludendorff now lived outside of Munich. He had little political sense, but in common with Hitler, he was in favor of an authoritarian counterrevolution. Because of Ludendorff's renown, Hitler thought that Ludendorff might be useful to him. So he cultivated the general.

The German mark began to depreciate in 1921, when it dropped to 75 to the dollar. In 1922, it fell to 400. To reduce the demands on the government's printing press, Germany petitioned the Allies for permission to delay payment of reparations. France turned down the request, but Germany decided to discontinue payments anyhow. As a result, when Germany defaulted on the delivery of timber to France, French troops occupied the Ruhr, the industrial heartland of Germany. The German workers in the Ruhr went on strike and were supported financially by the German government. This freezing of the German economy speeded up the mark's fall. In the four months preceding November, it moved from a million to the dollar to four billion.

Hitler saw the destruction of the German currency as an opening in his quest to topple the republic. The question was: How could he do it? The Nazis were far from the most prominent party in Bavaria. Outside of this German state, they were unknown. Hitler thought that, if he could get the support of the Bavarian government and the army stationed in Bavaria, he could lead a march on Berlin and bring down the republic, a tactic that Mussolini had used successfully.

By mid-September, Gustav Stresemann, the German chancellor, decided that, if Germany were to be saved from destruction, the strike in the Ruhr would have to be called off and reparation payments resumed. On September 26, he announced the adoption of these steps. Bavaria wasn't interested. It declared a state of emergency and set up a dictatorial triumvirate: Gustav von Kahr as State Commissioner; General Otto von Lossov, the army commander in Bavaria; and Colonel Hans von Seisser, the head of the Bavarian state police. The idea was that Bavaria might secede from Germany and form a union with Austria.

Hitler begged Kahr and Lossow to move on Berlin before Berlin moved on Bavaria. On November 6, they told him that they wouldn't be rushed into any precipitate action and that they alone would decide what to do and when to do it. Hitler then decided to kidnap Kahr, Lossow and Seisser and force them to support him in his march to overthrow the republic.

On November 8, Kahr addressed a meeting of about 3000 businessmen at the Buergerbraukeller, a large beer hall in Munich. Lossow and Seisser were present. After Kahr had been speaking for about half an hour, SA troops surrounded the beer hall, and Hitler took the rostrum and announced the beginning of the revolution. He then herded Kahr, Lossow and Seisser into a private room. Despite offers of key positions in Hitler's government followed by threats to shoot them, they refused to cooperate. Hitler then returned to the hall and announced that Kahr, Lossow and Seisser had joined him in his new government. He also stated that Ludendorff would take over army leadership. Hitler had previously sent for Ludendorff to join him at the beer hall but hadn't told him what was going to transpire.

Ludendorff now appeared. He and Hitler retired to the room where Kahr, Lossow and Seisser were being kept. Ludendorff was infuriated by having been put upon by Hitler and was even more upset when he found out that Hitler, not Ludendorff, was to be dictator. Nevertheless, Ludendorff said that it was a great national cause and that he would join it. He urged Kahr, Lossow and Seisser to do so, also. At this point, all five returned to the dais in the beer hall, where Kahr, Lossow and Seisser each swore loyalty to the new regime. Kahr, Lossow and Seisser then slipped out of the meeting.

In the meantime, Roehm had occupied the army headquarters at the war ministry building. But no other strategic points had been taken. Lossow called for reinforcements. By sunrise, there was an army cordon around the war ministry. At 11 in the morning, at Ludendorff's suggestion, he and Hitler led 3000 storm troopers out of the beer hall to march to the war ministry and take over Munich. They moved through the narrow Residenzstrasse, on the other end of which was a detachment of around 100 policemen. No one knows who fired first, but shots rang out from both sides. Firing then ceased, since both the SA and the police were Germans, and they recoiled from the idea of shooting each other. However, the SA troops had decided that they had had enough. The beer hall putsch (rapid takeover) was over.

When the police at the end of the street had been sighted, Hitler had linked arms with a colleague, Scheubner-Richter. Scheubner fell before the policemen's fire. In his fall, he threw Hitler to the ground, and Hitler's shoulder was dislocated. Hitler then fled and, two days later, was arrested. Ludendorff, who had marched calmly through the fire of the police detachment to the square at the other end of the street, was immediately arrested. Sixteen Nazis and three policemen had been killed.

People who are interested in discrediting Hitler (for what purpose, no one knows — Hitler did everything necessary to discredit himself and then some) have maintained that his rapid departure from the Residenzstrasse was because he was a coward. There's nothing else in his career to indicate that this was the case. He viewed the individual as nothing more than a means for continuing the race. In this respect, he seems to have generally thought of himself as being no different than any other German. The only exception he made was that he considered himself to have a special mission — leading the German nation to its proper place in the scheme of things. The reason he ran away was most likely because he saw that the game was over and that the best thing he could do for his cause was to remove himself from the danger zone so that he would be able to continue his quest another day.

Hitler's trial was an exemplar of German justice. As an authoritarian, he was permitted to address the court whenever he liked for as long as he liked. The leading German newspapers covered the proceedings, and by the end of the trial, Hitler had impressed the German people with his patriotism. For the first time, he was a national figure.

Ludendorff was found not guilty. Hitler was found guilty of treason. The German penal code required lifelong imprisonment for treason. Hitler was sentenced to five years. In less than nine months, he was free. He spent his prison term in the Landsberg fortress, on the Lech river, where he had his own room overlooking the river and was waited on like a guest. He occupied his time writing *Mein Kampf (My Struggle)*.

In *Mein Kampf*, Hitler spelled out many of his goals.
1. The unification of Germany and Austria was a "task to be furthered with every means."
2. France was "the inexorable mortal enemy of the German people." There must be "a final ... reckoning with France" in which France must be destroyed.
3. The German people must have living space, Lebensraum, and to get it, Germany must spread out into Russian territory.
4. There would be no "democratic nonsense" in the Nazi state. Germany would be ruled by a leader, the fuehrer.

5. All Germans, no matter where they were presently located, must become part of the German state.

From the time of Hitler's release from prison through 1929, Germany thrived, which lent credibility to the republic. These were poor years for an overthrow. However, Hitler was willing to wait until bad times returned, which he was sure would happen. In the meantime, be devoted himself to building up the Nazi party.

Despite efforts to upgrade the SA, the brown shirts never rose above their nature, which was that of street brawlers. To have more dependable troops, Hitler created the Schutzstaffel (SS), fitted them out with black uniforms, and had them pledge their loyalty directly to him. The SS was first led by Joseph Berchtold and then by Erhard Heiden. In 1929, Heiden was succeeded by Heinrich Himmler.

Hitler was not only working to build a political party but also to develop, within the party, a shadow government that would become a real government when the Nazis came to power. As a consequence, when the republic was overthrown, there'd be no awkward interval while the new government was being organized. Instead, the new government would already be in functioning order. All it would have to do is step in when the republic disappeared.

On April 7, 1925, Hitler gave up his Austrian citizenship. He was nationless until February 25, 1932, when the Nazi minister of the interior of the state of Brunswick made Hitler an attache of the legation of Brunswick in Berlin. This converted Hitler into a citizen of Brunswick and, therefore, of Germany.

We've concentrated on the great depression as it took shape in the US. But it was a worldwide phenomenon, and Germany was no exception to it. From 1929 to 1932, manufacturing output dropped by close to 50 percent. Millions were unemployed. Small businesses went bankrupt by the thousands.

On September 14, 1930, because of an impasse in the Reichstag over the financial program of Heinrich Bruening (the incumbent chancellor), new elections were called. Hitler and the Nazi party campaigned vigorously with the promise that every German would have a job and bread. As a result, the Nazis received over six million votes, which gave the party 107 seats in the Reichstag. It was now the second largest party in the Reichstag.

Bruening continued on as chancellor after the election. Unable to put together a functioning government, most of the time be ruled by presidential decree, which article 48 of the constitution allowed in emergencies. The president was Hindenburg.

On May 29, 1932, Hindenburg, having lost faith in Bruening, asked for his resignation and, on June 1, replaced him with Franz von Papen. On June 4, Papen dissolved the Reichstag and called for new elections on July 31. The Nazis once more campaigned energetically. In the election, the Nazis received almost 13,750,000 votes and won 230 seats in the Reichstag, which made them the largest party in the Reichstag but not a majority.

Even before this new Reichstag had met, Papen had gotten from Hindenburg a decree for its dissolution. In its first meeting, the Reichstag voted to censure Papen's government, Papen delivered Hindenburg's decree, and the Reichstag was once more dissolved, with new elections scheduled for November 6. This time the Nazis came in with two million fewer votes than previously, resulting in a loss of 34 seats. The Nazis still had the most seats, 196, of any of the parties but were further than ever from a majority. On November 17, Papen resigned. On November 9, Hindenburg offered the chancellorship to Hitler if be could get a workable majority in the Reichstag. He couldn't. On December 2, Kurt von Schleicher was named chancellor. Schleicher was also unable to command a majority in the Reichstag. On January 28, 1933, he resigned.

At noon the same day, Hindenburg and Papen agreed to see if Papen could put a government together with Hitler in charge but not in control. On January 30, Hitler became chancellor. The Nazis held only three posts in the 11 person cabinet. Papen was vice chancellor. He had friends in the remaining eight cabinet positions. He also had the support of Hindenburg, who said that he wouldn't see Hitler unless Papen accompanied him. As a consequence, Papen thought that he could manage Hitler. Little did he know.

Hitler's cabinet, made up of members of the Nazi and German National parties, would have a majority in the Reichstag only if joined by the Catholic Center party. Hitler talked with the Center leader and then returned to the cabinet. He reported that the Center had made impossible demands. Then, promising that, in no case, would the composition of the cabinet be changed, he said that new elections must be held. They were set for March 5.

The Nazis now had the resources of the government to help them win votes. Industrialists were promised that organized labor would be put in its place and were asked to finance the campaign. In general, they did. On February 27, the Nazis set fire to the Reichstag building and accused the Communists of committing the crime. On February 28, Hitler got Hindenburg to issue a decree suspending seven sections of the constitution that guaranteed individual and civil liberties as a "defensive measure against Communist acts of violence endangering the state". Hitler now had a free hand to arrest the leaders of opposition parties, close down their presses, and ban their meetings. Only the Nazis and their Nationalist allies were allowed to campaign without interference. On election day, the Nazis increased their all-time vote total by three and one half million but still received only 44 percent of the vote. However, with the Nationalists, the Hitler cabinet now had a majority of 16 seats in the Reichstag.

The next step was to pass a law conferring dictatorial powers on the cabinet for the next four years. Passage of such a law was dependent on a change in the constitution, which required a two thirds majority in the Reichstag. Through use of the decree of February 28, the Communists could be prevented from taking their seats and enough Social Democrats could be detained by the police so that the required two thirds vote could be achieved. On March 23, this charade was carried out, and the so-called "Law for Removing the Distress of the People and the Nation" was passed. The Reichstag remained in existence until Germany's defeat in 1945. But its members were, from then on, selected by the Nazis. Its main function was to serve as an audience for Hitler's speeches.

Dictatorial power for the cabinet was, to Hitler, just one thing — dictatorial power for him, and him alone. Papen and his eight man cabinet majority were left standing to one side with their mouths open while they watched Hitler push through his program. By the end of the year, Hitler had:

1. Destroyed all political parties but his own. A July 14 law decreed that "The National Socialist German Workers' Party constitutes the only political party in Germany." Formation or maintenance of any other political party was now a crime.
2. Smashed the state governments so that the states became nothing more than administrative units of the nation.
3. Wiped out labor unions. Late in May, Hitler outlawed collective bargaining. From now on, "labor trustees", appointed by the Nazi government, would "regulate labor contracts" and maintain "labor peace".
4. Decreed that Jews could no longer work in public service, universities, or the professions. On April 1, he also established a boycott of Jewish shops.
5. Eliminated freedom of speech and of the press.
6. Compelled all educators, from kindergarten through the universities, to enroll in the National Socialist Teachers' League, which was made "responsible for the execution of the ideological and political coordination of all teachers in accordance with National Socialist doctrine." All teachers swore to "be loyal and obedient to Adolf Hitler."

The Geheime Staatpolizei (secret state police; Gestapo, for short) was set up by Goering as a substitute for the Prussian political police, which he had disbanded. At the time, Goering was Reich governor of Prussia. In April 1934, Goering made Himmler deputy chief of the Gestapo, which then became a secret police organization within the SS. The Gestapo law, issued by Hitler on February 10, put the Gestapo above the law.

By the beginning of 1934, the SA was two and a half million strong. Roehm, who was now in Hitler's cabinet, proposed that the SA become the nucleus of a "People's Army" reporting to the ministry of defense, over which it was implied that he would have authority. Nothing could have been more abhorrent to the officer corps. As General von Brauchitsch later said, " ... rearmament was too serious and difficult a business to permit the participation of peculators, drunkards and homosexuals." Roehm was Hitler's friend (the only man with whom Hitler ever used the familiar personal pronoun), but Hitler agreed with the officer corps. In the meantime, the SA continued its roughhouse ways.

By midyear, Hindenburg was almost at the end of his patience. On June 21, he informed Hitler that Hitler had to clean up the situation quickly or he would put the nation under martial law and let the army do the job.

On June 30, urged on by Goering, Himmler and Goebbels, Hitler took action. It was "the night of the long knives". Roehm and several hundred other SA leaders were executed. At the same time, the Nazis took the opportunity to liquidate many others, some out of vengeance (Kahr, for example) and some because they knew too much (like the three SA men who were thought to have been involved in starting the Reichstag fire). By July 1, most of the slaughter was over. On July 2, Hindenburg thanked Hitler for his "determined action and gallant personal intervention which have nipped treason in the bud and rescued the German people from great danger."

Hindenburg died on August 2. Three hours after his death, it was announced that, in conformance with a law put in place by the cabinet the preceding day, the offices of the president and the chancellor had been combined and that Hitler was going to function as both. In the future, Hitler would be known as the fuehrer (leader) of Germany. Hitler then extracted from every member of the German armed forces a pledge of loyalty to himself.

Hitler had consolidated his power. He was now ready to concentrate on the goal of his life: creation of the greater Germany of which he had dreamed.

In one arena, he had already made himself clear. In his July 13, 1934 speech to the Reichstag, he said, with respect to the actions that he had taken to put down the SA, that he "was responsible for the fate of the German people" and therefore he was "the supreme judge of the German people." Thus, Hitler was the law, and he made no bones about it.

Hitler now began his campaign to militarize Germany and expand its borders. His modus operandi was straightforward. He consistently and repeatedly maintained that he loved peace, that he was revolted by the very idea of war — it was senseless, useless and horrible. He would then take his next step in his expansionary plans, after which he'd proclaim that the action had been necessary to safeguard Germany, that the action was the last that would have to be taken, and that it would never happen again. He would then return to the theme of his love for peace. If he got away with it, he'd then proceed to the next step in his plan.

On March 16, 1935, Hitler ordered universal military service and provision for an army of a half million men. That was the end of the military restrictions of the Versailles Treaty ... unless England and France acted. They didn't.

Beginning in June 1935, state employment offices assumed total command of the labor force. They decided who could be employed for what and where.

The Nuremberg Laws of September 15, 1935 stripped the Jews of German citizenship. Henceforth, they were "subjects" of Germany. It was forbidden for a Jew to have sex with, let alone marry, a German.

On March 7, 1936, German troops occupied the demilitarized zone of the Rhineland and began to fortify it. Neither England nor France took any action.

On June 16, 1936, a nationwide police force was set up under Himmler.

In September 1936, the Four Year Plan was launched, the purpose of which was to prepare the German economy for war by making it self-sufficient. Imports were cut to the bone, prices and wages were put under government control, dividends were limited to a maximum of six percent, and factories were established to make synthetic rubber and fuel, steel and textiles, among other goods essential to the war effort.

On December 1, 1936, Hitler outlawed all non-Nazi youth organizations.

By the end of 1936, the unemployment problem had been eliminated. Although the German worker had lost his freedom to choose his work and negotiate for his wage, he now at least had a job and a pledge that it wouldn't disappear. As the workers said, with Hitler, there was no more freedom to starve.

On February 4, 1938, Hitler took command of all of Germany's armed forces. All power was now concentrated in his hands.

March 12, 1938 was the date of the Austrian Anschluss (forced political union with Germany). Austria connived in its demise. Nazis were active in Austria. In the secret clauses of the

Austro-German agreement of July 11, 1936, Austria committed itself to amnesty for Nazi political prisoners and appointment of Nazis to posts of "political responsibility". On February 12, 1938, Hitler upped the stakes. He demanded that Arthur Seyss-Inquart, a pro-Nazi, be named minister of security, who was responsible for the Austrian police. On February 16, the appointment was made. Seyss-Inquart was instructed by Germany to send a telegram to Germany that asked "the German Government to send German troops as soon as possible" to "help" the Austrian government "establish peace and order". Why Seyss-Inquart strained at this gnat is hard to say, but he didn't send the telegram. However, it made no difference, since Germany acted as if he had and even printed the text of the telegram in its March 12 newspapers.

Czechoslovakian Sudetenland was next on the list. In contrast to the Austrians, the Czechoslovakians were ready to fight to defend the integrity of their borders, and they expected to be backed up by England and France. However, on September 30, 1938, Neville Chamberlain, prime minister of England, and Edouard Daladier, premier of France, signed the Munich Agreement, which provided for German occupation of the Sudetenland. This was Chamberlain's "peace in our time".

Concurrently with Germany's occupation of the Sudetenland, Hungary appropriated 7500 square miles of Czechoslovakian territory and Poland 650 square miles. Poland? Was that the innocent whose invasion ignited World War II? It was, and although Germany's invasion of Poland can't be justified (anymore than can its invasion of Austria or Czechoslovakia), it should be borne in mind that Poland had been a dictatorship since 1926.

November 10, 1938 was Kristallnacht. Organized by the SS and approved of by Hitler, "spontaneous demonstrations" resulted in the looting and burning of Jewish synagogues, homes and shops all over Germany, and the killing of somewhat under 100 Jews — men, women and children. The insurance money due the Jews for damage was confiscated by the state, and the Jews were collectively fined one billion marks "for their abominable crimes", which consisted of killing a German official. Goering, among other things, the economic czar of Germany, balled out Reinhard Heydrich, the number two man in the SS and the organizer of

Kristallnacht, for breaking so much plate glass, a primarily imported product of which Germany was in short supply. According to Goering, Heydrich should have killed more Jews and broken less glass.

The Czechoslovakian provinces of Bohemia and Moravia were next. They disappeared into the German maw on March 15, 1939. On the same day, Hungary occupied the province of Ruthenia. On March 16, the province of Slovakia fell under the benevolent protection of Germany. Czechoslovakia had disappeared from the map.

On March 23, under German pressure, Lithuania agreed to "hand back" (as the German demand put it) the district of Memel to Germany. Also in March, Hitler conscripted all German youth into the Hitler Youth movement.

With Hitler's demands that Danzig become a free city and that Germany be granted a route through the Polish Corridor with extra-territorial status, demands to which Poland was unwilling to accede, it became obvious that Poland was next on Hitler's list. By now, England and France's policy of appeasement, fed by distaste for war and guilt over how Germany had been treated at the end of the First World War, had reached its limit. On March 31, Chamberlain told Commons (and therefore, Hitler), "In the event of any action which clearly threatened Polish independence and which the Polish Government accordingly considered it vital to resist with their national forces, His Majesty's Government would feel themselves bound at once to lend the Polish Government all support in their power ... I may add that the French Government have authorized me to make it plain that they stand in the same position on this matter."

The English and French guarantee of the inviolability of Polish borders had an interesting aspect: it related to an invasion by Germany only. At the time, it may have seemed that this was the only guarantee necessary. As events subsequently developed, the wording turned out to be fortuitous.

On August 23, 1939, Germany and Russia signed a nonaggression pact with an accompanying secret protocol delimiting the "spheres of interest" of the two countries in eastern

Europe. In other words, they agreed on how they were going to split eastern Europe between them.

At the time of this agreement, Russia had been negotiating for some time with England and France over the possibility of a common stance against Germany. For several reasons, the talks were getting nowhere. Russia maintained, logically enough, that if it were going to be able to take effective action against Germany, it had to have freedom to move its armed forces within Poland. Given the nature of past Russian-Polish relations, Poland found itself between a rock and a hard place. But it finally decided to not grant Russia this permission. Russia wanted to get down to the nitty-gritty of the agreement and asked England and France for all kinds of details — manning levels, troop dispositions, plans for action, etc. England and France, on the other hand, were interested in reaching some kind of general agreement and were understandably loath to reveal such details. But both sides continued the negotiations, each hoping that the other would ultimately make some kind of concession.

These talks were held in Moscow. Russia's side of the conversation was carried on by Kliment Voroshilov, an old intimate of Stalin's. When the nonaggression pact with Germany had been concluded, Stalin instructed Voroshilov's adjutant, General Khmelnitsky, to tell Voroshilov that he could terminate his discussions with England and France. Khmelnitsky gave Voroshilov a note that read, "Klim! Koba (Stalin) said you should shut down the barrel organ." Koba was a fictional outlaw who led Georgian mountaineers against the tsar. The book in which he appeared, *The Patricide* by Kazbegi, was read by Stalin as a child, and Koba was the underground alias he chose for himself before he finally took the name of Stalin.

At 4:45 am on September 1, German armies moved into Poland. At 11 am on September 3, England declared war. Six hours later, France followed suit. On September 17, Russia invaded Poland. On September 29, Germany and Russia agreed on how they would split the spoils: Germany would retain the Polish land that it had already occupied, even though the area had originally been in the Russian sphere of interest; in return, Germany allowed Russia to gobble up Latvia, Lithuania and

German Expansion to 1939

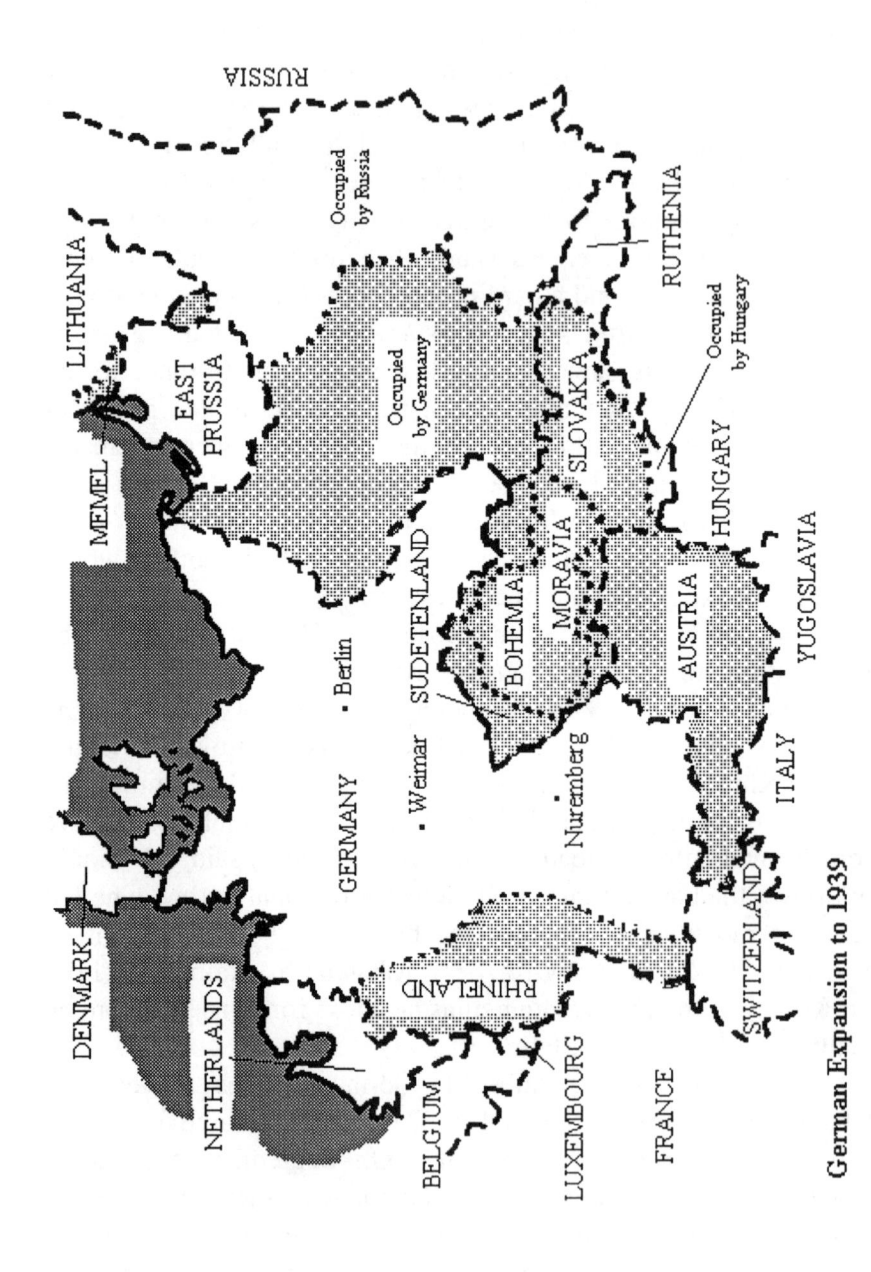

Estonia. Even after this deal, Russia ended up with almost half of Poland. And because they had committed only to declaring war on Germany if Poland were invaded, the Allies didn't declare war on Russia. On the Western Front, there was no fighting, and it remained that way.

Germany wanted bases in Norway so that an English blockade couldn't bottle up the German navy in the Baltic. It also wanted bases in Denmark for air attacks against England. On April 9, 1940, the Danish and Norwegian governments were presented with demands that they accept German "protection". Denmark capitulated. Norway decided to resist and was supported by the Allies.

On May 10, the German offensive on the Western Front began. The first matter of business was to occupy the Netherlands, Belgium and Luxembourg. The Allies had anticipated such an approach. They moved their forces forward from the Belgian border to the Belgian line of defense along the Dyle and Meuse rivers. However, they weren't ready for the attack that the Germans launched. It was a new kind of warfare. Elements of it had been tried in Poland and Norway. But it was in northern Europe that the world first saw blitzkrieg (blitz-krieg, lightning war) in its full power.

Airborne troops, landed by parachute or glider, seized bridgeheads behind enemy lines before defenders could destroy the river crossings. If no bridges existed, combat engineers constructed ones made of pontoons. Divisions of tanks, concentrated at a single point in the defense, established a breakthrough. Dive-bombing Stukas weakened the defenses in front of the lines of advancing tanks, which moved forward 30 to 40 miles a day. Each tank constituted a self-propelled artillery unit. Following the tanks were motorized infantry that moved in to consolidate the positions opened up by the tanks. This agglomeration of fire and steel set on wheels and watched over by air cover was coordinated through a network of radio, telephone and telegraph.

On May 14, this juggernaut rolled over the Allied lines. Divisions of tanks, lined up in columns miles long, broke through the defense just west of Sedan, reached open country, and began

The Western Offensive

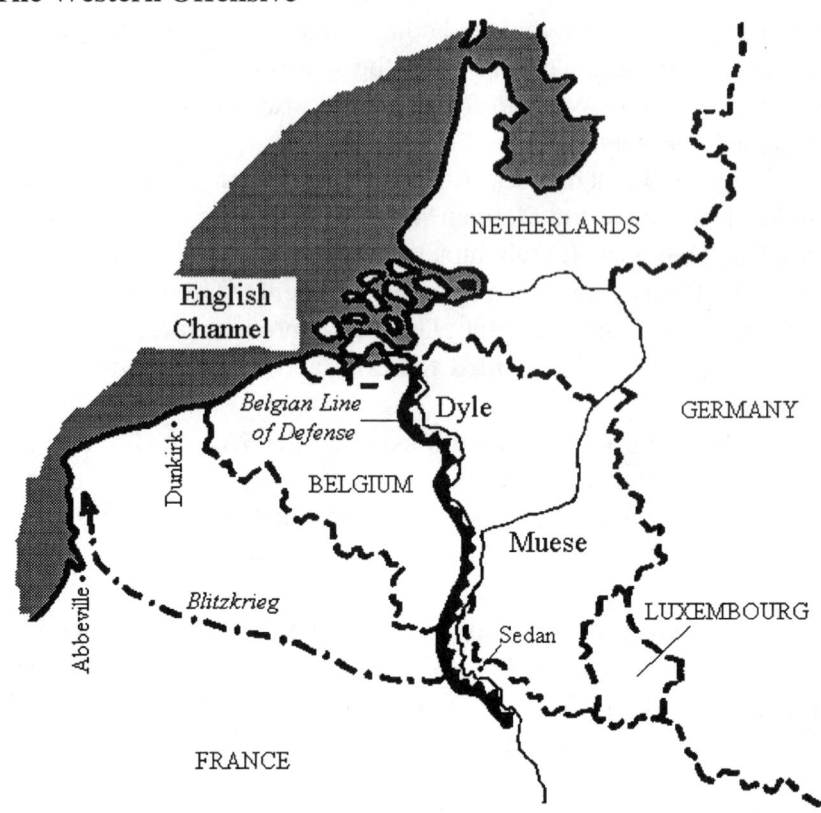

the race to Abbeville on the Channel. They reached it on the evening of May 20. By May 24, the Belgians, the English, and ten French divisions were trapped in a triangle with its base on the Channel and its peak about 70 miles inland. King Leopold III of Belgium surrendered on May 28. Two days earlier, the evacuation of the Allied forces from Dunkirk had begun. By the time it was over, on June 4, almost 340,000 men had been moved across the Channel. It was a reprieve for the Allied forces. But nevertheless, England had been driven from the continent.

By now, the Allied forces in Norway had been withdrawn to contend with the Germans in France. On June 7, the Norwegian government was transferred to exile in London. The occupation of Norway by Germany was complete.

On June 5, the Germans began their drive into France. There was little resistance. On June 10, the French government left Paris.

On June 14, the city was occupied. On June 22, France capitulated. Hitler now dominated the European continent.

The next move was to invade England. The prerequisite was that the RAF be destroyed. On August 13, Goering launched his air offensive. Until August 24, the RAF had the better of the battle. Its achievement was primarily due to its sector stations, underground centers from which the English fighters were directed by radiotelephone on the basis of the latest information collected from radar, ground observations, and pilots. On August 24, Goering ordered the Luftwaffe (air weapon) to concentrate on RAF installations. By September 6, six of the seven key sector stations were so badly damaged that the RAF communications system was threatened with annihilation.

To describe what happened next, it's necessary to backtrack. On August 24, a dozen German bombers got lost and, instead of bombing their intended targets, released their bombs over the center of London. The English thought the act was planned and, in reprisal, bombed Berlin the next night. The RAF repeated the bombing on the nights of August 28 and 30. In retaliation, Hitler switched his tactics from assaults on the RAF by day to bombings of London by night. The change occurred on September 7.

Night after night, London was pounded. But the RAF was saved. It continued to inflict damage on the Luftwaffe. On September 15, the Luftwaffe decided to carry out an attack on London by day. About 200 bombers, escorted by some 600 fighters, started to cross the Channel around noon. They were being tracked. Although some bombers got through, most were turned back. Two hours later, an even more powerful German formation approached but was completely overcome. On September 17, Hitler decided to postpone the invasion of England indefinitely. It was never again considered.

Failure to invade England was a setback to Hitler. And the Battle of Britain inflicted damage on the Luftwaffe from which it never fully recovered. But basically, Hitler's military machine remained intact.

In September 1935, the US passed a neutrality act which incorporated an arms embargo preventing it from supplying arms to any belligerent. This measure lasted only six months, but in

1936, the arms embargo was continued for a year. On May 1, 1937, the arms embargo was made permanent. On November 9, 1939, the embargo was lifted. But all purchases had to be paid for in cash and carried on non-US ships (the "cash and carry" policy). The policy was restrictive. But now, at least, the US could supply England with arms. In March 1941, the Lend-Lease bill was passed. It put the cash part of "cash and carry" out of its misery. The object was to supply England with whatever it needed to carry on the war, with the hope that, sooner or later, the loans would be repaid in kind. Ultimately, most of the loans were repaid. It wasn't until November 1941 that the US decided to allow its ships to enter the European combat zone.

Long before he had given up on invading England, Hitler was entertaining thoughts of conquering Russia. On December 18, 1940, he made his decision. The invasion would begin in mid-May 1941, its objective was to bring Russia to its knees by destroying the Russian army, and it was all to be over before the Russian winter set in.

On the night of March 26, 1941, an anti-Nazi coup took place in Yugoslavia. Hitler was so incensed that he decided that Yugoslavia would have to be crushed immediately. It was estimated that this action would result in a delay of about four weeks in the start of the Russian invasion. On April 6, German armies attacked Yugoslavia and Greece, which had been mauling Italy since Germany's ally had invaded it on October 28, 1940. By the beginning of May, Germany had occupied all the invaded areas with the exception of Crete, which was captured by airborne forces near the end of May. On June 22, 1941, the invasion of Russia began, about one month late, as predicted.

At the time of the invasion, the Russians weren't having it easy under Stalin. With the right treatment, the Germans might have turned these dissatisfied Russians into compliant collaborators. However, to the Nazis, the Russians were subhumans. They had no right to live, except as slaves. Russian prisoners of war died of hunger and cold by the hundreds of thousands. Russians were shipped to Germany as slave labor. Russia's food production went to Germany, while the Russians were left to the tender mercies of starvation. As a result, the Russian soldier fought fiercely and tenaciously even when surrounded.

The Germans also underestimated both the depth of the Russian reserve and the quality of its equipment. No matter what losses the Germans inflicted, the Russians just kept pouring in more men, more tanks, and more planes.

Nevertheless, the advance of the German armies into Russia was impressive. By December 2, a reconnaissance battalion had moved to within sight of the Kremlin spires. But there, the Russian winter and the indomitable Russian soldier brought the German forces to a halt. On December 6, the Russians launched a counteroffensive, on a 200 mile front arcing around Moscow, with troops trained and equipped to fight in sub-zero weather and deep snow. These troops had been stationed in Siberia as a defense against any possible Japanese action.

The first retreat of the Nazi army began. Neither Moscow, Leningrad, Stalingrad, nor the Caucasian oil fields had been captured, and the lifeline to England and the US remained open. After the war, the German high command testified that, in their opinion, if Hitler hadn't turned aside to punish Yugoslavia, the Russian winter wouldn't have overtaken the German offensive before it had reached a successful conclusion.

On December 7, Japan attacked Pearl Harbor. On the next day, the US declared war on Japan. Japan had a pact with Germany, but it was a defensive one. Since Japan hadn't been attacked, Germany could have stayed out of the war with the US. Nevertheless, on December 11, Germany declared war on the US.

At first, the Japanese looked invincible. They captured the Philippines, the East Indies, Thailand, Malaya, Singapore, and Burma. But Japan's advance southward was halted at the Battle of the Coral Sea (May 7 and 8, 1942), and its eastward movement was stopped at the Battle of Midway (June 3 and 4). In both engagements, for the first time in operations at sea, the offense was exclusively aerial. The opposing fleets never came within sight of each other.

The summer of 1942 saw a return of German fortunes on the Russian front. But it was no longer a purely German army making the advance. Casualties from the previous winter's fighting were

The Maximum Extent of Japanese Advance

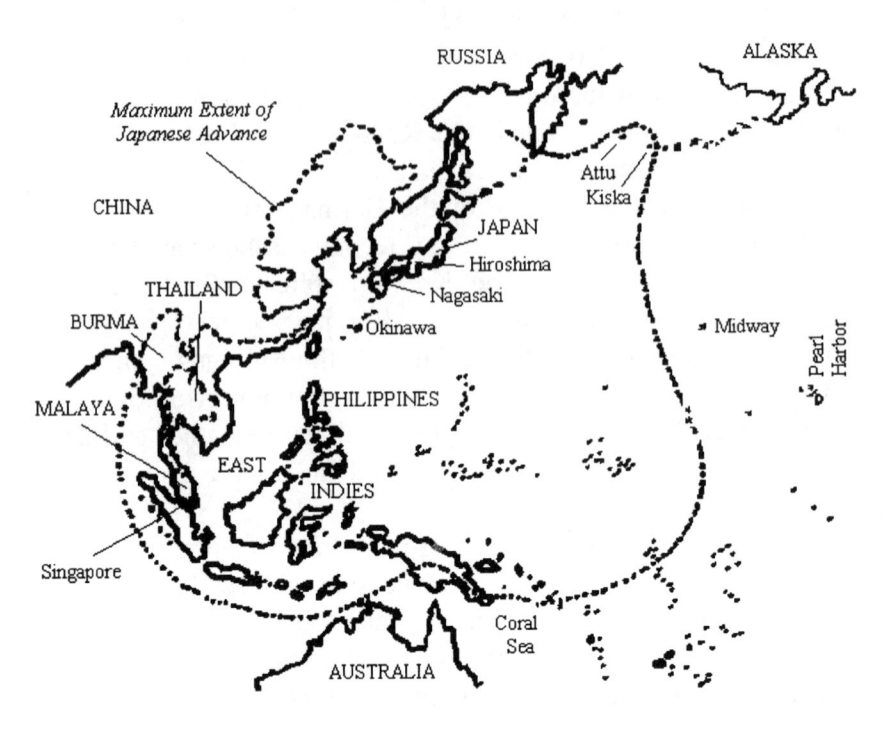

over a million (dead, missing and wounded). As a consequence, the German divisions were now supplemented by ones made up of Rumanians, Hungarians, Italians, Slovaks and Spaniards. Moreover, the goal of destroying the Russian army in one summer was replaced by the more modest aim of capturing the Caucasus oil fields, the Donets industrial basin, and the Kuban wheat fields.

Concurrently with the turnaround in Russia, General Erwin Rommel advanced to El Alamein, in North Africa, just 65 miles from Alexandria. Reinforcements would have probably allowed him to take Egypt, cut off the Suez canal, sweep through the oil fields of the Middle East, and join the German armies advancing on the Caucasus. Hitler sent him none. All manpower was needed in Russia. Even a steady flow of supplies would have helped. For this to happen, the English would have had to be driven from Malta. Plans were made, but Hitler called them off. The troops and planes were needed for the Russian offensive. So three quarters of Rommel's supplies continued to end up at the bottom of the Mediterranean.

On August 8, the Maikop oil fields were taken. On the 23d, German troops arrived at the Volga just north of Stalingrad. And on the 25th, the German advance reached Mozdok, just 50 miles from the Russian oil complex near Grozny. It was the last Axis offensive action. The term Axis was coined by Mussolini on November 1, 1936. He used it to describe the first German-Italian agreement as a "vertical line between Rome and Berlin ... around which can revolve all those European states with a will to collaboration and peace." Later, the term came to include Japan.

From this point on, Germany and Japan were on the defensive. As the war aged, the availability of men and munitions tipped more and more in the Allies' favor. But the fighting went on. Both Hitler and the Japanese preferred Gotterdammerung to what they considered the dishonor of surrender.

On April 25, 1945, US and Russian troops met some 75 miles south of Berlin. What was left of Germany had been cut in two. Hitler was holed up in a bunker 50 feet under the ruins of what had been the chancellery. On April 30, he committed suicide. On May 7, Germany surrendered unconditionally.

In the Pacific, the offensive against the Japanese was based on the strategy of "island hopping". Forces were poured into the islands that had to be taken. Those of secondary importance were left to the impotent occupation of enemy troops. Implementation of this strategy culminated in the capture of Okinawa. The way was now open for the assault on Japan proper. However, on July 16, 1945, the first atomic bomb was set off at Alamogordo, New Mexico. On August 6, an atomic bomb was dropped on Hiroshima. On August 9, a second was released over Nagasaki. On August 14, Japan surrendered.

Waged on three continents, characterized on both sides by an unwillingness to consider defeat, witness to the birth of the blitzkrieg, the extensive use of radar, and the atomic bomb, World War II was monumental in it proportions. Even so, it was overshadowed by the developments that followed.

In Japan, a nexus of improbable factors resulted in surprisingly positive results. An autocrat who believed in democracy, General

The Maximum Extent of German Advance in 1942

Douglas MacArthur became the virtual dictator of Japan. For close to five years, MacArthur told the Japanese exactly what to do. The Japanese, a people who were almost infinitely adaptable at the same time as they clung tenaciously to their uniquely Japanese character, developed their own singular form of capitalism within the framework of their own peculiar type of democracy. As in Germany, the major war criminals were tried, convicted and executed. But the bulk of those involved in conducting the war and its related atrocities were allowed to blend back into the general population and, not infrequently, ended up in positions of importance, both in industry and government.

Unlike Japan, which was exclusively a US concern, in Germany, Russia was involved, and developments were more complicated. Germany's unconditional surrender meant that the German government had ceased to exist. What remained was a geographic area under the control of the victors. It was assumed that the issues remaining after the surrender would be resolved in a forthcoming peace treaty. But no such development occurred. The US was absorbed with the war in the Pacific, the English and Russians were consumed by the need to recover from the devastation wrecked by the war on their own countries, and France, which had been occupied since 1940, was working to breathe life back into its moribund institutions. As a consequence, the occupation of Germany solidified around existing and prearranged circumstances. There were four occupation zones: English, French, Russian and US. Berlin, deep in the Russian zone, was similarly divided into four sectors. Because the four powers couldn't agree on how to deal with Germany as a whole, each set the tone for life in its German zone.

In 1947, the US sponsored the Marshall Plan for European economic recovery. Russia refused to allow its zone to participate. However, the three Western zones did share in the program, which ultimately amounted to $13 billion in funding when it wound down in 1952. The plan was a success, which was quite an achievement, considering the fact that the US had previously poured $10 billion of aid into Europe with no discernible effect. A major factor in this accomplishment was the way in which the plan was conceived and carried out. It wasn't thought of as a handout to people in distress. Nor was it to be a program relating the US to each of a number of European nations. Instead, it was up to the European nations to get together, determine their collective needs and resources, and decide how they could best help each other. Only then would the US step in to make available the material and financing required to bridge the remaining gap between needs and resources. Food, clothing and shelter had to be provided, of course. But not as a matter of humanitarian concern. The object was to promote a healthy work force that could cooperate with

The German Occupation Zones

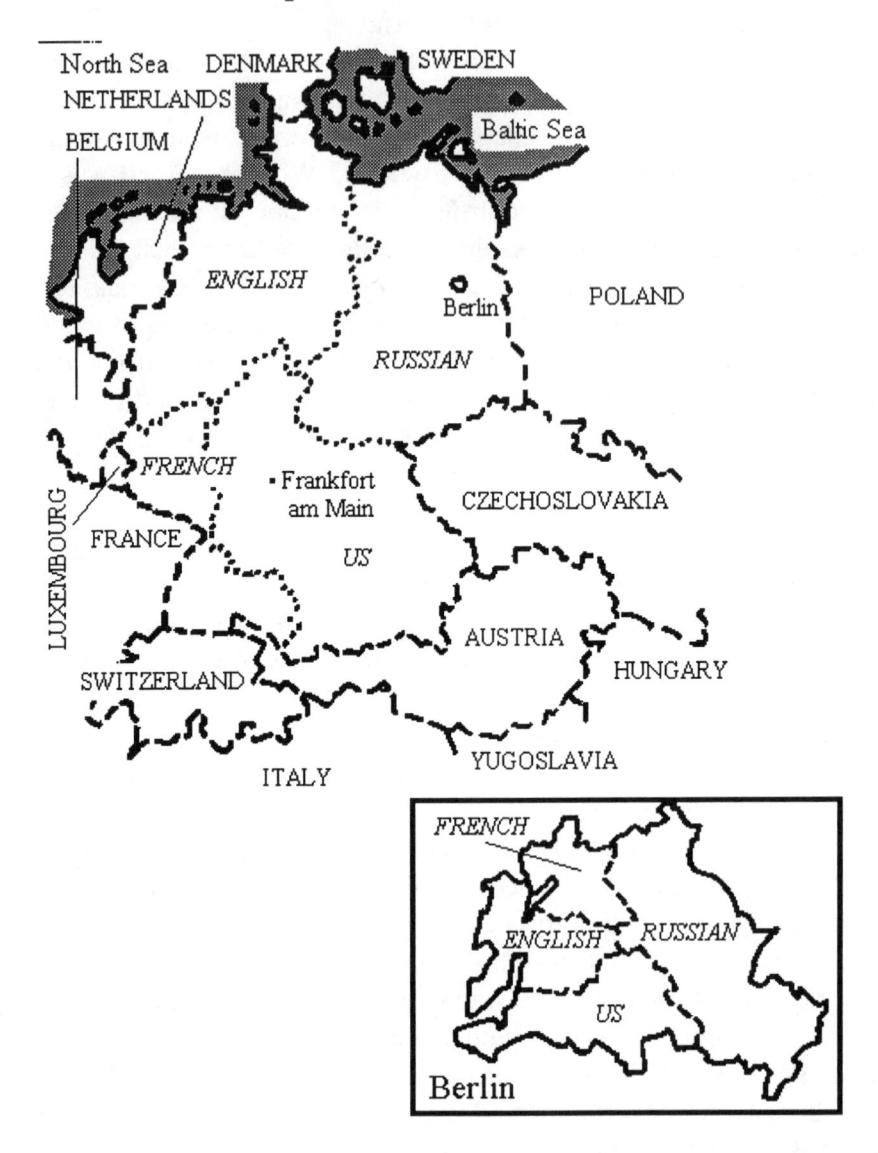

management and capital in the development of an engine of production capable of sustaining an independent, viable economy. Moreover, this was all to be done in just four years.

Other things (primarily Russia) being equal, Europe would probably have recovered even without the Marshall Plan. But the Plan did have three long-term consequences.

1. It speeded up Europe's recovery, which stymied the Russian effort to further penetrate Europe.
2. By forcing Europe to depend first on itself, the European countries had no choice but to create the conditions that would allow unimpeded trade across their borders. It was the first step toward a united European economy. This journey is not yet complete. But considerable progress has been made. Without the stimulus of the Marshall Plan, there's doubt that the process would have even started.
3. The time limit of four years for achieving self-sufficiency eliminated the possibility of concentrating on the development of new production facilities. Instead, it was necessary to confine efforts to the rehabilitation of existing plant. Since most of this plant was in Germany, the question of whether to rebuild Germany was resolved. Life would be breathed into Germany's moribund economy, despite France's protests.

Also in 1947, England and the US formed an economic unit known as Bizonia and consisting of the English and US zones. The object was to make the area more economically self-reliant and, therefore, less dependent on food subsidies. By March 1948, Bizonia was being run by an Administrative Council (a protocabinet) chosen by an Economic Council (a quasi-parliament) whose members were named by the state parliamentary assemblies in proportion to the strength of the parties in these assemblies. The major political parties were the CDU (Christian Democratic Party), the SPD (Social Democratic Party), and the FDP (Free Democratic Party). The CDU was committed to welfare state capitalism, the SPD to socialism, and the FDP to laissez faire. The first Administrative Council was formed by the CDU in coalition with the FDP. This council selected Ludwig Erhard, a relatively unknown economist without party affiliation, as chief economic architect. He established a free enterprise economic system in Bizonia.

In the spring of 1948, the three Western governments asked the Germans in their zones to convoke a constituent assembly to write a constitution for a new government. Because the West Germans didn't want to do anything to obstruct ultimate unification with the Russian zone, they called what they drafted a Basic Law rather

Frankfurt am Main. *Courtesy of the German Information Center.*

In 1945

In the Late 1970's

than a constitution. On May 24, 1949, under the Basic Law, the three Western zones became the Federal Republic, more commonly known as West Germany. To keep intact the four-power status of Berlin and, thus, the occupation rights of the Western governments in the Russian sector, West Berlin (the Western sectors) wasn't incorporated into West Germany.

A coalition of the CDU, FDP, and the German party formed the first cabinet in West Germany. Konrad Adenauer, a 73 year old Rhinelander who sat out the war at his country home, was elected chancellor by one vote, his own. Despite his age, der Alte (the Old Man), as he was known, remained chancellor for 14 years.

Adenauer appointed Erhard as economics minister. Erhard implemented the CDU program of welfare state capitalism. Government social insurance was established for the elderly, disabled and unemployed. Government regulated, private health insurance made medical treatment available when needed. Government funds were used for child support and to help with the rent of those who couldn't otherwise pay for housing. Government funds also financed the private firms that put up apartment buildings to help alleviate the housing shortage. On this welfare state underpinning, free enterprise was erected. Tax and other laws were enacted to stimulate investment and risk taking. Cartels and other combinations were attacked. Low tariffs and related policies were adopted to encourage foreign trade.

The result was the West German "economic miracle". In response to a tight money policy, hoarded goods appeared on the market. Saving and investment were also stimulated. Marshall aid complemented this capital accumulation. New, technologically leading edge industrial machinery was installed in West Germany's plants. Production grew at an average annual rate of 8.2 percent in 1950 - 54 and 7.1 percent in 1955 - 58. By 1960, exports had expanded to the point where West Germany stood second only to the US in world trade. Wages increased as employers bid for employees. West Germans were now well clothed and fed. Millions of housing units were constructed. Electric household appliances were commonplace. Millions bought cars.

On May 5, 1955, in accordance with the Paris Treaties executed in October 1954 by all concerned, the remnants of West

Germany's status as an occupied territory were removed. As a consequence, West Germany became sovereign. The same treaties accepted West Germany as a member of the North Atlantic Treaty Organization. When the European Economic Community, also called the Common Market, was formed in 1957, West Germany was a key member.

Thus, the outcome of World War II was the opposite of that of World War I. The Western nations had learned how to convert their former enemies into, if not friends, at the least, allies.

After recounting these success stories, it's perhaps only appropriate to look at developments in England, where things ultimately turned out to be less encouraging. We've seen that England was a partner in the Allied effort, in the two World Wars, that resulted in the defeat of the forces of aggression. Before that, we followed, in some detail, England's development into a constitutional monarchy with an independent judiciary practicing the common law in the defense of the individual's right to life, liberty and property, a framework within which the English built the first industrial society.

By 1870, England was producing more pig iron than the rest of the world combined, was mining almost half of the world's coal, was without peer in shipbuilding, and was the world's primary textile supplier. The foundation for this industrial activity was gentry agriculture, which fed the nation.

As times changed, England changed with them. The large-scale farming in the US midwest, combined with the rail transportation to the east coast of the US and the trans-Atlantic shipping industry, began to place (on England's doorstep) more and more grain that was less expensive than that grown at home, which undermined gentry agriculture. Increasing numbers of English laborers left the farmlands for the industrial towns. Other countries began to develop their own industrial bases, and by the early part of the 20th century, England had experienced a serious decline in its export staples of iron, steel, coal and textiles. But by now, London had become a financial capital of the world, and a movement into high technology areas compensated for losses in the more basic industries. However, shortly after the Second World

War, it became clear that England was starting to suffer from what has come to be known as the English Disease.

Like all nations, England has had its share of labor unrest, which sometimes involved violence. As already noted, England was the first country to industrialize, and some segments of labor saw the introduction of machinery as the cause of their problems. The most well known of such groups was undoubtedly the Luddites, named after a probably mythic leader, Ned Ludd, who sought to destroy textile manufacturing equipment. But such animosity was general. Agricultural machinery was another favorite target. Agricultural agitators also had their mythic leader. His name was Captain Swing.

Laborers also associated to improve their lot. As in the US, labor unions were initially combated as combinations in restraint of trade. However, in 1824, it became lawful for laborers to come together to determine wages, hours, and conditions of work. Again as in the US, the first unions were trade unions. They had a central agency, the Trades Union Congress. This agency was able to place a few workingmen in Commons, where they tended to vote with the Liberal (Whig) party. For this reason, they were known as Lib-Labs.

Then, in the early 1890's, unionization of unskilled workers began. These newer unions wanted a political party of their own. As a result, Keir Hardie, a miner and socialist, formed the Independent Labor Party and was elected to Parliament in 1892. His first entry into the House of Commons was a bit of an spectacle. He wore his miner's clothes and was preceded by a man blowing a horn.

In 1899, a joint committee, named the Labor Representation Committee, was sponsored by the Trades Union Congress, the Independent Labor Party, the Fabian Society, and another socialist society. Its function was to support the election of laborers to Parliament. The committee's first secretary was Ramsay MacDonald, subsequently England's first Labor party prime minister. England's Labor party grew out of this organization. It was the unions' creature, for which the unions largely paid. In 1918, the Labor party drew up a new constitution that committed the party "to secure for the producers by hand and by brain the full fruits of their industry, and the most equitable distribution thereof that may be possible, upon the basis of common ownership of the means of production and the best obtainable system of popular administration and control of each industry and service."

All well and good. But the ability of the unions to have adopted, through the efforts of their political party in Parliament, legislation, that the judiciary (with no tradition of judicial supremacy) had no way of preventing from encroaching on individual rights, created a body of statutory law bestowing extraordinary legal privilege uniquely on unions. The unions had the right to break contracts and enjoyed immunity from civil actions for damages. Employers were obliged to recognize unions and respect closed shops. In time, as a result of these measures, over 50 percent of the work force became unionized. In the US, France, and West Germany, the highest figure attained was about 25 percent or less. Nationalization of industries went forward. Regulation of industrial activity was broadened. Restrictive labor practices were established. Introduction of productivity-increasing technology was resisted. And social services were extended.

The results were catastrophic. Productivity was suffocated. Investment fell off. Labor costs soared. Inflation approached 40 percent a year. And the government ballooned. By 1975, it was absorbing almost 60 percent of the gross national product.

In 1979, the Conservative (Tory) party was returned to power, retrenchment began, and England's health has improved. But its prognosis is uncertain.

CHAPTER TWENTY ONE

Russia

The original Russian people were slavs who occupied the area north of the Khazar kaganate (state) in the 7th century. The Khazar kaganate reached from the Crimea to the Caspian sea and north to the mid-Volga. The military power of the kaganate shielded these slavs from the Asiatic nomads of the steppes.

In the 9th century, the Vikings worked their way up the rivers feeding into the Baltic and reached the headwaters of the rivers that flowed into the Black sea. Early in the 11th century, the Khazar kaganate was overrun by nomads from the steppes. Later in the century, the Vikings moved down the Black sea rivers, won ascendancy over the area, and settled down to a life of trading. The center of this trading empire was at Kiev on the Dnieper. But the trade articles were mainly forest products, which the Vikings collected from the slavic hinterlands, primarily in the form of tribute. By the middle of the 11th century, these Vikings had become slavicized (they adopted slavic names, the slavic language, and slavic customs), but they bequeathed their name to the slavs, which was the Rus.

In the 12th century, the trading state dominated by the Viking Rus began to disintegrate and left in its wake numerous self-contained principalities. The next development occurred in the region surrounding the entry of the Oka river into the Volga. This remote area, almost completely covered with forests, was made up of essentially uninhabited principalities, which the princes thought of as their property. Over time, peasants immigrated to this area. When a group of peasants settled on a prince's land, he conceived of them as nothing more than an appendage to his land, as a building or other structure would be. In other words, they were just another part of the domain over which he was the autocrat. Within a prince's domain, his rule was absolute. His domain was no more than an extension of himself. There was no distinction between them. They were one. As a consequence, everything in his domain (land, people, buildings and tools)

The River System between the Baltic and Black Seas

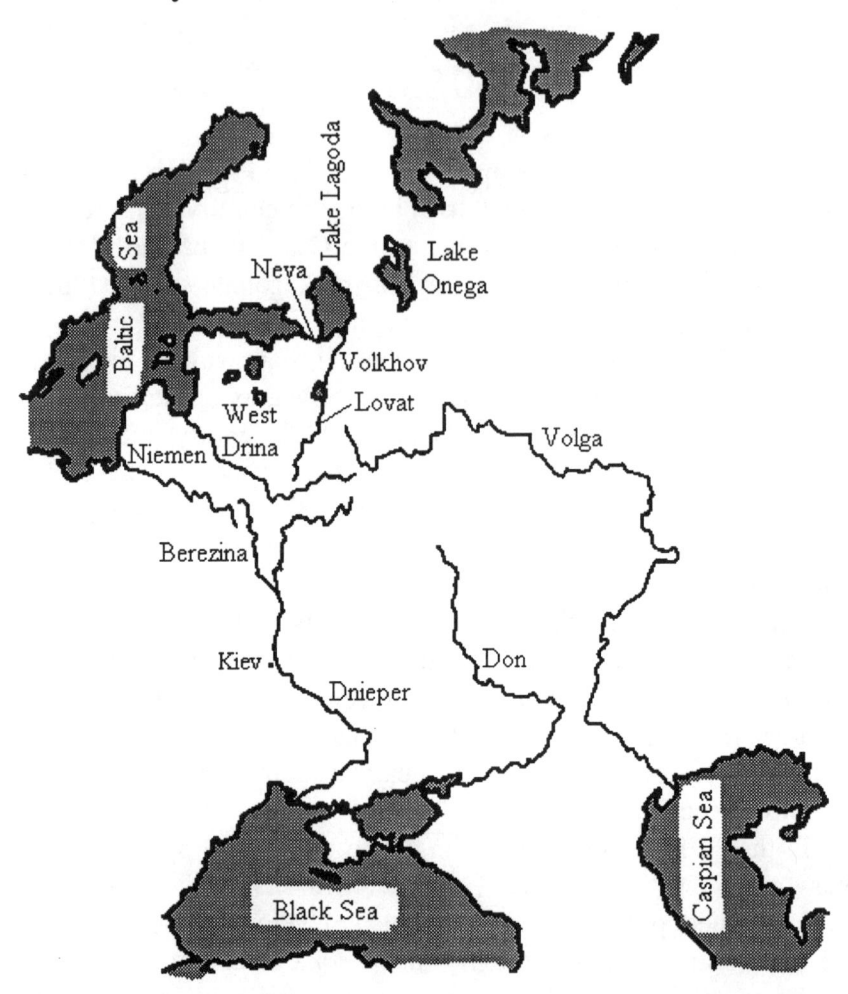

belonged to him absolutely, just as his body did. There was no such thing as law, because he was the law. The relationship between the prince and his people wasn't one of sovereign and subjects. Instead, it was one of seigneur and the bonded work force on his lands.

In 1237, the Russian principalities became, by conquest, subsidiary to the Golden Horde, a branch of the Mongol empire with its capitol at Sarai on the lower Volga. Thus, the Mongol khan of the Golden Horde became the Russian ruler. The Russians called him Tsar (Caesar).

The Golden Horde had no interest in occupying Russia. What they wanted was money, goods and service. So they didn't take over Russia. They just demanded tribute. None was more competent in performing the unattractive job of collecting tribute and delivering it to the Golden Horde than Prince Alexander Nevsky and his descendants. Prince Alexander was called Nevsky because of his triumph over the Swedes in an engagement conducted on the banks of the Neva river in 1240.

The first known prince of Moscow was Daniel, the son of Alexander Nevsky. On his death in 1303, Daniel was succeeded by his son, Yuri. In 1325, Yuri was murdered by a rival for the favor of the Golden Horde. Yuri's brother, Ivan, then became the prince of Moscow. In 1327, another principality, Tver, rebelled against the Mongols. Ivan, leading a combined Mongol Russian force, crushed the rebellion. In return, the Mongols gave Ivan the title of Great Prince (that is, prince over all the other Russian princes) and Farmer General of tribute throughout Russia. He thus became Ivan I, known as Kalita (literally, Moneybag).

Moscow maintained its position of dominance in Russia throughout the suzerainty of the Golden Horde. The Horde was mortally shaken by the onslaught of Tamerlane (Timor the Lame), who in 1395, destroyed Sarai. In the middle of the 15th century, the Golden Horde shattered into pieces, the most prominent remnants of which became the khanates of Kazan, Astrakhan and the Crimea. In 1480 (traditional date), during the reign of Ivan III (the great great great grandson of Ivan I), Moscow stopped paying tribute to these successors of the Golden Horde.

Ivan III was the first to refer to himself as tsar. In 1547, his grandson, Ivan IV, formalized the title. Ivan IV is commonly known in English as Ivan the Terrible, but a better translation of the Russian name would be "Ivan the Awesome".

Starting with Ivan III, Moscow began annexing other Russian principalities. By 1598, Muscovy was equal in size to the rest of Europe. With the acquisition of Siberia in the first half of the 17th century, Russia doubled its size. During this one and one half centuries of expansion, autocracy remained the ruling principle.

Russia's geographic location predicated a short farming season, six months at the most, in comparison to the usual eight or nine

The Trading Empire of the Viking Rus

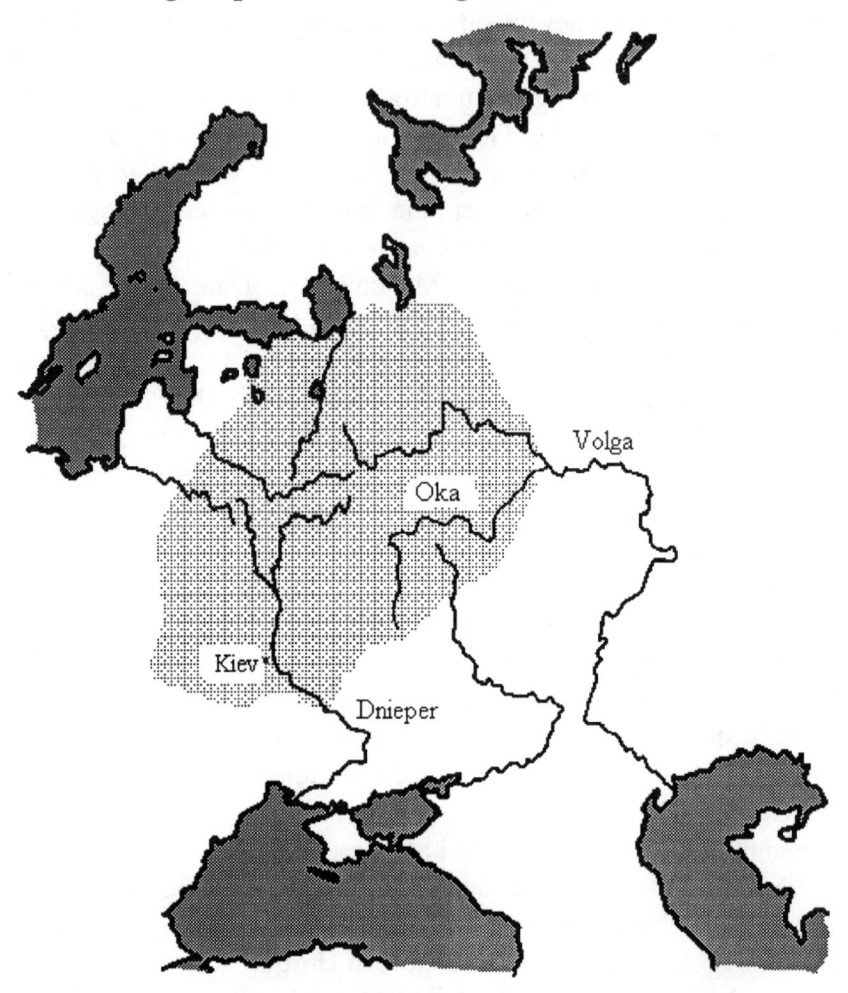

months in most agricultural regions. As a result, farming required concentrated effort and created pressure to work collectively. The communal work organization was an extended family consisting of a father, mother, children, and married sons with their wives and offspring. This extended family was a work team led by a bolshak (the big one), usually the father, who directed the team's work.

A number of extended families lived in a mir, or community, with which the land worked by the families was associated. This land was divided into strips allotted to families on the basis of the number of adult members, both men and women, in each family.

These land strips were worked privately by each family. Thus, although each family was a collective, the community wasn't.

Every 12 to 15 years, in a process known as "black repartition", a community reallotted its land among its families, so that the relation of the number of strips and number of adults remained roughly proportional. Not only could the number of adults in an extended family increase or diminish, but when a bolshak died, the result was typically the creation of several new extended families, each headed by a son of the former bolshak. "Black" land was land subject to taxation, as opposed to "white" land, which wasn't taxed. Clerical land, for example, was white land. The land the peasant worked was black land — thus, peasant land reallocation was a "black" repartition.

The community made up its mind by acclamation. It viewed as antisocial any disagreement with the decisions of the majority.

A community's land didn't belong to it. Instead, the land was held in trust by a landlord, who was responsible for seeing that each peasant on the land paid his taxes. In effect, the landlord was liable for the taxes and either had to collect them from his peasants or pay them himself. You can imagine what he did.

The peasant couldn't formally complain about his landlord and, in fact, wasn't even allowed to appear in court. He was defenseless in the face of authority. As a consequence, when told what to do, he had no choice but to obey. But his only real allegiance was to his community.

Because of this anti-authority attitude, the peasant was as resistant to suggestions made in his own interests as he was to arbitrary commands. To the peasant, authority was something that was used to compel people to do what they otherwise wouldn't do, such as pay taxes and serve in the army. Therefore, there was no such thing as a benevolent or well meaning authority. There was only strong authority and weak authority. Between the two, his preference was for strong authority. That, at least, got things done, which was something he could respect. Thus, the significance of the name, Ivan the Awesome. In the face of weak authority, the peasant tended toward acts of indiscriminate violence.

Being so subservient, the peasant's most cherished desire was to not be subject to any restraint whatsoever. The most available

The Growth of Muscovy

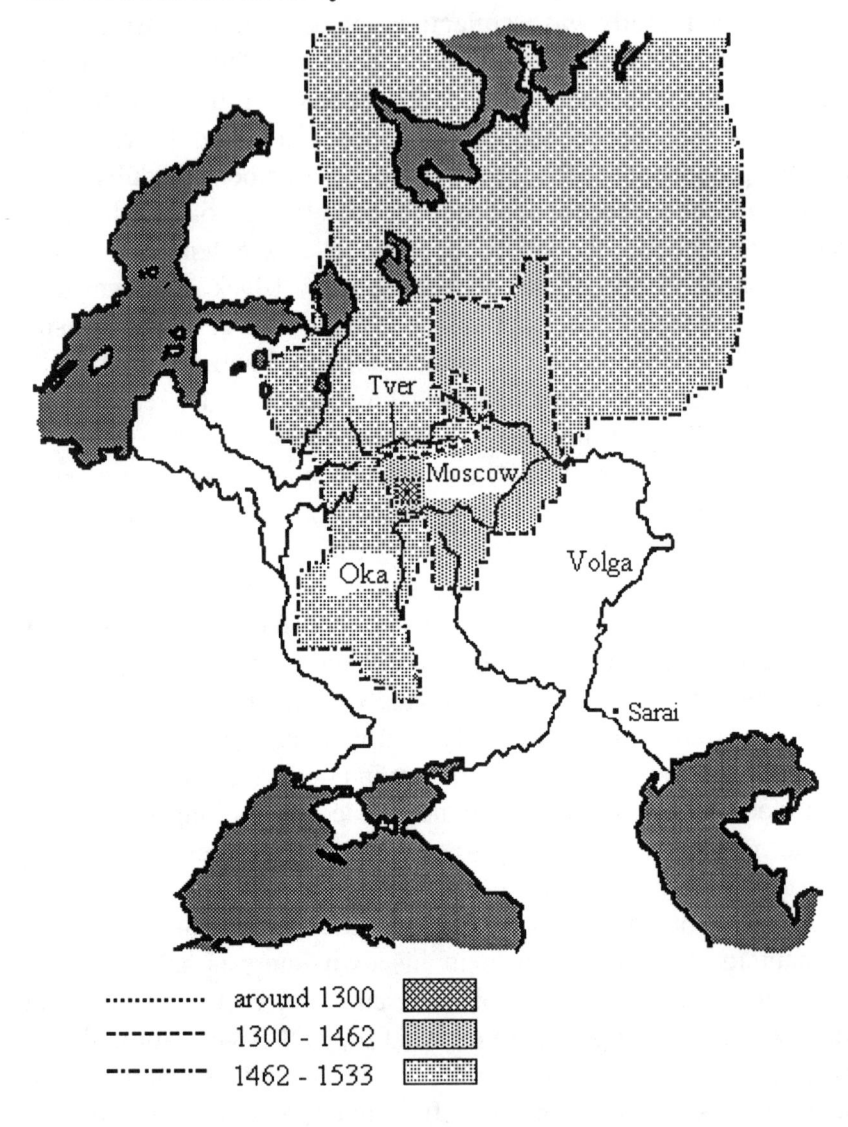

············· around 1300	
-------- 1300 - 1462	
—··—··— 1462 - 1533	

method of attaining this state was vodka. The peasant's drinking habits were an alternation between abstinence (when farming consumed his waking hours) and complete stupor (whenever he got any time off).

Since the peasant was restricted to his community, his world view was constricted. He had difficulty in conceptualizing anything outside of his immediate surroundings. In fact, the peasant's concept of his country was couched in terms of his limited world view. To him, Russia was like one large community. He could never be dissuaded from the idea that, one day, the tsar, who was conceived of as some kind of super bolshak, would redistribute the land in a kind of grand black repartition, so that each family would share according to its size and all the land would be properly cared for. It's perhaps no accident that the Russian word mir, which as we've seen, refers to a peasant community, also means world.

Unable to grasp an abstract concept such as law, and reflexively antagonistic to any form of authority, the peasant was a poor basis on which to found any government other than an authoritarian one. Even when the social fabric was torn and the peasant had the opportunity to revolt, the most he was capable of was local, irresponsible acts, such as murdering his landlord, burning down his landlord's manor, cutting down his landlord's trees, harvesting the crops grown by others, and confiscating goods.

We've said that neither the peasant nor his community owned the land he worked. But even the landlord, who constituted the authority with whom the peasant dealt, held his position only on royal sufferance contingent on providing service to the crown, for all land was just part of the tsar's domain. To the extent that the term was appropriate, these landlords constituted Russia's nobility. But unlike the nobility in other lands, they weren't a class with landed wealth, the origins of which reached back to feudal times. Instead, they held the land, from which their living came, at the pleasure of the tsar. They also depended on him both to see that their peasants remained enserfed (that is, bound to their land) and to provide the police muscle necessary to keep them from going on murderous rampages.

The tsar's domain also extended to trade and industry. All imports had to pass through the hands of tsarist agents who purchased whatever they felt was appropriate on the tsar's behalf at fixed prices. Any foreigner who turned down these "offers" was prohibited from trading in Russia. The goods the tsar acquired in this way were either used in his household or resold at market

Russia Expands

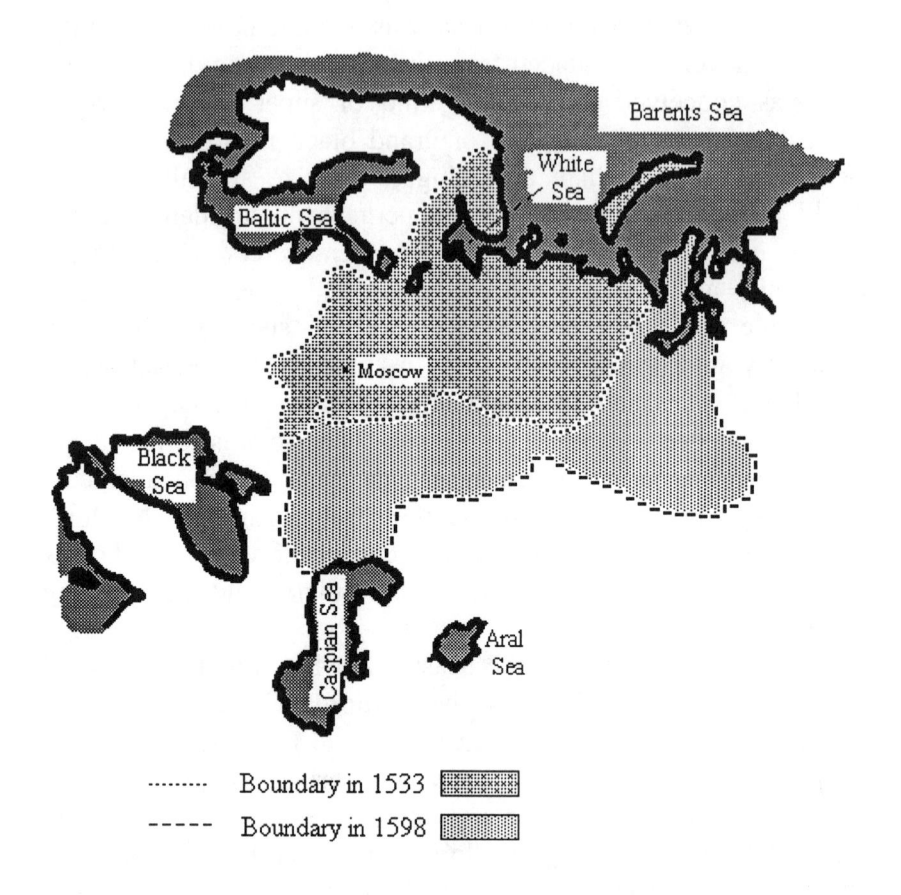

Map showing Russian territorial boundaries in 1533 and 1598, with labeled seas: Barents Sea, White Sea, Baltic Sea, Black Sea, Caspian Sea, Aral Sea, and the city of Moscow.

- - - - - - - - Boundary in 1533
- - - - Boundary in 1598

prices.

Whenever private initiative developed an export market, the government characteristically imposed a royal monopoly. From that point on, the commodity was sold at a fixed price exclusively to the tsar's treasury, which then traded it on the export market at negotiable prices. Among other exports monopolized were caviar, flax, tar, potash, leather, madder (a dye), meerschaum, and beef fat.

Industry was also monopolized by the government. Most Russian industry was established by foreigners (sponsored and financed by the crown) and directed by the tsar's personnel, who were, again, generally foreigners. All industries, including those that had developed independently in Russia (iron, salt, and coarse cloth), were run the same way. All were monopolies of the monarchy, to which they sold at cost whatever part of the production was needed. Profits came from the sale of the surplus on the open market.

During the 17th century, strains in the autocratic regime began to show. The first sign was the increasing ineffectiveness of Russia's army. It consisted of cavalry made up of the nobility and supported by a peasant infantry. The cavalry charged into battle and sucked the infantry in behind it. From that point on, it was every man for himself. In the meantime, the western European states were developing military techniques that exploited the advantages of the flintlock and bayonet, and that placed primary emphasis on corps of infantry in close order ranks that advanced and fired as units under the control of a chain of command.

To rectify this situation, Tsar Peter I (the Great) created a standing army. One of the requirements of this army was that, at least, the command hierarchy had to be literate and understand such things as maps and setting artillery ranges. Since even Russian nobles were, for the most part, illiterate, Peter had no alternative but to set up an extensive education program.

Peter's attitude was, "We need Europe for a few decades, and then we must turn our back on it." But this turned out to be impossible. The changes introduced couldn't be made at a superficial level. What Peter was doing was saying that the public should educate itself — get involved with Russia and support the government. It was the first time Russia had recognized a difference between authority and the domain over which that authority was exercised. The first crack in the concept of autocracy had appeared.

From that point on, changes cascaded. In 1736, Empress Anne reduced the nobility's service to a maximum of 25 years and let one of each landlord's sons remain home to look after the family's interests. In 1762, Peter III removed the nobility totally from compulsory service and abolished most of the crown's trading and industrial monopolies. In 1785, Catherine II (the Great) invested the landlords with legal ownership of the lands that they had

Russian Peasants *from the Orel region in the second half of the 19th century. From a photograph in the George Kennan Archive of the Library of Congress.*

previously managed at the government's sufferance. And in 1861, Alexander II emancipated the serfs. In total, the monarchy had conferred on its subjects considerable civil, economic and intellectual freedom.

It was anticipated that the next development would be for the populace to begin participating in the political process. However, this step was never taken. The imperial government resolutely refused to share political power. The monarchy held on tenaciously to its unlimited authority with regard to Russia's foreign policy and the disposition of the funds in the treasury, the bulk of which were spent on the court and the armed forces. The method of replenishing the treasury's funds was for the tsar to fix the annual amount necessary to conduct his business. Responsibility for providing this amount was then split among the bureaucrats who carried out the tax collection. The government spent virtually nothing in support of this bureaucracy. It was expected that the bureaucrats would "feed themselves from official business." The system encouraged corruption.

There was no countervailing institution in Russia to challenge the tsar's monopoly on political power. The peasants, their faith in the coming grand black repartition never failing, resolutely supported the tsar.

The landlords, even after they acquired property rights in their lands, also failed to coalesce into any kind of political amalgam. Nine tenths of them were so poor that they were indistinguishable from peasants. The rich landlords were content to live the life of grandees. The remaining middle group, who could have formed a political base, were haunted by their memory of compulsory state service and shied away from taking any part in the country's political life.

The commercial and industrial interests, also freed from the grasp of government monopoly, were still dependent on the monarchy for preservation of a high tariff wall, without which they wouldn't have been able to maintain themselves. Consequently, they had no desire to come into conflict with the tsar.

As a result, resistance to autocracy fell to the intelligentsia, whose only basis for their position was ideological. The first goal of the intelligentsia was to enlist the newly emancipated peasants in their cause. The peasants would have nothing to do with them. Instead, the peasants stuck with the tsar and their anticipation of the coming grand black repartition. In frustration, in 1878, a group of the intelligentsia turned to terrorism, the purpose of which was to demonstrate the vulnerability of the autocratic system. This approach was effective, because the precautions designed to safeguard government officials were weak. But it called up within the government a radical response: the intensive use of a political police force, which was already in existence.

The first such police force was created by Peter the Great in 1697. It was the Preobrazhenskii Prikaz, which was responsible for dealing with antigovernment actions. Preobrazhenskii is the town outside of Moscow in which Peter grew up. Prikaz is council.

This special police force operated without restraint. It had the right to conduct any investigation it deemed appropriate and to engage in any action it found necessary to collect evidence and combat sedition.

Peter III (1761 - 1762) and Catherine the Great (1762 -1796) disbanded Peter the Great's special police, although to some extent, the functions continued on a more private basis. Catherine created an internal security organization, called the Secret Expedition, which made secret arrests and used torture. In 1802, Alexander I (1801 - 1825) established the Ministry of the Interior, which performed the functions of a police ministry. In 1811, he set up a Ministry of Police. But eight years later, the Minister of the Interior convinced him that the Ministry of Police was redundant, he eliminated it, and its functions were transferred to the Ministry of the Interior.

Then in December 1825, in the confusion that followed the death of Alexander I, a group of young officers attempted a coup d'etat. These men, from distinguished families, had spent a year or more in Europe during the 1813 - 1815 campaigns followed by three years of occupation in France. On March 31, 1814, Alexander I had entered Paris at the head of his victorious troops.

During this sojourn in Europe, these young officers had become imbued with republican principles. Their attempt at a coup d'etat was inept and quickly disposed of by Nicholas I as the opening act of his reign. However, as a result of this Decembrist revolt, in 1826, Nicholas I established a Third Section in His Majesty's Private Imperial Chancellery. This chancellery was the agency that dealt with the questions that demanded the personal attention of the tsar. This Third Section was a secret police organization. Its responsibilities included ferreting out and forestalling subversion. Like Peter the Great's special police before it, the Third Section answered only to the tsar.

In 1845, a new Criminal Code was adopted. Under its provisions, not only were attempts to change the government outlawed, even questioning the government's actions became a crime.

In August 1880, the Third Section was superseded by a central political police force initially named the Department of State Police. In 1883, the name was shortened to the Department of Police. Political prisoners weren't dealt with by the judiciary. Their trial and punishment were the province of the Department of Police.

The response of the political police to terrorist activities gave a new cast to the Russian political situation. Because terrorist acts could be carried out with relative ease, and because these acts did demonstrate the vulnerability of a government whose claim to power was based on its impregnability, it became the goal of the police to stamp out even the possibility of terrorism. As a result, police regulation and proscriptions became an integral part of everyday life. To take part in Russian society, a citizen had to have a certificate of "trustworthiness". These certificates were issued by the police, whose decisions weren't subject to question and, consequently, could be as arbitrary as subjective opinion required. In an equally summary way, a person could be put "under surveillance". A person so classified had to exchange all of his official documents for special ones issued by the police, couldn't travel without police approval, was subject to search at any time, and was prohibited from working in a broad range of employment categories. The police definition of political crime was so broad that innocent acts, such as students forming an association or workers organizing a trade union, were outlawed.

The result of this police action was twofold.
1. Although designed to protect the tsar's authority, the comprehensive action of the political police tended to place the populace under the supervision of the police. In effect, the police became a kind of second government.
2. Dissatisfied people, shut off from more normal forms of expressing dissent, became radicalized and created centers of resistance dedicated to bringing down the regime.

The situation caused an explosion in 1905. In St. Petersburg on January 9 (Bloody Sunday), a monster demonstration of workers bearing a petition to the tsar, Nicholas II, and led by the priest George Gapon was fired on by troops. In February, the tsar's uncle, Grand Duke Serge Alexandrovich, was assassinated. In June, a mutiny broke out on the battleship Potemkin. Resistance to the royal regime was expressed in a number of violent ways. A general strike, begun in October, brought the country to a standstill. The tsar's reaction to this unrest had been to meet terror with terror. But on October 17, the tsar finally gave in and signed the October Manifesto proclaiming that no law would be promulgated without the approval of the Duma, the to-be-established Russian parliament.

The experiment didn't work. Neither side was willing to participate constructively in the compromise. Despite commitments to the contrary, Nicholas maintained that his autocratic prerogatives remained intact. He was willing to abide the Duma as a consultative body only. His position was that, since he had created the Duma of his own free will, he was also free to ignore it at will. Those opposed to autocracy saw the Duma as an arena for unbridled attacks on the monarchy with the goal of bringing it down. In this sense, they were effective in advancing their program, since their incessant assaults in a sanctioned forum tended to undermine the impression of omnipotence that the crown worked so strenuously to uphold. It was these circumstances that led to the Russian Revolution.

A characteristic of Russia under the old regime (before the Russian Revolution) was the violence associated with autocratic rule. We've already noted that Ivan I (1325 - 1341) came to power as a result of the murder of his brother, Yuri. Following the reign of Ivan I, a bloody dispute over the rule of Russia ensued and was finally resolved when Vasili II, the great grandson of Ivan I, gained ascendancy (1425 - 1462). Vasili then mercilessly eliminated all contenders for his position. Ivan the Terrible (1533 - 1584), the great grandson of Vasili II, while out of control with anger, killed his oldest son.

Ivan's son Fedor (1584 - 1598) succeeded his father and died without issue. Fedor was feeble minded. During his reign, the machinery of government was controlled by Boris Godunov, his brother in law. On Fedor's death, Boris was elected tsar (1598 - 1605). Godunov's position was, because of the manner of his elevation, none too firm. He thought he saw subversion in all corners. He dealt with these problems, both imagined and real, by eliminating all potential suspects. Among these was Fedor Romanov, who was compelled to take monastic vows and sent to an out-of-the-way monastery. Fedor's son, Michael, as well as all other members of the Romanov family, were exiled. Boris's son and successor was murdered a few weeks after his ascendancy. The First Pretender, who claimed to be the son of Ivan IV, assumed control and, within the year, was murdered in turn. Civil war (the time of troubles) then engulfed Russia and was finally resolved when Michael Romanov was elected tsar (1613 - 1645).

Michael was succeeded by his son, Alexis (1645 - 1676). Alexis was married twice, first to Maria Miloslavsky and, after Maria's death, to Nathalie Naryshkin. He had three sons, Fedor and Ivan by Maria and Peter (the future Peter the Great) by Nathalie. On Alexis' death, Fedor became tsar (1676 - 1682). When Fedor died, the Miloslavsky and Naryshkin families entered into a power struggle. The Naryshkin's maneuvered their way clear to making Peter tsar. But the Miloslavsky's invaded the Kremlin over and over again, and dispatched most of the Naryshkin's. To resolve this conflict, it was finally agreed that there would be two, concurrent tsars. As a result, Ivan was made the first tsar at the same time that Peter became the second tsar (1682 - 1696). On Ivan's death, Peter became the undisputed tsar (1696 - 1725). Peter's son, Alexis, died after he was put through an ordeal of torture for the third time. Peter conducted these "investigations" and was witness to his son's torture.

Ivan VI (1740 - 1741), the great great grandson of the Tsar Alexis, was overthrown, confined, and killed when an attempt was made to free him. Peter III (1761 - 1762), the grandson of Peter the Great, abdicated, was arrested, and a few days later was killed by his guards, under the direction of Alexis Orlov, whose brother, Gregory, was the lover of Peter's wife, Catherine. Catherine then ascended to the throne as Catherine the Great (1762 - 1796). She was succeeded by her son, Paul I (1796 - 1801), who was murdered

The Geography of Lenin's Youth and of the Revolution

in his bed by conspirators, with whom Alexander, Paul's son, was involved. Alexander then became the Tsar Alexander I (1801 - 1825).

Alexander II (1855 - 1881), the grandson of Paul I, was killed by a bomb set by revolutionaries. Finally, Rasputin was murdered. He had the Tsarina Alexandra under his thumb. She, in turn, dominated the Tsar Nicholas II, her husband and grandson of Alexander II, who became tsar in 1894. It's no wonder that Russian government has been described as "Absolutism tempered by assassination."

Another characteristic of Russia under the old regime was its insatiable drive to expand territorially. From the reign of Ivan III through that of Alexander III (1881 - 1894), the son of Alexander II, the border of Russia amounted to a fault line over which, at various times and in various combinations of alliance and opposition, Russia contested with Sweden, Poland, Turkey, Prussia, Austria, England and France for dominion. Although understandable in and of itself, Russia's emphasis on maintaining a militant military and pursuing a policy of expansion can also be interpreted in terms of the idea that Russia saw itself in a hostile environment peopled by enemies that, if not continuously played off against one another, could combine into a single alliance fatal to Russia.

The Russian Revolution produced Communist Russia. It was, in its initial stages, the creation of one person, Lenin. In 1887, Lenin's older brother, Alexander, was executed for participating in a plot to assassinate Tsar Alexander III. In 1887, Lenin entered Kazan University, where he was recognized as Alexander's brother and recruited into a People's Will group. The People's Will was an organization dedicated to fighting the tsarist regime through the systematic use of terror.

Lenin participated in a demonstration to protest university regulations. As a consequence, he was expelled from the university.

In the investigation that followed his expulsion, the police discovered both that Lenin was involved in the People's Will and that he was Alexander's brother. He was then classified as an "unreliable" and subjected to police surveillance. From then on, his petitions to be readmitted to the university were systematically turned down. Because they were the relatives of an executed terrorist, he and his mother were avoided in their home town of

Simbirsk. His father had died just before Alexander's execution. The name of Simbirsk was later changed to Ulyanovsk in honor of Lenin, who was born there as Vladimir I. Ulyanov.

As a result of this treatment at the hands of the police and his neighbors, by the fall of 1888, when he moved with his mother to Kazan, Lenin had developed a deep enmity for those who had ruined his career (the tsarist government) and ostracized his family (the "bourgeoisie").

In the fall of 1893, Lenin moved to St. Petersburg to begin his revolutionary career. He sought out the Social Democratic (SD) party, the basic position of which was that the Russian Revolution would take place in two stages. First, the party must cooperate with the "liberal bourgeoisie" to create a "bourgeois democracy". Then the working class would be rallied to the second, socialist phase of the Revolution. Lenin's background made him reluctant to cooperate with the bourgeoisie. But he was finally convinced by the more senior members of the SD that, during this cooperative period, the SD would be in control and would steer its temporary ally along the path that would be to its own best advantage. As a consequence, in the autumn of 1895, Lenin began work as an orthodox SD, organizing workers for the battle against autocracy in cooperation with the liberal bourgeoisie.

By 1900, Lenin's observation of worker behavior in and out of Russia led him to the conclusion that labor wasn't a revolutionary class. It didn't want to overthrow capitalism. Instead, it was interested in increasing its share of the profits of capitalism. Unless it was directed by a socialist party distinct from it, it would act contrary to its class interests. The startling outcome of this line of thought was that only the intelligentsia recognized labor's class interests for what they were. Moreover, since workers, by definition, had to spend most of their time working, the revolutionary movement (to see that the workers realized their class interests) would have to be led by a cadre of intelligentsia who could devote their lives to the movement. This reasoning fit right in with Lenin's predilection for indefatigable work in which he made no distinction between himself and the movement.

Lenin then began to lose faith in the ability of the SD to control its liberal bourgeoisie ally. He finally decided that, in fact, the liberal bourgeoisie were using the SD for their own purposes.

In sum, Lenin concluded that the Revolution had to be carried out by a dedicated minority. His experience with the People's Will led him to believe that, to be effective, this committed group would have to be organized along military lines and be headed by a Central Committee, the decisions of which would be binding on the membership.

The founding gathering of the international SD (where the SD parties of Russia, Germany, and other countries came together to form an umbrella international organization) was split on Lenin's theses. In the beginning, Lenin was consistently in the minority. But at one point, a number of delegates walked out, which gave Lenin a temporary majority. He promptly named his faction the Bolshevik (the majority), leaving to his opponents the name Menshevik (minority).

The First World War found Lenin in Austria, where he was arrested as an enemy alien and suspected spy. However, influential people in the Austrian and Polish socialist movements supported him as "an enemy of tsarism". On September 1, Lenin departed for Switzerland on an Austrian military mail train, which indicated that Austria had decided that he was of value to its cause.

The winter of 1916 - 1917 was unusually cold, which immobilized rail transportation in northern Russia. Toward the end of February, Petrograd (St. Petersburg, which sounded Germanic, was so renamed at the beginning of the war) still had adequate flour supplies. But fuel was running out, which idled both bakeries and factories.

The temperature then turned warm (46 F), where it stayed for the rest of the month. The cold weather had kept people indoors for months. When the temperature moderated, they poured outside. Because of the gravity of the food situation and the number of idled workers in the streets, the administration had barriers erected on the bridges that linked the workers quarters with the commercial center. At the time, the tsar was in Mogilev consulting with General Mikail Alekseev, the army chief of staff.

The workers made the barriers erected on these bridges nugatory by crossing on the still frozen river.

These laborers were peasants who had come to Petrograd to work in the factories. With the random violence characteristic of peasants in the face of what they sense as weak authority, they emptied food stores and caused other damage. The next day, the crowds became even more violent: three civilians were killed, a grenade was thrown, and a police officer was beaten to death.

That evening, a telegram was received from Nicholas, which ordered the authorities to put down the demonstrations with military force. The next day, military patrols were present all over Petrograd. Several incidents occurred, the most serious being when a company of the Volynskii Guard Regiment shot and killed 40 workers in Znamenskii Square.

The Guard Regiments stationed in Petrograd were draftees and long-out-of-service reserves in basic training preparatory to their move to the front. The only difference between them and the workers (peasants) in the streets was that they wore uniforms. In reaction to the Znamenskii Square incident, the Pavlovskii Regiment met that night and decided to disobey if ordered to fire on civilians. This resolve was communicated to the Preobrazhenskii and Litovskii Guard Regiments billeted nearby. They fell in with the plan. The next day, these regiments joined the workers in the streets. By evening, Petrograd was in the control of peasants in uniform. Of the 160,000 man garrison, half had rebelled and the rest had decided not to take sides.

The next day, the Duma established a Provisional Committee to take over government responsibility. On the same day, the Petrograd Soviet (Committee) of Workers' and Soldiers' Deputies was formed. It resembled a giant peasant-community assembly and, as such, was unable to do anything other than act as a vehicle for speechmaking. As a result, decision making was assumed by the Executive Committee of the Soviet, which wasn't elected by the Soviet but was, instead, appointed by the socialist parties.

The Executive Committee chose not to join the Provisional Government that the Duma had put together. As a means of controlling the unruly mobs, the Provisional Government asked the Executive Committee for support. This the Executive Committee was willing to provide as long as the Provisional Government adhered to policies of which the Executive Committee approved.

During the waning months of 1916, all politicians, from royalists through liberals to extreme socialists, agreed that, if a revolution in Russia were to be avoided, the monarchy must be replaced by a cabinet appointed by the Duma. Whether they were right is another question.

In any case, the politicians convinced the generals. Consequently, in the face of the Petrograd uprising, the generals (believing that, if disruption could be confined, the war could be carried on, and that, if the tsar gave up his crown, the unrest could be prevented from spreading across the country) urged the tsar to abdicate. The tsar did so, apparently out of patriotic feelings: he didn't want to see Russia's armed forces fall apart. The four century autocratic rule of a country making up one sixth of the earth's surface collapsed without noticeable concern.

Not a month after the tsar's fall, Lenin and a number of other Russian emigres crossed Germany in a train provided by the German government. The object was to return these activists to Russia as a kind of virus to infect the body politic of the Provisional Government and remove Russia as an opponent in the war. One of Lenin's sponsors was Parvus, a Russian revolutionist who, after the failure of the "revolution" of 1905 to topple tsarism, decided that success in Russia depended on the help of German armies. Consequently, he put himself at the service of the German government. In 1917, he was in Copenhagen, where he conducted intelligence activities for the Germans. He predicted that, if returned to Russia, the anti-war socialists would cause such disruption that Russia would have to withdraw from the war. He was particularly high on Lenin, whom he described as "much more raving mad" than others. Lenin arrived in Petrograd early in April.

It's hard to say what Lenin's long-term goals were. He left an expanse of papers from which it's possible to select statements supporting almost any position you choose. As a consequence, the surest guide to Lenin's motivations was his actions. In these terms, his one clearly identifiable long-term goal was to have the Bolshevik Central Committee rule Russia. His short-term goals varied with the circumstances, but each had the characteristic that it looked to Lenin like the next best step toward his long-term goal.

On his return to Russia, Lenin's first short-term goal was to overthrow the Provisional Government. He tried various strategies, including two massive demonstrations, one in April and one in July. The July putsch might have succeeded, but at the last minute, Lenin lost confidence and decided that the time to try for an overthrow was not yet. The overthrow occurred in October and took the form of a coup d'etat, which was effective, not because the Bolshevik forces were willing to fight (with one exception, they instantly retreated at the first sounds of gun fire), but because there was no resistance. The Bolsheviks took over all strategic points by just occupying them. The government guards accepted replacement with no questions asked.

When the promised support from outside Petrograd failed to appear, the forces guarding the Provisional Government's cabinet in the Winter Palace began to drift away. A day after the coup began, these ministers were captured. A rump Congress of Soviets, convened by the Bolsheviks and stacked with their members, named a new cabinet, the Council of People's Commissars, headed by Lenin and consisting of Bolsheviks.

The only military action took place six days after the coup, when 600 Cossacks, advancing on Petrograd to support the Provisional Government, were met by a Red force of at least 6000 at Pulkovo, a suburb of Petrograd located ten miles south of Petrograd. The Red force was made up of Red Guards, and rebel soldiers and sailors. When they came face to face with the Cossacks, the Red Guards and rebel soldiers retreated, but the sailors, 3000 in number, held their position, with the result that the Cossacks retired to Gatchina. If possible, the fall of the Provisional Government was reacted to with more indifference than that accorded to the end of tsarism.

With the October coup, Lenin had not only reached his first short-term objective, he had also, for the moment, gotten members of his party installed as the country's ruling council. However, he was faced with multiple problems, each of which was formidable.

1. The country as a whole was, if not anti-Bolshevik, at least, non-Bolshevik. Lenin didn't have popular support.

2. The Bolshevik council represented, not the Bolshevik party, but the All Russian Soviet, into which the Petrograd Soviet had evolved. With their lack of public support, the Bolsheviks could never have carried on their activities under the slogan of "All Power to the Bolsheviks" so the slogan that they adopted was "All Power to the Soviets" — just one more example of Lenin's pragmatism. As a consequence, the Bolshevik council was theoretically committed to work with the Executive Committee of the Soviet, on which sat members of the other socialist parties.
3. The Bolshevik council was temporary. It's authority was to last only until a Constituent Assembly established a permanent government. And the assembly was scheduled to convene in one month.
4. The council was the head of a government at war with Germany. Russia's troops were demoralized, and a German victory would mean the end of the current Russian government.
5. The Bolsheviks were almost immediately engaged in a Civil War with the White Russians, a collection of anti-Bolshevik military forces.

Lenin distracted the populace by turning over to it the wealth of Russia to divide. His slogan was, "Loot the loot." By decree, Lenin authorized the expropriation, without compensation, of all privately held lands. The expropriation was carried out by the peasant communities, which then distributed the newly acquired land among the indigenous peasants. To the peasants, it was the long-awaited-for grand black repartition. It occupied them until the spring of 1918. In the meantime, their interest in politics, which was small enough to start with, was reduced further.

The same sort of thing happened in industry. Lenin put plant management into the hands of factory committees, who pushed the owners and directors to one side. The committees also distributed, among themselves and the workers they represented, the profits, material and equipment of the plants.

The division also extended to the Russian state. Ethnic groups proclaimed their independence — Finland, Lithuania, Latvia, Ukraine, Estonia, Transcaucasia (now made up of Georgia, Azerbaijan and Armenia) and Poland. Provinces and non-Russian peoples (settled among Russians) declared themselves republics. One study determined that, by June 1918, at least 33 "governments" existed on the land of the defunct Russian empire.

With respect to Germany, Lenin's position was peace on Germany's terms, now. He felt that he couldn't immediately sue for peace, because it would seem to confirm the suspicion that he was a German agent. So he first asked all the belligerent powers to negotiate to end the war. Once this appeal was turned down, he would be in a position to work out a treaty with Germany. By the end of November 1917, all parties had rejected the appeal and discussions with Germany began. However, a treaty wasn't signed until March 1918.

The delay was due to the fact that Lenin was consistently outvoted by the majority of the Central Committee, which throws light on Lenin's concept of government. He insisted that the decisions of the committee were final. But within the committee, although he was the undisputed leader and, as time when on, considered more and more infallible, he never contemplated going against the will of the majority and refused to even consider removing someone from the committee just because he disagreed. From the time that the treaty with Germany was signed until the end of the war, it was Germany, over and over again, that intervened, with political support and money, to prevent the Bolsheviks from going under.

The Bolsheviks beat back the armed forces opposing them in the Civil War. Several factors were involved.

1. The populace wasn't pro-Bolshevik, but it wasn't in favor of the White Russians either, since their armies, of necessity, lived off of the land. What the common Russian wanted was an end to the strife, and the Bolsheviks at least had in their favor the fact that they were recognized as the government. Perhaps most importantly, the Bolsheviks had given the peasants their land, and the peasants were afraid that any other government might force them to return the land.
2. The White forces were geographically separated, they were united only in their opposition to the Bolsheviks, and they were unable to develop a unified program.

3. But perhaps the most important factor was Lenin's pragmatism. Before the coup, he supported the abolition of army discipline. He was also in favor of establishing a soldier committee in each military unit, which was to have control over the unit's equipment. All this undermined officer authority and reduced the effectiveness of the armed forces, which in turn, weakened the Provisional Government. But when it came to the Bolshevik Red army, personnel were drafted, military professionals from the Imperial army were relied on, and strict army discipline (including the shooting of deserters) was reintroduced. The only concession to Bolshevism was that "commissars" were appointed to supervise military commanders and ensure their "political reliability".

Almost as soon as the coup occurred, the white collar workers in Petrograd went on strike. The object was to make Bolshevik government inoperable. Involved were, among others, the ministries, banks, and the telephone and telegraph workers. The Bolshevik response was to replace management with their own personnel and give the employees the choice of working or being prosecuted.

Lenin and the Executive Committee first clashed over the demand of the committee that the council incorporate members of the other socialist parties. This Lenin categorically refused to do. The next question was whether the council or the committee had the right to legislate. The committee was to vote on this question. Because of the committee's composition, a tie of 23 to 23 was anticipated. Lenin and Trotsky (one of the council's commissars), although not committee members, declared that they would participate in the voting. As a result, by a vote of 25 to 23, the right to legislate became the prerogative of the council.

The Bolshevik campaign platform for representation in the Constituent Assembly consisted of three points: they endorsed the supremacy of the soviets, they wanted to stop the war, and they were in favor of replacing private landholding with communal redistribution. The results of the election weren't favorable for the Bolsheviks. The number of seats that they won made them a distinct minority in the assembly.

The first step of the Bolsheviks in combating this rejection was to indefinitely postpone the opening of the assembly. Nevertheless, on the originally scheduled date, elected delegates to the assembly began to show up at the Taurida Palace for deliberations. Three days later, armed troops, loyal to the Bolsheviks, surrounded the palace, prevented the delegates from entering, and ordered them home.

The next Bolshevik step was to outlaw the Constitutional-Democratic party, the "Kadets", who were dedicated to a parliamentary government. Kadet delegates to the assembly were declared to be "enemies of the people" and were prevented from taking part in the assembly.

The assembly finally met in mid-January 1918. On the opening day, demonstrators (estimated at around 50,000 in number) began a march on the Taurida in support of the assembly. They were met by Bolshevik troops, who fired into the demonstrators until they dispersed. The official starting time for the assembly had been set for noon, but at the time of Lenin's arrival (1 pm), proceedings had not yet begun. Lenin delayed the commencement of deliberations until the streets had been cleared of demonstrators (about 4 pm). He then permitted the meeting to start.

The Bolsheviks introduced a resolution that, if passed, would have caused the assembly to forsake the purpose for which it was formed. The resolution was defeated, at which point, the Bolshevik delegation asserted that the assembly was dominated by "counterrevolutionaries" and left. The meeting continued, peopled more and more by Bolshevik armed guards, until at 5 pm the next day, it adjourned. It never reconvened.

How could all of this have happened? One part of the answer is that the Bolsheviks didn't hesitate to let their armed support pull their triggers. Their socialist adversaries also had armed forces on which to rely, but they refused to use to use them. Why? The explanation is that the other socialist parties considered the Bolsheviks errant, but brothers, nevertheless. In addition to this compromising attitude, they were afraid that, if the Bolsheviks were toppled, it would be a prelude to the destruction of the whole socialist movement and a return to autocracy. The Bolsheviks weren't hampered by any such concerns. Their goal was everything or nothing.

In June, the Bolsheviks expelled all other socialist party members from the soviets. The one party state had been established.

In early December 1917, the principal institution of the Red terror, the Cheka, was founded. Like the tsarist political police before it, the Cheka was authorized to condemn political prisoners, in secret, to any sentence, including death. Its first use was in the suppression of the white collar strike in Petrograd.

The terror was an integral part of Bolshevik policy and substituted for their lack of popular support. The object of the terror wasn't so much to directly eliminate members of the opposition, although it was hoped that it would do that, also. To some extent, the terror was unfocused. Persecution of innocents wasn't something to necessarily be avoided. The purpose was to demonstrate that no one was safe. In such circumstances, the best hope was to avoid coming to the attention of officials by withdrawing completely from public life. Once the populace broke up into an unorganized collection of individuals, each afraid of being noticed by the authorities and struggling just to survive, a small minority could rule millions.

Of course, compared to Stalin's terror, Lenin's was small potatoes. Stalin claimed lives in the millions. Lenin's achievement was restricted to, at best, hundreds of thousands.

In addition to the use of execution, Lenin's terror invented forced labor camps as a method for stamping out dissent. The camps were directed by the Commissar of the Interior, who not accidentally, also ran the Cheka. In Stalin's time, the acronym for the group administering the labor camps became Gulag. By 1923, Russia had 315 labor camps and 70,000 inmates.

Also in conformance with long-standing Russian tradition, the tsar and his family, as a possible rallying point for the opposition, were wiped out, evidence indicates, on Lenin's orders.

Despite all the problems with which they had to contend, the Bolsheviks, almost immediately on coming to power, launched a concerted effort to convert Russia into a Communist economy. The program consisted of:

1. Nationalization of manufacturing and transportation
2. Replacement of private commerce with a national distribution system, in which government accounting was to take the place of money
3. Adoption of a monolithic economic plan
4. Compulsory labor

The most notable achievement of this effort was the formation of a huge bureaucratic mess that intruded into rather than managed the economy. But it did support thousands of intelligentsia. The state economy was accompanied by an illegal private economy that, with every advance in state control, grew in proportion. This development was partially a function of the government's inability to enforce its laws. However, the Bolsheviks also recognized that inflexible implementation of their program would lead to disaster. It was the illegal private sector that kept the urban population from starving to death.

The Communist program brought production to a standstill. What was happening was that the country was living off of the capital that had been accumulated before the coup. Recognizing that this practice couldn't go on forever, in March 1921, the Bolsheviks called an end to their experiment and switched to what they called the New Economic Policy (NEP), which amounted to officially adopting the principles of the private economic sector that had developed in response to the Communist plan.

The economic policy followed in 1918 through the first quarter of 1921 was referred to by the Communists as "War Communism", signifying recognition of its catastrophic results and implying that the whole thing was a temporary expedient necessitated by the Civil War. The lie to this claim is that the term, War Communism, was first officially used by the Communists in the spring of 1921, when the practice was being abandoned in favor of the NEP.

Lenin died on January 21, 1924. His death left a vacuum at the top of the Communist power structure. However, by 1929, the vacancy had been filled by Stalin, who was firmly in control of the party and the government. As circumscribed as Lenin's rule by Central Committee was, even such limited power sharing was unsatisfactory to Stalin. Nothing but complete consolidation of control under his dictatorship would do.

Stalin had a definite program to carry out. He saw the Russia of the 1930's as surrounded by hostile nations, just as he imagined that tsarist Russia had been beset by enemies. To protect its interests, Russia had to have a well equipped, modern army. To produce the tanks, artillery, planes, and other equipment necessary to make this army a reality, a concerted effort to develop the requisite heavy industry was required. And time was short. This industrialization would have to take place rapidly.

The only way to achieve such forced draft industrialization was to rely heavily on foreign technology and equipment. To finance this foreign technological transfusion, an increase in Russian exports was necessary. And the principle commodity in which this increase could be realized was grain, which had been the premier export product under the tsars. To experience grain export to such a degree, the Russian government wouldn't only have to effect a significant increase in grain production but also get grain distribution under its control.

Enticing the peasant to increase his production by means of a price increase was out of the question. The discrepancy between the minimal price the peasants received and the price that could be realized on the international market was from where the accumulation of capital for the expansion of Russia's industrial base was to come. It was akin to a tribute, and Stalin was known to refer to it as such.

The solution to the problem of how to increase and get control of grain production was to collectivize agriculture. With the exception of their dwellings and personal property, all the peasants' possessions — livestock, tools, and the land on which they worked — were to be appropriated by a government run commune, on which the peasants would work. This high-speed industrialization and mass collectivization was the object attributed to Russia's first five year plan by Stalin.

Collectivization didn't appeal to the peasants. Some policy would have to be adopted to encourage them to join the communes. The program chosen was to single out a minority, known as the kulaks, and subject them to such terror (deal them "such a blow") that the majority of the peasants would rapidly step into line ("snap to attention before us").

The term, kulak, is worthy of some elaboration. Theoretically, a kulak (literally, fist) was a kind of agricultural bourgeois, who hired labor and expanded his holdings at the expense of the community peasants. In fact, there were few peasants fitting this description. Consequently, in the case of many communities, the families, who (as a consequence of ability, luck and effort) were a little better off (they owned a calf as well as a cow, or a relative would come to help them at harvest), were chosen to play the role of the kulaks. Ultimately, in operation, the term came to mean any peasant who resisted collectivization.

In each district, collectivization was managed by a committee made up of the first secretary of the district party committee, the chairman of the soviet executive committee in the district, and the head of the local OGPU (the successor to the Cheka). The "kulak" families (men, women and children) were dispossessed (the seized property was turned over to the collective) and jammed into boxcars for transport to labor camps where they worked under wretched conditions. They built canals and roads, and worked at construction sites and in mines. The police also hired out such labor to state institutions. Estimates of the number driven from their homes range from seven to 15 million. Most of them perished from the rigors to which they were exposed.

Beginning in 1930, grain exports increased and industrialization went forward, but at great expense to the population. As the saying went, as the state swelled up, the people "grew lean". They subsisted on rations (when honored), were often hungry, were inadequately housed, were overworked, spent their spare time trying to acquire the most fundamental of living needs, and endured all kinds of privation. The year of 1933 was characterized as "hungry thirty-three". The government continued to export grain while peasants and their children starved. Estimates of the number of resulting deaths extend from three to four million on the low side to seven to ten on the high.

In early 1933, an internal passport system was established. Passport registration with the local police was necessary to establish legal residence. Travelers were required to register their passports with the police wherever they stopped. Any citizen whose residence was rural didn't get a passport. The effect was to bind the peasants to their communes. They had returned to serfdom.

By the end of 1933, the "war" of forced collectivization, as Stalin sometimes referred to it, had been won. There had been active opposition in the party to Stalin's policy. But he had been resolute in pushing through his program. In general, the party was now willing to accept the results and move on. However, a faction developed that thought it was time for Stalin to be replaced.

At the end of the Seventeenth Party Congress held in the beginning of 1934, the delegates voted on the makeup of a new Central Committee. The procedure followed was for each delegate to receive a ballot on which were listed the names of the nominees. Each delegate crossed out the names of the nominees for whom he didn't want to vote and handed in his ballot anonymously. In the vote, Kirov (a personally popular member of the party, an effective administrator, and currently the Leningrad (formerly Petrograd) party chief) received only three or four negative votes, while Stalin apparently garnered at least 166 (out of a total of 1225). Stalin had the results modified so that they indicated that he had received only three negative votes.

Presumably, these indications that Stalin didn't have the undivided support of the party played some part in his decision to undertake his great purge. In December, Kirov was murdered. The suspicions are strong that the act was committed on Stalin's orders. In any case, he attributed the murder to an opposition group and used the event as a pretext for the initiation of the purge. It lasted from 1935 through 1938 and exploded in 1937 and 1938.

Purge procedure was straightforward. Once a victim had been selected, he was arrested and forced to confess. Coercion varied. Sometimes the victim would be assured that he would be treated leniently if he confessed, a promise that was rarely kept. Sometimes his family was threatened. And torture was used. Popular methods were the "conveyor" (endless interrogation, by rotating teams, that lasted for days) and beatings with rubber truncheons. Confessions were unacceptable unless they included incrimination of others, which were filed away for potential future use.

The number of victims of the purge isn't known. One source says that between four and one half to five and one half million people were arrested in 1937 and 1938 alone, and between eight and nine hundred thousand of these were executed. Almost all of the others were sent to a labor camp by means of a month long trip in a packed railway car. Once at his destination, an inmate, fed 500 grams of bread or gruel daily and spending 12 hours a day at heavy labor, could look forward to an average life expectancy of about six months, which could be shortened by mass shootings, referred to as "cleansing actions", by the NKVD, the successor to the OGPU. Few victims reappeared from these camps.

To what end this obliteration of a generation? It's hard to conceive that Stalin's position of power was ever seriously threatened. A less massive, selective terror would have ensured a compliant elite. The best available explanation was given by Khrushchev when he said, on March 8, 1963, that "Stalin was seriously sick ... suffering from suspiciousness and persecution mania."

Invasion of Finland took place on November 28, 1939. Ultimately, in the Treaty of Moscow of March 1940, Finland ceded some territory to Russia. But it had given the Russian armed forces a serious mauling and retained its freedom. As a result, measures were taken to cure the military shortcomings revealed in the Finnish war. In consequence, the Russian army was in somewhat better shape than it might have otherwise been to combat the Nazi invasion in 1941.

In 1940, two decrees, which enserfed the industrial worker, were issued. One outlawed voluntary departure from a job and criminalized shirking. The other empowered industrial commissariats to transfer workers at will. Between two and three million people were sent to labor camps for violating these decrees.

After Russia had gobbled up eastern Poland and the Baltic states as its booty for supporting Hitler's invasion of Poland, it then, in June 1940, occupied Rumanian territory consisting of the province of Bessarabia and the northern part of the province of Bukovina. All these newly acquired territories were forcibly incorporated into the Russian system. Banks and plants were nationalized, estates were confiscated, agriculture was collectivized, and "socially alien" elements were repressed by means of large numbers of arrests in eastern Poland, imprisonment and mass execution of Polish soldiers, and arrests and deportations in the Baltic states, Bessarabia, and northern Bukovina. Victims totaled about two million. Most of these were either executed or met an early death in a labor camp.

At the Teheran conference, late in 1943, the allies allowed Russia to establish the Russian-Polish border at the Curzon line, which ceded large parts of Poland to Russia.

In the summer of 1944, Stalin recognized a Communist led Polish National Committee of Liberation, which moved to Lublin with the advancing Russian troops, as the government of Poland. This recognition was ratified by the Allies at Yalta in February 1945.

Also in the summer of 1944, Russian forces were advancing on Warsaw. Because they wanted to liberate their capital themselves (rather than let the Russians do it), on August 1, the Warsaw underground rose up against the occupying Germans. The Germans responded brutally. The Russian advance was brought to a halt, some say by Russian orders, while the Germans systematically wiped out the insurgents. There were large-scale executions, and the city was essentially leveled. England planned to air drop arms and supplies to the Poles in Warsaw, but its planes couldn't carry enough fuel for a round trip and would have to land in Russian controlled territory and refuel for the return trip. The Russians refused to allow them to do so. The Warsaw Poles were non-Communists.

In the spring of 1945, King Michael of Rumania was commanded by Russia to name a pro-Communist prime minister within two hours. He did.

Subsequently, Stalin unilaterally bestowed the German land east of the Oder and Neisse rivers on Poland. At the Potsdam conference in the summer of 1945, Truman, the US president, and Attlee, the English prime minister, endorsed this act, although they said it could only be considered "temporary". To this day, the boundary remains unchanged. In fact, it was recognized as legitimate in the treaties that resulted in the reunification of East and West Germany.

The Eastern Borders of Russia and Poland Redefined

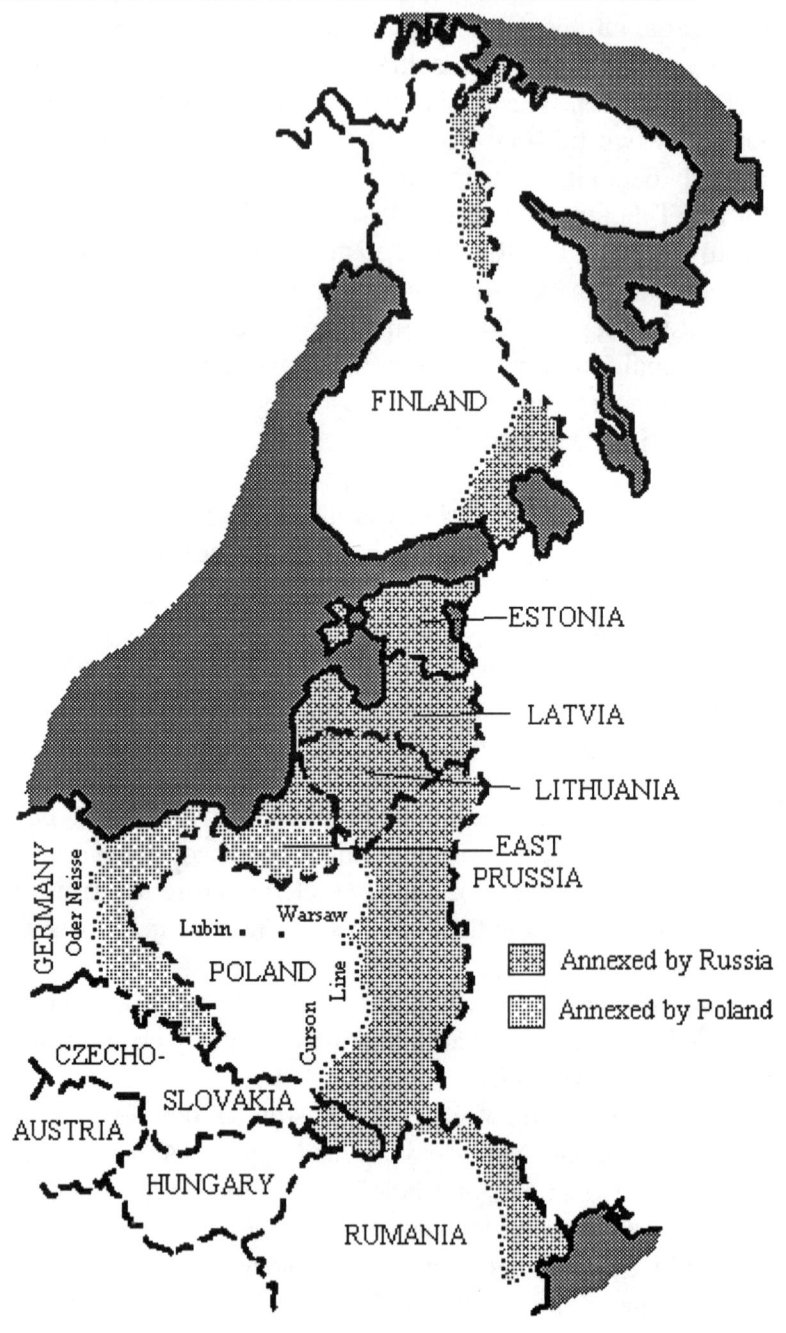

Because of the failure to agree on a peace treaty with Germany, Russian presence in eastern Europe continued after the end of the Second World War. As a result, wartime accords (on military occupation, demilitarization, denazification, and dismantling of industry) gave the Russians the blessing they needed to tear down what was left of the prewar social and economic structure of the east European countries and prepare the way for a takeover by local Communist parties under the sponsorship of the occupying Russian armies. Between 1947 and 1949, Communists assumed power in Poland, Rumania, Bulgaria, Hungary, Czechoslovakia, and East Germany to the accompaniment of purges, arrests, trials and executions. The 1948 break of Tito (dictator of Yugoslavia) with Stalin resulted in purges in Hungary, Bulgaria, Czechoslovakia and Poland, where committed Stalinists were then placed in power.

Stalin died on March 5, 1953. On his death, there were five men at the fore of the Russian government: Malenkov, Molotov, Bulganin, Kaganovich and Beria. By 1958, all but one of these men had been condemned as members of an "anti-party group" and had slipped into oblivion. The exception was Beria, who was executed for allegedly plotting the elimination of his colleagues so that he could become the uncontested dictator of Russia. Khrushchev, who in 1953, hadn't even been considered a credible candidate, succeeded to Stalin's position.

By then, the Cold War was in full swing. Two superpowers emerged from the Second World War, the US and Russia. They opposed each other in terms of ideology and political and economic systems. There were efforts at conciliation. But with the Berlin blockade (1948 - 1949), the final break occurred. The US was convinced that Russia was dedicated to destroying the US. Russia's opinion of the US was the mirror image of the convictions of the US. The conflict was carried on at two levels.

1. An arms race, the underlying principle of which was mutually assured destruction. The idea was that a superpower must be in possession of adequate supplies of nuclear missiles at hardened sites so that, if attacked by the other superpower, enough of its missiles would escape destruction to deliver a mortal retaliatory blow, thus negating any advantage to be gained by attacking first.

Russia's East European Satellites

2. Local struggles, fought by indigenous proxy forces supported by supplies, munitions and arms; sometimes additionally supported by advisory and technical personnel; and sometimes augmented by battle units supplied by a superpower or one of its surrogates. Vietnam, Angola, Afghanistan and Nicaragua were examples.

In this struggle, Russia had certain advantages. Being a command economy with a demonstrated indifference to the (at least, short-term) welfare of its people, it could direct as much of its effort as it desired to the construction of ever more awesome military might up to the limit of the minimum support needed to keep its work force in operation. On the other hand, it also had some disadvantages. Unlike the US, it was unable to carry out its part in the Cold War and still provide a decent living standard for its citizens. As a consequence, it had to shield its people from the evidence of this disparity.

As indicated by the relative mildness of the purge that put Khruschev in power and his willingness to unmask Stalin, Khruschev's term was, compared to its predecessors, less oppressive. It should be borne in mind that, in Russia, when power changed hands, a purge was inevitable, since contrary to the case in other countries (where a new leader was free to choose his cabinet), a new man in the Russian seat of power inherited the previous leader's hierarchy and had to put up with it until he could find a way to replace it with his own people.

Khruschev was ousted in 1964 in favor of Brezhnev, who was cut from the Stalinist mold. He saw Russia as a military empire. To him, technological advance meant improvement in the nuclear bomb and the means of delivering it. Under Brezhnev, economic and social life continued to decay. A Russian survey indicated that, by the late 70's, one fifth of the grain crop and one third of the potato crop never got to consumers because of ineptness and absence of storage facilities. Only two out of every five farming villages were accessible by paved roads. Trucks failed so often that four times as many men were employed to repair them as to make them. Farming equipment was so misused that, although 550,000 new tractors were turned out annually, the number of tractors in use on communes never increased.

The economy was characterized by corruption and inefficiency. Alcoholism was endemic. Crime was growing by leaps and bounds. The cost of energy and mineral extraction was going up rapidly. Russia could make high technology missiles and nuclear powered ships. But the household appliances, shoes and clothes that it produced were flawed. It had difficulty motivating people and encouraging innovation. The state was committed to providing for the people's welfare. Since everything was being taken care of by the system, why work? The Bolshevik concept of egalitarianism was part of its program of social justice. But the idea that all people had a right to equal economic treatment resulted in a situation in which envy snuffed out any indication of initiative.

Brezhnev died on November 10, 1982. Then came two short rules, that of Andropov (15 months) followed by that of Chernenko (13 months). On March 12, 1985, Gorbachev was elected the general secretary of the party.

Gorbachev was credited with recognizing Russia's problems. His attempts to right things seem to be unavoidably summarized in the two themes that he himself chose: glasnost and perestroika. Glasnost (openness) was the belief that, if the mass media revealed the operation of the government to the people, they would react to and discourage bureaucratic mismanagement by demanding change. Yet old habits die hard. In the wake of Russia's crackdown on Lithuania in January 1991, Gorbachev urged suspension of press freedom.

Perestroika is restructuring. Outside of taking punitive steps to reduce drunkenness, particularly on the job, and trying to tack free market mechanisms onto a socialist economy, such as freeing wholesale prices but not retail prices, Gorbachev's perestroika was confined to the structure of the government. Despite his remarks about change coming from the bottom, Gorbachev was a dedicated socialist and, as his actions with respect to alcoholism and his banning of strikes in May 1991 indicate, his efforts were primarily devoted to trying to effect change from the top of a command economy. Gorbachev didn't believe in private property, and his ineffective attempts to improve the economy reflected this prejudice. He was more of a politician given to maneuvering than a leader dedicated to change. Under his direction, the Communist empire didn't improve. Instead, it began to fall apart.

Between June 1989 and February 1990, Poland, Hungary, Czechoslovakia, Bulgaria, and East Germany disbanded their Communist parties and established electoral processes involving multiple parties. All these actions were taken in response to massive public demonstrations that went on for days until the governments capitulated. Gorbachev adopted a policy of noninterference in this process. Russia, he said, had "no moral obligation or political right" to interfere with moves toward democracy in eastern Europe. This attitude contrasted sharply with the previous Russian response to political liberalization in satellite nations — such movements in Czechoslovakia and Hungary had been crushed by Russian military force.

The process took a different turn in Rumania, where the Stalinist dictator, Ceausescu, reacted to public protest by stomping down with his iron boot. His security forces killed thousands of his countrymen. However, the army chose to support the popular revolt, overthrew the government, and executed Ceausescu and his wife.

In May 1990, elections were held in Rumania. In December of the same year, even Albania, the most Stalinist of the East European Communist states, agreed to the formation of opposition parties. Albania was a Chinese, rather than a Russian, client, but its techniques were Stalinist.

Beginning in March 1990, the republics, making up Russia, began to declare their sovereignty and elect non-Communist officials. By December of the same year, all 15 of these republics had proclaimed themselves sovereign states. Gorbachev approved of this process. He felt that it aided his effort to decentralize political power. But he denied the republics the right to secede unilaterally, thus providing some new kind of definition of sovereignty. Apparently, a republic could be as sovereign as it wanted as long as it remained part of Russia. When Lithuania tried to secede, Gorbachev had Russian troops occupy its capital.

In the fall of 1990, Gorbachev abruptly abandoned pending radical economic reforms (the 500 day plan). His more liberal aides then began to drift away. He replaced them with Communist party hard-liners. On August 19, 1991, a coup by hard-liners, led by Yanayev, Gorbachev's vice president, took place. The program with which Yanayev appealed for support was an end to the experimentation that had been going on and a return to central planning. For the Russian citizen, it offered state provided welfare services, equal economic treatment, and a strong central authority — just those things from which Gorbachev had been trying to wean Russia. Apparently, in this arena, he had been successful. Glasnost had done its work. The mass media had exposed the workers to the abundance in the West that, in Russia, was only a long overdue Communist promise. Huge crowds in

The Flag of the Russian Republic Flies Over the Barricades *during the abortive 1991 coup by Communist hard-liners. From a photograph taken by Anthony Suau and appearing in the September 2, 1991 issue of* Time.

metropolitan centers protested the coup. Workers began to go on strike. Just one day later (August 20), the leaders of the coup had begun to waver. By August 21, it was all over. Gorbachev had been returned to power.

The coup was a fiasco for the Communist party and sounded its death knell. Republics moved to declare their independence. On August 24, Gorbachev resigned his party chairmanship and barred Communist cells from all military, security and government organizations. Not long after, the Russian legislature (the Congress of People's Deputies) outlawed all Communist political activity. Early in September, the congress dissolved itself. On the same day, the independence of Latvia, Lithuania and Estonia was

The Soviet Russian Republics

[Map showing the former Soviet republics: Belarus, Moldova, Ukraine, Russia, Georgia, Armenia, Azerbaijan, Kazakhstan, Turkmenistan, Uzbekistan, Kyrgyzstan, Tajikistan, with Black Sea, Caspian Sea, and Aral Sea labeled]

recognized. In December, the Russian republic (one of the original 15 republics making up the Russian Soviet Union), Ukraine and Belarus formed a Commonwealth of Independent States (CIS), a loose association of independent republics. Gorbachev accepted the dissolution of the Soviet Union, after which eight more republics joined the CIS. The sole holdout was Georgia, whose liberal element expressed its intention of joining as soon as the political instability, under which it was currently suffering, had been resolved.

In addition to rebuilding their economies, the republics are now faced with the twin problems of seeing if their differences can be resolved without destroying their fragile association within the CIS at the same time as they contend with moves for independence by peoples within their borders. By mid 1993, Georgia had decided against joining the CIS, and Azerbaijan and Moldova had dropped out. In September 1993, Russia, Armenia, Belarus, Kazakhstan, Tajikistan and Uzbekistan agreed to accept the ruble as their common currency and unify their credit, banking, tax and customs policies. Later in the year, Belarus and Uzbekistan dropped out of this agreement. In the fall of 1993, Georgia joined the CIS in return for the support of Russian troops in putting down rebellion. Azerbaijan rejoined for the same reason. In January 1995, Kazakhstan agreed to, at least partially, unify its army with Russia's. In 1995, Russian troops were permanently stationed in a number of the republics, and the CIS began to look somewhat like a proxy for a greater Russia.

On March 29, 1996, Russia, Belarus, Kazakhstan and Kyrgyzutan signed an integration agreement. On April 2, Russia and Belarus created a supranational supreme council similar to the European Union, to which other republics were invited to join.

CHAPTER TWENTY TWO

India

India originated on the flood plains of the Indus river and its tributaries. The history of India before 500 BC is obscure. Indians have concentrated on the infinite and have cared little about everyday occurrences. The result has been that Indian writing has had little to say about the economic and political life of Indian civilization.

Two cities, Mohenjo-daro (Mound of the Dead) and Harappa (Hara is one of Siva's names), and many villages were present in the Indus valley between 2500 and 1500 BC. Several levels of these cities have been unearthed. Judging from the decreasing sophistication of the artifacts at the upper levels, one has to conclude that the vigor of the Indus civilization had undergone significant decay. The cities had been subjected to earthquake and resulting flood. For reasons unknown, the population was never able to recover from this catastrophe. Ultimately, the Indus valley was invaded and conquered by Aryan barbarians, an Indo-European race. Mohenjo-daro and Harappa became things of the past.

The movement of settlement from the Indus to the Ganges plain started around 800 BC, when the introduction of iron tools permitted the felling of jungle trees and cultivation of ground laden with roots. By 600 BC, India's most powerful kingdoms were located in the upper and middle Ganges valley.

At this point, at least the beginnings of a caste system were present in India. The history of caste is hazy. How much earlier the system first emerged can't be said. Why it arose also isn't known. The prohibition of the lighter skinned Aryans against marriage with the darker skinned native population may have been the start. Or the prohibition may have just reinforced the idea of caste already present in the native population. In any case, a person's caste was defined by the people with whom he could eat and marry. Once a caste system had insinuated itself into the structure of a society, it became self-reinforcing, since those

Ancient India

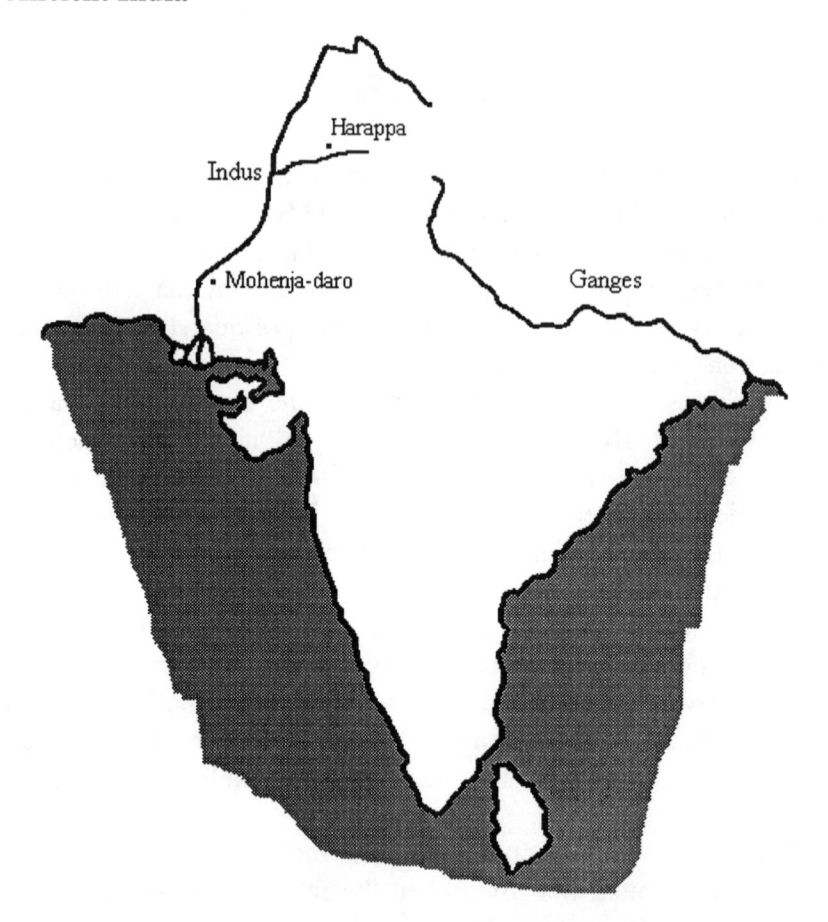

Map showing Ancient India with labels: Harappa, Indus, Mohenja-daro, Ganges

coming into a caste society from the outside were forced, by the habits of the native population, to form a new caste, because they had only themselves with whom to eat and marry. How a person behaved was defined by both his caste and the superiority or subordination of his caste to those of others.

The cement holding together the caste society of India was religion. We have no chronology of the religious history of India until the coming of Buddha, who died around 485 BC. The practice has been to identify four "stages" in the development of Indian religion, which seems acceptable as long as no attempt is made to relate these stages to time periods.

The oldest Indian literature of which we have knowledge is the

The Mauryan Empire

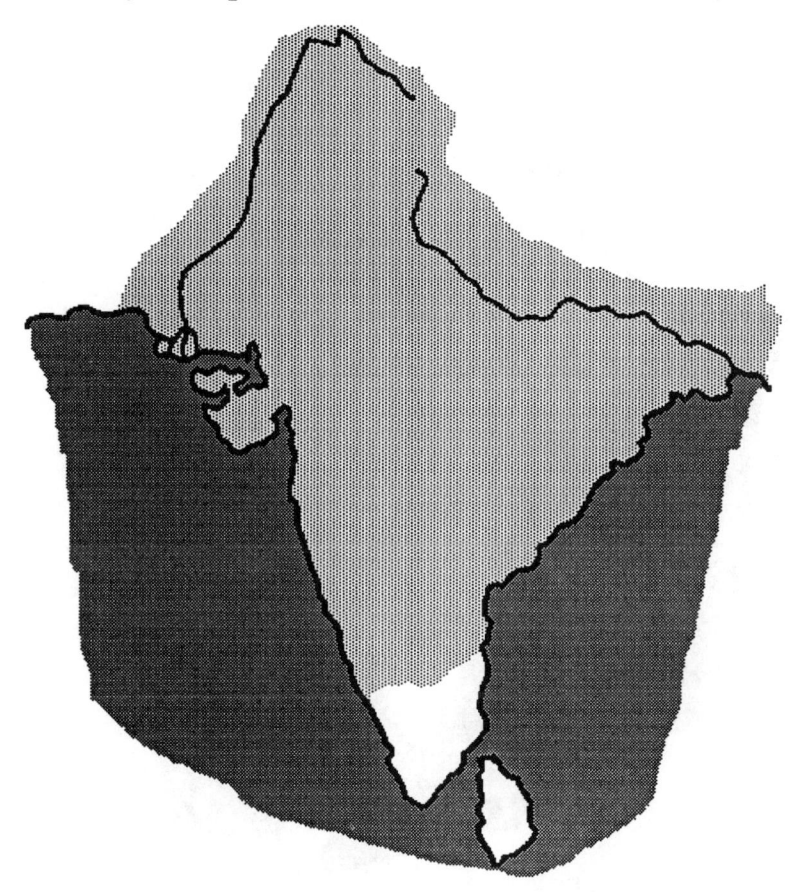

hymns called the Rig Veda. The gods of the Rig Veda were indistinct manifestations of natural forces. Worship involved animal sacrifice. Because of the vague definition of these gods, it was possible to change their nature without altering the language of the Vedic hymns. Such adaptability became characteristic of Indian religion, which frequently substituted one god for another.

The tendency to merge different gods into one was extended in the Brahmanas, a collection of Vedic interpretations. In the Brahmanas, the god Prajapati (Lord of Creatures) was depicted as the creator and lord of the universe. The sacrificial slaughter of animals was portrayed as a re-creation of Prajapati, and consequently, in a sense, a reincarnation of the universe. As a

The Gupta Empire

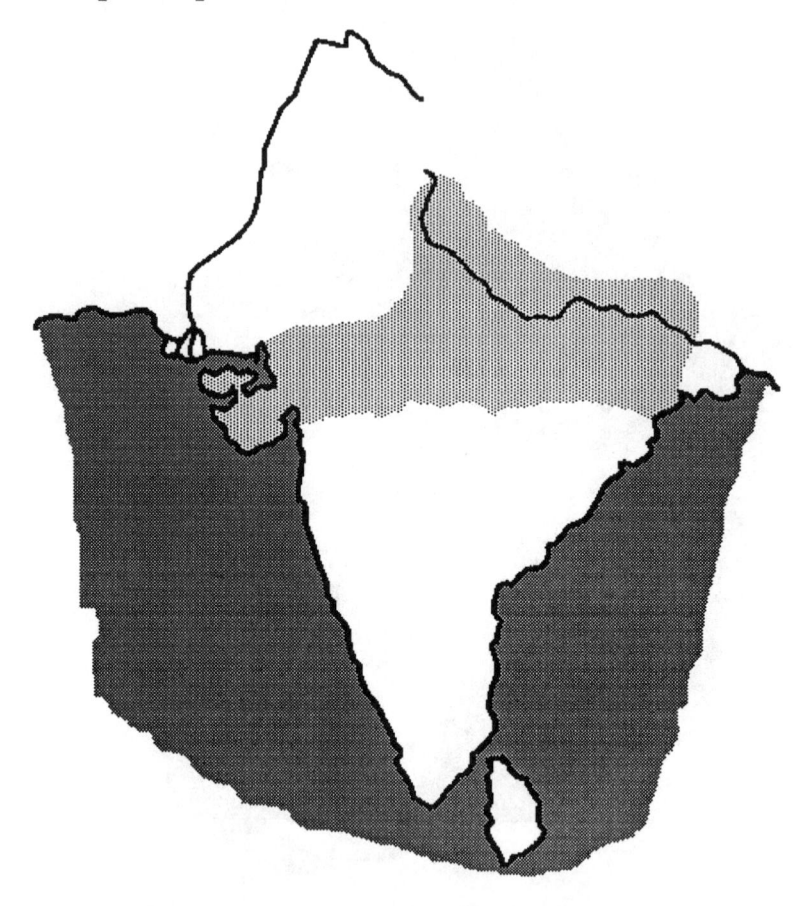

result, the priests, who carried out these rites, were (in being able to call both the gods and the universe into existence) greater than the gods — a claim asserted in the Brahmanas. Since these Brahmin priests represented themselves as being so powerful, they made up an elite caste.

Ascetic retreat within the jungle may have been practiced before the coming of the Aryans. In any case, by the 6th century BC, asceticism was common in India. Ascetics of exceptional piety were held in high repute and attracted disciples in proportion. The doctrines produced by these jungle institutions were documented in the Upanishads (literally, "to sit down in front of"), which constitute the third stage of Indian religion.

The Upanishads rejected sacrifice and priests, and maintained that the object of religious practice was an ineffable transcendent experience. The concepts of brahman, atman and karma were introduced. Brahman was the spiritual reality behind sense appearances, atman the human soul. In the mystic experience that constituted the culmination of a religious life, the identity between brahman and atman would be realized. The barrier to this experience was karma, the intellectual and moral shortcomings accumulated both in an individual's life and in his previous incarnations. By self-discipline, ascetic exercises, and instruction, an individual's karma could be sloughed off, thus allowing atman to realize its identity with brahman.

The principles stated in the Upanishads were incorporated into the teachings of Gautama Buddha. Buddhism was organized around "monks", seekers of enlightenment. It adopted reincarnation and the concept that the goal of life was to escape from the wheel of births and deaths by cultivating proper views and good habits. It was atheistic and offered the possibility of such escape without the help of priests or sacrifice. Two centuries after Buddha's death, India was on the brink of becoming Buddhist, particularly after the endorsement of Buddhism by Ashoka ("Sorrowless"), under whose reign the Mauryan empire reached its peak and occupied all India except for a small region in the south.

However, the weakness of Indian Buddhism was that it didn't provide people with rituals for their triumphs and trials — birth, marriage, illness and death. As a result, the Brahmin priests, armed with their sacred ceremonies, found the means to their survival.

In making their rituals available to the people, the Brahmins adapted themselves to the multitudinous variety of local deities held in awe by villagers. This accommodation took the form of accepting each local god as a manifestation of a supreme deity. Thus, gods, who had evolved independently, became avatars, incarnations of the gods Siva and Vishnu, who became preeminent in Hinduism.

The final triumph of the Brahmins was to incorporate the preexisting idea of reincarnation into the fabric of Hinduism and tie this belief to the concept of caste. Hinduism accounted for

Nataraja. *From a photograph of a sculpture by Tiruvalangadu, who lived in the 11th century. The sculpture is in the Madras Museum in India. Nataraja is the incarnation of Siva as the Lord of Dance. The bell in one of Siva's hands represents creation (it creates sound), his upraised hand represents protection, and the fire in a third hand represents destruction, the three main functions of Siva. He dances on the dwarf of ignorance. Siva wears a crescent moon and a serpent in his headdress. Everyone sees the moon as beautiful and is repelled by a serpent. But Siva accepts all and rejects nothing.*

caste as the result of karma built up in earlier incarnations. Piety in this life, which included total acceptance of (and strict adherence to the behavior defined by) a person's caste, could lead to reincarnation as a member of a higher caste, until ultimately, release from the wheel of rebirth was possible. These developments took place during the Gupta dynasty (320 - 490).

Hinduism organized itself around temples, which made available a more congenial alternative to the monasteries that had constituted the hubs of Buddhism. Hindu temples became the loci for all kinds of activity. Among others, priests, architects, artists, dancers, singers, teachers and writers practiced in the temples. By 600, religion and the gods had become the center of popular concern, and scientific activities such as mathematics and astronomy, which had shown all the signs of vigor under the Guptas, fell from favor. Buddha became part of the Hindu godhead as an avatar of Vishnu. Indian Buddhism was reduced to such a hollow husk that, when in the 10th century, Moslem raiders destroyed the Buddhist monasteries, no one had enough commitment to Buddhism to reconstruct them.

In this way, India was converted to Hinduism, with the result that Indian behavior became passive. In a world characterized by an endless repetition of birth and death, the particulars of a lifetime had little significance. In an existence where the only hope of salvation lay in unquestioning adherence to the dictates of caste, complete acceptance of the position to which a person was born was the only reasonable approach to life. The advent of a new conquering people from the outside was meaningful only in the sense that a new caste was introduced to the society.

Such an approach to life served the Indians well in terms of maintaining their identity, although the price was apathy. Even the Moslem conquest of India couldn't destroy the core of Indian society. Eventually, parts of northern India became Moslem, and an amalgam of Islam and Hinduism created the Sikh sect in Punjab. Sikh means Disciple. The leaders of the Sikh faith were teachers, known to the Sikhs as gurus. But despite these defections, the bulk of India remained steadfastly Hindu and passive.

An Indian Participating in the Annual Inauguration of Studies.
The way in which he holds his hands symbolizes his determination to study. From a photograph in Some Aspects of Indian Culture *by C. Sivaramamurti (National Museum, New Delhi, 1969).*

From time to time, Hindu mobs do break out in murderous frenzy, usually against another religious group, primarily Moslems. But such outbursts are uniformly and tearfully regretted, and anger remains among the most abhorred of emotions, not only in oneself, but even in the actions of others. Hindus are quick to remove themselves from the presence of those who show any inclination to descend into anger.

The most recent of India's conquerors was England. At first, England treated India as just another part of its colonial empire. However, ultimately, England's better nature won out, and it began to introduce far-reaching changes in India. In 1835, the English established schools to teach a European curriculum to Indian students in the English language. In 1857, universities were founded. The English also set up an administrative system for India and peopled it with English speaking Indians. Finally, they build an infrastructure in India, so that India ended up with, most notably, a nationwide railway system.

The court is still out on India's destiny. In territory, population, and intelligence of its people, it's a potential giant. English domination catapulted it into the modern world. The obverse side of this English gift was a pervasive and misleading example that modernization came from above. At the moment, one of India's feet is mired in Eastern mysticism, and the other is stuck in bureaucratic governmental direction of the country from the top.

The Shang Empire

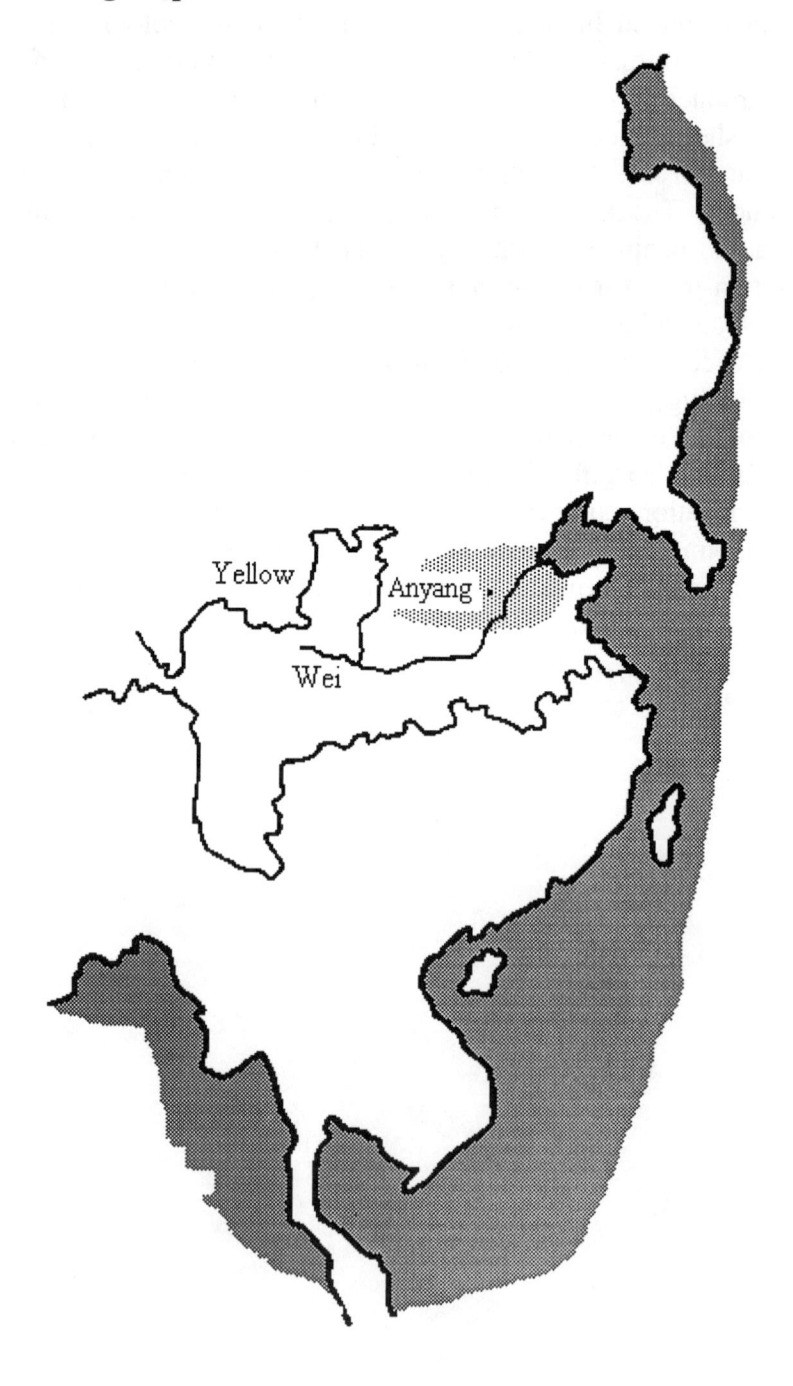

CHAPTER TWENTY THREE

China

Like the Mesopotamian, Egyptian and Indian civilizations, the Chinese civilization began on the flood plain of a great river, in the case of the Chinese, the Yellow.

Our knowledge of early Chinese history is sketchy. Archeologists have identified three Neolithic Chinese cultures in north China. Of these, the Black Pottery culture seems to be the precursor of later Chinese civilization. The way in which this culture evolved into civilization isn't known.

Tradition says that the Hsia was the first Chinese dynasty, but no archeological signs of this dynasty have been found. Chances are that the Hsia ruled over some Neolithic villages rather than a fully developed civilization. This isn't the case for the second dynasty, the Shang, established in 1523 BC. Anyang, the last of the three capitals identified with the Shang dynasty, has been unearthed. Indications are that the Shang rode to power on war chariots. All the devices and principles used in modern Chinese script are present in Shang writings.

In 1051 BC, invaders from the Wei valley in modern Kansu set up a new dynasty, the Chou. The political theory that held sway in China until the overthrow of the Manchu dynasty in 1912 may have begun with the Chou. This theory holds that the Chinese emperor, as the Son of Heaven, has a mandate from Heaven, but that the mandate would be revoked if he failed to conform to the will of Heaven. This concept led to several unavoidable conclusions.

First was the notion that the Son of Heaven should rule all true people. This idea was positive in the sense that it encouraged dynastic consolidation within China. It was negative in that it led the Chinese to consider all those not under the rule of the emperor — that is, all foreigners — to be inferior to the Chinese.

A second conclusion was that the dictates of a person of such eminence as the Son of Heaven weren't to be questioned, since whatever he decided must be in the best interests of the Chinese.

Chinese Principalities Around the Beginning of the 3d Century BC

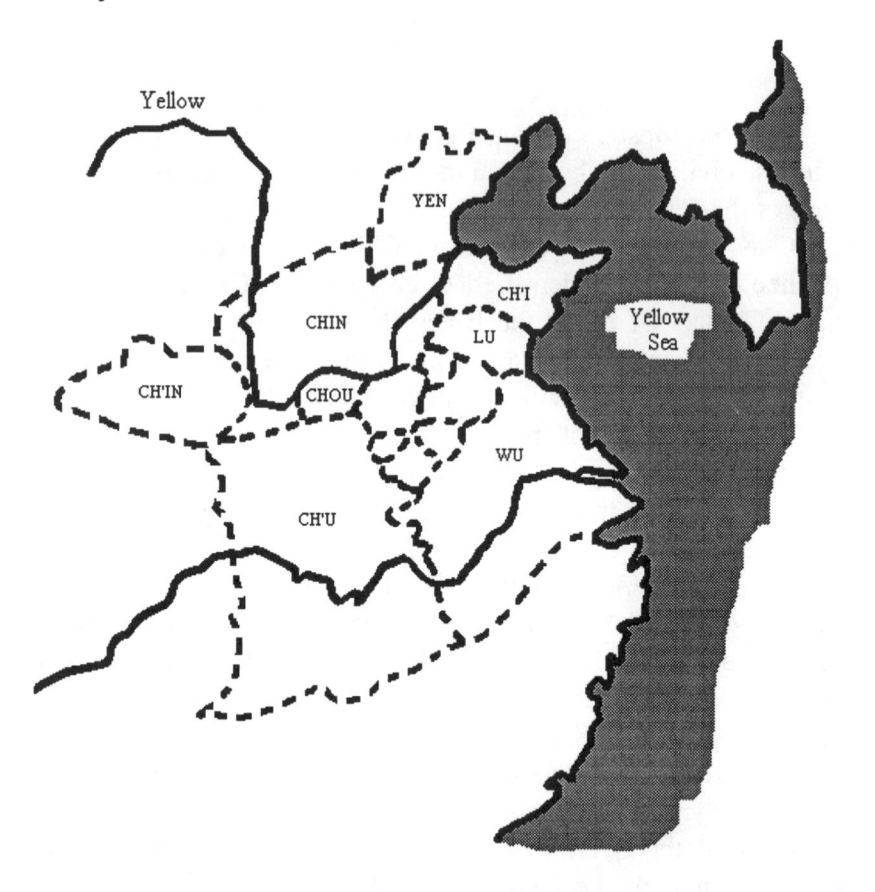

A third conclusion was that, if the Son of Heaven maintained his position only as long as he conformed to the will of Heaven, it became important to know what this will was. It was on this peg that Confucian thought was hung.

In 771 BC, barbarians pillaged the Chou capital in western China. China then split into over a dozen principalities. By the 6th century BC, warfare between these principalities had become endemic. The recurrent question was: How could the will of Heaven be determined, so the land could once more become unified under the peaceful rule of the Son of Heaven?

This was the question that Confucius (traditional dates 551 - 479 BC) addressed. His answer was that the will of Heaven was

A Kylin *(a mythical beast) guarding the tomb of Emperor Wen Di (560 - 567) of the Chen dynasty. From a photograph in the book* China *published by Gallery in 1980.*

Tao, "The Way". Tao consisted of the mannerly conduct found in a genteel family. The traits that personified gentility were goodness, wisdom and courage — traits that called for moderation in conduct, knowledge of traditional rites and customs, trustworthiness, loyalty, and not associating with those who weren't genteel. Gentility was a function of education and behavior. Thus, anyone could be a gentleman. Such a gentleman should be happy practicing his genteel life. But the natural habitat of gentlemen was government.

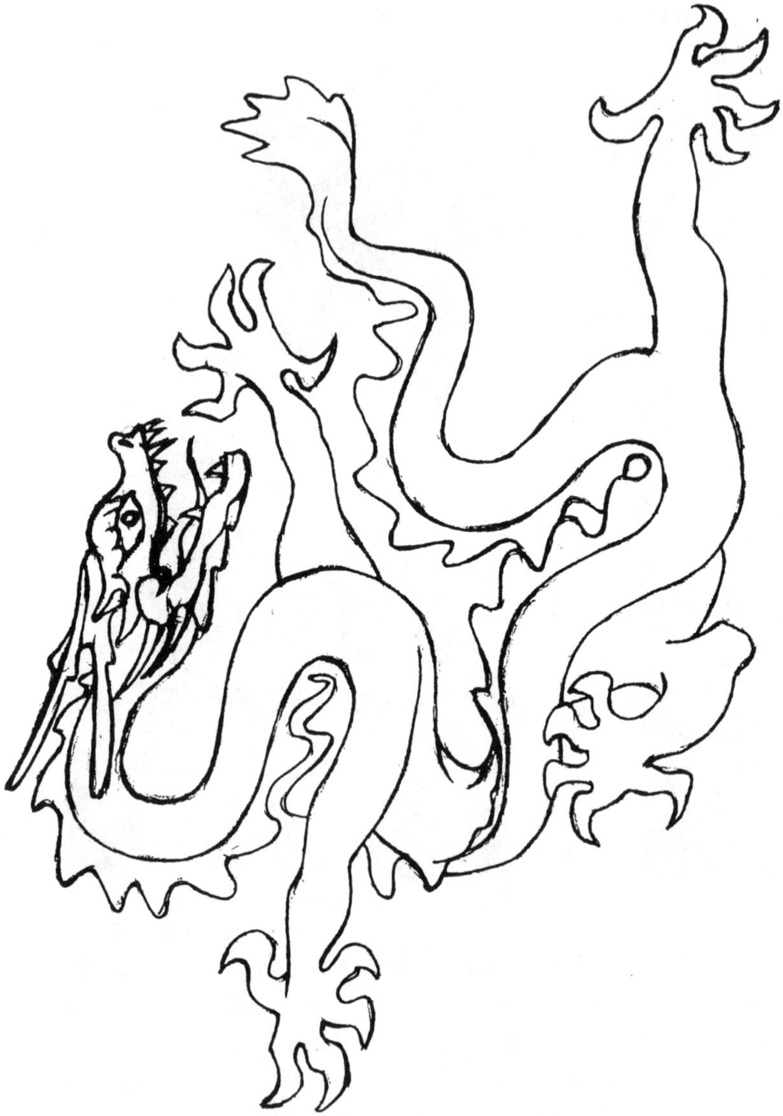

Between the 5th and 2nd centuries BC, a landlord class (the gentry) grew up in the principalities constituting China. These landlords owned their land, which they paid peasants to work.

In 221 BC, Shih Huang-ti, the prince of Ch'in, reunited China. The key to his victories was his light cavalry, a new military phenomenon in China. Ch'in is the source of the present-day name of China.

Shih Huang-ti divided his empire into provinces administered by a hierarchy of officials. This organization was adopted by all succeeding Chinese emperors. He established a method of writing, derived from Ch'in calligraphy, a method that, made easier over time, became standard. He also created an extensive road and postal system.

When Shih Huang-ti died in 210 BC, an uncertain succession resulted in a short but violent period of warfare, as a consequence of which, Kao-tsu, a petty official turned general, became, in 202 BC, sovereign of China and founder of the Han dynasty.

Kao-tsu continued Shih Huang-ti's centralized government. There was, however, a difference. Kao-tsu replaced Shih Huang-ti's cruelty with gentleness.

The core of Kao-tsu's administration was his old comrades in arms. But from the beginning of Kao-tsu's reign, positions in his bureaucracy were available to "men of excellent reputation and manifest virtue". In practice, this referred to the gentry. Within two generations, it meant gentry modeled on the Confucian pattern. The Han emperor Wu-Ti (140 - 87 BC) decreed that, to enter public office, a person had to pass a state examination that was based on Confucian teachings and that was open to all. Thereafter,

---

A Chinese Dragon. *From a photograph of a detail of the wall of dragons in Beijing. The photograph appears in* The World of Ancient China, *written by J. B. Grosier and published by Minerva in 1972. Credit for the photograph is given to Weiss. You can tell that this is a Chinese dragon, because it has no wings. In addition, this dragon is one of the emperor's, because it has five claws on each foot. Other people could also have dragons, but their dragons could have only four claws per foot.*

China in the Sui and T'ang Dynasties

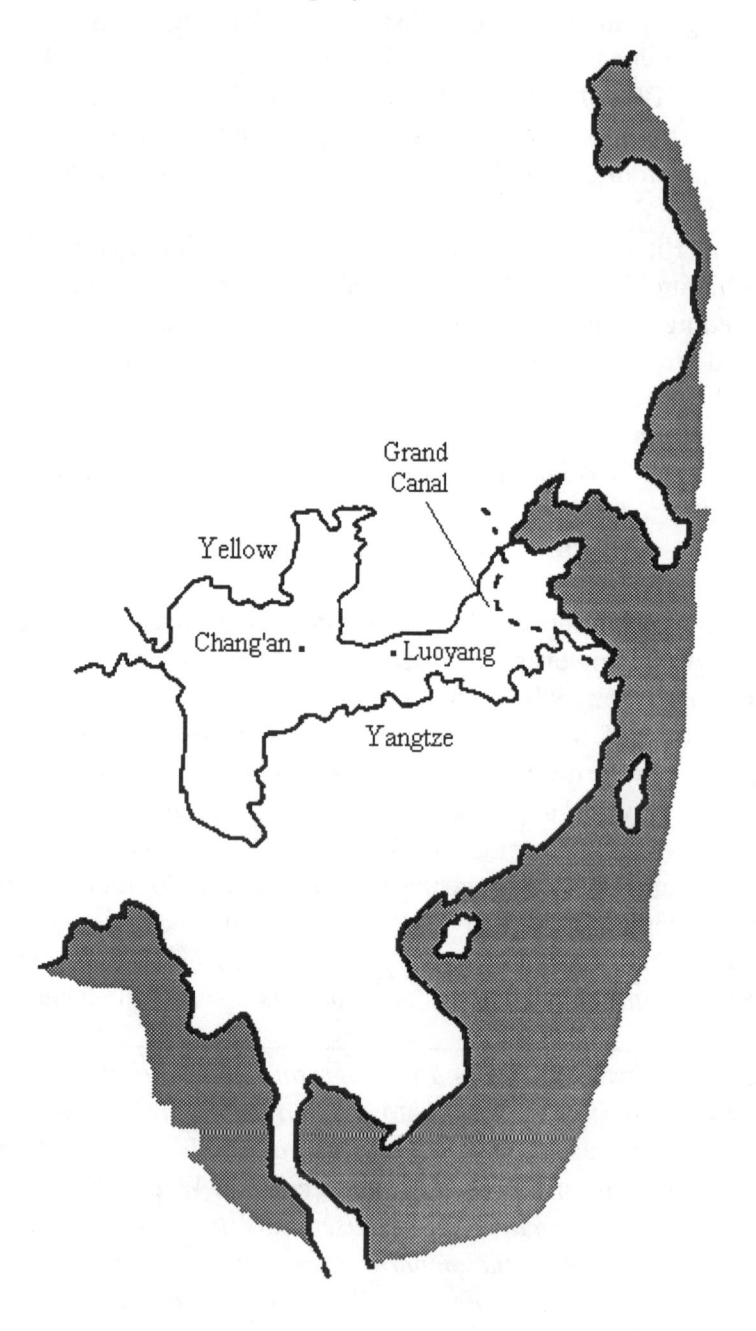

Grand Canal
Yellow
Chang'an
Luoyang
Yangtze

an official position became the objective of every respectable person.

In this way, the path of China was set for the next 2000 years. Even today, the Chinese refer to themselves as the Sons of Han. And Mao Tse-tung began his adult life as a student of the Confucian classics. He didn't become a Communist until he was 27.

Of course, during these 20 centuries, the Chinese were subject to the two ills of all empire — dissolution from within and invasion from without. But after each internal breakup, when imperial power had been restored, the Confucian civil service system was there, with its organization, trained personnel, examinations, and schools, ready to take up where it had left off. And an invader found that, without this civil service system, China was ungovernable. Once he had taken the compromising step of adopting the system for his own, it was only a matter of time before he became as Chinese as the people he had conquered.

Confucian thought placed merchants with soldiers at the bottom of the social hierarchy. As a result, merchants never became an important class in China. A large number of them were foreigners. And native merchants tended to take their earnings, buy land, become gentry, and finally, undertake the study needed to become a government official and attain complete respectability. All this inhibited the development of trade and the accumulation of capital. Even Chinese agriculture continued to be intensive, relying on manual rather than animal labor. To the end, Confucian China remained an agrarian society. Even in 1989, over 70 percent of the Chinese population were peasants.

The Han dynasty came to an end in 220. For the next three and one half centuries, China was in disarray. It was finally reunited under the Sui dynasty (589 - 618). During the Sui dynasty, and the T'ang dynasty (618 - 905) that followed it, the Chinese had, for the first time, the advantage of two agricultural bases, one in the Yellow river valley, the other in the Yangtze. Many canals were constructed, the most significant of which was the Grand Canal connecting the Yangtze with the Yellow river. Finished in 611, this accomplishment was possible because of the conscript labor of millions of peasants. As a result, rice and other products from the

The Great Wall

Yellow

south could be transported to the capital city, first Chang'an and then Loyang, in the north. Storehouses were set up at suitable points to gather, preserve and dispense grain and other products, all these functions being carried out by the imperial bureaucracy.

In 755, a military uprising occurred and crippled China for eight years. The T'ang dynasty endured, but only because it was supported by the Uighurs, a Turkish speaking tribal federation originating in the steppes. Subsequently, the Chinese began paying tribute to the Uighurs. In 840, the Uighur state fell apart under the onslaught of barbarians.

The Uighur aristocracy had adhered to the Manichaean religion since 762. The Chinese used the overthrow of the Uighur empire as an opportunity to eliminate all Manichaeans, who were primarily merchants of Uighur or other foreign extraction and had lorded it over the Chinese from under the cover of protection by the Uighur military. Other religious interlopers — Nestorians, Zoroastrians and Moslems — soon experienced the same fate. In 845, 44,600 Buddhist monasteries were demolished and 150,000 Buddhist monks and nuns enslaved. After that, there remained no religious challenge to Confucianism.

China could have become an important naval power and, in the early 1400's, conducted several impressive maritime undertakings. But these naval activities took place in south China, the capital of China was in the north, and the government was more concerned with a new Mongol invasion in the northwest than any potential gains from naval activity. As a result, the Chinese government not only gave up its own maritime role but also outlawed private enterprise at sea.

During the Ming dynasty (1368 - 1644), the Great Wall of China was built as a defensive measure against the Mongols. It was ineffective but stands as a massive monument to China's siege mentality. It can be seen from the moon.

The Chinese tended to protect their borders through diplomacy and payment of tribute rather than through use of military power. When European traders appeared off China's coast, they were considered to be just one more instance of barbarians at the border and were rebuffed by restricting them to a few designated seaports from which they could operate and appointing officials with whom

China in 1842

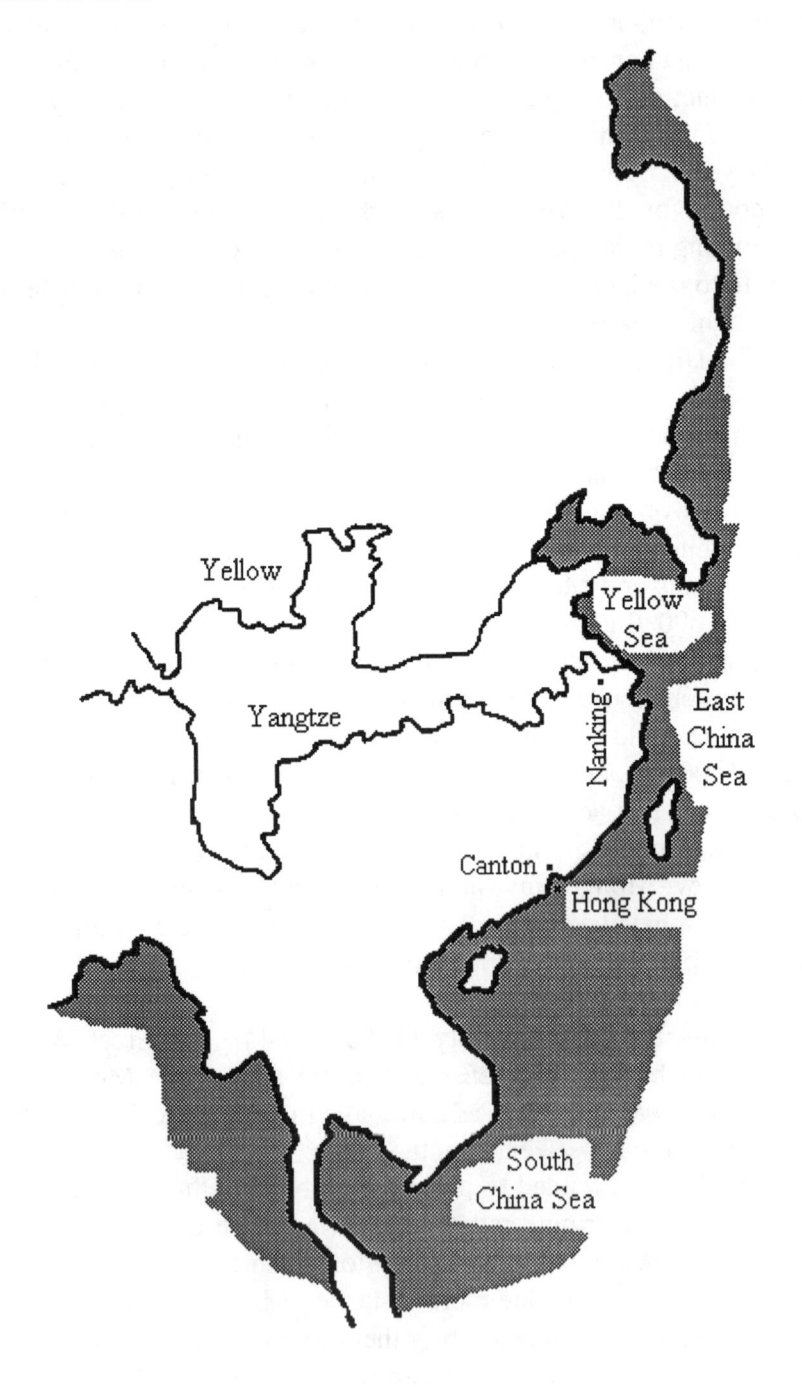

they had to deal.

Thus, while the Western world was exploding, China sat behind its borders, self-satisfied with the assumed superiority of its way of life and disdainful of the "barbarians" who weren't fortunate enough to be Chinese. The Chinese invented movable type, paper, gunpowder, and the compass — tools that revolutionized the Western world. In China, they scarcely caused a ripple.

The first inkling that things weren't all right was the First Opium War (1839 - 1842), during which a small number of English gunboats and marine landing parties moved against the Chinese essentially at will. The war ended with the Treaty of Nanking, under which the ports open to English trade were extended from one (Canton) to five and Hong Kong became an English territory.

From that point on, it was all downhill. Out-of-the-way regions of the empire declared their independence, while uprisings and foreign encroachment shook China proper, until in 1949, control was once more established under the Chinese Communist government. Imperial examinations based on the Confucian classics were eliminated in 1905. On February 12, 1912, the last Chinese emperor gave up his throne.

This century of disruption resembled earlier transitions from one dynasty to another. Since 1949, resurgence of Chinese domination in border areas have also adhered to the typical imperial pattern.

The difference was that, this time, neither the emperor nor the Confucian civil service reappeared. However, the head of the Communist government is treated much as the emperor was: his dictates aren't questioned and are assumed to be for the benefit of the people. The pattern of employing state power on behalf of the people and, thereby, rationalizing tyranny, remains. The bureaucracy no longer follows a Confucian ideology. It follows a Communist one. But both ideologies are anti-merchant (only the name has changed; it's now anti-profiteer), anti-outsider, and anti-religion.

In its saner moments, the Chinese government seems to recognize that, if China is to flourish, it must industrialize according to Western principles. Yet true to its cultural heritage of 3000 years, the government remains obsessed with the perceived need to maintain internal control at the expense of all other goals. As a result, China continues to take actions that assault the world's sense of propriety, with the consequence that China remains a nation of questionable virtue with which it's considered risky to associate.

CHAPTER TWENTY FOUR

Latin America

The term "Latin America" was coined by the mid-19th century French, who thought that, since French culture, like the Spanish and Portuguese, was "Latin" (romance-language speaking), France was destined to assume leadership in the area. France's dream of dominance never came to pass, but the term stuck.

It's a disservice to Latin American countries not to discuss them individually, since they are different. Yet they exhibit enough common characteristics that viewing them as an entity doesn't create a completely distorted image. This is particularly the case when it comes to the question that we want to address in this chapter: Given that Latin America is a treasure house of natural resources, why is it that, while the US has become thriving, powerful and free, Latin America remains mired in the Third World?

The original inhabitants of Latin America, like those of North America, were Indians of Asiatic origin who came to America by crossing the land bridge that existed between Siberia and Alaska some 20,000 - 40,000 years ago. They were conquered by the Spaniards and Portuguese from the Iberian peninsula. The conquest wasn't difficult, which was due to a number of factors. The Portuguese were never faced with the need to conduct a war of conquest, since there was no Indian civilization in Brazil, where the Portuguese concentrated, just tribes. In the case of the Spaniards: they had guns and horses, and the Indians didn't; the Indians were split by internal dissensions, while the Spaniards were single-minded in their conviction that they were destined to conquer and convert; and the Indians had no resistance to European disease, such as smallpox, typhus, measles, chicken pox, and influenza, which the Spaniards brought with them and which literally slaughtered the Indians. For example, in 1519, when Cortez invaded Mexico, the Indian population was about 11 million. By 1605, it had dropped to somewhat over one million.

A Conquistador. *From an illustration by Leonard Everett Fisher for the book* Vasco Nunez de Balboa *written by Emma Gelders Sterne and published by Knopf in 1961.*

In Peru, after Pizzaro's incursion, population fell from about seven million to under two million in 1580.

For administrative purposes, Spanish Latin America was divided into vice royalties, each of which was headed by a viceroy (deputy king). This arrangement worked well enough to keep the colonies under royal rule for about 300 years. The Iberian monarchs appointed, as colonial officials, only those of unswerving devotion to the king. Native-born colonists, known as criollos, were by definition, of questionable loyalty. So all the significant colonial offices were filled by peninsulares, people born in Iberia. For those who could meet the requirements, the assignment was worth the effort, for at the end of their tours of duty, the peninsulares returned to Iberia much more well off than when they left.

In addition to a demanding selection process, colonial officials were subjected to many checks on their performance, which necessitated a large amount of paperwork, a characteristic of Iberian bureaucracy that was passed on to Latin America.

Initially, it was the troves of gold and silver, of which the Spaniards relieved the Indians, that constituted the flow of wealth from Latin America to Spain. When the worked precious metals gave out, the Spaniards turned to mining. To the output of the mines were added the products of the land: sugar, tobacco, cacao, indigo, wood, cotton and hides.

This production required that Iberians settle in Latin America, for the Indian had no concept of property or of producing for export. These settlers needed land. And land they got, in vast amounts. But as large as the original grants were, over time they grew: land owners bought out their neighbors, unclaimed land was expropriated, and the Iberian laws of entailment (the firstborn male must inherit) and primogeniture (not only that, but he must inherit it all) prevented the division of land among heirs. Thus were born the latifundia, or haciendas, of Latin America. Some reached a prodigious size, exceeding a million acres.

The Iberian colonist knew how to extract wealth from the land. But unlike his counterparts in North America, he had no intention of dirtying his hands with manual labor, particularly when all those Indians were available. The Iberians forced the Indians to swear

The Latin American Vice Royalties

allegiance to a new king, worship a new God, and speak a new language. The technique varied, but the Iberians also saw to it that the Indians made their labor available.

Again unlike their counterparts in North America, where the typical colonist was a married man with his family, the Iberian settler was characteristically an unaccompanied male. As a result, in Latin America, the white men consorted with Indian women, though they commonly didn't marry them. The mixed-blood children who resulted were called mestizos. Ultimately, the Latin American population became predominately mestizo.

The concentration of Indian work forces in proximity to the colonists contributed to the continuing spread of European disease, which to the Indian was fatal. The result was disaster. Much of the Indian population was obliterated. To offset the decline in the Indian work force, the colonists began importing black slaves from Africa.

In the 1760's, Charles III of Spain founded a colonial militia to assume some responsibility for colonial defense. The militia soon outnumbered the royal troops. For example, by 1800, the vice royalty of New Spain had a militia of 23,000 as opposed to 6000 royal troops. Militia officers enjoyed immunity from civil law, which created a special military class above the law.

By 1800, the colonists had several grievances. For one thing, the criollos resented the flow of wealth to the peninsulares. "Spaniards," they said, "Not only don't allow us to share in the government of our country; they also carry away all our money." Second, the restriction of colonial trade to the Iberian peninsula was constraining, because the colonists knew that they would be better off if they could trade freely with all countries.

The action that precipitated the revolt of the colonies occurred in 1808, when Napoleon occupied Madrid and placed his brother, Joseph, on the Spanish throne. This change in imperial government freed the colonies from any lingering sense of loyalty to the mother country.

A group of the colonial aristocracy, including Francisco de Miranda, Simon Bolivar, Manuel Belgrano, Bernardo O'Higgins, Jose de San Martin, and Jose Bonifacio, had studied and traveled in Europe. There they became imbued with the ideas of Locke and Rousseau. Inspired by the example of the American Revolution, they returned to Latin America to use the colonial militia in freeing their homeland from foreign rule. The leaders realized that a declaration of independence in one vice royalty meant little as long as a Spanish army remained in one or more of the others. Consequently, they didn't rest in their struggle until all of Latin America was independent. Only Brazil moved into nationhood

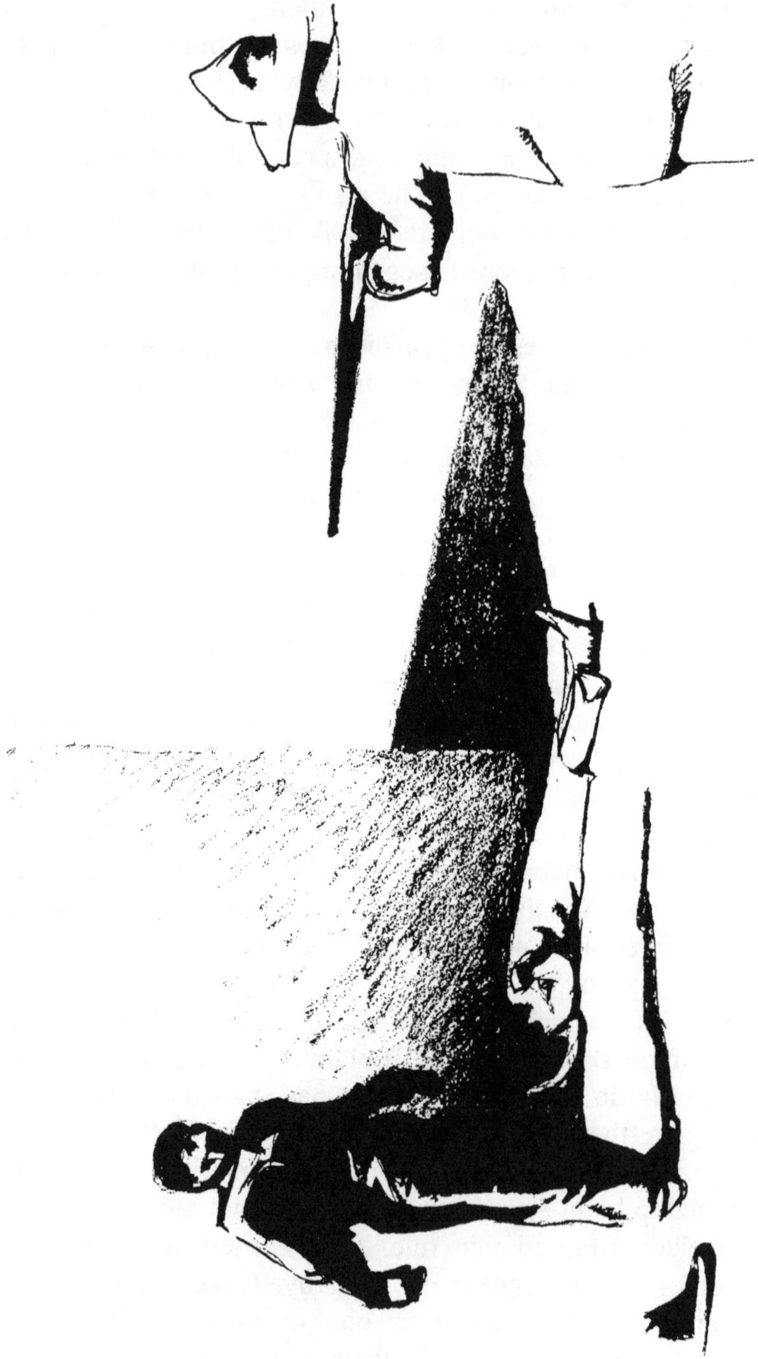

without bloodshed. When Napoleon occupied Portugal, the royal family moved to Brazil, and it became independent by default.

The immediate results weren't impressive. In 1830, Bolivar lamented, "America is ungovernable. Those who have served the revolution have plowed the sea." Bolivar had dreamed of a single Latin American nation. Instead, decentralization set in. Eventually, the four Spanish vice royalties split into 17 nations. Only Brazil moved to nationhood without partition. Compounding this move toward fragmentation, land owners retreated to their haciendas.

In the fight for independence, the army took its talent where it found it. As a result, the army became an avenue of social advance for mestizos. When their wars of liberation were over, the new nations emerged with large military establishments, often led by mestizos with no alternative careers. These mestizos stepped into the vacuum left by the land owners and became political bosses, known as caudillos. Once in office, they faced empty treasuries; were unable to reward their supporters, who drifted away; and were then overthrown by new caudillos.

The economies of the new nations were almost totally dedicated to agriculture and mining. After 1850, economic activity in Latin America quickened. The cause was the increasing industrialization in the US and Europe, which demanded ever expanding amounts of food and raw material. The need for more efficient transportation grew. Railroad construction, in which English capital was heavily involved, began. The rails ran primarily from the haciendas and mines to the ports. The rising requirement for metal tools, small machines, instruments, and construction equipment was met by imports from England, France,

---

A Latin American Set Piece. *This is a characterization borrowed from Paul Johnson, which he used to describe the situation where a faction lines up members of its opposition against a wall and executes them as bandits. In the case of the illustration at hand, Carrancistas are shooting Villistas in Mexico. The illustration is from a photograph appearing in the book* Revolutionary Mexico, *written by John Mason Hart and published by the University of California Press in 1987.*

and the US.

For Latin America, the great depression was cataclysmic. The economic decline in Europe and the US resulted in a spectacular contraction of the demand for Latin American goods. This economic disaster coincided with a period of increased intensity in nationalistic feeling. As a consequence, Latin America embarked on a program to gain control of its economic destiny. The goal was twofold: to achieve greater economic independence and to create jobs for the working classes, which were becoming increasingly unionized.

One aspect of this program was a plan for industrial development. The particular type of industrialization chosen was what's known as import substitution. That is, the plan was to manufacture domestically the products that heretofore had been imported. And the state assumed a major role in this industrialization. It established trade barriers, gave preference to domestic producers in government contracts, invested in firms, and established government owned and operated companies. The other aspect of this economic program was the nationalization of foreign owned industry: the oil companies, mines, railroads, and communication firms.

Ultimately, the program was unsuccessful. Domestic demand was inadequate to support the national industries. Protected industries, assistance for unprofitable firms, and arrangements to preserve jobs led to inefficient production of products that couldn't compete internationally. To prop up their faltering economies, the Latin American countries resorted to foreign borrowing and the printing of paper money. The outcome was burdensome foreign debt and runaway inflation. As these threats to the prevailing social order mounted, ruling elites imposed repressive regimes, often through military coups, to both maintain the status quo and institute policies designed to combat the rising financial problems. Grass roots free market activity remained bound by excessive regulation and paperwork, and found expression only in the underground economy.

At this writing, Latin America remains in an unenviable state.

Charts and Lists

Time Line

ABOUT 15,000,000,000 YEARS AGO — UNIVERSE BEGINS

ABOUT 4,500,000,000 YEARS AGO — SOLAR SYSTEM FORMS

FIRST LIFE (ALGAE)

ABOUT 3,000,000,000 YEARS AGO

FIRST CELL WITH NUCLEOUS
ABOUT 1,500,000,000 YEARS AGO — FIRST MULTICELLED ALGAE

PRESENT

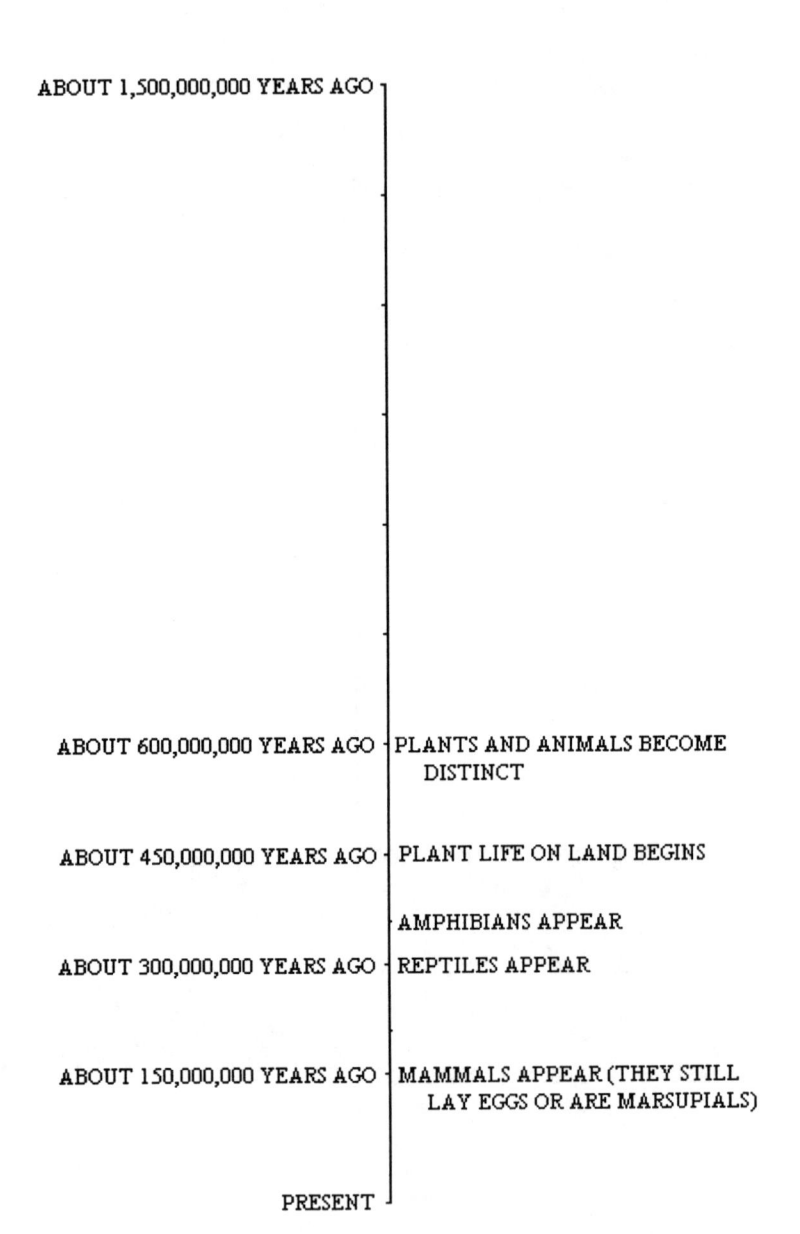

```
ABOUT 1,500,000,000 YEARS AGO ─┐
                               │
                               │
                               │
                               │
                               │
                               │
                               │
                               │
                               │
ABOUT 600,000,000 YEARS AGO ───┤ PLANTS AND ANIMALS BECOME
                               │ DISTINCT
                               │
ABOUT 450,000,000 YEARS AGO ───┤ PLANT LIFE ON LAND BEGINS
                               │
                               │ AMPHIBIANS APPEAR
ABOUT 300,000,000 YEARS AGO ───┤ REPTILES APPEAR
                               │
                               │
ABOUT 150,000,000 YEARS AGO ───┤ MAMMALS APPEAR (THEY STILL
                               │      LAY EGGS OR ARE MARSUPIALS)
                               │
                  PRESENT ─────┘
```

ABOUT 150,000,000 YEARS AGO	
ABOUT 105,000,000 YEARS AGO	PLACENTAL MAMMALS APPEAR
ABOUT 90,000,000 YEARS AGO	
ABOUT 75,000,000 YEARS AGO	PRIMATES (E. G., LEMURS) APPEAR DINASAURS DIE OUT
ABOUT 60,000,000 YEARS AGO	
ABOUT 45,000,000 YEARS AGO	ANTHROPOIDS (SUCH AS MONKEYS — THEY HAVE NAILS RATHER THAN CLAWS) APPEAR
ABOUT 30,000,000 YEARS AGO	HUMANOIDS (SUCH AS GIBBONS — THEY HAVE NO TAILS) APPEAR
ABOUT 15,000,000 YEARS AGO	GREAT APES (SUCH AS GORILLAS) APPEAR
PRESENT	

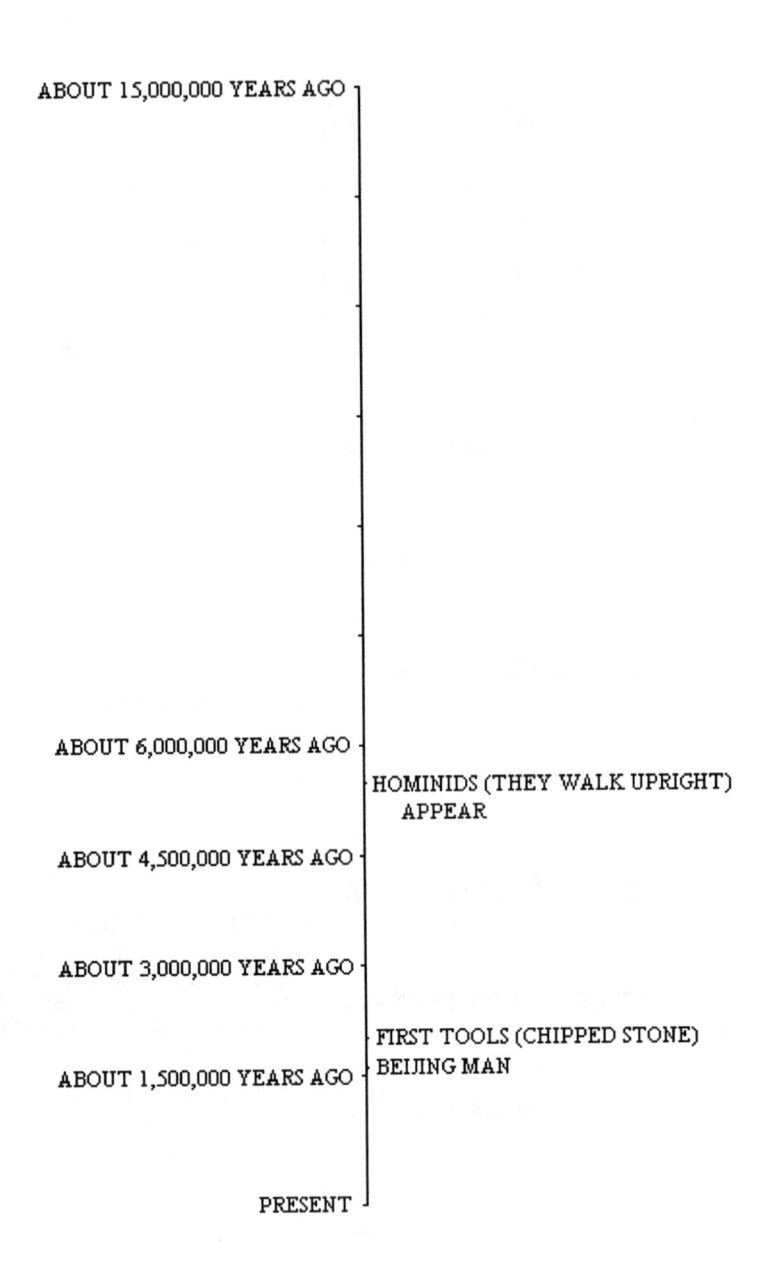

ABOUT 15,000,000 YEARS AGO

ABOUT 6,000,000 YEARS AGO — HOMINIDS (THEY WALK UPRIGHT) APPEAR

ABOUT 4,500,000 YEARS AGO

ABOUT 3,000,000 YEARS AGO

FIRST TOOLS (CHIPPED STONE)
ABOUT 1,500,000 YEARS AGO — BEIJING MAN

PRESENT

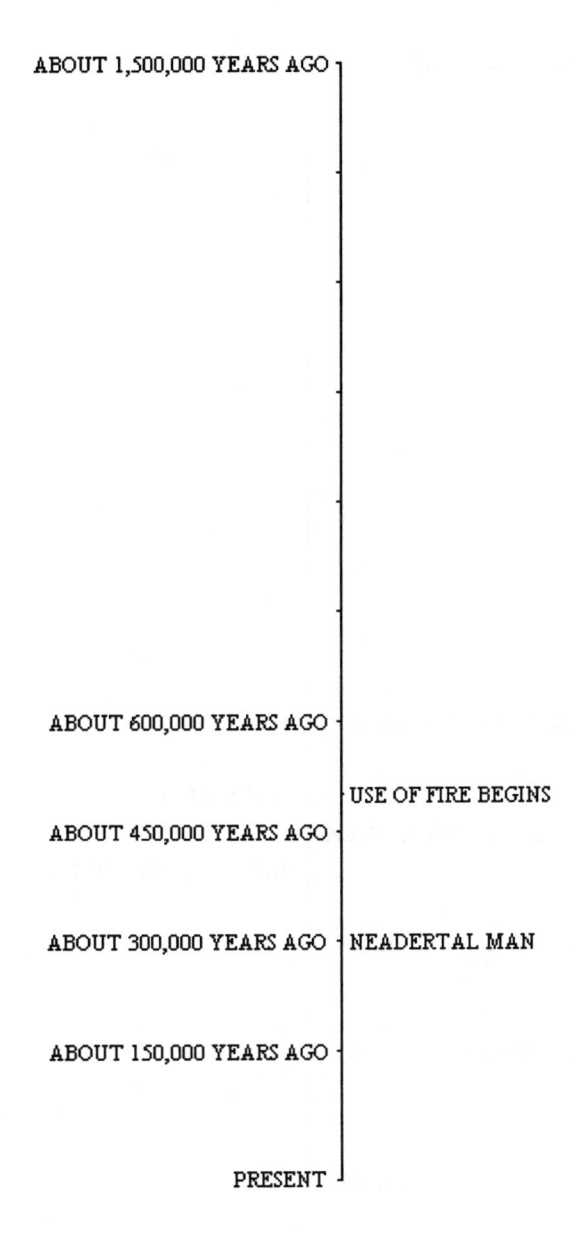

ABOUT 1,500,000 YEARS AGO

ABOUT 600,000 YEARS AGO
USE OF FIRE BEGINS
ABOUT 450,000 YEARS AGO

ABOUT 300,000 YEARS AGO — NEADERTAL MAN

ABOUT 150,000 YEARS AGO

PRESENT

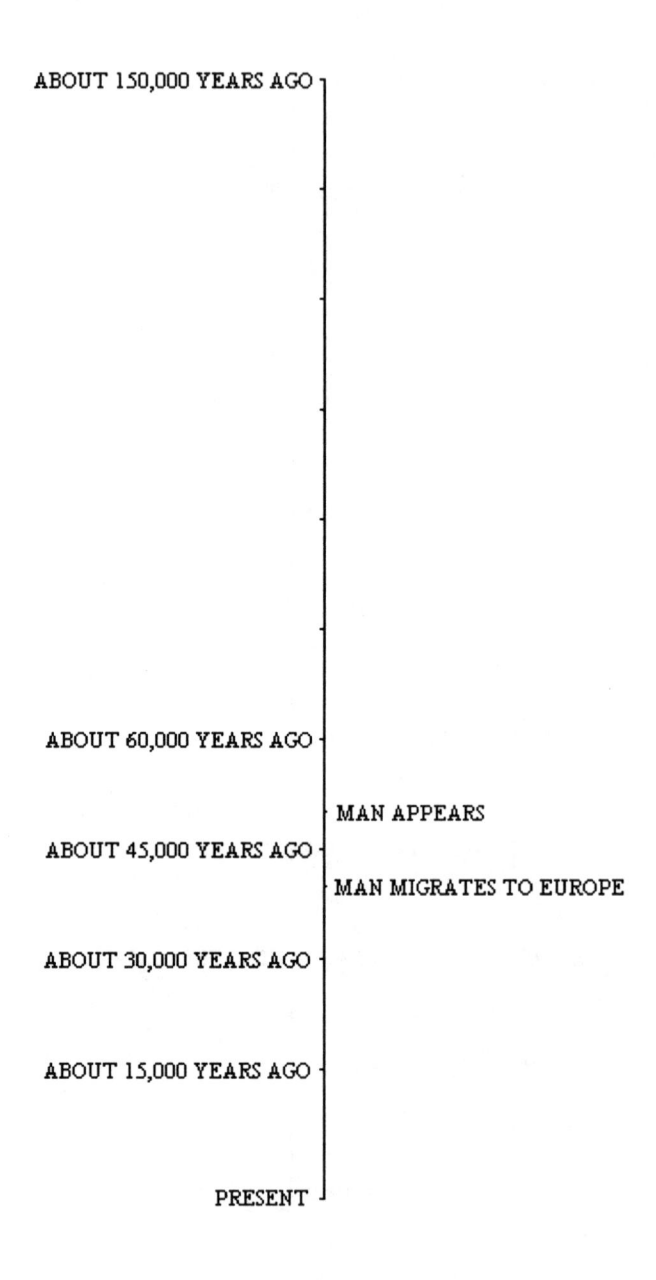

ABOUT 150,000 YEARS AGO ⊣

ABOUT 60,000 YEARS AGO ⊢
⊢ MAN APPEARS
ABOUT 45,000 YEARS AGO ⊢
⊢ MAN MIGRATES TO EUROPE

ABOUT 30,000 YEARS AGO ⊢

ABOUT 15,000 YEARS AGO ⊢

PRESENT ⊣

```
13,000 BC ┐


  7000 BC ┤
          ├ MAN BECOMES A FARMER-DROVER

  5500 BC ┤


  4000 BC ┤ SUMERIAN CITIES DEVELOP


  2500 BC ┤ MOHENJO-DARO AND HARAPPA DEVELOP ON THE INDUS
          │ AKKADIAN EMPIRE
          │ THIRD DYNASTY OF UR
          │ HAMMURABI; MYCENAE
          │ SHANG DYNASTY IN CHINA
  1000 BC ┤ CHOU DYNASTY; GANGES CIVILIZATION BEGINS; ASSYRIAN EMPIRE
          │ BUDDHA; CONFUCIUS; PERSIAN EMPIRE; ROMAN REPUBLIC
          │ ALEXANDER CONQUERS PERSIA; HAN DYNASTY OF CHINA
          │ DIOCLETIAN; GUPTA DYNASTY OF INDIA
     500  ┤ WESTERN ROMAN EMPIRE FALLS TO BARBARIAN ASSAULT


 PRESENT ┘
```

```
500 ─┐
     │
     │ MOHAMMED IS BORN
     │ THE HEGIRA (MOHAMMED'S FLIGHT TO MEDINA)
650 ─┤
     │
     │ CHARLES MARTEL TURNS BACK THE MOSLEMS AT POITIERS
800 ─┤ CAROLINGIAN EMPIRE ESTABLISHED
     │
     │ KING ALFRED OF ENGLAND
     │
950 ─┤ ENGLAND UNITED UNDER THE WESSEX CROWN
     │
     │ KIEVIAN RUSSIA; NORMAN CONQUEST OF ENGLAND
1100 ┤ HENRY I OF ENGLAND INTRODUCES ITENERANT JUDGES
     │
     │
     │ RUSSIA BECOMES SUBJECT TO THE GOLDEN HORDE
1250 ┤ EDWARD I OF ENGLAND ESTABLISHES THE PRACTICE OF CALLING
     │     PARLIAMENT FREQUENTLY
     │ HUNDRED YEARS WAR BEGINS
1400 ┤ PARLIAMENT DIVIDED INTO TWO HOUSES
     │ BATTLE OF AGINCOURT; JOAN OF ARC
     │ HUNDRED YEARS WAR ENDS; GUTTENBERG PRINTS HIS BIBLE
     │ COLUMBUS; VASCO DA GAMA; CORTEZ; REFORMATION BEGINS
1550 ┤ FIRST ENGLISH JOINT STOCK COMPANY; SPANISH ARMADA
     │ CAPITALISM REPLACES GUILD SYSTEM
     │ FIRST ENGLISH COLONY IN AMERICA; OLIVER CROMWELL
     │ WILLIAM AND MARY DEPOSE JAMES II IN ENGLAND
1700 ┤ JUDICIARY COMPLETELY SEPARATED FROM CROWN IN ENGLAND
     │ AMERICAN REVOLUTION; RUSSIAN LANDLORDS GIVEN OWNERSHIP
     │ NAPOLEON; WAR OF 1812; PANIC OF 1819; ERIE CANAL
     │ PANIC OF 1837; ANNEXATION OF TEXAS; MEXICAN WAR
1850 ┤
     │
     │
     │
PRESENT ┘
```

- 1850
  - THE GADSDEN PURCHASE
  - PANIC OF 1857
  - US CIVIL WAR BEGINS; RUSSIAN SERFS EMANCIPATED
- 1865
  - FIRST VOLUME OF MARX'S DAS KAPITAL PUBLISHED
  - GERMANY FORMED; PANIC OF 1873
  - END OF RECONSTRUCTION
- 1880
  - US RETURN TO GOLD STANDARD; AUSTRO-GERMAN ALLIANCE

  - SHERMAN ANTI-TRUST ACT
- 1895
  - PANIC OF 1893; FRANCO-RUSSIAN ALLIANCE
  - GASOLINE-DRIVEN CARS BECOME AVAILABLE

  - RUSSIAN "REVOLUTION" OF 1905; FORD MASS PRODUCTION
  - AUSTRIA ANNEXES BOSNIA
- 1910
  - FABRICATION OF RAYON BECOMES COMMERCIALLY FEASIBLE
  - WORLD WAR I BEGINS
  - UNRESTRICTED SUBMARINE WARFARE; LENIN ASSUMES POWER
  - WEIMAR CONSTITUTION; RUSSIAN NEW ECONOMIC POLICY
- 1925
  - BEER HALL PUTSCH; LENIN DIES
  - THE GREAT DEPRESSION; STALIN IN POWER
  - PRESIDENT ROOSEVELT; HITLER BECOMES CHANCELLOR
  - NRA DECLARED UNCONSTITUTIONAL; STALIN'S PURGE BEGINS
  - THE MUNICH AGREEMENT; WORLD WAR II BEGINS
- 1940
  - GERMANY INVADES RUSSIA; JAPAN ATTACKS PEARL HARBOR
  - WORLD WAR II ENDS
  - MARSHALL PLAN; BERLIN BLOCKADE (COLD WAR BEGINS)
  - GOVERNMENT OF WEST GERMANY FORMED; STALIN DIES
- 1955
  - WEST GERMANY JOINS NATO; COMMON MARKET FORMED
  - KHRUSHCHEV COMES TO POWER IN RUSSIA
  - BREZHNEV TAKES OVER IN RUSSIA

- 1970

- 1985
  - GORBACHEV COMES TO POWER IN RUSSIA
  - RUSSIAN SATELLITES THROW OUT THEIR COMMUNIST PARTIES
  - COMMONWEALTH OF INDEPENDENT STATES FORMED

English Royalty

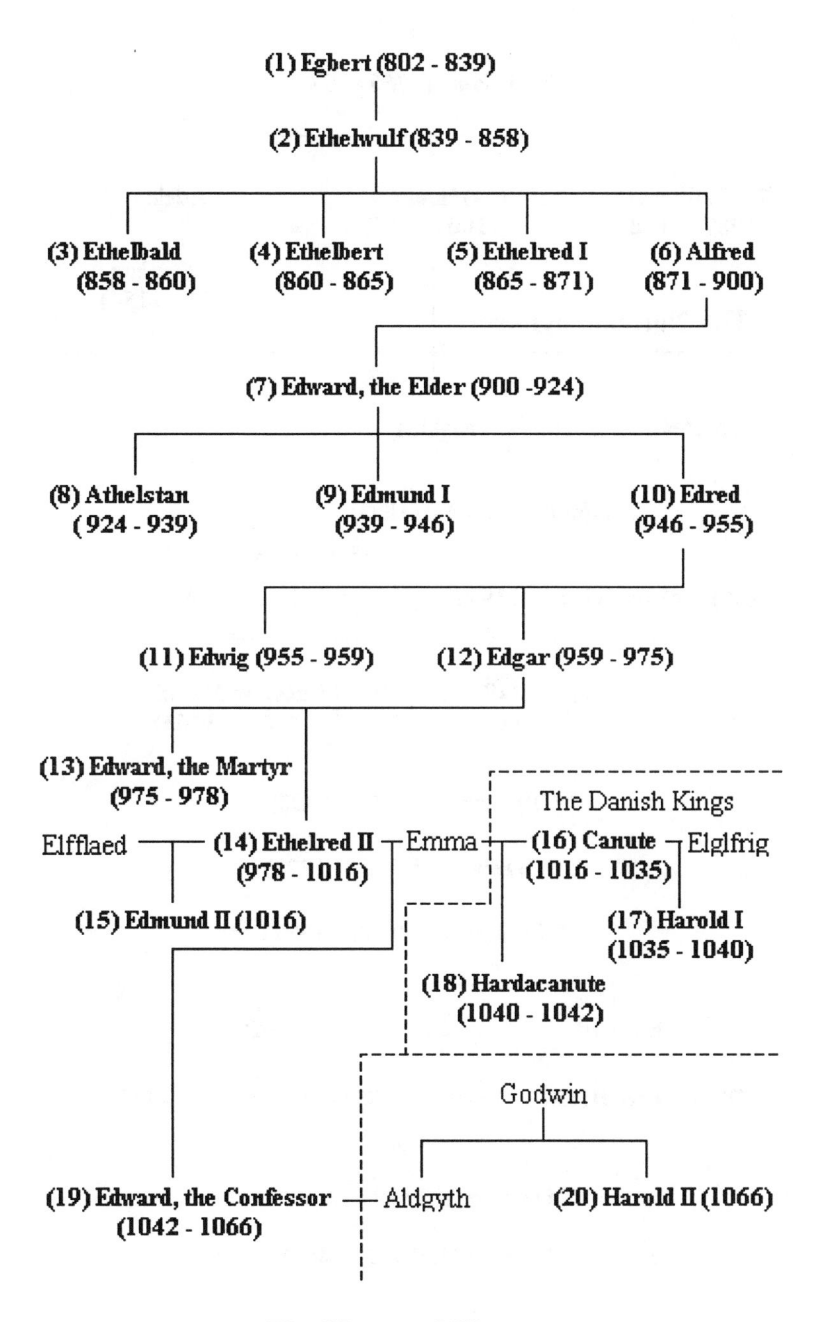

```
                        (1) Egbert (802 - 839)
                                 |
                        (2) Ethelwulf (839 - 858)
                                 |
      ┌──────────────────┬───────────────────┬──────────────────┐
  (3) Ethelbald      (4) Ethelbert       (5) Ethelred I      (6) Alfred
   (858 - 860)       (860 - 865)         (865 - 871)         (871 - 900)
                                                                  |
                        (7) Edward, the Elder (900 - 924)
                                 |
         ┌───────────────────────┼───────────────────────┐
     (8) Athelstan          (9) Edmund I            (10) Edred
      (924 - 939)            (939 - 946)            (946 - 955)
                                 |
                  ┌──────────────┴──────────────┐
            (11) Edwig (955 - 959)      (12) Edgar (959 - 975)
                                                 |
                  ┌──────────────────────────────┤
         (13) Edward, the Martyr                 :     The Danish Kings
              (975 - 978)                        :
  Elfflaed ─── (14) Ethelred II ─┬─ Emma ─┬─ (16) Canute ─┬─ ElgIfrig
                (978 - 1016)              :   (1016 - 1035)
         (15) Edmund II (1016)            :          (17) Harold I
                  |                       :           (1035 - 1040)
                                  (18) Hardacanute
                                    (1040 - 1042)
                  |              ─ ─ ─ ─ ─ ─ ─ ─ ─ ─ ─ ─ ─ ─ ─
                                           Godwin
                                    ┌────────────┐
         (19) Edward, the Confessor ─┬─ Aldgyth    (20) Harold II (1066)
              (1042 - 1066)

                         The House of Wessex
```

455

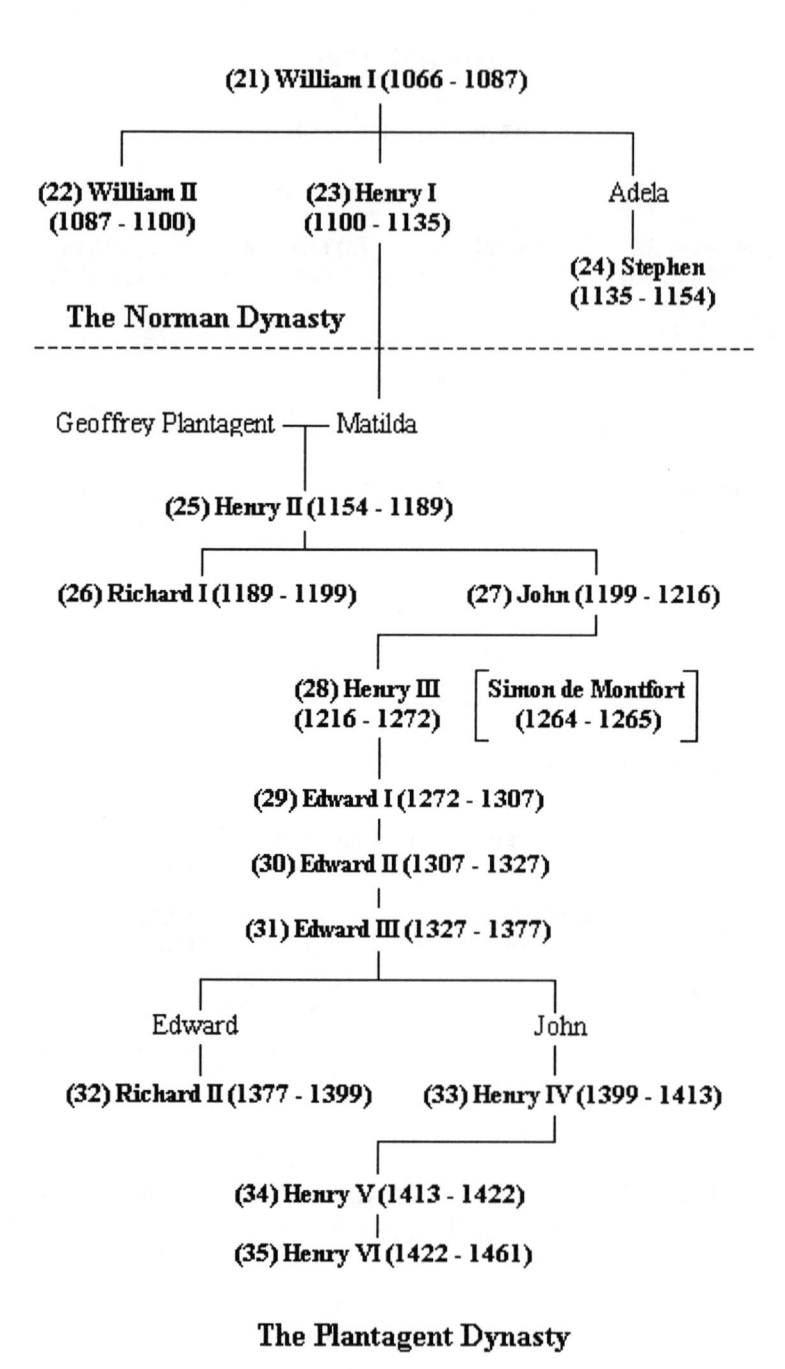

```
                    (21) William I (1066 - 1087)
        ┌───────────────────┼───────────────────┐
  (22) William II      (23) Henry I          Adela
   (1087 - 1100)       (1100 - 1135)           │
                                          (24) Stephen
                                          (1135 - 1154)
              The Norman Dynasty
- - - - - - - - - - - - - - - - - - - - - - - - - - - - -
    Geoffrey Plantagent ── Matilda
                    │
            (25) Henry II (1154 - 1189)
         ┌──────────┴──────────┐
  (26) Richard I (1189 - 1199)   (27) John (1199 - 1216)
                                        │
                        (28) Henry III   ⎡ Simon de Montfort ⎤
                        (1216 - 1272)    ⎣   (1264 - 1265)   ⎦
                              │
                    (29) Edward I (1272 - 1307)
                              │
                    (30) Edward II (1307 - 1327)
                              │
                    (31) Edward III (1327 - 1377)
                    ┌─────────┴─────────┐
                 Edward                John
                    │                    │
        (32) Richard II (1377 - 1399)  (33) Henry IV (1399 - 1413)
                                        │
                        (34) Henry V (1413 - 1422)
                                │
                        (35) Henry VI (1422 - 1461)
```

The Plantagent Dynasty

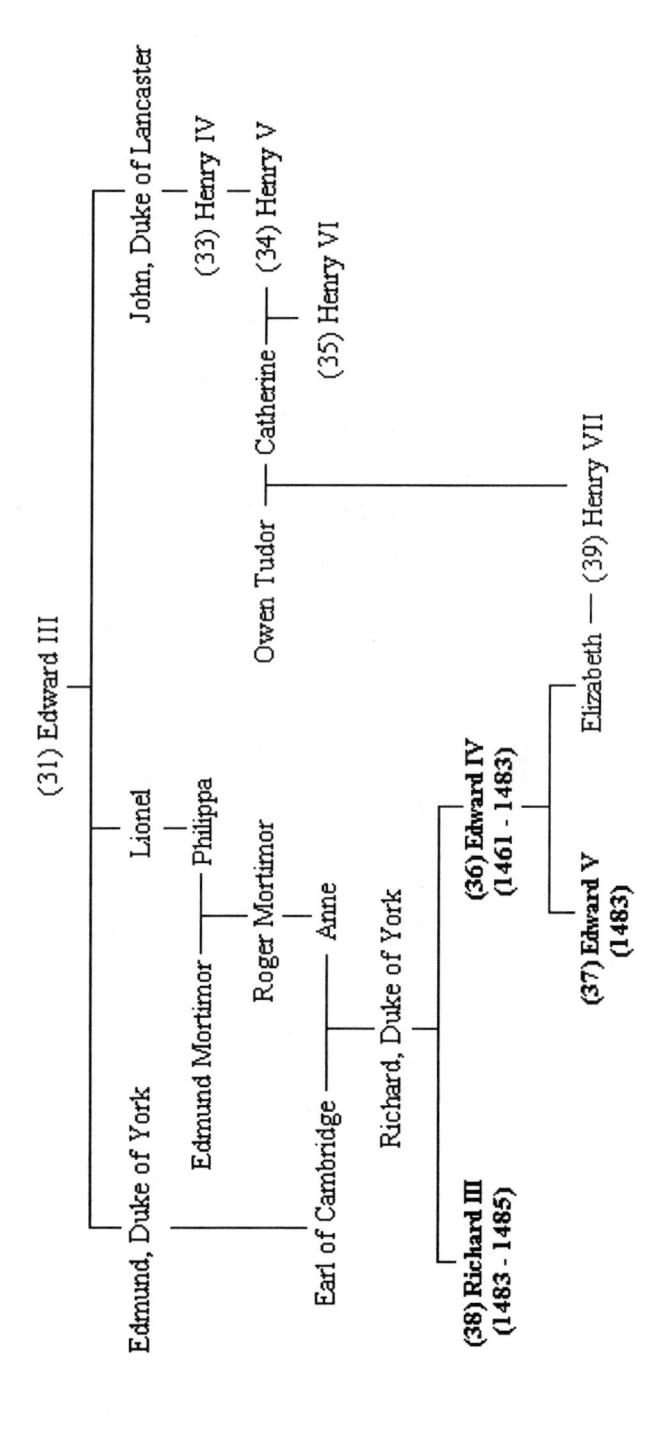

```
                                    Edmund, Duke of York
                                            |
                                    Edmund Mortimer ─── Philippa
                                                          |
                                    Roger Mortimer
                                            |
                Earl of Cambridge ─── Anne
                                            |
                                    Richard, Duke of York
                                            |
    ┌───────────────────────────────────────┤
    |                                       |
(38) Richard III                      (36) Edward IV       Elizabeth ─── (39) Henry VII
(1483 - 1485)                         (1461 - 1483)
                                            |
                                      (37) Edward V
                                           (1483)
```

(31) Edward III
├── Lionel
│   └── Philippa (see above)
└── John, Duke of Lancaster
        └── (33) Henry IV
                └── (34) Henry V
                        Catherine ─── Owen Tudor
                        | |
                   (35) Henry VI   (→ Henry VII above)

The Houses of York and Lancaster

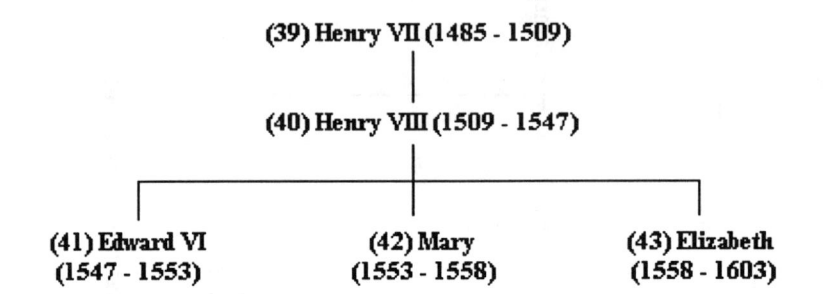

```
(39) Henry VII (1485 - 1509)
                │
(40) Henry VIII (1509 - 1547)
    ┌───────────┼───────────┐
(41) Edward VI  (42) Mary   (43) Elizabeth
(1547 - 1553)  (1553 - 1558) (1558 - 1603)
```

The House of Tudor

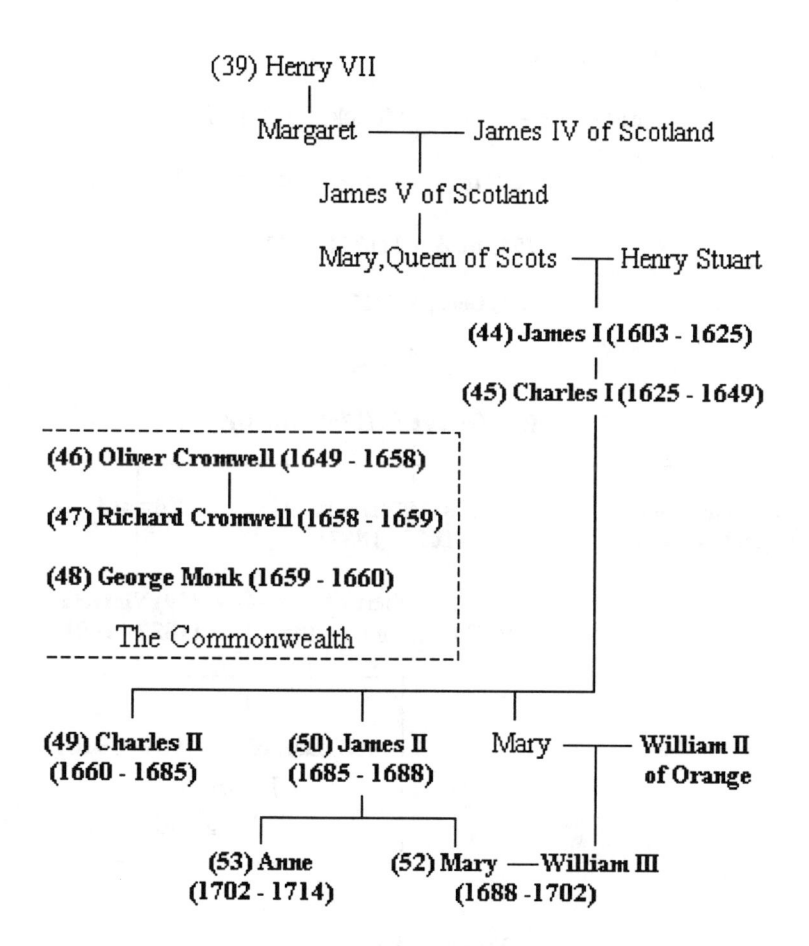

```
(39) Henry VII
      |
    Margaret ——┬—— James IV of Scotland
                |
        James V of Scotland
                |
    Mary, Queen of Scots ——┬—— Henry Stuart
                            |
              (44) James I (1603 - 1625)
                            |
              (45) Charles I (1625 - 1649)
```

- **(46) Oliver Cromwell (1649 - 1658)**
- **(47) Richard Cromwell (1658 - 1659)**
- **(48) George Monk (1659 - 1660)**

The Commonwealth

- **(49) Charles II (1660 - 1685)**
- **(50) James II (1685 - 1688)**
- Mary —— William II of Orange

- **(53) Anne (1702 - 1714)**
- **(52) Mary (1688 - 1702)** —— William III

The House of Stuart

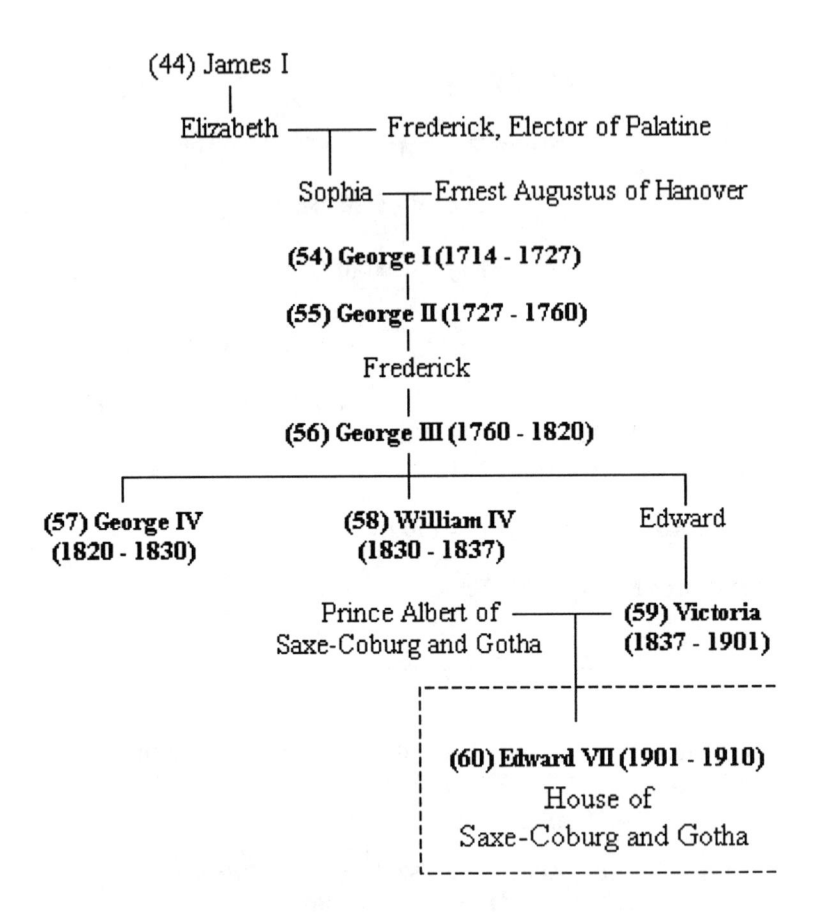

```
(44) James I
      |
   Elizabeth ——┬—— Frederick, Elector of Palatine
              Sophia ——┬—— Ernest Augustus of Hanover
                       |
              **(54) George I (1714 - 1727)**
                       |
              **(55) George II (1727 - 1760)**
                       |
                   Frederick
                       |
              **(56) George III (1760 - 1820)**
         ┌─────────────┼─────────────┐
**(57) George IV**  **(58) William IV**   Edward
**(1820 - 1830)**   **(1830 - 1837)**       |
                  Prince Albert of ——┬—— **(59) Victoria**
                  Saxe-Coburg and Gotha    **(1837 - 1901)**
                                  |
                        **(60) Edward VII (1901 - 1910)**
                              House of
                          Saxe-Coburg and Gotha
```

House of Hanover

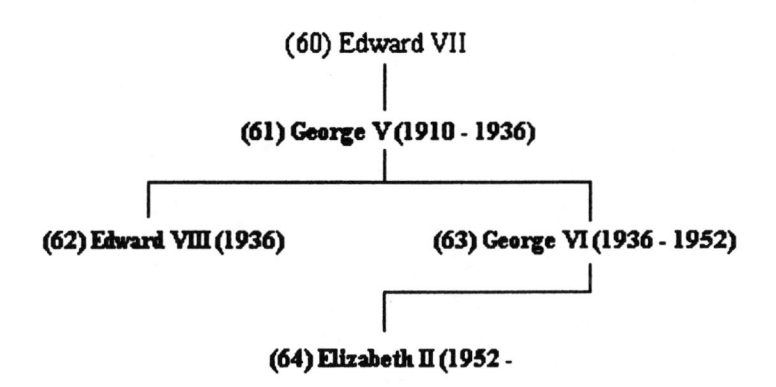

```
                    (60) Edward VII
                           |
              (61) George V (1910 - 1936)
                           |
        ┌──────────────────┴──────────────────┐
(62) Edward VIII (1936)            (63) George VI (1936 - 1952)
                                             |
                                   ┌─────────┘
                          (64) Elizabeth II (1952 -
```

The House of Windsor

During the First World War, King George V decided that the name of his House, Saxe-Coburg and Gotha, was too Germanic sounding, so he changed it to Windsor, an uncompromisingly English name. In response, the kaiser said that, from now on, the Shakespearian play would be known as "The Merry Wives of Saxe-Coburg and Gotha".

Russian Rulers

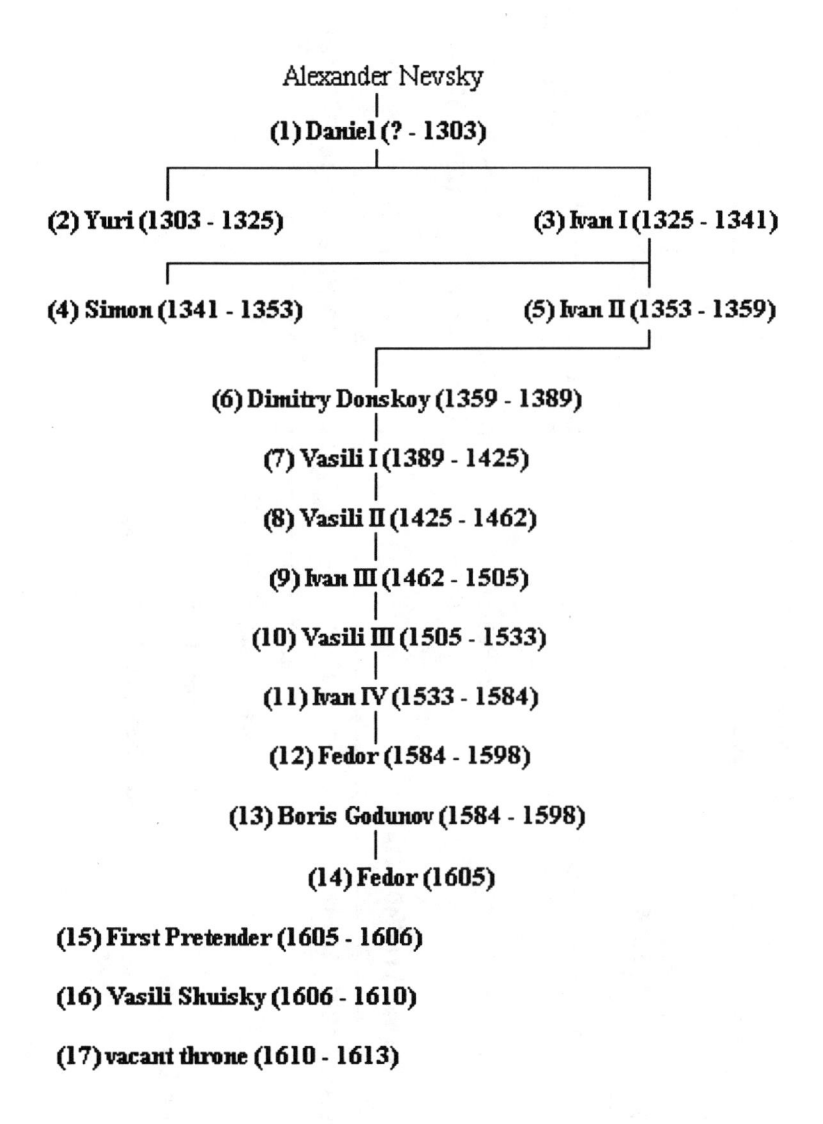

```
                    Alexander Nevsky
                           |
                  (1) Daniel (? - 1303)
         ┌─────────────────┴─────────────────┐
(2) Yuri (1303 - 1325)              (3) Ivan I (1325 - 1341)
         ┌─────────────────┴─────────────────┐
(4) Simon (1341 - 1353)            (5) Ivan II (1353 - 1359)
                                             |
                         (6) Dimitry Donskoy (1359 - 1389)
                                   |
                         (7) Vasili I (1389 - 1425)
                                   |
                         (8) Vasili II (1425 - 1462)
                                   |
                         (9) Ivan III (1462 - 1505)
                                   |
                         (10) Vasili III (1505 - 1533)
                                   |
                         (11) Ivan IV (1533 - 1584)
                                   |
                         (12) Fedor (1584 - 1598)
                                   |
                         (13) Boris Godunov (1584 - 1598)
                                   |
                         (14) Fedor (1605)
```

(15) First Pretender (1605 - 1606)

(16) Vasili Shuisky (1606 - 1610)

(17) vacant throne (1610 - 1613)

Riurik Dynasty

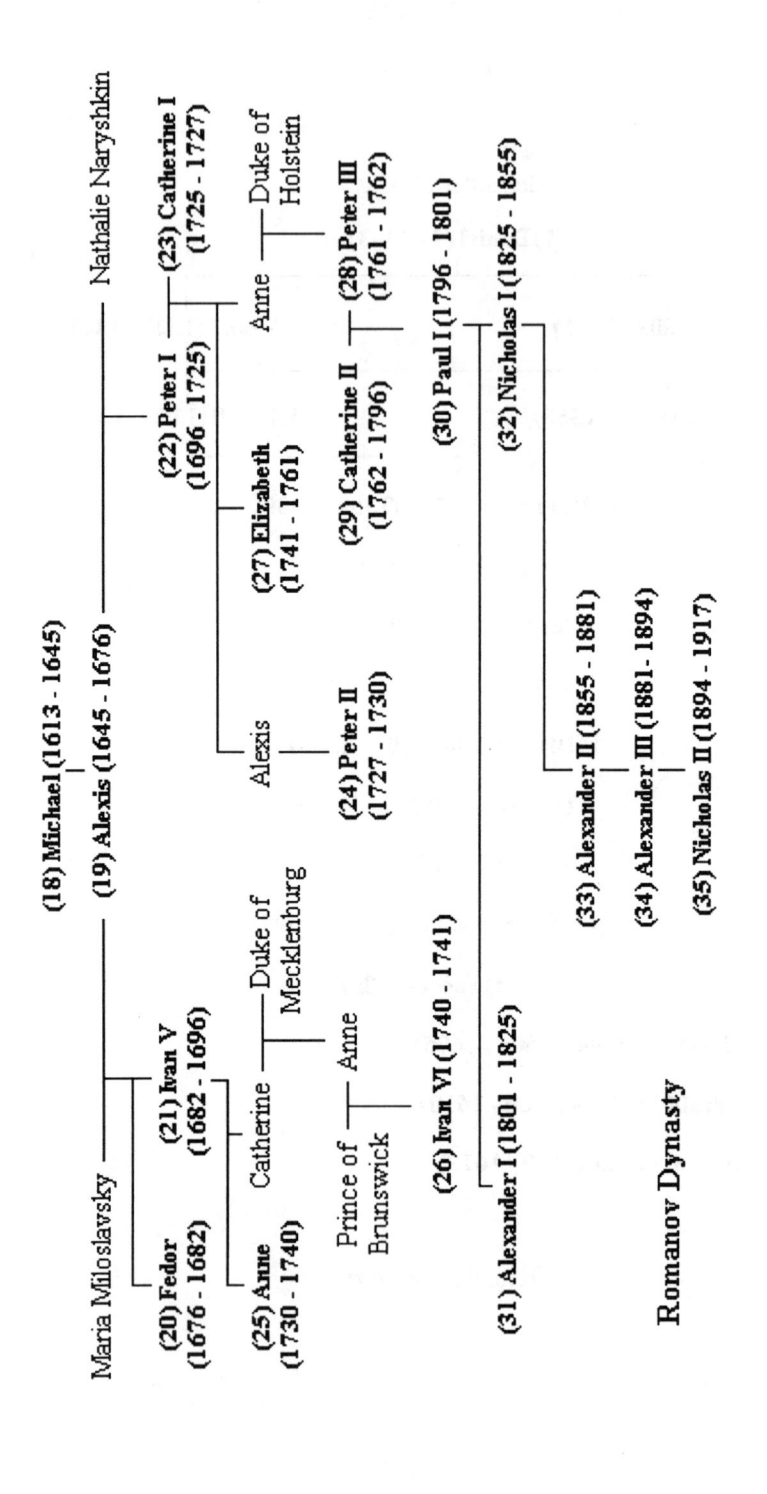

Maria Miloslavsky ─┬─ (18) Michael (1613 - 1645) ─┬─ Nathalie Naryshkin
                   │   (19) Alexis (1645 - 1676)
                   │
┌──────────────┬───┴──┐   ┌─────────────────┬──────────────┐
(20) Fedor   (21) Ivan V   Alexis   (22) Peter I ─┬─ (23) Catherine I
(1676-1682) (1682-1696)   (1696-1725)   │ (1725-1727)
             │   │   │
(25) Anne ─ Catherine ─ Duke of   (24) Peter II   ┌─────┴─────┐
(1730-1740)   Mecklenburg   (1727-1730)   (27) Elizabeth   Anne ─ Duke of
             │   (1741-1761)   Holstein
   Prince of ─┬─ Anne   │
   Brunswick │   (29) Catherine II ─┬─ (28) Peter III
              │   (1762-1796)   │ (1761-1762)
        (26) Ivan VI (1740-1741)   │
                                                              (30) Paul I (1796-1801)
                                                                            │
                                          (31) Alexander I (1801-1825) (32) Nicholas I (1825-1855)
                                                                            │
                                                              (33) Alexander II (1855-1881)
                                                                            │
                                                              (34) Alexander III (1881-1894)
                                                                            │
                                                              (35) Nicholas II (1894-1917)

Romanov Dynasty

(36) Provisional Government (1917)

(37) Lenin (1917 - 1924)

(38) Joseph Stalin (1924 - 1953)

(39) G. M. Malenkov (1953 - 1955)

(40) Nicholas Bulganin (1955 - 1958)

(41) Nikita Khrushchev (1958 - 1964)

(42) Leonid Brezhnev (1964 - 1982)

(43) Yuri Andropov (1982 - 1984)

(44) Konstantin Chernenko (1984 - 1985)

(45) Mikhail Gorbachev (1985 - 1991)

(46) Boris Yeltsin (1991 -

Order of Entry of States into the US

1787 Delaware
     Pennsylvania
     New Jersey
1788 Georgia
     Connecticut
     Massachusetts
     Maryland
     South Carolina
     New Hampshire
     Virginia
     New York
1789 North Carolina
1790 Rhode Island
1791 Vermont
1792 Kentucky
1796 Tennessee
1803 Ohio
1812 Louisiana
1816 Indiana
1817 Mississippi
1818 Illinois
1819 Alabama
1820 Maine
1821 Missouri
1836 Arkansas

1837 Michigan
1845 Florida
     Texas
1846 Iowa
1848 Wisconsin
1850 California
1858 Minnesota
1859 Oregon
1861 Kansas
1863 West Virginia
1864 Nevada
1867 Nebraska
1875 Colorado
1889 North Dakota
     South Dakota
     Montana
     Washington
1890 Idaho
     Wyoming
1896 Utah
1907 Oklahoma
1912 New Mexico
     Arizona
1959 Alaska
     Hawaii

Presidents of the US

1. George Washington (1789)
2. John Adams (1797)
3. Thomas Jefferson (1801)
4. James Madison (1809)
5. James Monroe (1817)
6. John Quincy Adams (1825)
7. Andrew Jackson (1829)
8. Martin Van Buren (1837)
9. William Henry Harrison (1841)
10. John Tyler (1841)
11. James Polk (1845)
12. Zachary Taylor (1849)
13. Millard Fillmore (1850)
14. Franklin Pierce (1853)
15. James Buchanan (1857)
16. Abraham Lincoln (1861)
17. Andrew Johnson (1865)
18. Ulysses S. Grant (1869)
19. Rutherford Hayes (1877)
20. James Garfield (1881)
21. Chester Arthur (1881)
22. Grover Cleveland (1885)
23. Benjamin Harrison (1889)
24. Grover Cleveland (1893)
25. William McKinley (1897)
26. Theodore Roosevelt (1901)
27. William Howard Taft (1909)
28. Woodrow Wilson (1913)
29. Warren Harding (1921)
30. Calvin Coolidge (1923)
31. Herbert Hoover (1929)
32. Franklin Roosevelt (1933)
33. Harry Truman (1945)
34. Dwight D. Eisenhower (1953)
35. John Kennedy (1961)
36. Lyndon Johnson (1963)
37. Richard Nixon (1969)
38. Gerald Ford (1974)
39. Jimmy Carter (1977)
40. Ronald Reagan (1981)
41. George Bush (1989)
42. Bill Clinton (1993)

Bibliography

Aronson, Theo *Crowns in Conflict* (Salem House, 1986)
Barr, Stringfellow *The Mask of Jove* (Lippincott, 1966)
Black, Donald Chain *Spoonerisms, Sycophants, and Sops* (Harper & Row, 1988)
Blum, Jerome *In the Beginning, The Advent of the Modern Age, Europe in the 1840's* (Charles Scribners' Sons, 1975)
Bosher, J. F. *The French Revolution* (Norton, 1988)
Brodie, Bernard and Fawn M. *From Crossbow to H-Bomb* (Indiana University, 1973)
Brogan, Hugh *The Longman History of the United States of America* (Morrow, 1985)
Bryson, Bill *The Mother Tongue* (Morrow, 1990)
Burns, E. Bradford *Latin America* (Prentice-Hall, 1972)
Burns, Edward McNall, Lerner, Robert E., and Meacham, Standish *Western Civilizations* (Norton, 1984)
Cantor, Norman F. *Inventing the Middle Ages* (William Morrow, 1991)
Cantor, Norman F. *The Civilization of the Middle Ages* (Harper Collins, 1993)
Carman, Harry J. *A History of the American People* (Knopf, 1952)
Catton, Bruce *The Coming Fury* (Doubleday, 1961)
Churchill's History of the English-Speaking Peoples
Conquest, Robert *Stalin* (Viking, 1991)
Craven, Avery *Reconstruction* (Holt, Rinehart and Winston, 1969)
Davidson, James West and Lytle, Mark Hamilton *After the Fact* (Knopf, 1982)
Divine, Robert A., Breen, T. H., Fredrickson, George M., and Williams, R. Hal *America Past and Present* (Harper Collins, 1991)
Doder, Dusko and Branson, Louise *Gorbachev* (Viking, 1990)
Donald, David Herbert *Lincoln* (Simon & Schuster, 1995)
Dunn, John *Locke* (Oxford University, 1984)
Durant, Will *The Life of Greece* (Simon and Schuster, 1939)
Elkins, Stanley and McKittrick, Eric *The Age of Federalism* (Oxford University, 1987)
Fairbank, John King *China* (Belknap, 1992)
Falls, Cyril *The Great War* (Putnam, 1959)
Ferguson, Wallace K. *A Survey of European Civilization, Ancient Times to 1660* (Houghton Mifflin, 1939)
Fischer, David Hackett *Paul Revere's Ride* (Oxford University, 1994)
Flexner, James Thomas *Washington* (Little Brown, 1974)
Florinsky, Michael T. *Russia: A Short History* (Macmillan, 1964)
Foote, Shelby *The Civil War* (Random House, 1958)
Foner, Eric *Reconstruction* (Harper & Row, 1988)
Freehling, William W. *The Road to Disunion* (Oxford University, 1990)
Galbraith, John Kenneth *The Great Crash* (Houghton Mifflin, 1988)
Garraty, John A. *The Great Depression* (Harcourt Brace Jovanovich, 1986)
Gies, Frances and Joseph *Life in a Medieval Village* (Harper & Row, 1990)
Ginger, Ray *Age of Excess* (Macmillan, 1965)
Goodwyn, Lawrence *Democratic Promise* (Oxford University, 1976)

Grant, Michael *The Classical Greeks* (Scribner's, 1989)
Grant, Michael *The Founders of the Western World* (Scribner's, 1991)
Green, Peter *Alexander of Macedon* (University of California, 1974)
Greer, Thomas H. *A Brief History of Western Man* (Harcourt, Brace & World, 1968)
Groner, Alex *The History of American Business & Industry* (American Heritage, 1972)
Hallahan, William H. *Misfire* (Scribner, 1994)
Hampson, Norman *The French Revolution* (Scribner's, 1975)
Hart, B. H. Liddell *History of the Second World War* (Putnam, 1970)
Hawke, David *John D* (Harper & Row, 1980)
Hession, Charles H. and Sardy, Hyman *Ascent to Affluence* (Allyn and Bacon, 1969)
Hobsbawn, E. J. *The Age of Capital 1848 - 1875* (Charles Scribner's Sons, 1994)
Holton, Gerald *Introduction to Concepts and Theories in Physical Science* (Princeton University, 1985)
Howard, Michael *The Lessons of History* (Yale University, 1991)
Hubbard, J. T. W. *For Each, the Strength of All* (New York University, 1995)
Jannen, William Jr. *The Lions of July* (Presidio, 1996)
Johnson, Paul *The Offshore Islanders* (Holt, Rinehart and Winston, 1972)
Johnson, Paul *The Birth of the Modern* (Harper Collins, 1991)
Johnson, Paul *Modern Times* (Harper & Row, 1983)
Josephson, Matthew.*The Robber Barons* (Harcourt, Brace, 1934)
Josephson, Matthew *The Politicos* (Harcourt, Brace & World, 1938)
Keegan, John *The Face of Battle* (Viking, 1976)
Keller, Morton *Affairs of State* (Belknap, 1977)
Kennedy, Paul *The Rise and Fall of the Great Powers* (Random House, 1987)
Kindleberger, Charles P. *Manias, Panics and Crashes* (Basic Books, 1978)
Klein, Maury *The Life and Legend of Jay Gould* (John Hopkins University, 1986)
Lafore, Laurence *The Long Fuse* (Lippincott, 1965)
Langguth, A. J. *A Noise of War* (Simon and Schuster, 1994)
Longford, Elizabeth *The Oxford Book of Royal Anecdotes* (Oxford University, 1989)
Madlow, Ben *A Sunday Between Wars* (Norton, 1979)
Maleska, Eugene T. *A Pleasure in Words* (Simon and Schuster, 1981)
Manchester, William *American Caesar* (Little, Brown, 1978)
Markham, Felix *Napoleon* (New American Library, 1963)
Martin, Albro *Railroads Triumphant* (Oxford University, 1992)
Massie, Robert K. *Dreadnought* (Random House, 1991)
McElvaine, Robert S. *The Great Depression* (Times Books, 1984)
McGrane, Reginald Charles *The Panic of 1837* (Russell & Russell, 1924)
McNeill, William H. *The Rise of the West* (University of Chicago, 1963)
McNeill, William H. *A World History* (Oxford University, 1971)

McPherson, James *Battle Cry of Freedom* (Oxford University, 1988)
Mee, Charles L. Jr. *The Marshall Plan* (Simon and Schuster, 1984)
Middlekauff, Robert *The Glorious Cause* (Oxford University, 1982)
Morison, Samuel Eliot, Commager, Henry Steele, and Leuchtenburg, William E. *The Growth of the American Republic* (Oxford University, 1969)
Myers, Margaret G. *A Financial History of the United States* (Columbia University, 1970)
Oates, Joan *Babylon* (Thames and Hudson, 1979)
Ollard, Richard *This War Without an Enemy* (Atheneum, 1976)
Parkes, Henry Bamford *The Divine Order* (Knopf, 1969)
Patterson, Orlando *Freedom in the Making of Western Culture* (Basic, 1991)
Perrett, Geoffrey *America in the Twenties* (Simon and Schuster, 1982)
Peters, F. E. *Allah's Commonwealth* (Simon and Schuster, 1973)
Peterson, Merrill D. *The Great Triumvirate* (Oxford University, 1987)
Pipes, Richard *Russia under the Old Regime* (Scribner's, 1974)
Pipes, Richard *The Russian Revolution* (Knopf, 1990)
Price, Harry Bayard *The Marshall Plan and Its Meaning* (Cornell University, 1955)
Quinn, Arthur *A New World* (Faber and Faber, 1994)
Ratner, Sidney, Soltow, James H. and Sylla, Richard *The Evolution of the American Economy* (Basic.Books, 1979)
Rayback, Joseph G. *A History of American Labor* (Free Press, 1966)
Roaf, Michael *Cultural Atlas of Mesopotamia and the Ancient Near East* (Facts on File, 1990)
Roberts, J. M. *The Triumph of the West* (Little, Brown, 1985)
Roux, George *Ancient Iraq* (World, 1964)
Safire, William *Freedom* (Doubleday, 1987)
Schama, Simon *Citizens* (Knopf, 1989)
Shachtman, Tom *The Day America Crashed* (Putnam, 1979)
Shirer, William L. *The Rise and Fall of the Third Reich* (Simon and Schuster, 1960)
Skidmore, Thomas E. and Smith, Peter H. *Modern Latin America* (Oxford University, 1984)
Sloat, Warren *1929* (MacMillan, 1979)
Snyder, Louis L. *Great Turning Points in History* (Van Nostrand Reinhold, 1971)
Solomon, Robert C. *History and Human Nature* (Harcourt Brace Jovanovich, 1979)
Soren, David, Ben Khader, Aieha Bed Abed, and Slim, Hedi *Carthage* (Simon and Schuster, 1990)
Spitz, Lewis W. *The Protestant Reformation* (Harper & Row, 1990)
Thomas, Benjamin P. *Lincoln* (Knopf, 1952)
Thomson, David *Europe Since Napoleon* (Knopf, 1982)
Todd, John M. *Luther* (Crossroad, 1982)
Treasure, Geoffrey *The Making of Modern Europe 1648 - 1780* (Methuen, 1985)

Trevelyan, G. M. *History of England* (Longman, 1973)
Tuchman, Barbara W. *The Guns of August* (Macmillan, 1962)
Tuchman, Barbara W. *A Distant Mirror* (Knopf, 1978)
Tuchman, Barbara W. *The March of Folly* (Knopf, 1984)
Tucker, Robert C. *Stalin in Power* (Norton, 1990)
Turner, Henry Ashby Jr. *The Two Germanies Since 1945* (Yale University, 1987)
Vadney, T. E. *The World Since 1945* (Facts on File, 1987)
Weintraub, Stanley *A Stillness Heard Round the World* (Dutton, 1985)
Weir, William *Fatal Victories* (Archan, 1993)
Willson, David Harris *A History of England* (Holt, Rinehart and Winston, 1967)
Wilson, Colin *A Criminal History of Mankind* (Putnam, 1984)
Wolpert, Stanley A. *A New History of India* (Oxford University, 1977)
Yergin, Daniel *Shattered Peace* (Penguin, 1990)
The Wall Street Journal

Index

500 day plan   405

Abbisid   95
abolition   267
absolute monarchy   139, 141
Abu Bakr   91, 93, 97
Achaean   45
Act of Settlement   179
Adams, John   207, 237, 238, 246, 247, 251
Adams, John Quincy   251, 252
Adams, Sam   192
Adenauer   363
Agamemnon   45
Agincourt   130, 134
airplane   315, 316
Akkad   27, 28, 29
Alamanni   79
Alaric   81
Albert   311
Alekseev   385
Alexander the Great   57, 58
Alexander Nevsky   369
Alexander (Lenin's brother)   383, 384
Alexander I   378, 382, 383
Alexander II   376
Alexander III   383
Alexander VI   143
Alexandra   383
Alexis (son of Peter I)   381
Alexis (Tsar)   381
Alien and Sedition Acts   247, 248
Alfred   101
Ali   93, 97
All Russian Soviet   389
Allah   91
Allen   195, 245
alphabet   49
American Relief Administration   324
American Revolution   234, 435
Amorite   29, 32
Andropov   404
Angles   79, 83

Anglo-Saxons   84
Anne (Empress of Russia)   375
Anne (Queen of England)   177, 178, 180
Anschluss   346
Antiochus III   71
Antonius Pius   76
Appollonius   62
apprentice   117, 164
Arabia   91
Arabic numerals   95
Aramaean   37
archbishop   79, 81
Archduke Ferdinand   307, 308
Archimedes   63, 64
Aristotle   62
Armada   162
armee revolutionaire   227
armistice   315
Arnold   195
Articles of Confederation   197, 202-205
Aryans   409, 412
Ashoka   413
assembly   184, 189
Assembly of the Notables   213
Assyria   27, 36 - 39, 41
Ataulf   81, 82
Athelstan   101
atman   413
atomic bomb   357
Attlee   399
auditeur   233
Augustine   145
Augustus   75, 76, 84
Austro-German Alliance   305
autocracy   367, 368, 369, 375
Avicenna   95
Axis   357

Baal   69
Babylonia   27, 33, 34, 39, 50, 63
Bactria   59
Baekeland   299
Bank of England   179, 180

bank loan   242, 300
bank note   242, 243, 251, 253
bank run   243
barbarian   10, 27, 34, 35, 37, 45, 75, 76, 79, 80, 81, 84, 87, 89, 90, 99, 108, 130, 317
Barras   232
Baruch   323
Bastille   217
Batchelder   263
Battle of Britain   353
Battle of the Coral Sea   355
Battle of Midway   355
Battle of New Orleans   250
Becket   125, 126
Bede   101
Bedouin   91, 92
beer hall putsch   338, 339
Beijing man   15
Belgrano   435
Berchtold   341
Beria   401
Berkeley   187
Berlin blockade   401
Bethmann   311
Bill of Rights   205, 207
bishop   78, 79, 81
Bismarck   305
bit   35
Bizonia   361
Black Codes   286, 287
Black Death   139
Black Hand   307
Black Pottery culture   419
black repartition   371, 373, 377, 389
Blacker   173
blitzkrieg   351, 357
blockade   279
Bloody Sunday   380
Boeotia   53
Boethius   101
Boleyn   153
Bolivar   435, 437
bolshak   370, 373

Bolsheviks   385, 387-394, 403
Bonaparte, Joseph   435
Bonifacio   435
Borgia, Cesare   143
Borgia, Lucrezia   143
Bosnia   307
Boyle   179
brahman   413
Brahmanas   411, 412
Brahmins   412, 413
Brandenburg   99, 100
Brauchitsch   344
Breckinridge   269, 272
Brewster   168
Brezhnev   403, 404
Brown   262
Bruening   341, 342
Bryan   302, 303
Buddha   410, 413, 415
Buddhism   413, 415, 427
Bulganin   401
Bunker Hill   196
Bureau of Internal Revenue   279
bureaucracy   42, 279, 323, 330
burgher   114, 120, 128, 129, 137, 150
Burgoyne   198
Burgundians   79
Burr   246, 247, 248
Bute   189, 190
Byzantine empire   88, 89, 90
Byzantium   60, 78, 88

cabinet (English)   128, 155
cabinet (US)   238
Caesar   73, 87, 88
calendar   24
Calhoun   249, 252
California   254
caliph   93
call loan   255, 329
Calvert, Cecilius   187
Calvert, George   187
Calvin   151
Cambyses   41

canals 261, 262, 293
Cannae 69
Canute 121, 122
capital 294
capitalism 163, 164, 302
capitalist 295, 297
Captain Swing 365
Carlyle 235
Carnegie 295
Carolingian empire 103, 107, 108, 149
carpetbagger 289, 290
Carter 320
Carteret 187
Carthage 68, 69, 71, 83
cash and carry 354
caste 409, 410, 413, 415
Catherine of Aragon 152, 153
Catherine II 375, 378, 381
Cato 71
caudillos 437
Ceausescu 405
Celts 83
Central Committee 387, 390, 394, 397
Chaeronea 57
Chamberlain 347, 348
chancery 137
Charlemagne 102, 103, 104, 142
Charles Martel 95, 142
Charles I 169-174, 176, 177, 187
Charles II 176, 177, 187
Charles III 435
Charles V 148, 149, 151, 153, 161
Charles VII 135
Cheka 393, 396
Chernenko 404
China 10, 150
Chou dynasty 419, 420
Christian Democrats 361, 362
Christianity 77, 78
Church of England 167, 168, 169
Cicero 88
Cimbri 87
Cimon 60

city-state 47
civil rights 283, 292
Civil War 293, 299, 302, 321, 323, 329
Civil Works Administration 326
Civilian Conservation Corps 326
civilization 9, 10, 15, 22, 27, 31, 34, 80, 97, 99, 107, 109, 317
Clay 249, 251, 252
Clement VII 153
clergy 114
Clermont 257
Cleveland 321
Clinton 261
Code Napoleon 233
Coercive Acts 193
Coinage Act 242
Coke 168, 169, 207
Cold War 401, 402, 403
collectivization 393, 396, 397
colonization 276
Columbus 158, 159
Commission for Relief in Belgium 323
Committee of Public Safety 224, 227, 229
committees of correspondence 192
Commodus 76
common law 124, 125, 137, 171, 207, 364
Commons 127, 137, 138, 155, 162, 170-174, 177, 181
Commonwealth of Independent States 407, 408
compass 157, 429
compound bow 35
Compromise of 1877 283, 292
Confederacy 269, 271, 272, 273, 276, 277, 279, 283, 286
Confucianism 420, 423, 425, 427, 429
Confucius 420
Congress of Berlin 307
Connecticut 186

487

Conservatives 366
conspiracy 209, 211, 215
Constantine 77, 78, 89
Constantinople 78, 90
Constantius 82
Constituent Assembly 389, 391, 392
Constitution 204-208, 237, 238, 239, 246-249, 289
Constitutional Democrats 392
constitutional monarchy 138, 364
Consuls 233, 234
continental 240
Continental army 196
Convention of 1800 247
convoy 315
Cooke 295, 299
Copernicus 164
Corday 225, 226
Cornwallis 198
Cortes 141
Cortez 160, 431
Council of People's Commissars 388
Council of State 233
Counter-Terror, the 231
county 123
court of common pleas 128
Crawford 251
Crecy 130, 134
criollos 433, 435
Cromwell, Oliver 173-177
Cromwell, Richard 176
Cromwell, Thomas 155
Cumberland Road 257
curse of Cromwell 176
Curzon line 399
Cyrus 39, 41

da Gama 159
Daladier 347
Daniel 369
Danton 217, 222, 223, 229
Darius 41, 50
Dark Ages 107

Davis 275, 280
Decembrist revolt 378
De La Ware 187
de Lisle 221
de Miranda 435
de Montfort 127, 128
de San Martin 435
Declaration of Independence 197, 198, 207
Declaration of the Rights of Man and of the Citizen 235
Deep South 267, 269, 271
Deere 263
Delaware 188
Delian Confederacy 55, 56
democracy 49, 50, 54, 55
Democrats 239, 252, 253, 257, 269, 275, 285, 287, 291, 292, 302
Descartes 165
Desmoulins 217, 228, 229
Diaz 159
diet 148
Diocletian 76, 77, 79, 84
Diodorus 53
Directory 231, 232, 247
divine right of kings 128, 167, 169, 170, 177, 210
Donation of Pepin 142
Douglas 268, 269, 275
draft 279
Dred Scott 253, 275
Drexler 336
DuBois 290
Duc de Chartres 215
Duma 380, 386, 387
Dunk 197
Dunkirk 352

East Florida 251
East India Company 180, 192
Ebert 332, 333
Edward, the Elder 101
Edward I 128, 129
Edward II 129

Edward III   122, 129, 130, 131, 137
Egypt   10, 24, 36, 37, 39, 41, 42, 43, 50
Eisenhower   257
Elamite   32
electoral college   246, 247, 248
Elizabeth (daughter of James I)   179
Elizabeth I   161, 162, 167, 168, 169, 183
Emancipation Proclamation   274
England   83, 101, 112, 121, 123, 129, 130, 138, 140
English Bill of Rights   178
English Constitution   137
English Disease   365, 366
English Revolutions   234
enrages   224, 229
equality before the law   287
Erasistratus   62
Erhard   361, 362
Erie Canal   261
Erzberger   332, 333
Ethelred II   121
Etruscan   65
Euboea   50, 51
Euclid   62, 63
Eudoxus   62
European Economic Community   364
Evrard   227
executive   25, 26, 65, 205
Executive Committee   386, 387, 389, 391

Fabian Society   365
faith   145, 147, 154
fallow   31, 109
Farm Credit Administration   326
farmer-drover   18
Fatima   97
Federal Deposit Insurance Corporation   326
Federal Reserve System   254

Federalists   237, 238, 239, 245-250
Federalist Papers, The   207
Fedor (son of Tsar Alexis)   381
Fedor (son of Ivan IV)   380, 381
Ferdinand   141, 152
feudalism   122, 123, 130, 134, 140, 209
fiat money   279, 302, 303
fief   111, 123
fire   17
First Continental Congress   193
First Consul   233
First English Civil War   173
First Opium War   429
First Pretender   381
Fluvia   88
Foch   332
food domestication   18, 19
Ford   299
Forquier   228, 229, 231
Fort Sumter   271
fractional reserve banking   242, 243
Franco-Russian Alliance   306, 307, 310
Franks   79, 103, 104, 105
Frederick, Elector of Saxony   149
Frederick the Great   189
Frederick (son of George III)   189
Frederick William I   99, 220
Free Democrats   361, 362
free silver   302
freedmen   285, 286, 287
Freedmen's Bureau   279, 280, 285
French empire   234
Frick   295
fuehrer   340, 345
Fulton   257, 260
fyrd   103, 121

Gadsden   254
Gadsden Purchase   254
Gage   193
Gaiseric   83

Gaius Marius   87
Galileo   164
Galla Placidia   82
Gapon   380
Gaspee   192
Gates   198
Geisenhainer   263
General Will   210
gentry   129, 137
George I   180, 188
George II   188, 189
George III   189, 191
Georgia   188
Gestapo   344
Girondins   220, 221, 225, 227, 228
glasnost   404, 405
Godunov   381
Goebbels   337, 345
Goering   337, 344, 345, 347, 348, 353
gold standard   300, 303, 330
Golden Horde   368, 369
good works   145, 147
Gorbachev   404-407
Gould   295
Goulding   263
government   9
Grafton   191
grain domestication   18, 20
Grand Canal   425
Grant   277, 289, 290
grape-olive agriculture   49, 50, 56
Great Council   123, 127, 128
great depression   341, 438
Great Wall of China   427
Greeley   274, 275
Green Mountain Boys   245
greenback   279, 302
Gregory   101
Grenville   189, 190, 191
Grey   311
guild   103, 115, 116, 117, 119, 163, 164
Guillotin   214
Guitian   29

Gulag   393
Gupta dynasty   415
guru   415
Gutenberg   150

haciendas   433, 437
Hadrian   76, 85
Hamilcar Barca   69
Hamilton   203, 207, 237-245, 247-250
Hammurabi   32, 33
Han dynasty   423, 425
Hannibal   69, 72
Harappa   409
hard money   241, 244, 302
Hardie   365
Harding   317
Harriman   295
Hasan   97
Hawkins   161
Hayes, Edward   173
Hayes, Rutherford   291, 292
headright system of land allotment   184
heavy plow   107, 108, 109
Hebert   224, 229
Hebrew   37
Hegira   92
Heiden   341
Henrietta Maria   187
Henry the Navigator   157, 159
Henry, Patrick   190, 195
Henry I   123, 124, 125
Henry II   125, 126, 127
Henry III   127, 128
Henry V   131, 133, 134, 135, 139
Henry VI   139
Henry VII   152, 155, 167
Henry VIII   152, 153, 155, 161
Hermandad   141
Herodutus   41, 51, 53, 54
Herophilus   62
Hesoid   61
Heydrich   347, 348
Hieron   63, 64

High Middle Ages   107
Hill   295
Himmler   341, 344, 345, 346
Hindenburg   331, 342, 343, 345
Hinduism   413, 415, 416
Hipparchus   63
Hippocrates   62
history   9
Hitler, Adolph   331, 333-348, 353-357, 398
Hitler, Alois   334, 335
Hitler, Johann   334
Hittite   36
Hobbes   210
Hohenzollern   99, 100
Holy Roman empire   148, 149
Home Owners' Loan Corporation   326
Homer   61
Honorius   81, 82
Hoover   319, 320, 323, 324, 325
hoplite   47, 49
Hotel de Ville   218, 222, 231, 232
House of Lancaster   139
House of Representatives   205
House of York   139
Howard   285
Howe, Elias   263
Howe, William   196
Hsia dynasty   419
Hundred Years War   112, 122, 130, 131, 137, 138, 139
hungry thirty-three   396
Huns   80
hunter-gatherer   18
Hurrian   36
Husayn   97
Huss   150
Hyksos   36, 37

imam   97
immigration   300, 301
impressment   245, 249
Incas   161
Independent Labor Party   365

Independent Treasury   254
Independents   173, 174
India   10
Indo-European   36, 65
indulgence   147, 148
Indulgents   229
inflation   329, 330
Innocent I   81
insurrection   211
Insurrectionary Commune   222, 223, 224, 229, 230
Inquisition   141
intelligentsia   377, 384, 394
intendants   224
interest   163
Internal Revenue Service   279
Intolerable Acts   193
Isabella   141, 152
Islam   107
Ivan I   369, 380
Ivan III   369, 383
Ivan IV   369, 380
Ivan V   381
Ivan VI   381

Jackson, Andrew   250-253, 257
Jackson, Claiborne   271, 272
Jacobins   219, 220, 224, 225, 227-234
Jafar   97
James I   167, 168, 169, 177, 179, 187
James II   177, 178, 187
James IV   167
James V   167
Jay   207, 238, 245
Jay Treaty   245, 246
Jefferson   193, 197, 199, 238, 239, 240, 246-249, 279
Jellicoe   315
Joan of Arc   135
John   124, 127
Johnson   283, 285, 289
joint-stock company   163
Josephson   295

journeyman 117, 164
Joyce 174
judicial 25, 26, 65, 128, 179, 205, 364
judicial supremacy 168, 207, 366
jury 55
just price 115, 209
Justinian 85, 89
Justinian law 85, 119, 124
Jutes 79, 83

Kaaba 91, 93
Kaganovich 401
Kahn 320
Kahr 338, 339, 345
kaiser 331, 332, 333
Kansas-Nebraska Act 268, 269
Kao-tsu 423
karma 413, 415
Kassite 34, 36, 45
Kepler 164
kerosene 294
Key, Francis 273
Key, John 273
Khmelnitsky 349
Khrushchev 398, 401, 403
king 26, 33, 43, 45, 47, 102, 103, 112, 119, 120, 123, 124, 127, 168, 189, 205
King 250
king's bench 128
Kirov 397
knight 89, 108, 109
Knox 238
Koba 349
Koran 93, 97
Korff 219
Kristallnacht 347, 348
Ku Klux Klan 290
Kublai Khan 157
kulaks 393, 394

Labor Representation Committee 365
Laborites 365

Lafayette 217-222
Lancaster Pike 255, 256
language 17
latifundia 72
Laud 169, 185, 186
Laurium 50, 51
law code 31, 33, 39, 43, 75, 85, 115
Law of Prairial 230
Law of Suspects 227, 228
le Coq 138
League of Nations 316, 317
Lebensraum 340
legal tender 279
legislative 55, 65, 127, 138, 205
Legislative Assembly 220, 221, 222
Lend-Lease 354
Lenin 383, 384, 385, 387-394
Leo I 83
Leo III 103
Leo X 148
Leonidas 51, 60
Leopold of Austria 220
Leopold III 352
Lepidus 88
Lexington 194, 195
Liberals 365
Licinius 77
Liebknecht 332, 333
limited government 155, 168
Lincoln 239, 269, 271-277, 279, 283, 285, 286
Locke 177, 178, 188, 205, 210, 435
Lombards 79
lord 105, 109, 110, 112, 113, 114, 118, 119, 120, 123
Lossow 338, 339
Louis, Antoine 214
Louis XV 212
Louis XVI 212-215, 217, 218, 219, 221, 222, 223
Louisiana Purchase 248, 249, 268
Loyalist 197, 198, 199

Lublin government   399
Luddites   365
Ludendorff   331, 333, 337, 339, 340
Ludwig   336
Luftwaffe   353
Lugalzaggisi   26, 27
Luther   144, 145, 147-152, 154
Luxemburg   332
Lyons   271

MacArthur   358
MacDonald   365
machine gun   315
Madison   203, 205, 207, 249, 250
Magna Carta   124, 127
mahdi   97
Maillart   138
Malcolm   333
Malenkov   401
Manchu dynasty   419
Manichaeans   427
Manifest Destiny   253, 254
manor   109, 111, 119
Mao Tse-tung   425
Marat   217, 222, 223, 225, 227
Marathon   50, 60
Marbury   207
Marcel   138
Marcellus   64
marcher lord   27, 73, 80, 89
marchland   27, 29, 317
Marco Polo   157
Marcus Aurelius   76
Mardonius   53
Margaret   167
Marie-Antoinette   209
Mark Antony   88
Marne   313
Marseillaise   221, 222
Marshall   207, 260
Marshall Plan   359, 360, 361, 363
Martin   295, 296
Marx   298
Mary of Modena   177

Mary Queen of Scots   167
Mary (daughter of Charles I)   177
Mary (of William and Mary)   177, 178, 179
Maryland   187
Mason   187
Massachusetts   185
master   117, 164
Matilda   125
Mauryan empire   413
Maxentius   77
Maximian   77
Maximus   77
Maysville Road   257
McClellan   273
McCormick   263
McKinley   303
Mecca   91, 93
Medes   36, 39
Medina   92, 93
Mein Kampf   340
Melqart   69
Menes   42
Mensheviks   385
merchant   24, 42, 43
Mesopotamia   10, 18, 23, 24, 26, 28, 29, 32 - 35, 41, 42, 43
mestizos   435, 437
Mexican War   254
Michael   399
Middle Ages   85, 96, 99, 164
Miloslavsky   381
Miltiades   60
Ming dynasty   427
Minie   281
minimum wage   327
minnie ball   281
Mirabeau   215
Missouri Compromise   268
Mitanni   36, 45
Mithradites   87
mobilization   309, 310
Mogul   96
Mohammed   91, 92, 93, 97, 98
Mohenjo-daro   409

Molotov 401
money 119, 163, 243, 244, 302, 330
Monk 176
monopoly 297, 298
Monroe 250, 251
Moor 140, 141
Morgan 295, 298
Moslems 91, 415, 416, 427
movable type 150, 429
muckraker 295
Munich Agreement 347
Muscovy 369
Mussolini 338, 357

Napoleon Bonaparte 228-234, 247, 248, 249, 251, 435, 437
Napoleon III 305
Naram Sin 28, 29, 33
Narmar 42
Naryshkin 381
nation 120, 150, 151, 153, 154
National Assembly 214, 215, 217-222
national bank 243, 244, 250-253
National Convention 223, 224, 225, 227, 229-232
National Guard 217, 218, 222, 232
National Old Trails Road 257
National Recovery Administration 326
National Youth Administration 326
Nazi 337-347, 354, 355, 398
Neandertal 15, 17
Necker 213, 215, 217, 218
Ned Ludd 365
Neolithic age 18
Neolithic village 20, 21
Nerva 76
New Deal 325
New Economic Policy 394
New Hampshire 187
New Jersey 187

New Mexico 254
New York 187
New York Stock Exchange 241, 255
Newcastle 189
Newton 179, 180
Nicene Creed 78
Nicholas (Grand Duke) 313
Nicholas I 378
Nicholas II 309, 380, 383, 386
Niezsche 154
night of the long knives 345
NKVD 398
Norman 122, 123
North, Simeon 263
North (Lord) 191, 192, 193, 199
North Atlantic Treaty Organization 364
North Carolina 187
Northwest Ordinance 203

Octavian 73, 75, 88
October Manifesto 380
Odoacer 83
OGPU 396, 398
O'Higgins 435
Olive Branch Petition 197
Omar 91, 93, 97
Omayyad 93, 95
Oregon 253
Orlov, Alexis 381
Orlov, Gregory 381
Osborne 177
Osgood 238
Ostrogoths 79, 80

paladin 102
Paleolithic age 17
panic 319, 320, 321, 328, 329
Panic of 1819 251
Panic of 1837 253
Panic of 1857 255
Panic of 1873 300
Panic of 1893 300, 321
Papen 342, 343

paper 150, 429
paper money 242, 279
Parlement 213
Parliament 127, 128, 129, 137, 155, 164, 167, 169, 170, 205
Parthia 59, 88, 89
Parvus 387
patrician 65
Paul (Saint) 145
Paul I 381
Pausanius 53, 60
Peace of Paris 189
Peace of Westphalia 188
Pearl Harbor 355
peasant 114
Peloponnesian War 56, 60, 61
peninsulares 433, 435
Penn 187
Pennsylvania 187
People's party 303
People's Will 383, 385
Pepin 142
perestroika 404
Pergamum 59
Pericles 56, 60
Perseus 71
Persia 36, 39, 41, 50, 51, 53-58, 60, 89, 95, 96
Peter I 375, 376, 381
Peter III 375, 376, 381
Petition of Right 170
Petrograd Soviet 386, 389
petroleum 293, 294, 297
pharaoh 43
Pheidon 47
Philip the Fair 130, 138
Philip of Macedonia 57
Philip II 161, 162
Philip V 69, 71
Philistine 37
Phoenicia 49, 68, 69
Phrygians 37
Pierpont 272, 273, 283
Pinckney, Charles 247
Pinckney, Thomas 246, 247

Pitt 189, 191
Pizarro 160, 433
Plataea 50, 53, 60
plebeian 65, 67
plow 21
Plutarch 53
Pocahontas 183
Poitiers 130, 134
political police 377, 378, 379
Polk 253, 254
pope 83
populism 302, 303
portolan 157
Potemkin 380
Potsdam conference 399
Prajapati 411
predestination 145, 147, 154
predatory pricing 297
president 205
prime minister 180, 205
Prince Max 331, 332
Princip 307
Privy Council 155, 162
protestantism 143, 151, 153, 154
Provisional Government 386, 387, 388, 391
Prussia 99, 100, 101, 305, 318
Ptolemy 58, 59, 63
public land sale 244, 253
Public Works Administration 326
Publius 207
Punic 68
Purge, Stalin's 397, 398
Puritan 168, 169, 171, 173, 185
Pythagoras 62

radar 353, 357
Radical Reconstruction 289, 290
railroads 261, 262, 263, 293, 297, 299, 300
Randolph 238
Rasputin 383
Reagan 327
Reconstruction Finance Corporation 324

495

redemption (of bank notes or checks)   242, 300
redemption (of the South)   289, 292
regulation   297
Reichstag   331, 332, 341, 342, 343, 345
reincarnation   413, 415
Renaissance   99
representative government   127, 181, 234
representatives on mission   224
Republicans (before 1835)   239, 246-251, 253
Republicans (after 1859)   239, 269, 271, 272, 275, 283, 287, 288, 289, 291, 292
Restraining Act   193
Revenue Act   191
Revolutionary Tribunal   224, 230
Reynolds   168, 169
Rhode Island   186
Richard I   127
Richard II   137
Richardson   268
Richelieu   215, 224
rifle   280, 281
Rig Veda   411
roads   248, 252, 255, 257, 261, 293
Robespierre, Augustin   229, 230, 231
Robespierre, Maximilien   213, 220, 222-225, 229-232
Rockefeller   295, 297, 298
Rockingham   191, 199
Roehm   337, 339, 344, 345
Roland   102
Roman church   84, 99, 103, 125, 143, 150, 153, 154
Romanov, Fedor   381
Romanov, Michael   381
Rommel   356, 357
Romulus Augustulus   83

Roosevelt, Franklin   239, 324, 325, 331
Roosevelt, Theodore   298
Royal Air Force   316, 353
royal court   123, 128
royalists   231-234
Rousseau   210, 235, 435
Rubicon   73
rule of law   126, 127, 234
Rump Parliament   174, 175, 176
Rural Electrification Administration   326
Rus   367
Russian Revolution   235, 383, 384

SA   337, 338, 339, 341, 344, 345
Saint-Just   229
Salamis   53
Samnite   67
Sandys   184, 185
sans-culottes   224, 225
Sanson   228, 231
Santa Fe Trail   257
Santa Maria   158
Saracen   95, 97
Saratoga   198
Sargon   27, 28
Sassanid empire   89
satrap   41
satrapy   41
Saxa Rubra   77
Saxon   79, 83, 84, 101, 103, 121, 122, 123
Sazonov   309
scalawag   289, 290
Scheer   332
Scheidemann   332
Scheubner   339
Schicklgruber   334
Schleicher   342
Schlieffen   310
Schlieffen plan   310
Schmidt   214
scientific attitude   62, 88, 95, 98, 119, 164, 179

Scipio Africanus 69
Scott 254
secession 205, 269, 271, 286
Second Continental Congress 195
Second English Civil war 174
Sedan 305, 312
Seisser 338, 339
Seleucid empire 59, 60
Seleucus 59
Senate 205
separation of church and state 155, 187
Serbia 307, 308, 309
serf 109, 123, 129
Serge Alexandrovich 380
Seven Years War 189, 195, 198
Seward 271
Seyss-Inquart 347
Shaftsbury 177
Shakespeare 135
Shang dynasty 419
sharecropping 290, 291
sharia 97, 98
Shelburne 199
sheriff 103
Sherman 277
Sherman Anti-Trust Act 298
Shih Huang-ti 423
shiite 97
shire 103, 123
Shreeve 259
Shulgi 31
Sieyes 213, 214, 223, 232, 233, 234
Sikh 415
Silver Purchase Act 327
Simon Magus 143
Sims 315
Siva 413, 414
Sixtus IV 141
slash and burn 18
Slater 262
slavery 185, 197, 205-208, 248, 265, 267, 268, 269, 274, 275, 279, 283, 285, 286, 287, 435

Smith 183
Smythe 184
social contract 210
Social Democrats (German) 332, 343, 361, 385
Social Democrats (Russian) 384, 385
Social Security Act 327
socialism 302
soft money 302, 303
Solon 49
Sophia 179, 180
South Carolina 187
South Sea Company 180
Spain 140, 141, 161, 162
Spanish American War 254
Spartacists 332
speaker 129
specie 241, 242, 250, 253, 254, 302
Specie Circular 253
SS 341, 344, 347
Stalin 349, 354, 393, 394, 395, 397, 398, 399, 401, 403
Stamp Act 190, 191
Stamp Act Congress 190
Standard Oil 297, 298
States General 138, 139, 213, 215
steamboats 257, 260, 261
steel tools 37, 38
Stephen 124
Stilicho 81
stirrups 108
Stresemann 338
Stuart 167
subinfeudation 111
submarine 315
subsidized loan 302, 303
Sui dynasty 425
Sulla 87
Sumer 23, 24, 26, 27, 31, 34, 35
Sumerian king list 29, 34
sunnah 97
sunni 97
Supreme Court 207, 238, 253

suspension of redemption 243, 253, 255
suspension of the writ of habeas corpus 271, 273
Syria 60, 71

Taft 298
Tamerlane 369
Taney 252
T'ang dynasty 425, 427
tank 315
Tao 421
tariff 243, 244, 252, 299
Tarleton 199
Taylor 254
Tea Act 192
Teheran conference 399
Tennessee Valley Authority 327
Terror, the 227, 229, 231
terrorism 377, 379
Tetzel 147
Texas 253, 254
Themistocles 51, 53, 60
Theodosius I 80, 81
Thermidorians 230, 231, 232
Thermopylae 51, 53, 60
Third Dynasty of Ur 29, 33, 34
Third Estate 138, 213, 214, 215
Tiglath-Pilestar III 38
Tilden 291
Tito 401
tobacco 184, 185
Toleration Act 179
tools 16, 17
Tories 177, 366
Torquemada 141
Townshend 191
Trades Union Congress 365
Trajan 76
treason 174
Treaty of Ghent 250
Treaty of Paris 199
Treaty of Versailles 317, 318, 346
trench warfare 281, 313
Tribonian 85

tricolor 217
Trotsky 391
Truman 399
Tsar 368, 369
tyrant 55

Uighurs 427
ulema 97, 98
Ulfilas 79
unions 298, 301, 302
university 119
unrestricted submarine warfare 313, 315
Upanishads 412, 413
Ur-Nammu 29, 31
US Steel 298
usury 115, 163
Uthman 97

Valens 80
Valentinian III 83
Van Buren 252, 254
Vandals 79, 81, 83
Vanderbilt, Cornelius 295
Vanderbilt, William 295, 296
Vasili II 380
vassal 111, 112, 118, 119
Vendee 223, 230, 231
Vermont 245
Vespucci 159, 160
vice royalties 433, 435
viceroy 433
Vietnam 276
Vikings 105, 108, 111
Virginia 183, 184, 185
Vishnu 413, 415
Visigoths 79, 80, 81
Vitruvius 63
Voltaire 149
von Steuben 201
Voroshilov 349

Wagner National Labor Relations Act 327
Wallia 81

498

Walpole   180
war chariot   34, 35, 36
War Communism   394
War Hawks   249
War of the Roses   139, 140
War of 1812   244, 249, 250, 251, 262
Washington   195, 196, 197, 199, 217, 237-240, 244, 246, 251
Waterloo   251
Weber   154
Webster   260
Weimar Republic   333, 334
Wells   318
West Florida   249
Western civilization   11, 43, 61
wheel   24
Whigs (in England)   177, 365
Whigs (in the US)   253, 254, 268
Whiskey Rebellion   244
whiskey tax   244, 245
White Russians   389, 390
white supremacy   289, 291
Whitney   263
William the Conqueror   122, 123, 125
William Rufus   123, 124
William III   177, 178, 179
Williams   186
Wilson   316, 317, 323, 331
Winthrop   185, 186
Witan   101, 103
Wolsey   155
Woodward   283
Works Progress Administration   326
World War I   281, 293, 323, 331, 348, 364, 385
World War II   318, 328, 329, 330, 401
writing   29, 31, 32
Wyclif   150

Xerxes   50, 51

Yanayev   405
Yathrib   91
Yorktown   198, 199
Yugoslav   307
Yuri   369, 380

Zama   69
zero   95
Zwingli   151

Order Form

Fax orders: (203) 656-4002

Telephone orders: (203) 656-3446
Please have your VISA or MasterCard ready

Postal orders
HEP Publications, PO Box 2192, Rowayton, CT 06853-0192

Please send me the specified number of copies of
History, An Interpretive Overview

I understand that I may return all or any part of these books for a full refund — for any reason, no questions asked.

Name _____

Address _____

City _____ State _____ Zip Code _____

Number of copies _____

Payment $ 36.95 per book

❏ Check   ❏ VISA   ❏ MasterCard

Card Number _____

Name on Card _____

Expiration Date ____/____

Order Form

Fax orders: (203) 656-4002

Telephone orders: (203) 656-3446
Please have your VISA or MasterCard ready

Postal orders
HEP Publications, PO Box 2192, Rowayton, CT 06853-0192

Please send me the specified number of copies of
History, An Interpretive Overview

I understand that I may return all or any part of these books for a full refund — for any reason, no questions asked.

Name _____

Address _____

City _____ State ____ Zip Code _____

Number of copies _____

Payment $ 36.95 per book

❏ Check   ❏ VISA   ❏ MasterCard

Card Number _____

Name on Card _____

Expiration Date ____/____